WITHDRAWN

Leopardi

A STUDY
IN
SOLITUDE

GIACOMO LEOPARDI

Leopardi

A STUDY

IN

SOLITUDE

BY

IRIS ORIGO

HAMISH HAMILTON

LONDON

First published in Great Britain, 1953
by Hamish Hamilton Ltd
90 Great Russell Street London WC1

PRINTED IN GREAT BRITAIN
BY WESTERN PRINTING SERVICES LTD BRISTOL

CONTENTS

ILLUSTRATIONS

GIACOMO LEOPARDI   *frontispiece*

Portrait by Domenico Morelli, painted in 1839 from the poet's death-mask, and claimed by his friends to be a 'miraculous likeness'.

For

ELSA

FOREWORD
TO THE FIRST EDITION

THIS book speaks for itself. To the gallery of romantic poets of the early nineteenth century it adds for the English-speaking reader a life-like portrait of Leopardi. I have no competence and no wish to retouch the picture, painted as it is with a fine perception of character and a deep knowledge of Italy, yet without surrendering the English point of view that serves to frame the perspectives in and to bring out the colours.

There is only one thing that the purely English reader may miss, because it is only communicable to those who have some familiarity with the Italian language and some sympathy with the classic temperament: I mean the poignant accent, the divine elevation of this poet. The student, the writer, the sufferer, the wanderer was only Conte Giacomo Leopardi, but the poet was Orpheus himself. Long passages are fit to repeat in lieu of prayers through all the watches of the night. How shall I express their quality? Suppose you were held up in some minor Italian town where by chance an itinerant company was to perform *Il Trovatore*. Suppose that having nothing better to do you strolled into the theatre, resigned in advance to a meagre stage-setting, a harsh orchestra, a prima donna past her prime, a rhetorical little tenor saving his breath for the gymnastic prodigy of his final high note. But suppose also that, having found things in general much as you expected, suddenly you heard, coming from behind the wings, an unexampled heavenly voice, a voice pure as moonlight, rich as sorrow, firm as truth, singing *Solo in terra*. Alone on earth that voice might indeed seem, and far from earth it would carry you; and no matter how commonplace the singer might look, or even ridiculous, when he stepped before the footlights, if ever that sheer music sounded again, there would be something not himself that sang and something not yourself that listened.

I speak of voice and of music, but that is only a metaphor. What works the miracle in Leopardi is far from being mere sound or diction or the enigmatic suggestion of strange words. His versification is remarkable only when a divine afflatus blows through it, which is not always. This afflatus is intellectual, this music is a flood of thoughts. We are transported out of ourselves ascetically, by the vision of truth. Leopardi lived in a romantic tower, a dismal, desolate ruin; but through the bars of his prison he beheld the same classic earth and Olympian sky that had been visible to Homer, Pindar, and Sophocles. The world is always classical, the truth of human destiny is always clear, if only immersion in our animal cares does not prevent us from seeing it. Lifting the eyes would be so easy, yet it is seldom done; and when a rapt poet compels us to do so, we are arrested, we are rebuked, we are delivered.

The misfortunes of Leopardi were doubtless fortunate for his genius. Every classic poet has his romantic accent, corresponding with the scope of his intuition and the degree of harmony or conflict that the vision of the truth creates in his heart. In Leopardi this vision was saturated with anguish; narrowed by it, no doubt, but not distorted. The white heat of his anguish burned all anguish away, and cleared the air. Beneath the glorious monotony of the stars he saw the universal mutation of earthly things, and their vanity, yet also, almost everywhere, the beginning if not the fullness of beauty; and this intuition, at once rapturous and sad, liberated him from the illusions of the past and from those of the future.

GEORGE SANTAYANA

PREFACE
TO THE NEW EDITION

THE first edition of this Life of Leopardi, which I have now revised and enlarged, appeared eighteen years ago. Since then the centenary of Leopardi's death has been celebrated, with much pomp and many speeches, in both Naples and Recanati, and on the 22nd of February 1939, the little that is left of his bones was transferred from the church of S. Vitale to the slopes of the hill above Mergellina, beside 'Virgil's tomb'.

A considerable amount of new material—including four more volumes of Leopardi's *Epistolario* and many of the papers left in Ranieri's possession—has either come to light, or has been rendered available. It is listed in the Bibliography at the end of this book. Moreover, two excellent Italian *Lives* of the poet—by Giovanni Ferretti and by Michele Saponaro—as well as several interesting critical studies and monographs, have appeared, and two new critical editions of Leopardi's *Works* have been made by Francesco Flora and by Giuseppe De Robertis.

All this recent material, while it has made me aware of the deficiencies of my first effort, does not, I think, lead to any essentially different conclusions about Leopardi, either as a writer or as a man. My apology for this edition is rather the one I would give if I were asked after eighteen years to describe an old friend: in the interval I have perhaps got to know him a little better.

It is sometimes a good plan, however, to go back to one's starting-point; and while I was re-reading Leopardi's works, I thought I would also visit his birthplace again. I arrived there on a grey November evening. In the little square before Palazzo Leopardi a piercing wind was raising little eddies of dust and dead leaves, and an old woman—the only human figure in sight—was hobbling up the church steps, with a little straw chair under her arm, her black shawl

xi

drawn tightly around her. I followed. In the centre of the nave, beyond the font where Leopardi was baptized, a bier, draped in black velvet, with a great waxen candle at each corner, was prepared for a funeral. The long wooden bench where I knelt still bore the inscription, *gentis Leopardae*. I came out and wandered up the long, winding street. The shutters of the *palazzi* were closed; an unusually high proportion of the people I met seemed to be either crippled or infirm; and another blast of biting wind came with renewed vigour up one of the narrow side streets, at the corner where Leopardi's hat was blown off, and the little boys jeered, as he wrapped his cape over his head.

I rang the bell of Palazzo Leopardi and was shown into the library; its chill—though it was only November—entered my bones. On the table, in a case, I saw the brown rugs which the poet used to wrap round his shoulders and knees: they seemed thin. Beside his inkstand the petals of the carnation left there by Carducci had shrunk to a pinch of dust. But everything else in the library was unchanged. Still a metal grating enclosed the books forbidden by the Church and among them Leopardi's own *Operette Morali*; still the traveller may see the beautiful copperplate hand in which, at ten years old, the poet wrote out his dissertations and his translations of Horace; still he may handle Leopardi's Virgil, his Tasso, and his great lexicons; and still, across the little square, he may see the window where Leopardi watched Silvia at her loom.

But here, unfortunately, there is a change. For the citizens of Recanati—with belated and perhaps excessive piety—have celebrated the centenary of the poet's death by putting up, on every site mentioned in his poems, a number of white marble tablets, inscribed with some of his lines, and on Silvia's little house we may read all too plainly the verse about

la man veloce
Che percorrea la faticosa tela.

The whole town is bestrewn with these tablets, white and incongruous on the faded brick walls. They may be seen on the doorway of Palazzo Leopardi, on the *torre del borgo*, on the tower of *il passero solitario*, on what was once a lonely country path, leading to the hill of *L'Infinito*—and, worst of all, on the wall encircling the hill itself, which has now been turned into a trim public garden.

But perhaps, after all, it is not very important. For as I stood on the hill in the fading light, the wind dropped; a pale autumnal gleam caught the far snow-capped peak of the Gran Sasso and lingered upon the long trellises of yellow vine-leaves in the fields below, and on the orange flames of the bare willows. '*Le vie dorate e gli orti*'—there they lay. And suddenly it seemed very easy to understand the mixture of love and aversion that Leopardi had felt for his native city. Bitterly as he railed against it, he never ceased to belong there and to feel the tie that tugged him back. He belonged to Recanati as Flaubert did to Rouen, as Joyce to Dublin. This was the town that in his youth he called 'horrible, detestable, execrated', a prison, a den, a cave, an inferno, a 'sepulchre in which the dead are happier than the living', and 'the deadest and most ignorant city of the Marches, which is the most ignorant and uncultivated province of Italy'; this the city of whose 7,000 inhabitants he said that they were 'only remarkable for their endurance in remaining there', while he himself vowed 'never to return there permanently until I am dead'. And yet, and yet— hardly had he got to Rome than he wrote to his brother that life in a big city was only bearable if a man could 'build himself a little city within the great one'. Hardly had he got to Bologna than he was walking upon the hills, 'seeking for nothing but memories of Recanati'. When he returned there from Rome, it had become '*la mia povera patria*'; when he published his *Canti* in Florence, he put the name of his birthplace upon the title-page; and when, in the following year, he felt his strength decreasing, he wrote to a friend that if he got any worse he would return to Recanati, 'since I wish to die at home'. And certainly many of his greatest poems were either written there or directly inspired by his memories of youth and of home, of the night wind stirring in his father's garden, and the stars shining above his native hills.

There is, moreover, I think, a more fundamental sense in which Leopardi belongs to Recanati. Many men of genius, perhaps most, have been, in the botanical sense, *sports* (Shelley is the first instance that comes to mind). But Giacomo Leopardi was a very direct product of his inheritance and environment: he was a very great poet, but he also always remained a provincial aristocrat, the son of Conte Monaldo and Contessa Adelaide. From his stock he derived his fastidiousness, his pride, and his ill-health—the heritage of the *fin de race*. From his mother, his melancholy, his sense of grievance, his reserve—and, perhaps, some of his sensibility. From his father, his gentle manners, his love of books, more of his mental attitude than he would have liked to admit—and not his genius, but his talent.

There are two Leopardis: the poet and the man. The man, as he revealed himself in many of his letters and his diaries, was a querulous, tortured invalid, mistrustful of his fellow-men, with a mind sometimes scornful and cantankerous, and a heart intolerably sad and lonely. But to this unhappy man was granted the poet's gift: a capacity for feeling so intense and an imagination so sensitive and lively that he could perceive, in the most common sights of daily life, the 'heavenly originals' of which, according to Plato, all earthly objects are but copies. 'To a sensitive and imaginative man', he wrote, 'who lives, as I have lived for a long time, constantly feeling and imagining, the world and its objects are, in a way, double. He sees with his eyes a tower, a landscape; he hears with his ears the sound of a bell; and at the same time his imagination sees another tower, another bell, and hears another sound.' And it is of these sights and sounds that poetry is made.

The key to Leopardi's character and to the peculiar flavour of his work lies, I think, in this passage. He saw the whole world and the people in it, as it were, at one remove; his only contact with reality was through his own imagination. Thence his fore-destined unhappiness in love: the only woman he ever knew was the one in his own mind—'*la donna che non si trova*'. Thence, too, his unfailing disillusionment with every new scene, his incurable restlessness, and, at the same time, his deep attachment to anniversaries and to familiar places, however unhappy he had been in them, merely because they had become part of the furniture of his mind.

This book does not claim to be a critical study of Leopardi's work. It is only an attempt to describe rather more fully than before his life and character, and to perceive, through his letters and notebooks, something of the imaginative background of his mind. In some fragmentary notes for an autobiography, which he was planning in 1828—'before knowing', he wrote, 'whether I shall ever do anything that will make men want to hear about me'—he said that he intended to call it *The Story of a Soul* 'because I do not intend to tell anything else, and indeed, have no other material; for so far I

have experienced no great changes of fortune, nor any outer events
that are unusual or worth mention'. This was true then, and remained
so until his death, at the age of thirty-nine. But for the story of his
inner life, which alone he thought worth telling, he has himself
supplied all the material a biographer could desire. 'Almost all
writers of real feeling,' he wrote, 'in describing their despair and
their total disenchantment, have drawn the colours from their own
heart.' Tedium and disillusion, love unfulfilled and dreams unsatisfied, nostalgia, loneliness and grief—these are the colours of his pal-
ette. With them he painted—in his poems, in his notes about his
childhood and youth, in his letters, and in the four thousand pages
of his encyclopaedic day-book, the *Zibaldone*—a merciless and tragic
self-portrait.

My grateful acknowledgments are due to Dottoressa Guerrieri,
the librarian of the Biblioteca Nazionale in Naples, for permission to
reproduce the two holographs of Leopardi's poems; to Cav. Polve-
rigiani, the archivist of the Commune of Recanati, for permission to
photograph the death-mask of Leopardi and the bronze bust by
Monteverde reproduced on the jacket; and to Prof. Astolfi, the
librarian of the Sodalizio dei Piceni in Rome, for assistance in con-
sulting a number of books and periodicals not easily accessible.

I should also like to thank Duke Antonio Carafa d'Andria for his
kind permission to reproduce Domenico Morelli's portrait of
Leopardi, the Contessa Vittoria de Gavardo for her courtesy in allowing me to visit the Villa della Ginestra, and the Contessa Rosita
Leopardi for permission to visit the private rooms and garden, as well
as the library, of Palazzo Leopardi.

I am most grateful to Mr. Julian Trevelyan for allowing me to make
use of the translations of Leopardi's poems by R. C. Trevelyan
quoted on pages 190, 245 and 247. All the others are my own.

I can only thank Elsa Dallolio for greater help than can be listed
here by dedicating to her a book which, in some ways, is as much
hers as mine.

Rome, January 1953   IRIS ORIGO

Leopardi

I

GENS LEOPARDA

*Del mio nascimento dirò solo che io nacqui di famiglia nobile in una città ignobile della Italia.**

THE little city of Recanati, in the Marches, stands on a low hill some fifteen miles from the Adriatic. It is, at first sight, indistinguishable from a hundred other hill-towns of provincial Italy, like them presenting an aspect which combines distinction and squalor, dignity and dreariness. One long winding street stretches along the crest of the hill: tall shuttered palaces—Renaissance and Baroque—of faded brick and stone, face each other in a stateliness that has lost all splendour. The narrow, sunless little side-streets come to an end with startling suddenness, framing a view of an astounding beauty: hillsides of olives and of vines stretching down to the Adriatic, with the orange sails of the Venetian *paranze* far out to sea—and to the west, fold upon fold of blue mountain ranges, rising to the Gran Sasso and the Maiella. The piazza has a great square watch-tower, to guard against the pirates; the numerous churches are adorned by a Romanesque portal, a Renaissance façade, the figure of the Virgin or of a patron saint. The palaces mostly belong to a later period, to the prosperous seventeenth and eighteenth centuries. Through the wide arches of their doorways one has a glimpse of an inner courtyard and of a great stone staircase—occasionally, of a garden beyond: a desiccated palm tree or a bed of dusty geraniums, sometimes a pillared balustrade or a sponge-stone fountain.

At the beginning of the nineteenth century, when Leopardi spent his childhood in one of them, no less than forty of these palaces were

---

* 'Of my birth I will only say that I was born of a noble family in an ignoble city of Italy.' From Leopardi's projected autobiography: *Storia di un' anima.*

inhabited by noble provincial families. They all 'kept a carriage'; they gave formal entertainments several times a year; they prided themselves on their box at the theatre, on their footmen in liveries, and on being able to afford the maintenance of at least one priest in the house, as the children's tutor. The Leopardi family, at the time of the birth of their son Giacomo, had four such ecclesiastics living with them—but they were one of the oldest families in Recanati, and their *palazzo* was the most important in the city. Standing at the edge of the town, where the main street winds into a small cobbled square and emerges as a white country road, it presents a dignified, rather sombre façade of dusty red brick, with a few balconies of wrought-iron, and an arched doorway. Within, a double staircase, adorned with balustrades and classical busts, leads to the main rooms of the *palazzo*, and to the library in which Giacomo Leopardi spent his youth.

Here we may still see—stretching back to the beginning of the thirteenth century—the documents relating to the *gens Leoparda*, as well as a great family tree, and a long manuscript narrating the *Istoria gentilizia* of the family, compiled by the poet's father, Conte Monaldo. It is a typical record of the clerical *noblesse de province*: in each generation, down the centuries, we find few men of action, and none illustrious, but a long line of magistrates and city priors, of bishops and canons and knights of Malta, while the women are either mothers or nuns.[1] At one time, indeed, at the beginning of the seventeenth century, there were no less than fifteen nuns of *casa Leopardi* alive at the same time, and nine of them in the same convent, in which some of them dwelled for sixty years.[2] And we hear of one of the poet's aunts, Donna Margherita delle Oblate dell' Assunta, who, after a great many years of conventual segregation, 'showed a great passion for the sun, so that once, when its rays reached her cell, she spread a sheet on the spot where they fell, and began to dance upon it'.[3]

A slight strain of madness, or at least of eccentricity, is to be observed among the male ancestors, too. One, in the eighteenth century, Conte Paolo, went mad—according to his great-nephew Monaldo—'from excess of scruples. He lived very quietly in perpetual silence, never answering anything but yes or no when spoken to . . . and spending the greater part of his days in bed.'[4] And the poet's own great-uncle, Don Luigi Bernardino (also a priest), was so anxious to be perpetually at the service of his parishioners that he kept in his bedroom at Palazzo Leopardi a little bell, fastened to a long cord which hung down into the street, so that the faithful might be able to call upon him at any hour of the day or night.

Conte Monaldo, the poet's father, prided himself on his ancestry, on his palace, and on his town—further than that, he considered, a man's pride should not extend. 'One's patriotism is not due to the whole nation,' he wrote, 'not even to the state; one's true country is only that morsel of the earth in which one is born and spends one's life. That alone should awaken any interest in its citizens.' In this view, if there was a genuine local patriotism, there was also a keen awareness that it is pleasanter to be a large frog in a small pond. 'Being very proud', he himself wrote, 'of my abilities and personal independence, I neither want nor need a great town. I would always choose a hut, a book, and an onion at the top of a mountain, rather than hold a subordinate position in Rome.'

To Monaldo, as to most members of his caste, the boundaries of the Papal States were also those of the universe. To them the invasion of the Papal territory, in 1796, by the troops of the French Republic, partook of the nature of sacrilege; and when the news came to Recanati that the troops had reached Ancona, Conte Monaldo was among the first to join a solemn procession of the whole population and clergy which made its way from Recanati to Loreto, to implore the miraculous aid of the Madonna. For Loreto, the most famous sanctuary of central Italy—'that great market of ignoble superstitions', as Giordani called it—was only twelve miles distant from Recanati, and from the windows of the Palazzo Leopardi one could see the church's great dome outlined against the sky. In this church of Baroque magnificence, fortified against pirates by massive bastions and turrets constructed by Sangallo, under Bramante's imposing dome, and enclosed by a marble screen adorned by Sansovino, stands the little house of the Virgin Mary. This dwelling, according to the legend, took flight from Nazareth, assisted by angels, precisely on the 10th of March 1291—on one of the many occasions when Palestine was invaded by the Moslems—and, after trying several other less favourable sites, finally settled down in its present position. And, according to Conte Monaldo, it was a Leopardi, Ciccotto di

Monaldutio, a 'Doctor-in-law', who was 'one of the sixteen deputies sent from our province in 1296 to Dalmatia and Palestina, to verify the miraculous departure from those lands of the Holy House'.[5]

To Loreto, throughout the Middle Ages, came pilgrims from every Catholic country in Europe; princes and emperors were among them, and like the Magi, they brought their gifts. But, alas, less than a year after the Republican troops' invasion, the Emperor Napoleon entered Loreto—not to bring gifts, but to take them away: jewels worth half a million *scudi*, according to one account, besides gold and silver, statues and brocades. For the prayers of the pilgrims from Recanati, which at the time had appeared marvellously efficacious —since the Virgin in the cathedral of Ancona was seen to move her eyes 'in compassion' for the people's suffering—were only able to delay for a short time the progress of the Republican troops. In the following spring French soldiers were billeted in Recanati—and a few days later Napoleon himself rode through, on his way to Rome. He rode hastily, Conte Monaldo related, surrounded by guards with their hands on the trigger of their muskets, and all the population turned out to see him. 'But I', wrote the Count, 'refused to approach the window, thinking it too great an honour for such a villain, that an honest man should rise to see him pass.'

The pages of Conte Monaldo's autobiography tell us a great deal about the education and the manner of life of a Catholic nobleman in the provinces at the end of the eighteenth century. Conte Monaldo was born in Recanati on the 16th of August 1776, lost his father before he was five years old, and spent the years of his childhood in the Palazzo Leopardi, 'in perfect harmony', with his mother, his great-uncle, four of his uncles, his brother and sister, and no less than four ecclesiastics. 'Indeed,' he adds, 'I did not dream of ascribing this harmony to any merit of theirs or mine, not imagining that any family could live otherwise.' It is plain that Monaldo himself was both a docile pupil and a faithful friend. Of the family chaplain, Don Vincenzo Ferri, he said that he must leave a portrait, 'since probably no one else will ever speak of him again until the day of the Last Judgment', and he then proceeded to describe him as 'the ugliest man in the city', but commented: 'The affection I felt for him made his features so attractive to me that to this day I feel inclined to love anyone who combines in his appearance an African complexion, cat's eyes, a large mouth, and a snub nose.' Of his next tutor, Don Giuseppe Torres, a Jesuit from Vera Cruz, he wrote that he was not only his preceptor, but his father and friend. 'To him I owe my manners, my principles, and my whole formation as a Christian and an honest man.' But sincerity compelled him to add that this same tutor, owing to the manner in which he insisted on his pupils saying all their lessons by rote, had been 'the assassin of my studies'—an opinion which did not prevent him, in later years, from entrusting to Don Giuseppe the education of his own sons. For both these tutors stayed on in *casa Leopardi*—the latter for thirty-seven years— as much part of the background of the poet's boyhood as the walls that looked down upon him.

At the age of sixteen, during a visit to the neighbouring city of Pesaro, Conte Monaldo fell in love with a charming young lady of the same age as himself, Contessa Teresa Ondedei Zongo, whom he met in his grandmother's house, and who, he ventured to believe, returned his affection. But their shyness in each other's presence was such that neither of them dared so much as to speak to the other. Finally, one evening, a jovial and tactless family friend rallied Monaldo before the whole company: 'Come, speak up, since we all know it—confess that you are in love with the Contessina Teresa.' But the unfortunate young man was so overcome by bashfulness that, blushing furiously, he could only stammer: 'No, no, it isn't true!' and thus himself brought his first romance to an end.

Two years later, when barely eighteen, he assumed, as head of the family, the complete management of the whole property—yet he was still forbidden by his mother to go out of the house, unless accompanied by his preceptor. This restriction, although not unusual in families such as his, was particularly galling to Monaldo. 'To this day,' he wrote in his Memoirs, 'although I am the father of twelve children (living and dead), a magistrate of the city, and forty-eight years of age, I still feel a very great satisfaction when I find myself alone in a street, without a tutor by my side.' Indeed this early humiliation may well have contributed, in later life, to his intense punctilio in dealing with both equals and inferiors, and to his insistence on all outward signs of dignity. From the age of eighteen he dressed from head to foot in black, with knee-breeches and a sword at his side, and in later years he prided himself on being the last man in Italy habitually to wear a sword, and to be clothed 'in a noble and decorous manner'. 'With a sword by one's side,' he wrote, 'and always in full dress, it is not possible to fall very low, even should one wish to.' In his Memoirs he advised his sons to follow a similar practice, partly on the grounds of economy—'five or six yards of black cloth have always formed the whole of my wardrobe'—but also because 'to be clothed in a noble and decorous manner' invariably, in his opinion, aroused respect. 'When I go out in a rather finer suit and cloak, I am bowed to more deeply than usual. . . . Dress', he advised, 'with dignity, be select in your company, greet everyone courteously, give a few pence to beggars, and you will be respected always and everywhere.' These precepts he was himself the first to follow. 'Your servant, your servant' (*schiavo, schiavo*) he would say, as he took his leave, and in the street he would be greeted by so many acquaintances and beggars that he would hold his hat permanently in one hand, and scatter pence with the other—until, the money being exhausted, he put his hat on his head again—and the beggars, who understood the sign, would give up and go home.[6]

A kind man, a self-important man—and also an extremely opinionated one. 'All that I have ever come in contact with, has been done according to my will, and all that has not accorded with it seemed to me ill done.' So the Count wrote in his Memoirs, but unfortunately his first act as the official head of the family was a conspicuously imprudent one—the hasty marriage of his sister Ferdinanda, at the age of sixteen, to the Marchese Pietro Melchiorri, a Roman nobleman who required an extremely large dowry with his bride, and supplied her in return with the permanent company of his stepmother and of nine brothers- and sisters-in-law, all living in the same house. 'This', wrote Monaldo, 'enabled her to find ample exercise for her many virtues.'

His second independent action was even less fortunate: a contract of marriage between himself and a young lady of Bologna, Marchesa Diana Zambeccari, whom he never had seen, but who had been offered to him—'since the placing of young women is a difficult business'—by a merchant of that city. But before signing the contract, Monaldo expressed a natural desire to see his bride, and finally

CONTE MONALDO LEOPARDI

set out for her parents' *palazzo* in Bologna, accompanied by a
mutual friend, Conte Gatti, who had taken charge of the whole
affair. It had been arranged beforehand by the two young men that,
if his bride did not displease him, Monaldo would pull a white
handkerchief out of his pocket—and leave the rest to his companion.
On arrival they found the *palazzo* filled with the young lady's relations and friends, all profuse in compliments and consumed with
curiosity. Only the bride herself was not yet visible. Poor Monaldo,
bewildered alike by the attentions of the company and the admoni-
tions of Conte Gatti, became convinced that he had now gone too
far to retreat, and kept his hand continually upon his handkerchief,
ready to pull it out. At last the young lady appeared: 'a bow, two
words, one glance, and out came my handkerchief. Gatti whispered
something in the bride's ear, and then everyone cried out: "Long
live the happy pair! Bravo, Conte Gatti, how clever you are, how
well you have managed!"—and so the marriage was arranged.'

But a few hours later, on further acquaintance with the young lady,
Monaldo began to be convinced that 'the handkerchief had been
drawn out with too great a precipitancy'. He found in his bride,
who was several years older than himself, 'those qualities that
deserve respect and esteem', but none of the lighter graces—and in
short, it seemed to him 'that our union was not written in heaven'.
But how could an escape be found? Here Monaldo first exhibited a
combination of qualities that he was to show throughout the rest of
his life: vacillation in conjunction with profound obstinacy. At first
he allowed himself to be convinced by the persuasions of his friend,
who told him that his doubts were 'temptations of the devil', and
he prepared himself 'to drain the bitter cup and poison myself for
life'. The bride's portion was decided upon: 20,000 *scudi*. The
date of the wedding was fixed for the following February, and
Monaldo embarked on preparations on a scale proportionate to his
own distaste for the whole enterprise: jewels and gowns for the
bride, furniture for a whole new apartment, horses and carriages and
liveries. But on returning home and reviewing the prospect of his
marriage from a distance, he decided that it was not endurable. Was
there, he wondered, any conceivable way of escape? A loophole was
offered him by his future father-in-law, who refused to pay him the
half of the dowry that was due 'in advance', on the pretext that his

coffers had been depleted by the levies of the French troops. But
Monaldo felt a creditable distaste for haggling over his bride,
although, he admitted, this ray of hope 'changed the whole aspect of
my future to a splendid and seductive one'. Unwilling to use the
opportunity here offered, he hit upon another plan: he composed an
anonymous letter to his father-in-law. 'Conte Leopardi considers
his bride most worthy of respect and of esteem, and would wish to
regard her with passion: but the heart is not subject to laws. . . .
Leopardi will marry your daughter, and treat her as befits a Christian
and a man of honour, but . . . if these young people are unhappy all
their lives, you will have willed it by disregarding this warning.'

This disconcerting letter was followed by two others to the same
effect, with the consequence that soon after, on a market-day in
January, an 'honoured merchant' of Bologna visited Recanati, and
asked Monaldo, in the name of his future father-in-law, whether or
not the thought of this marriage was pleasing to him. After some
hesitation, the future bridegroom replied that he disliked the prospect so intensely that he would prefer to enter a monastery. The
contract was accordingly dissolved, but at a severe price: Conte
Monaldo had to return to the Marchese Zambeccari the full sum
expended on his daughter's jewels; he had to pay for the new carriages, the new liveries, the stables, for a lady's maid who had been
engaged for the bride, and even for 'the damage suffered by the
trousseau owing to the changes of fashions' (this alone was estimated
at 400 *scudi*). In all, his imprudence cost him 20,000 *scudi*—with no
return, except the meagre satisfaction that the Marchese Zambeccari
remained his friend, 'and was perhaps the more pleased with me in
that he had saved a good deal of his own money, and tasted a little
of mine. . . . So true is it,' he sententiously concluded, 'that a facile
error may lead to most bitter penitence. But let us leave this melancholy subject, and pass on to other events.'

Other events, indeed, crowded the next two years of Conte
Monaldo's life. In the spring of 1797 the French Republican troops
had made their first invasion of the Papal States, and now the Pope
—having failed in various efforts to conciliate the enemy—decided
to fight against France without arms, without fortresses, without
provisions, without soldiers, and without time to prepare his un-
armed and trembling subjects, numbering only two and a half mil-

lion, for warfare against forty million Frenchmen. Among these unprepared soldiers was Monaldo's brother Vito, then a boy of seventeen, whom Monaldo decided to equip and send to the wars. They set out for Rome together, where Vito, 'inflamed by the sound of martial trumpets', entered the Papal troops as a private, became a second-lieutenant within four days, and a lieutenant within eight—all 'without knowing a single word of what is necessary to be an officer or a soldier'. On the first occasion, however, on which this youth might have been called upon to fulfil these functions—after the defeat of the Papal troops at Faenza—Monaldo reflected, on his brother's behalf, 'that neither religion nor honour require an unprofitable death'. So he hurried to meet the troops and, after convincing the head of the battalion that his brother's services could be dispensed with in exchange for those of 'two fine horses', brought Vito home, 'to hide his military ornaments in the attic'. Four days later, after the fall of Ancona, a regiment of Papal troops occupied Recanati, and began to prepare for its defence; but Monaldo succeeded in persuading its colonel ('whom I found in *casa Massucci*, eating a fat boiled pigeon') that Recanati was indefensible, and that it would be better 'to take his troops away in peace'. After this story it is not difficult to agree with Monaldo that the citizens of the Papal States 'lacked the preparations, the temper, and the inclination for warfare'.

During the next two years, a constant succession of troops—French, Papal, and Austrian—occupied the Marches, and Monaldo had to exercise all his ingenuity to placate each one of them in turn, following the principle, which he expressed to the population of Recanati, that 'wars should be fought by soldiers, and citizens should remain quiet spectators'. His indignation against the iniquities of the French Republican government was intense. The taxes imposed by it, he said, were terrible—amounting, in his own case, to over twelve thousand *scudi*, besides a carriage, four horses, wood, oil, fodder, beds, sheets, clothes, and even chickens and eggs. He was deeply shocked, too, by the impiety of the Republicans: two of the churches of Recanati were turned into stables, the black robes of the priests were requisitioned, and the monks (as well as the rest of the population) were compelled to wear a *coccarda tricolore* and to take their turn, still clothed in their monk's habits, in mounting guard at the

city gates. Finally, a 'tree of liberty' was erected in one of the
squares, and some coins were scattered on the ground around it, so
that the populace might applaud. They did indeed pick up the
money, but put the tree of liberty to a baser use. This government
was temporarily brought to an end in Recanati by the arrival of a
large number of insurgent 'brigands' (the expression is Conte
Leopardi's own), who turned out the French, cut down the tree of
liberty, and elevated Monaldo himself, much against his will, to
the position of governor of the city. A week later the French
returned again with reinforcements—the brigands fled—and Monaldo
was left to face the returning enemy. His position was rendered
worse by the fact that he had recently married and that his wife was
expecting her first baby. He hoped to find comparative safety for
her in the house of one of their peasants, just outside the walls, but
during their first night there his wife—of whose determination we
shall hear more later—was so tormented by fleas that she insisted on
their all returning to Recanati, 'although', he adds, 'I could not be
persuaded that the fleas were even more to be feared than the French'.
Indeed, on his return, Monaldo was immediately arrested. The first
sentence was that he should die; then this was altered to the destruction of his *palazzo*, and finally he considered himself fortunate in
escaping with the payment of a large fine.

But he did not allow himself to be depressed for long. A few
months later the tables were turned again. With the help of Austrian
troops the Marches were being freed from the French domination,
and in 1799 the Republican army, in its turn, was shut up in Ancona
and besieged there. Monaldo and his wife hurried down to the plain,
camping out in a peasant's house (this time, without fleas) to enjoy
the delights of the siege. 'We slept as peacefully in the cannon's
mouth', he wrote, 'as if we were in the shade of a peaceful olive
tree.' The troops then besieging Ancona belonged to every country
in Europe, for the Austrian allies included Germans, Hungarians,
Turks, Croats, Dalmatians, Lombards, and Venetians; there were
even some English sailors, and a cavalry troop of French Royalists.
Such a variety of foreigners, Monaldo wrote, 'rendered this resi-
dence a most agreeable one'. He had no praise warm enough for the
'charming courtesy of the Austrians', and the manners of their
Turkish allies seem to have pleased him no less. 'One morning, a

Turkish soldier passed by under our windows, holding by the hair
a Frenchman's head, so newly beheaded that it still seemed to have
some remnants of life, the mouth and eyes still grimacing. The Turk
held it up mockingly, saying: "Look! The Frenchman's laughing!"'

One more important event brought Recanati into the annals of
history. On 25 June 1800, the new Pope Pius VII, on his triumphant
return from France to Rome, went to Loreto, and even paid a
morning visit to Recanati. The little city was decked in its best; the
sailors of the port of Recanati, halfway to Loreto, unharnessed the
horses of the Papal carriage and themselves drew it up the hill to the
cathedral, where a large congregation of reinstated monks and nuns
and an exulting congregation of the faithful came to kiss the Pope's
toe, Monaldo of course among them. 'This was the precise anniver-
sary of the sack of our city, and I reminded the Holy Father that in
the preceding year, at the very moment when I was kissing his toe, I
had been condemned to death.'

This year, however, was the last in which Conte Monaldo played
a conspicuous part in the affairs of his city. After Marengo, the Papal
States again fell into the 'abhorred power' of France, and as long as
this rule lasted, Monaldo remained in complete retirement. His conduct, however, of his private affairs continued to be venturesome and
ill-advised. He speculated disastrously on the price of wheat and
made an unfortunate attempt to redeem a part of the Roman Campagna, by introducing new agricultural methods there. This enterprising effort may well command our sympathy now, but its
immediate result was the death from malaria of the peasants sent
from the Marches to those fever-stricken lands—and Monaldo had to
face yet another financial disaster. It is at this point that a new figure
steps into the foreground of our scene—a figure who from now
onwards will dominate it: that of Monaldo's wife, Contessa Adelaide.

His marriage, of which he gives us a detailed account in his autobiography, had taken place three years before, in 1797—in the same
year that marked the termination of his unlucky engagement to the
Bolognese young lady. Another man than Monaldo might have
been influenced by this experience to a certain prudence in affairs of
the heart, but less than six months had elapsed before he embarked
on a fresh alliance, which this time was to be irrevocable. On the
15th of June, he tells us, the feast of St. Vitus, while he was attending

a Mass in honour of this saint, his eyes fell upon the daughter of a nobleman of Recanati, Marchesa Adelaide Antici. Three days later, at the Corpus Domini procession, he saw her again, and although he knew that she was half-engaged to another man—'I was so dizzy that I could think of nothing else'. Two days after that, he went to see her brother, and asked if his addresses would be welcome—and so, 'on the 15th of June I was as free as a bird, and by the 21st, of my own accord, I had walked into a net'. The engagement was approved by the Antici family, but was violently opposed by the Leopardis, though their reasons do not appear to have included one which would seem important: the fact that this would be the eighth time that the Leopardi family intermarried with the Antici. According to Conte Monaldo, his mother even went so far as to kneel before her son, to implore him to alter his decision. Monaldo knelt down too, kissed her hand, and stuck to his determination; and subsequently as he himself wrote, 'endured for a whole lifetime the severe punishment of this fault'. He decided that, under the circumstances, it was not possible to take his bride home after the wedding, so he intended to go with her instead to live in an apartment in Pesaro. None of his family, except his great-uncle, came to the wedding, but after the ceremony, while the carriages were waiting to start, he determined to make a last attempt at a reconciliation. Taking his bride by the hand, he said, 'Let us go and kiss my mother's hand', and on entering the old lady's room, they received complete forgiveness. His uncles, too, wisely accepted the *fait accompli*, and one of them, on hurrying to *casa Antici* with the good news, found 'the street full of people, and all the relations and friends who had come to the wedding, waiting at the window to hear the result of this visit'; so he declared that peace had been restored, ordered the horses to be unharnessed, and invited the whole party to *casa Leopardi*.

'And so', Monaldo concluded, 'I became a husband.' His relations with his wife, throughout their married life, were very odd and his feelings for her extremely mixed. Many years after their marriage he still wrote love-letters to her, and in his Will, in which he still left the whole of the family property in her hands, he wrote: 'I feel sure that my children will respect and obey their worthy and venerated Mother, remembering that she has not only been the edification and blessing of her family, but also, by her wise energy and prudence,

has restored our domestic fortunes. If our House has been preserved
in the midst of so many storms, it is due, after God's mercy, to the
care, diligence, and labour of this wise and loving woman.'[7]

But in his autobiography his description of his wife ends with the
following words: 'I was unmoved by the tears that my mother shed
at my feet, and I have been terribly punished. The arsenals of the
Divine wrath are inexhaustible; let those sons tremble who dare to
provoke them. My wife's character and temperament are as far
apart from mine as the earth is from the sky. Every married man
knows what that means—and let the unmarried beware of finding it
out.'

Such, after twenty-six years of marriage, was Monaldo's estimate
of his wife's nature: she was 'at once a divine blessing and a divine
chastisement'. The force of her character began to reveal itself in full
measure six years after their marriage, when the vast extent of his
financial imprudences could no longer be concealed. The mere
interest on his debts now amounted to a sum equal to the whole
family income, so that ruin seemed both imminent and inevitable.
Monaldo, continually pressed and harassed by his creditors—vacillating, proud, confused—was at his wits' end, and now it was that
Contessa Adelaide, once and for all, assumed complete command.
She summoned a family council, laid bare the whole situation, persuaded Monaldo to resign the management of the estate to an ad-
ministrator, signed an agreement with his creditors, and herself
became the undisputed mistress of the household.

Thus did Monaldo fall into the position of 'her penniless and
restricted pupil', a position he was often to rebel against in later
years, even complaining about it to his own children. But he never
succeeded in regaining independence, although he was, within his
limitations, a man of culture and learning. A poet, or at least a writer
of verse, in his youth, he later on became the author of many—too
many—theological and political treatises, and revived in his native
city a 'poetical Academy' which had previously existed there in
1400, under the name of '*I Disuguali Placidi*'—literally, the Placidly
Unequal, or those who can agree to disagree. Its meetings were held
in the Palazzo Leopardi. 'Such Academies', the Count wrote, 'excite
a spirit of emulation, inflame a desire for glory, awaken a love of
study, or at least the necessity of pretending to it, bring about social

life, civilize our manners, render familiar the fine phrases and the
elegance of our language, and are even sometimes of service to religion, since they oblige men to speak of it in high and respectful
terms.'

In these assemblies Monaldo, like his fellow-members, could
'placidly agree to disagree'; but when it was a question of standing
up to his wife, his spirit failed him. 'My father has a good heart and
is really fond of us,' wrote his daughter Paolina, 'but he lacks the
courage to face Mama's sulks for even the slightest cause. . . .
When I was quite small, perhaps even before I was born, my father's
legs became entangled, I know not how, in my mother's skirts—and
he has never since been able to free himself.'[8] Monaldo too confirms this: 'My wife, if I dared to conceal from her the reason for
one sigh, would take my letters out of my pocket, sue me, make an
uproar over the whole town.'

A remarkable woman, Contessa Adelaide. On the day when the
family affairs passed into her hands she decided that everything should
be sacrificed to the family prestige. She sold all her jewels; she
deprived her husband and children of pocket-money; she even
measured, 'with a little wooden hoop', the size of the eggs brought
by the peasant-women as part of the owner's dues; she cut down
every pleasure and every luxury. She herself always wore, for
economy's sake, clothes that never varied in cut or fashion: straight
gowns with short skirts and high peasant's boots, in the manner
of the French Revolution, but with a broad *jabot* to mark that she
was not dressed '*à la guillotine*', short hair, and when she went out,
an enormous straw hat which concealed her face, and nodded of its
own accord, as she drove by in her carriage. Nor did she think it
necessary for the other members of her family to indulge in the
luxuries of which she deprived herself. When Giacomo's overcoat
became too short for him, she told the tailor merely to add to it a
strip of *pelone*.* But when it came home, 'You've done a fine piece
of work,' said Giacomo to the tailor, gently, 'but, you know, I really
can't wear this.' 'Perhaps for sitting at home at the fire?' hazarded
the man. 'But it's the only one I've got!'[9] And even Conte Monaldo
himself, when he required a little pocket-money, was forced to
resort to subterfuge; he would plot with the bailiff, to sell a barrel of

* Heavy hairy cloth.

wine or a sack of wheat behind his wife's back, or he would take to her two books from his own library, saying that he needed a few *scudi* to pay for them. 'Thus,' he remarked, 'I used to steal from myself.'

It must be added that often these subterfuges were practised by Conte Monaldo in the cause of charity: the cloister, for instance, of the monastery of the *Minori Osservanti* was built entirely at his expense, but, to avoid his wife's vigilance, the building materials had to be carried there at night. And the story is even told that on one winter's evening, on being accosted by a half-naked beggar, the Count retired into the shadow of a doorway, took off his trousers, gave them to the wretched man—and thus, wrapping himself in his cloak, made his way home.[10]

But meanwhile, Contessa Adelaide held upon her undeviating course, and year after year, *scudo* by *scudo*, the family fortunes were built up again, while—whatever the sacrifices at home—outward decorum was observed in the sight of Recanati. The great rooms of Palazzo Leopardi still remained open, and the household was not diminished by one footman, one coachman, or one priest. Similarly, in the conduct of Contessa Adelaide's spiritual life, she admitted no inner relaxation: the thought of the Kingdom of God wholly occupied her mind—and it was a kingdom as narrowly circumscribed as the little temporal world in which she spent her days. She was possessed by two ruling passions only, or perhaps it might be said by one alone, which had a double face: the laying up of coin—temporal for this world, and spiritual for the next. Everything else—the ideals and dreams, the little ambitions and passing distractions that go to make up the variegated life of ordinary men—all this was dismissed as vanity. 'In all her life', wrote her husband, 'she knew no wish, no pleasure, and no interest, but those of her family and of God.' To her children she appeared in a similar light. 'She is an utter excess of Christian perfection,' wrote her daughter Paolina; 'you cannot imagine the severity with which she regulates every detail of our family life. Dear Marianna, I wish you could spend just one day in our house, to realize how it is possible to lead an existence that is bodiless, soulless, lifeless.'[11]

For indeed Contessa Adelaide demanded from her children, as from herself, a total submission to her uncompromising ideals. Religion—not as doctrine and precept alone, but also as a meticulous daily practice of every ordinance prescribed by the Church—this was the basis of their earliest education, and everything else was secondary. When, in their babyhood, the children burned their tongue in the soup and cried, their mother bade them 'offer it up to Jesus'; when, later on, they wished for the distractions and interests of a wider world, she condemned the cravings which would only take them further away from God. The most terrible indictment of her is contained in her son's own words. 'I have known intimately a Mother who was not in the least superstitious, but most orthodox and scrupulous in her Christian faith and practice. Yet not only did she deny pity to those parents who lost their children in infancy, but she went so far as to regard them with a deep and sincere envy, inasmuch as those children, escaping all perils, had flown to heaven, while their parents had been freed from the trouble of bringing them up. When, as several times happened, she seemed likely to lose an infant child, she did not pray God that it should die, since religion forbids it, but she did in fact rejoice. . . . She was indeed scrupulous in her care of the poor sufferer, but even so she hoped at the bottom of her heart that her care would be of no avail, and one day she let fall the confession that her only fear in questioning the doctor was to hear of some improvement. When she saw the death of one of her infants approaching, she experienced a deep happiness, which she attempted to conceal only from those who were likely to blame her; and the day of her child's death, if it came, was for her a happy and pleasant one, nor could she understand how her husband could be so foolish as to lament it. She considered beauty a true misfortune, and, seeing her children ugly or deformed, gave thanks to God. . . . In no way did she attempt to help them to hide their deficiencies, but required rather that on this account they should give up all semblance of youthful life. If they resisted, or attempted to follow their own bent, and if their endeavours met with any success, she was annoyed, and in both her thoughts and words did her utmost to diminish that success. Similarly she never neglected an opportunity of pointing out to them their faults, while expatiating, with a ferocious and merciless veracity, upon the consequences, and the inevitable misery to which such defects must lead. In these and other matters the short-comings of her children were a comfort to her, and to tell

CONTESSA ADELAIDE LEOPARDI

them what she had heard said against them was always her deliberate choice. All this to free them from spiritual pride. . . .'[12]

The picture is, indeed, a terrible one. But at the end of the passage—which was written by Giacomo at the age of twenty-one—there is another sentence, not usually quoted: 'This woman had been allotted a most sensitive nature, and had been brought to this state by religion alone.'

What are we to make of this? May it not be, perhaps, the key to a better understanding of this formidable woman? For indeed other stories about her also make us feel that perhaps Giacomo's terrible portrait holds only one facet of the truth. We hear, for instance, that this cold and stiff woman, who habitually, after an absence of her husband's, only kissed him on the shoulder, once, after a long absence, fainted from emotion as she came down the stairs to greet him. She never fondled one of her children, yet she kept in her bedroom all her life the little chair on which they used to sit in childhood. Usually so cold and dignified, and stoical in all physical pain, she would have sudden bursts of weeping, in which she would retire to her room, alone.[13] And the only earthly possessions she cared for were her flowers—violets, lilies of the valley, cherry-pie, small yellow acacias—delicate flowers that make no show, and give their scent only to those who hold them close.[14]

As for her relationship with her son, we can hardly deny that there was a severity on one side, bitter resentment on the other. But against this there are letters in which, perhaps in affectionate reference to his having begun to earn a few *scudi* by his works—Giacomo signs himself 'your golden son', *tuo figlio d'oro*.[15] And when, in 1825, Monaldo wrote to thank Carlo Antici for Giacomo's prospective appointment as Secretary of the Academy of Bologna, he added, 'For all Adelaide's severity, when she read your letter, her eyes were wet'.[16] There are letters, too, of Contessa Adelaide's own, written to Giacomo just after he had left home for the first time, which show, through a formal pietistic style, an awkward, constrained tenderness. 'You know', she tells him (in a letter which begins '*caro, carissimo figlio*') 'that I love you sincerely, and that it is a thorn in my heart to see you always discontented and out of humour. I shall pray, although unworthy, to Our Lord and to our dear advocate the Blessed Mary, to render you completely happy. Take great care of yourself, and have no dealings with unworthy persons. Love me, and believe always in the sincere affection of your most affectionate mother, who embraces and blesses you.'[17]

This is the letter of a woman unaccustomed to show emotion, but not to feel it. And to it we may add a phrase of Paolina's, long after her brother had left home. 'The truth is, my dear Giacomuccio, that in those days [she is speaking of their youth] we did not understand you—except Mama, who understood you very well.'[18]

What was the link between the rigid, pious, *bornée* woman and her brilliant, unhappy son? What, but their depth of hidden feeling, their common capacity for self-torment? Giacomo too—as we shall see—drew away, when wounded, into silent, solitary grief. He, too, after the first spontaneous demonstrativeness of early childhood, learned to conceal his sensitiveness beneath an armour of silence.

Giacomo's suppressed emotions found an outlet in his poems—Contessa Adelaide's, in the practices of her religion. But in the mother, as in the son, the abiding note was self-torment. Giacomo has recorded, as an example of her insensibility, that when she heard of a young person's death, she had no thought to spare for the sadness of a life cut short; all her concern was for the *manner* of death—was the sufferer at peace with God? Yet if indeed she believed, as undoubtedly she did, that to die without being shriven was to be condemned to eternal hell-fire, was not her concern rational? Even Conte Monaldo, who loved his children more simply, wrote in his diary, when his wife had a still-born child, that his chief cause for grief was that 'my daughter will never see the beautiful face of God'; and when another little boy died, at the age of nine months, found his consolation in having given 'another Angel to Paradise'.[19]

Perhaps, to understand Contessa Adelaide's character, we should above all remember a prayer found among her papers: 'My God, you are the first father of my children. . . . Suffer them to die, rather than offend you.'[20] Here, perhaps, is the key to the rigid rules, the pious practices, of *casa Leopardi*: they were instituted by a woman haunted, for herself and for her children, by a sense of sin.

The character and will of Contessa Adelaide were never to suffer change. A few years after Giacomo had died in Naples, his mother, still alive and vigorous, was able to declare that she had succeeded in restoring the family fortunes to their original prosperity. But neither her son's renown nor his early death could alter her conviction that, in the sight of God, virtue alone was of any consequence, nor dispel her haunting fear that he had not used his gifts according to the Divine Will. Some ten years after his death an admirer of Leopardi's, Filippo Zamboni, went to Recanati 'on a pilgrimage' to his friend's house. There, in the room where the poet was born, 'beside his bed I saw his mother standing, majestic, austere, with snow-white hair. I pointed to Giacomo's portrait, and cried out: "Blessed be she who bore thee!"—whereupon she neither moved, nor bent her head nor turned to me; only lifting up her eyes to heaven, she exclaimed, "God forgive him!"' [21]

II

THE MAKING OF A POET

A voi ripenso, o mie speranze antiche,
*Ed a quel caro immaginar mio primo.**

AN evening party in *casa Leopardi*. The long reception gallery,
where Conte Monaldo and Contessa Adelaide were married,
has been opened for the occasion; a chill mustiness still hangs on the
air. The great chandelier has been lit; the marble busts in their niches
have been dusted, the floor polished and waxed. Presently the footmen bring in the meagre refreshments: dry home-made biscuits,
glasses of Marsala and of *vin santo*. A little later the guests begin to
arrive; the reception has begun.

The company that gradually assembles includes all that is notable
in Recanati. Conte Monaldo's mother, the Marchesa Virginia
Mosca, has come down for the occasion from her little apartment at
the top of the *palazzo*, and in attendance on her is her querulous old
cavalier servente, Volunnio Gentilucci. Don Giuseppe Torres, the
'assassin' of Conte Monaldo's studies, is talking to an Alsatian priest,
Johann Anton von Altkirch, who has taken refuge in Recanati after
his expulsion from his own country—a jovial, acute, and learned
man. The bishop from Loreto holds a central position under the
great gilt chandelier—as is suitable to his rank—and is conversing
with his host. Seated on stiff sofas against the walls are the gentry of
Recanati—a gentry as pious and austere, as narrow-minded and
parsimonious, as the Leopardis themselves. The ladies all sit together
in a group, talking of the dowry of Contessa Maria's daughter, of

* My mind is dwelling on my early hopes,
And on my first fond fancies.
                                        Le ricordanze.

20

the new images in the church; at the other end of the room the men discuss local politics and the unsatisfactory price of wheat. The candlelight flickers on their faces, reveals for a moment features puffed with over-indulgence or pinched with avarice, vacant with stupidity and pride. The air is heavy with the smell of unwashed garments, of stale powder and pomades. Hidden in the embrasure of a window, a small boy, whose fragile body is already dressed as a priest, peers out from behind a curtain of heavy red brocade; his large, inquiring eyes travel round the room, his glances falling upon each member of the assembly in turn. 'There is no place here upon which the eye can rest'—and with that Giacomo rushes out of the room.[1]

The little boy—Giacomo Leopardi himself—was then only eight years old, but he had already been dressed for two years as a little *abbé*, and when he was twelve he received the tonsure. At his birth on the 29th of June 1798, the news was sent by his father to all his friends in a letter informing them that his joy at the birth of his eldest son was all the greater 'in that it was preceded by forty-eight hours of anxiety, occasioned by the severe pains of the mother'.[2] Giacomo Leopardi, as was fitting, made his entry into the world with pain. On the following day he was baptized in the little parish church with the names of Jacobus, Taldegardus, Franciscus Sales, Xaverius, Petrus, and was laid in a cradle of cream and gold.[3]

His childhood, like that of his brothers and sister, was dominated by the indomitable will and unrelenting virtue of his mother, Contessa Adelaide, in a deliberate shaping of both their bodies and their souls. In illness she alone nursed them; even the ointment on their chilblains might be applied only by her hands. But above all she watched, day by day, the development of their spirit. 'Her eyes followed us unceasingly,' wrote her son Carlo in later years, 'it was her only caress.'[4]

In early childhood Giacomo slept with both his brothers, in a *boudoir* opening out of his mother's bedroom, and even when, later on, the boys were moved to an apartment looking over the garden, they could only reach it through the Contessa's rooms.[5] She accompanied Giacomo, who was then six, to his first Confession, and, to the boy's extreme discomfort, did not even move out of earshot while he knelt in the confessional.[6] Moreover, even

when Giacomo was fully grown-up, he complained that both his
parents were liable to open any letters addressed to him, or even
any which they thought might refer to him.[7] At meals the eldest
son sat on his father's right hand, and Monaldo has recorded that,
since the boy could not be bothered to use a knife, but tore at his
meat with a fork, he himself cut up every mouthful that his son ate,
and continued to do so until he was twenty-seven.[8] For indeed
Conte Monaldo was hardly less assiduous than his wife in watching
over both the moral and the physical welfare of his children.
When the three eldest were vaccinated—a daring innovation in those
days, which the Count was the first in Recanati to practise, sending
for the vaccine all the way to Genoa—he kept in his diary a daily
record of their progress,[9] and he also put up (this too was very
modern) swings and parallel bars for them in the garden. But further
than this the Count's innovations did not go, and it may be noted
that when, in his Will, he drew up a plan of education for some
young gentlemen of the Marches at his expense, he stipulated that
they should never be taught 'dancing, riding, fencing, or the use of
weapons', since 'these exercises are partly immoral and partly
dangerous, and should never be allowed in a wise and Christian
education'.[10]

This unceasing parental control, this semi-divine parental omni-
presence, strikes the reader of today with a sense of unbearable
oppression. And indeed Giacomo himself has left a record of his
feelings. 'The most beautiful and fortunate age of man', he wrote
in his notebook many years later, 'is tormented to such a degree
with a thousand anxieties, fears, and labours of education and instruc-
tion, that a grown-up man, even in the midst of all the unhappiness
caused by the disillusionment and tedium of life, and the deadening
of the imagination, would yet not accept to return to childhood, if
he had again to suffer what he suffered then.'[11]

This suffering was not caused merely, or even chiefly, by his
parents' strictness: many families have prospered under a rule quite
as severe as that of Contessa Adelaide. What was lacking was the
one thing that this particular child could not dispense with: an
atmosphere of love. 'I need love, love, fire, enthusiasm, life', he
wrote to his brother at the age of twenty-four.[12] His childhood
had held none of them. *Casa Leopardi* was a cold house, and he

needed warmth; a grey house, and he needed light. Conte Monaldo loved his children, but he was too much afraid of his wife to show them indulgence, and too much inhibited by his own prejudices to be easy-going. And Contessa Adelaide—perhaps she did love her children, too; but she thought it wrong to show it. As implacably as she snuffed out, between finger and thumb, a superfluous candle, she quenched her children's spontaneity. Giacomo was a child who needed praise: 'with a ferocious and merciless veracity'[13] she analysed his faults. He needed reassurance: she spoke to him, 'by preference', of what she had heard in his disfavour. Like most other children, he was naturally communicative and 'inclined to share any new impression, whether inner or outer'.[14] He would run up to his mother, crying, 'Look! Listen!' Beneath her cold grey eyes the new treasure dropped from his hand, the words from his lips. Very soon the habit of silence and secretiveness was formed, for ever.

When his mother scolded the servants sharply, he ran away, his fingers in his ears; and he has recorded that one day, when a poor woman had come to her, weeping over some lost opportunity, he overheard her comment: 'If you had only thought of it sooner, you might have got it,' and the cold unimaginativeness of this reply struck him as almost worse than cruelty.[15] Very possibly, as much as the words, it was the sheer harshness of the voice that he found intolerable. All his life long, he retained an acute sensibility to the timbre of people's voices, or indeed to any sharp sound. This became—not only in childhood but in later years—real suffering during a thunderstorm, or during the fireworks which enliven any Italian village *festa*. 'I did not believe that there was any danger,' he wrote, 'but I was no less frightened than if I had known the contrary.'[16]

His father was not unaware of his 'warm, lively, and apprehensive imagination'—but appears to have prided himself on it, rather than to have attempted to shield the child. At the age of four Giacomo was led into the great *salone*, which the children were only allowed to enter on special occasions, and there, in the centre of the hall, he saw a table covered with red velvet and with cushions of red damask, with a lighted taper at each corner. The little boy ran up to the table, stood on tiptoe—and saw the corpse of his baby brother, 'dressed as a little St. Louis!' 'He has gone to Paradise,' Giacomo was told; 'say a prayer and kiss him good-bye.' He tried to obey, but as his lips touched the cold baby hands, he was seized with such a fit of sobbing that his father, in describing the scene, commented with complacency on the precocious sensibility of his eldest son.[17]

On another evening in the same year Giacomo was taken, after dark, to watch a penitential procession through the streets of Recanati. Down the long street the penitents came, preceded by members of the various religious confraternities carrying lighted torches, and followed by monks with black cowls over their heads. The torches, the dark, moving shadows, the corpse-like whiteness of the monks' faces under their black cowls—all this struck such terror into the child that for many nights he could not sleep, and —according to Monaldo's own account—his parents feared for his reason.[18]

This may well have been the origin of his fear of seeing people in masks—a frequent occurrence in carnival time, but to him so unpleasant that at the age of twenty the impression still endured. 'No misfortune,' he wrote, 'no fear or danger, however formidable, at a later time seems to me strong enough to produce in us such anguish, torments, horrors, terrors, insomnia, as those so-called childish apprehensions.'[19]

But most unpardonable of all, in Leopardi's own opinion in later years, were the fears deliberately instilled by unscrupulous nurses, who terrified their charges into docility by telling them ghost-stories at bedtime—'so that the impression made upon their souls by these tales heard in the darkness, should be indelible'. And he proceeded to describe the results, in a manner which makes it plain that he was speaking of himself. 'Hardly can he lisp and make the sign of the Cross upon his forehead and breast, to show that he is born into the true religion, than tales of imps and apparitions have already found a place in his fearful and wondering mind. . . . He becomes aghast and afraid; he looks upon the coming of night as a torment, and on dark places as terrifying caverns; he shakes with anguish in his bed, sweats, and draws the sheets over him, tries to speak, and can only shudder from head to foot. The educator has achieved her intention. . . . She has taken from a child the one gift that can render human life as little unhappy as possible: Courage!'[20]

Thus Giacomo's imagination came to harbour all the menacing

phantoms which, since the days of the Ancients, have haunted the
dark recesses of men's minds: *Lamie* or *Striges* ('from which word
comes our name for *Streghe*, witches') and Fauns and Satyrs, 'more
insolent than words can tell', who would hide along the roads 'and
mock at everyone who passed, terrifying them and laughing at their
fears', while others 'would lie in ambush, and attack the passers by,
murdering them and barbarously tearing them to pieces'. Then, too,
there were the *larvae*, 'who were said to be evil men who had become
demons and who had the faculty of terrifying children and croaking
in dark corners. . . . Such', he wrote, 'were the fearful objects that
made the ancient peoples tremble, and that, it must be said, still
cause fear in us, too.'[21] For hours, rigid with terror, the child would
lie awake listening to the creaking of the weather-cocks and the
bells of the city watch-tower, and counting the chimes that brought
the dawn a little nearer.

> . . . Era conforto
> Questo suon, mi rimembra, alle mie notti,
> Quando fanciullo, nella buia stanza,
> Per assidui terrori io vigilava,
> Sospirando il mattin.*

Yet seldom, surely, has there been a boy who was less in need of
this rule of fear. Conte Monaldo described him as 'a most docile
and amiable child', and he himself has recorded that he believed
every word his parents told him, even to the extent of thinking 'that
everything tasted good that was praised by those who gave it to
me'[22] and waiting, in any trouble or anxiety, 'to determine the
degree of my own affliction or apprehension, until I had seen or
conjectured what my father's was'.[23] He looked upon his father
as a being immeasurably superior to all others, and showed 'a blind
submission to his authority', and an equal faith in his kindness.
Moreover he showed an unusual degree of infant piety. He took a
deep pleasure in going to church and serving Mass, 'calling that day
a happy one, in which he had been able to attend more Masses than
usual';[24] and at home he set up a little altar, at which he played

* This sound was a solace, I remember, during the nights when, as a child, in a
dark room, I was kept awake by haunting fears, sighing for the dawn.

Le ricordanze.

with his brothers. (It is reassuring, however, to hear that they sometimes made so much noise at this game that their father, sitting in
the library below, would have to tap in protest on the ceiling with
his long stick!) He bore the Cross at the reconsecration of the
church's font; he wrote a little poem on the Three Kings, which
obtained the praise of his great-uncle, Cardinal Antici,[25] and he
enthusiastically took part, at Christmas-time, in a little Nativity play
written by Conte Monaldo for his children, 'so that they may be
good, and love him, and pray to Jesus and Mary for him'.[26]

What was going on in Giacomo's head, he himself has told.
'Seeing some pictures of St. Louis riding through the streets of
Rome, and people calling out, "There goes the Saint!" the boy said
to himself, "I too, when I am grown-up, will be like that—and the
people, when they see me pass, will cry, 'There goes the Saint!'"
And his devout parents,' the poet added, 'took it for devotion and a
heroic inclination to sanctity—as indeed he still did himself.'[27]

There was, indeed, a 'heroic inclination' in the boy, but it was
hardly for sanctity. He was overwhelmed with compassion, he
wrote, 'with everyone who, I saw, never could be great'[28] and he
was determined to excel in everything. 'I am the strongest!' he would
boast, when he had defeated another child in a race, or knocked
down his brother Carlo. Indeed, forty years later, Carlo said that he
could still remember the strength of his blows. But what he was
seeking was not so much victory, as *le beau rôle*. When the boys
played at Pompey and Caesar, it was always Carlo who was the
hateful '*Roman tiranno*', and Giacomo who played the heroic part
of Pompey. And one year, at Christmas, he proudly presented his
father with a tragedy entitled *Pompey in Egypt*, in which the future
author of the ode *All' Italia* plainly saw himself in the title rôle:

> Me sol pugnar, me sol cadere estinto
> Del fier tiranno appiè. . . .*

But the best game of all was that of the Roman Triumph, using
as a war-chariot the cart in which the lemon and orange trees were
carried out of the orangery in spring-time, and back again into
shelter in the autumn. On these occasions Giacomo was in his

---

* 'I fighting alone, I alone falling dead at the feet of the proud tyrant.' This
'tragedy' was written in 1812, when Giacomo was fourteen.

greatest glory, for the small peasant-boys joined his brothers to swell the train of his lictors and slaves.

That he was an attractive little boy appears from all accounts—even his own. 'My face,' he wrote, 'when I was a little boy, had a slightly serious and wistful look which, being without any affectation of melancholy, gave it charm.'[29] He had 'simple, natural, unaffected manners', deep-blue eyes, and a gentle little voice. The ladies of Recanati were kind to him, and one 'mature lady' told him how much she preferred him to his brothers, and tried to question him about his troubles. But he, according to his own account, 'avoided her, more than any other'.[30] Already his private world was his alone.

He was, however, delighted to go to the house of another lady of Recanati, Marchesa Volunnia Roberti—an intelligent, kindly woman, whose *conversazioni* were also Conte Monaldo's only resource of an evening, when the atmosphere at home had become unbearably oppressive. Here the Count played cards and chess with a few old friends, and held an innocuous flirtation with his hostess, while Giacomo ate her cakes and rearranged her books. And we have a letter to her from the boy, written at the age of twelve in the highest of spirits and purporting to be from *la Befana*—the witch who on Twelfth Night brings presents to Italian children, riding on her broomstick. In this letter he told the Marchesa to treat the children well, 'not only with coffee, of course, but with pastry, jam-tarts, pancakes, cream-puffs, and other gifts—for those who give *conversazioni* must be open-handed—and so yours will be called "the pastry *conversazione*".'[31] Here is a lively, mischievous Giacomo whom we have not seen before.

Fits of uncontrollable high spirits would suddenly come over him. Sometimes, in one of these wild moods, he would rush upstairs, with his brothers at his heels, to the little apartment at the top of the house where his grandmother, Marchesa Virginia Mosca, lived, and where, every evening, she received a visit from her old *cavalier servente*. The children would rush in yelling, hugging their grandmother and overturning the chairs and tables, while the old bachelor tried to conceal his annoyance. '*Che specie graziosa!*'* he would say with thin lips, holding up his *lorgnon*—'as if we were a sort of

* 'What a charming species!'

monkey', the boys commented. And then Monaldo from below would hear a crash and a cry. 'They've upset the lamp again,' he would sigh—and hope that his wife had not heard, too.[32] And we have, too, a highly spirited account in verse of the day when Giacomo and his brothers terrified their severe old tutor, Don Vincenzo Diotallevi, by demanding his money or his life, in masks, on a lonely country road.[33]

In all these pranks Giacomo's inseparable companions were his brother Carlo and his sister Paolina. Of Contessa Adelaide's twelve children, seven died still-born or in infancy—thus freeing their parents (in the Contessa's own words) 'from the trouble of bringing them up'—and the other two who survived, Luigi and Pierfrancesco, were too young to be Giacomo's playmates. But Carlo and Paolina, who were respectively one and two years younger than himself, were his only friends—and his first audience. Paolina, who afterwards learned to copy out his work in a writing almost indistinguishable from his own, was a grave, clever, ugly little girl, whom her brothers called 'Don Paolo'—partly because her natural seriousness, her short hair, and the straight dark tunic in which she was dressed did indeed give her the air of a little priest, and partly because her favourite amusement, like Giacomo's, was to play at saying Mass. For some years she shared her brothers' studies and took part in their monthly examinations, and we read of her being presented by them with a wreath made, not of laurel, but of sausages! And in the evening, as she grew a little older, there were long confidential conversations with Giacomo, the brother and sister pacing up and down in the dark, because the light was painful to his eyes.

But gradually Paolina's life became more and more restricted; even the slight degree of liberty that was allowed to her brothers was taken away from her. Her only distraction was to write long intimate letters to two young women whom she herself had never seen —Marianna and Anna Brighenti, the daughters of Giacomo's publisher—and these letters she was obliged to write in secret at night, while her friends' answers had to be sent to her under cover to her brothers' preceptor, Don Vincenzo. When a letter arrived for her, he would place a flower-pot upon his window-sill, to convey the good news, and then at night Paolina would steal to the library to fetch it. For in this, too, the insurmountable obstacle was Contessa Adelaide's intense possessiveness—not for herself, but for God. 'My mother', wrote Paolina, 'cannot bear my making friends with anyone, because, she says, it distracts me from the love of God—nor can she bear to see any letter addressed to me.' And once, when her friends came to stay nearby, Paolina was obliged to inform them not only that it would be impossible to pay them a visit, but that when they drove into Recanati to church, she would not even be free to catch a glimpse of them out of the window. 'My mother wanders round the house and is everywhere at every time, and all that I see out of the window is controlled by her.'[34]

Yet she was not without spirit. No less violently than Giacomo did she rebel against the narrowness of their daily life, and her hatred of Recanati was no less intense. 'Among the causes', she wrote, 'that have dried up the source of happiness in me, is the fact of having to live in Recanati, that odious and abominable spot.' Poor Paolina! She had all her brother's melancholy, without his genius. 'I could wish no human being', she wrote, 'to lead a life like mine, deprived of every hope except that of soon leaving this world. Dear Antonietta, you cannot imagine how one can suffer in a prison like mine, in this horrible and detestable village—with a past of painful memory, a soul-destroying present and a desolate future. No, you would not believe it possible to live like this. And yet live I do, I live with a heart that is naturally warm, but is gradually becoming colder; with a nature that used to be sensitive, but which the evil of men and my experience of life have rendered dull and indifferent—I do live, but sometimes I ask myself whether I am indeed alive, and often I should prefer not to be.'

Paolina shared with Giacomo an intense desire to travel. 'If I could enter a post-carriage,' she wrote, 'and travel round the world, embarking from time to time on a great ship, and so spend the rest of my life living *alone* and seeing all the beauty and ugliness of nature—then I should be happy! Imagine then how much I must suffer, who cannot even get to see the pretty parts of this village, which are few enough, imagine what I feel when I read travel-books or descriptions of lovely places—then I burst into tears and throw the book away. I *cannot* get accustomed to my sad state.' And, in a later letter: 'There is no single thing on which my mind can rest with joy. Oh, there is no single serene day—not one, of which I can say: "Today I have been happy!" '³⁵

Throughout his life Giacomo remained devoted to his sister and continued to correspond with her, but an even closer friend was his brother Carlo. At the age of nineteen he wrote about him: 'Of my many brothers, there is one with whom I have always been brought up (he being only one year younger than I), so that he is my universal confidant, and shares my studies.' He was Sancho Panza to Giacomo's Don Quixote—though, as they grew up, Carlo tried to hold his own. Their political and literary opinions differed: Carlo was a pure Romantic, an admirer of all that was French; Giacomo, at that time, a Classicist, with a violent hatred of France. Their discussions enlivened the tedium of the interminable Recanati evenings; and when Giacomo, at last, escaped to a wider world, his letters to Carlo continued the old intimacy. 'No friendship', he wrote, 'will ever be equal to ours, which has its foundation in so many memories. You, your love, and the thought of you, are the pillar and the anchor of my life.'

Meanwhile, in these first years, Carlo was not only confidant and playmate, but also a willing audience. From his earliest childhood, Giacomo had had an insatiable passion for fairy-stories. At the age of three or four, he would run to everyone in the house, pestering to be told another one—and these, when he was a little older, he repeated in bed, in the early mornings, to his brother. But soon these tales gave place to long serial stories of a different kind. They described the fantastic adventures of members of his own family— Monaldo being the cruel tyrant Amostante, Carlo the handsome but stupid young gallant, Lelio Testadura—while the hero, Filsero the brave, the eloquent, the invincible, was of course Giacomo himself. And so witty—at least to the ears of the faithful Carlo—were some of Filsero's retorts that, forty years later, he could not hear a good joke without exclaiming: '*Ah, questa è Filserica!*'*

These myths were Giacomo's instinctive defence against his life of subjection; he found a measure of freedom in telling them, and his brothers, in listening. But many other fantasies—too elusive to be fully captured, too precious ever to be told—haunted the child's imagination, and belonged to him alone. They were his retreat from

* 'Ah, this is like Filsero!' Carlo Leopardi's *Reminiscences* to Prospero Viani.

the world of love, which had cast him out, into the world of fantasy. Only very rarely can we catch a glimpse of the strange, solitary little boy, in this new world of his own. What did he see there? 'A house suspended in the air'—so runs an entry in his notebook—'held by a rope to a star.'[36] And here he is, peering out 'at the moon and a clear sky', from a little window at the top of some garden steps, 'like Noah in the Sacred History'.[37] 'It was his delight'—this is another note—'to walk, counting the stars.'[38] One evening, when everyone else was asleep, he crept up to the attic and, holding up some lighted candles in different positions, tried to make the shadows dance.[39] Another day, he 'made experiments with darkness', on his little brother, Pietruccio. And here is a longer note: 'Lying under the haystack at S. Leopardo at dusk and seeing a man coming towards me from the far horizon . . . a tower in the midst of all that space—how frightened I was by infinity!'[40] The picture of St. Cecilia in the dining-room made him 'wishful to contemplate beauty'; the songs of peasant-girls in the fields, or of workmen trudging home at night, down the empty village street, moved him to tears. But still sweeter were other sights, other sounds. . . . 'I remember', he wrote, 'hearing in fancy in my childhood strains sweeter than can be heard in our real world. I remember looking up at pictures of shepherds and their flocks, painted on the ceiling of my rooms, and imagining a pastoral life so lovely, that were it to come true, this would not be our earth, but paradise—a home for gods, not men.'[41]

The years of childhood, he wrote, are 'the fabulous years' of a man's life, as the early years of its history are to a nation—the time of infinite promise, the golden age. 'For what the ancients once were, we all have been, and what the world was for some centuries, we were for a few years.'[42] During that short and happy time Giacomo, too, lived in an anthropomorphic world, in which trees and furniture and 'even the letters of the alphabet' took on a human aspect. 'Thunder and winds, sun and stars, animals and plants, and even the walls of the house, all seemed friends or enemies—none indifferent and none meaningless. . . . The colours of things, starlight, fire, the flight of insects, the song of birds, the transparency of water, all was new and unusual; no incident seemed commonplace, nor did we know the cause of anything, but made it up for ourselves; tears were daily events, and all passions still vivid and un-ruled. How easily at that time one's imagination took fire . . . how it enlarged small things, and adorned ugly ones, and lit up darkness—what living images, what happy dreams, what por-tents, what pleasant countries, what romantic inventions—what stuff for poetry, what richness, vigour, strength, emotion and delight!'[43]

In this Garden of Eden all inanimate objects were living and sentient creatures: 'Never alone, we asked questions of the pictures on the walls, of trees and flowers and clouds, we embraced stones and trees.' Every grove had its shrine, every stream its nymph. 'What a fine time that was,' Leopardi cried, 'when everything came to life, according to the human fancy . . . when we were sure that beautiful Hamadryads and Sylvans and Fauns and Pan lived in the woods, and Naiads in the springs. And, clasping a tree to your breast you almost felt it tremble in your hand, and believed it to be a human being, like Cypress.'[44] This was the state of mind which, in his arid later years, Leopardi most longed to recapture. 'The truly strong, green, fruitful, creative imagination', he wrote, 'belongs to children only.' And in his essay *In Praise of Birds*, he suggested the pleasing conceit that, of all living creatures, it is per-haps in birds that we may find an imagination most akin to that of children. 'Not the deep, fervid and tempestuous imagination of Dante and Tasso . . . but the rich, varied, light and unstable imagina-tion of childhood, which gives birth to light and gay thoughts, and sweet errors, and varied delights and comforts—the greatest and most fruitful gifts that Nature has courteously awarded unto human souls.'[45]

'What stuff for poetry', indeed! It was a world on which, in later years, he looked back with infinite nostalgia—claiming that with the end of those 'illusions' and the advent of reason, the creative spirit began to shrivel. And even at the time, he clung to it with an un-childlike, almost desperate, tenacity. His imagination, he wrote later on, was fixed with great intensity on a very few ideas ('unlike that of most children, which leaps from one thing to another') and this caused him to be terrified of anything unusual that might be disturb-ing and to clutch at all that was customary and familiar, 'outside of which he could not find peace'.[46]

Never, perhaps, was there a child more precociously tormented by self-awareness. 'He already knew almost all the good and evil in himself,' he wrote, in some fragmentary autobiographical notes, 'and was always going *au devant* of his own progress.'[47] What he held in his hand was already valueless; what lay before him, might never be attained. 'When we hoped for some good thing,' he wrote, 'what were our anxieties, our terrors, our tremblings . . . at every little obstacle!' Even when the treat, so anxiously hoped for, was reached, it lasted so short a time, and was followed by 'such dark and intense sorrow' at its termination! 'Indeed our sorrow then was inconsolable—not so much because the pleasure was over, as because it had not come up to our expectations, and in consequence we sometimes suffered from a sort of remorse, as if our lack of enjoyment had been our own fault. For experience had not yet taught us to have few hopes, and to be prepared to have those hopes destroyed . . .'[48]

One day his mother came upon him 'weeping because he was a man', and laughed at him. (But little Pietruccio, on his knee, tried to comfort him, stroking his cheek.) How could he tell her that his grief was nothing less than an awareness of mortality? Long before he could formulate his knowledge, the boy knew that nothing is stable, nothing ours; that the whole of life is but a process of losing. 'When I saw someone going away—even a person to whom I was quite indifferent—I would consider whether it was possible or probable that I should ever see him again. And if I decided that it was not, then I would watch and listen, following our guest with all my eyes and ears, always revolving within my mind this thought: "This is the last time, I shall never see him again!"'[49] Once, when he was taken to play with some other children, and was called away before the game was over, the pain of this disappointment was so intense that, many years later, he could find no more vivid image for the insecurity of human life. 'The life of man seemed to me to be as when, in childhood, I was taken to see friends, and began to play with the other children, seated around a table—and then my parents got up and called me, and my heart was heavy—but I had to go, leaving the game unplayed and the chairs upset and the children weeping.'[50]

So the first ten years of Leopardi's life went by: in dreams and

D

fantasies, in early grief, in premature self-awareness, in repressed affection. A child observant, silent, fearful, passionate, secretive, vulnerable—playing with shadows, counting the stars.

The portrait is one that the future hardly changed. But one more door was still to be opened—into the world of books.

IN CONTE MONALDO'S LIBRARY
(1812—1817)

. . . e intanto vola
*Il caro tempo giovanil.**

THE year 1812, when Giacomo Leopardi was fourteen, was an important one in the annals of Conte Monaldo: it was the year in which he formally opened, for the use of his fellow-citizens, the great library in his own house, which he had been preparing for the past ten years. Ever since his early childhood Giacomo had watched, wide-eyed, the arrival of cart-loads and barrow-loads of books, and had seen the bricklayers and carpenters who, under his father's direction, knocked down walls and put up shelves in the three long rooms at the head of the main staircase—while Contessa Adelaide tightened her lips in disapproval. But Conte Monaldo was in his element. The small nucleus of books he had inherited had been enriched, in the years before his marriage, by any others that he could lay hands on. There were French books, bought on barrows at random before the Count had learned the language; there was the whole library of a neighbour, bought by weight; there were the books of his uncle, of the town doctor, of the parish priest, all hastily snatched up by Monaldo as soon as their owners died; there were 'several cart-loads' that had been stored in an empty church, belonging to some suppressed monasteries. There was even the complete collection of an old priest, Don Pietro Pintucci, who said he would give the Count his books 'for nothing', that is, for a modest annuity of forty *scudi*. Monaldo agreed, the priest lived for another eighteen years—and in

---

* And, meantime, sweet youth is flying by.
Le ricordanze.

the end the worthless little pamphlets came to cost 729 *scudi*! With the passage of time the Count's discrimination increased, but without diminishing his enthusiasm. When a French ship landed at Ancona, laden with books from the sacked monasteries of Corfu, he hurried down to the harbour for them; he bought Greek books for Giacomo's studies, and English for Carlo's; and eventually the library was also enriched by 300 books given to Giacomo by his friends or by other authors. In the end the collection was a very odd mixture of valuable works and sheer trash—'grammars and dictionaries and glossaries and commentaries, histories and orations and dissertations, erudite works of Hebrew, Greek, Latin, and medieval scholarship, subjects sacred and profane . . . great works and mediocre ones, all mixed up together'.[1]

The library is to be seen today, just as it was at that time. A small vestibule, adorned by busts of the four great Italian poets, leads into four long narrow rooms, their walls lined with books, their ceilings gaily painted with eighteenth-century designs, and their windows looking out on to a peaceful square. The traveller can still see the table at which Giacomo wrote, his white china inkstand, in which lie the desiccated remains of a carnation romantically left there by Carducci, and the brown woollen rugs which, on winter evenings, he wrapped around his shoulders and his shivering knees. In the first room, on the wall, hangs a large family tree; in the centre of the room are some glass cases in which one can see several early manuscripts of Giacomo's, including his ode *Ad Angelo Mai*, his *Inno a Nettuno*, his translation of the *Aeneid*, and many childish works— among them, painstakingly penned in a copperplate hand, a *Dissertation upon happiness*—a curious subject to set a boy of ten, even if that boy were not Giacomo Leopardi. Each division of the bookshelves is surmounted by a title in eighteenth-century lettering, marking the contents of that section: *Literae humaniores, Philosophia, Historia profana, Historia sacra, Jurisprudentia, Geographia, Polemica, Dogmatica, Moralia*, etc., while one shelf, which was locked, contained the books proscribed by the Church—among which, after Giacomo's death, his sister Paolina solemnly placed his own *Operette Morali*.

Conte Monaldo's study, beside the three rooms with bookshelves, still holds his desk (on which stands a small metal skeleton—*memento mori*), some shelves holding the bound manuscripts of his innumer-

THE LIBRARY OF PALAZZO LEOPARDI

(Here the poet worked. In the foreground, his table and inkstand.)

able works, and, on the wall, beneath a prayer of resignation in the
Count's own hand, the Crucifix clasped by his younger son, Luigi,
on his death-bed. And over the entrance-door of the second book-
room there is a marble tablet with the Count's inscription: '*Filiis
amicis civibus, Monaldus de Leopardis bibliothecam.*'*[2]

His fellow-citizens, alas, made little use of it. 'Over the door',
Leopardi wrote several years later, 'is inscribed that it is open to
every citizen. How many do you think come there? Never a one.'[3]
But he himself spent seven years of his youth there, and said it was
the happiest time that he had ever known. 'This divine state,' he
called it, 'when I was quietly occupied with my studies, without any
disturbance and with the quiet and certain hope of a most happy
future.'[4] A clever and precocious boy, he lived almost entirely in
the life of his mind. After learning the alphabet and his catechism
from Don Vincenzo Diotallevi, the family chaplain, he had received
his first lessons from the 'assassin' of his father's studies, Don
Giuseppe Torres; but he was soon handed over to a new teacher, the
Abate Sebastiano Sanchini from Pesaro, while the boy's first French
lessons were given him by a French refugee priest, l'Abbé Borne.
Certainly none of these ecclesiastics can have complained of laziness
in their pupil. Before he was twelve he had acquired a solid basis of
Latin, and enough rhetoric, theology, and physics to enable him to
dispute with his teachers on these subjects, not only in the presence
of members of his family, but of other 'fellow-citizens' of Recanati.
Monaldo issued the formal invitations and even had copies of the
programmes printed, with a list of the questions, to which the small
candidates (for Carlo and Paolina shared in these studies) had to
answer in Latin. The first of these programmes, dated 30 January
1808, may still be seen in Palazzo Leopardi: 'The three Leopardi
children—Conte Giacomo Tardegardo, aged nine, Conte Carlo
Orazio, aged eight, and Contessa Paolina, aged seven—will present
themselves in an exercise dedicated to their most loving great-uncle
Conte Ettore Leopardi—the two boys answering questions in grammar and rhetoric, and the Contessa Paolina in Christian doctrine and
the history of the world, up to the fall of Carthage'![5] Four years
later, in 1812, the last of these examinations took place, and this was
the end of Giacomo's studies under a tutor, for—so his father

* 'For his sons, friends, and fellow-citizens, the library of Monaldo Leopardi.'

proudly informs us—'the master had nothing more to teach him'.[6]

So Giacomo, at the age of fourteen, entered into possession of his father's library, and took his education into his own hands. He began —this at least is agreeably childish—by compiling an 'Index of the works produced by me, Giacomo Leopardi, from 1809 to 1812'.[7] These included his first sonnet, *La morte di Ettore*, written at the age of eleven after reading Homer, a translation of the first two books of Horace's Odes, a parody of the *Ars Poetica*, a poetic epistle (dedicated 'To his dear Father, after two months' study of philosophy'), and—perhaps in rivalry with his father, who also fancied himself as a dramatist—two full-blown tragedies.[8] All these are still, of course, merely scholastic exercises; Giacomo was playing with words, as other boys with toy soldiers—marshalling his troops into formations, making reconnaissances into unfamiliar country, conquering new positions. But all the time he was acquiring the tools of his trade. By the time he was fourteen, he could make free use of almost every verse form; he could write odes, octets, sextets, free endecasyllables, and above all, could make a free use of the Dantesque *terzina*. 'It is not yet poetry,' comments De Robertis, 'but it is literary art—and that is something.'[9]

And by the time Giacomo was fifteen, the apprenticeship was already over; Giacomo had become an independent, an indefatigable scholar. 'Segregated from the world,' says De Sanctis, 'his father's library became to him a sort of Pompei, in which he shut himself up to excavate, as best he could, the past.'[10] It was a room neither sombre nor depressing, but in winter it was bitterly cold; and here, in every season, Giacomo spent the whole day, only interrupting his studies by an hour of talk with his brothers in the evenings, while he walked up and down in the dark, to rest his aching eyes. And when, at bedtime, he retired to his own room, we know that his studies were continued far into the night, for his brother Carlo has recorded that, if he woke up, he would see him 'kneeling by the table to write by the last dim light of the guttering candle'.

Already he was possessed by the conviction that his life would be short, that not one hour—no, not one minute—could be wasted, if he was to reach the fame for which he thirsted. It was upon the Classics that he fastened, and soon, not satisfied with Latin, he decided to teach himself Greek. A month later he was proficient enough to write a letter to his uncle in that language, and from that time onwards he left no shelf of the library unexplored. What the boy accomplished within the next four years it is almost impossible to believe. 'He entered those rooms', wrote De Sanctis, 'a citizen of Recanati; he left them a citizen of the world.' He had the enthusiasm, and also the leisure and insatiable curiosity, of a medieval scholar. 'He came to know', Giordani wrote, 'the world of two thousand years ago, before he knew that of his own time; and what is more surprising, from this lost ancient world he learned what his own was, and how to value it.'[11] He lived surrounded by lexicons and grammars—Greek, Latin, Hebrew—he commentated, annotated, dissertated, imitated. No classical scholar was too obscure, too erudite, to please him: 'they formed', he wrote, 'my whole delight'.

His first choice of an original subject, however, is suggestive: a *History of Astronomy*. It is, naturally enough, merely a compendium of other men's erudition, turgidly and awkwardly presented; but the lines of Ovid which he chose for his frontispiece are significant:

> . . . iuvat ire per alta
> astra, iuvat terris et inerti sedes relicta
> nube vehi, validique umeris insidere Atlantis.*

Already the boy, for all his heavy cargo of learning, knew by instinct that the high heavens would be his dwelling-place.

But this was only the beginning. In the course of the next two years we meet with a prodigious, a truly terrifying output of erudite compositions, of which only a few need even be listed here. His genius for philology developed as suddenly, as astonishingly, as Pascal's for mathematics. His first Greek work was a translation of the works of Hesychius of Milo; then followed a commentary on the writings of four Greek rhetoricians of the second century, and notes for a work on the Early Greek Fathers of the Church. How great his father's pride was, may be inferred from the inscription on the flyleaf of the work which Giacomo gave him on his sixteenth birthday, a translation into Latin of Porphyry's *Commentary on the*

---

* It is good to wander among the high stars, it is good to float over lands and deserted places on an idle cloud, and to seat oneself on the strong shoulders of Atlas.

Life of Plotinus: 'Today, August 31st, this work of his was given to
me by my eldest son Giacomo Leopardi, who has had no master in
the Greek language, and is sixteen years old, two months, and two
days.'[12] In his satisfaction, the Count even sent off the manuscript
to the Abate Cancellieri, a well-known Roman philologist, who not
only added his own praise upon the fly-leaf but also referred to the
work in Rome in a 'Dissertation on men endowed with great memories'. 'What may not be expected', he wrote, 'in maturity, of a
young man of such astonishing ability?'

Monaldo's gratification was no less great than his son's, and great,
too, was his satisfaction when a party of learned Jews came to
Recanati from Ancona, and—or so the Count relates—Giacomo was
able to converse fluently with them in Hebrew![13] But greatest of
all was his paternal pride when Giacomo produced a series of 'Dis-
courses on Sacred Subjects' and held two of them in Recanati, before
the members of a religious confraternity. Little could the poor Count
guess, from such beginnings, what a very different course his son's
genius soon would take!

And meanwhile, with undiminished enthusiasm, Giacomo was
continuing his studies. After his first taste of praise from Rome, he
was impatient to reach a larger audience. He had just finished a long
Essay on the Popular Errors of the Ancients, when an exciting piece of
news reached him: the Abate Angelo Mai, the librarian of the
Biblioteca Ambrosiana in Milan, had discovered a new manuscript
by Fronto—an author almost wholly, and perhaps deservedly, unknown. With great difficulty he succeeded in obtaining the book,
and feverishly set himself to translating it. Might not this be the first
step to fame? The whole family shared in the boy's hopes—Paolina
and Carlo copying out his work, and Conte Monaldo hastening to
send it off to a printer in Milan, Antonio Stella. And at the same
time Giacomo himself sent to Angelo Mai his graceful dedication:
'Others, when they dedicate, make a gift—I return to you a gift I
have received.' But the Abate's acknowledgment, though civil,
was not warm; Stella seemed disinclined to publish; and so the
matter dropped.

It was, however, at this time that—fortunately for literature—the
young man's mind was again taking another turn; he was returning
to the fabulous world of his boyhood. Had he indeed ever wholly

left it? 'Sometimes,' he wrote later on, 'when I was sitting quite still and thinking of other things, I would hear some verse of the Classics, quoted accidentally by a member of my family, and I would catch my breath and find myself obliged to take heed (*tener dietro*) to those lines.'[14] And indeed his brother has recorded that, when any member of the family wanted to draw Giacomo out of the brown study in which he often sat at meals, this was the only way to do so.[15] He read Virgil, and noted the 'marvellous childishness' of Circe's song; he read Ariosto—and as he was reading, some boys in the street were singing, '*Amore, amore, amore!*'[16] Many years later, he could hear their voices still.

But still nothing was further from his thoughts than that he himself could become a poet; it was only through scholarship that he hoped to be famous. 'My head was full of modern ideas, I scorned and rejected the study of our own language. . . . I despised Homer, Dante, all the Classics. . . . What has made me change my tune? The grace of God.'[17]

This change, which he himself called his 'conversion', and which he also compared to a gradual falling in love, took place between his seventeenth and his eighteenth year. 'My passage', he says, 'from erudition to poetry, was not sudden, but gradual—that is, I began to note in the Classics something more than I had before.' He discovered that the *Iliad* or an ode of Anacreon's aroused in him 'a crowd of phantasies, that people both my mind and my heart'; and when he read the *Aeneid*, and reached the second book, he found that inadvertently he was 'reciting it aloud, and changing tone, and catching fire, and perhaps sometimes letting a tear fall'.[18] Could he render such great art as this, he wondered, in his own language? 'Constantly and arduously I tried to find a way of making mine, if it were at all possible, that divine beauty.'[19] Moreover, in the boy's enthusiasm, the writer's deep instinct of assimilation and selection, for his own purposes, was already at work. 'When I have read a classical author, my mind is all in a turmoil and confusion. Then I begin to translate the best passages and their beauties, perforce examined and recollected, one by one, take their place within my mind, and enrich it, and bring me peace.'[20]

First he translated, in verse, a fragment of the *Odyssey*, the *Idylls* of Moschus, and the *Battle of Frogs and Mice* (of which, later on, he

made a second translation), and then the second book of the *Aeneid*;
and all were published between 1815 and 1817, in a literary review
of Milan, *Lo Spettatore*.²¹ They are works still at times scholastic
or imitative; the strains of Moschus reach us by way of Tasso, of
Politian: '*Sicule Muse, incominciate il pianto.*' Yet sometimes faintly,
on the breeze, another note is borne. '*Nelle mie quiete stanze.*' . . .
'*Pure alla rana Donar le ninfe interminabil canto.*' To those whose ear
is attuned the accent, already, is prophetic.

At all these translations, but especially at the *Aeneid*, Leopardi
laboured with meticulous, anxious care. 'Innumerable passages are
corrected and altered,' he wrote, and yet in the end he rejected the
whole translation as insufficiently polished. In his hands, he said rue-
fully, Virgil's brush had become a mere pen. Yet with what high
hopes and fears these works were sent off—to receive, as he hoped,
the verdict which would shape his whole future! 'On my knees,' he
wrote, in a short preface to the *Odyssey*, 'I implore the literary men
of Italy to give me their opinion.'²² He was 'torn between hope
and fear'; he wrote to his publisher, 'forgive this importunity from
a man who has no other thoughts or pleasures in his life but these'.²³

The phrase about the *Odyssey* was then thought ridiculous, and
no one took the pains to answer. But now the young man's amazing
versatility had taken another turn. Might he not follow, he thought,
the example of Michelangelo, 'who buried a Cupid he had sculpted,
and when the man who had dug up the statue believed it to be
antique, brought him the missing arm'?²⁴ Giacomo's Cupid was
a *Hymn to Neptune* which—so he informed the readers of *Lo Spettatore*—had recently been discovered by a Roman scholar in 'a torn
codex, of which only a few pages remain in a small library',²⁵
and had been translated by himself from the original Greek; and this
was followed by two Greek odes—the *Odae adespotae*—purporting
to have been found in the same codex, and to be by Anacreon, but
of course really composed by Leopardi himself, and by him, too,
translated into Latin verse.²⁶ Always Anacreon's poems had pleased
Leopardi greatly. 'Were I to attempt to describe the indefinable
effect that Anacreon's odes have upon me, I could find no more
suitable image than the passing of a summer breeze, scented and
refreshing . . . that opens your heart to a delight that is already fled,
before you have fully felt or savoured it.'²⁷ And now it was this

elusive melody that the young poet sought to capture, and his verses bring us to the threshold of the world that, afterwards, he made his own. The first poem, indeed—a madrigalesque address *To Love*—still has something of the workshop, but in the second, *To the Moon*, there is already a clearer promise.

> Medium per caelum tacite
> Nocturna solaque iter facis.
> Super montes, arborumque
> Cacumina, et domorum culmina.*

Have not these lines—to the reader of the *Canto notturno* and *La sera del dì di festa*—a strangely familiar ring? And in the same year the young writer composed another poem, *Le rimembranze*, which began:

> Era in mezzo del ciel la curva luna.†

Thus, in the first faint foreshadowing of a theme by a single flute, we may hear already the violins and trumpets, the oboes and the drums, of a great orchestra.

So Giacomo spent his youth, and it was the only period of his life of which, later on, he could say that he was happy. 'The days passed without my knowing it, and all their hours seemed short; and I myself at the time often marvelled at the happiness I felt. . . . And this state', he added, 'I shall never find again.'[28] No, it would not return. For at some moment between his seventeenth and his eighteenth year—how or why, we do not know—a sudden anguish seized him. He realized what, in these mole-like years, he had done to himself. For seven years he had lived only in his books; he had allowed himself no time for recreation, for exercise, for intercourse with friends of his own age; he had grudged even the short time snatched for his meals. 'What a life,' cried the ladies of Recanati, 'what a way to spend one's youth!'[29] Perhaps one morning his eyes ached so much that he was forced to stop reading, and looked in a mirror; perhaps he tried, as in the old days, to run a race with his brother, and discovered how quickly he became exhausted, how his head hammered and his pulses beat; perhaps his eyes fell upon some

---

* Silently through the skies you take your nightly path alone; above the mountains, the tree-tops, and the roofs.

† The sickle moon, in the sky's zenith.

ridiculous, but none the less painful, verses, addressed to him by a
young lady of his acquaintance:

> Non ti crucciare, almo giovinetto,
> Se il dorso 'ai curvo, se ansimante il seno.*

Suddenly his eyes were opened, and what he saw aroused in him
not only despair, but rage. The seven happy years at his books he
now called 'seven years of mad and desperate study'; and his father's
indulgence, 'criminal blindness'; while to his mother he attributed a
still more sinister motive. 'She considered beauty a true misfortune,
and seeing her children ugly or deformed, gave thanks to God.' Such
thoughts are not healthy food for a boy of eighteen; their bitterness
warped and haunted him for the rest of his life. 'I have miserably
and irremediably ruined myself', he wrote, 'by rendering odious
and contemptible my outer appearance . . . the only part of a man
which most people take into account. And not only the common
herd, but also all those who desire that virtue should have some
physical adornment, when they find me utterly wanting in this
respect, will hardly dare to love me—will hardly dare to love a man,
in whom nothing but his soul has beauty.'[30]

What was the appearance of the young man who wrote these
despairing words? It was not, surely, as unpleasing as he thought it.
He was slight and pale, and not very tall, but his face still had the
'serious and wistful' look which had charmed the ladies of Recanati
when he was a child; and his blue eyes held not only intelligence,
but tenderness. But the rather large head was sunk deeply between
his shoulders, and a very slight double hump had just begun to be
perceptible. To himself—for self-deception was never Leopardi's
weakness—he was quite plain about it. He was not like other young
men: in a society where to be different was to be an outcast, he was
a *gobbo*. Medical opinion seems to agree that what he suffered from
was scoliosis—a curvature of the spinal column which generally
takes place in adolescence, and which throws the frame of the
thorax out of place in such a way as to produce a slight double
hump, on the back and chest, and eventually—as in Leopardi's case
—may affect the functions of both the lungs and the heart. But how

---

* 'Do not distress yourself, noble youth, if your back is crooked and your
breath is short.' Quoted by Ferretti, *Vita di G.L.*, p. 35.

soon this deformity began, we do not know. All we know is that in
childhood Giacomo was as strong and straight as Carlo himself, and
that when, in 1816, his publisher Stella saw him for the first time,
the deformity was already noticeable. The silk cape of his ecclesiastical cloak, 'which is lifted up by the slightest breeze', concealed it a
little, and this, in Carlo's opinion, was one of the chief reasons why
his family wished him to become a priest.[31]

For Conte Monaldo was not indifferent to his son's welfare, nor
was he wholly blind; he merely walked in blinkers. Undoubtedly
the long years that the boy spent, while he was growing, bent over
his books, may have aggravated the condition of his spine, as well as
straining his eyesight. But none of this would Conte Monaldo admit.
Yet he was, in other ways, a careful father. We have seen how he
watched over the children's health when they were small, and in a
long letter to Ranieri after Giacomo's death he said with pride that,
although the boy had had 'a dangerous inflammatory illness of the
chest' (pneumonia?) at the age of six, he had had no other severe
illness, 'and, although never very robust, never spent a day in bed'.
He related, however, a number of nervous symptoms of his adolescence, and observed with some complacency that, however
foolish his son's caprices might be, 'with me he was always docile,
and yielded to my arguments and my prayers'.[32] On one point
only was he silent: he never referred, even by implication, to his
son's deformity.

In vain did the other members of the family try to arouse his
alarm. In 1813, when Giacomo was fifteen, his uncle, Marchese
Carlo Antici, sent his father a long letter of warning. 'You tell me
that your unequalled Giacomo is learning Greek without a teacher,
and hopes to master it in the course of one year, and afterwards to
teach himself Hebrew. I congratulate you, him, and the priesthood,
to which he already seems dedicated—but allow me to express my
apprehensions for his health. Were Giacomo to mitigate his exhausting concentration by some exercise in horsemanship, my fears would
be greatly diminished; but knowing that his long hours of study are
broken only by the discharge of ecclesiastical duties, I cannot escape
the distressing thought that his body is likely to become as frail as
his intellect is strong.'[33] And Marchese Antici begged his brother-
in-law to send Giacomo to stay with him in Rome, where the boy,

while still pursuing his studies with eminent scholars, could lead a more active life.

But Conte Monaldo—was it only owing to his satisfaction in his son's brilliance, or from a deeper, less acknowledgeable pride of race?—would not heed. He denied that Giacomo's health was being undermined, and though he agreed that a visit to Rome might benefit his studies, he firmly refused to let him go. 'For the present my preference is, that he should be less learned, but belong to his father, and live peacefully and cheerfully in the town in which Providence has placed him. . . . Depriving myself of him, I should lose the only friend I have, or hope to have, in Recanati, and I do not feel disposed to such a sacrifice.'[34] This at least is frank, and there is something pathetic in Monaldo's belief that his son was also his friend. Little did he foresee that Giacomo was soon to revolt against all the principles he had been at pains to instil; little did he realize that his rule already seemed a tyranny.

The months dragged on, and the years, and the boy was still in Recanati—and subject to long attacks of black, capricious melancholy. Sometimes it drove him to a more violent frenzy of study than ever before; sometimes, instead, it manifested itself in a total apathy, in which, far from studying, he could not even read. Periods of intense emotionalism alternated with others of complete aridity; sudden bursts of gaiety, with attacks of anguish. At one time he would take interminable daily walks across the hills in total silence, even if his father or brother were with him; at another, he shut himself up for weeks, with no exercise at all. Sometimes he played with the thought of suicide. Leaning over the rim of the deep round well in the garden, he longed to sink down, down into its brown depths, never to return:

> Pensoso di cessar dentro quell'acque
> La speme e il dolor mio.*

But an hour later he would admit to himself—and note, with characteristic self-appraisal, in his diary—the inconstancy of even that desire. 'If I were to throw myself in, I would climb up on to the rim

---

* Hoping to drown within those waters
My sorrow and my hope.
Le ricordanze.

again, as soon as I reached the surface . . . and feel some moments of pleasure at having saved myself, and of affection for this life, which I now so deeply despise.'[35]

For several months he was convinced that he had, at most, only a year or two more to live, and it was then that, in eleven days, he wrote a long visionary poem entitled *The Approach of Death*. 'Composition of *Cantica*', he noted in his diary, 'at night, in the midst of grief.'[36]

> Dunque morir bisogna, e ancor non vidi
> Venti volte gravar neve il mio tetto,
> Venti rifar le rondinelle i nidi.*

Then this apprehension, too, receded. He would live, he believed, but 'clinging on to life by my teeth and doing only the half of what other men can do',[37] and 'torn always and without relief between acute pain and lack of all pleasures, between chronic tedium and burning shame at [my] physical deformities'.[38] What could life hold for such a man? 'I have not yet seen the world,' he wrote, 'but when I shall see it and have some experience of other men, I shall certainly have to retreat within myself. . . . What I fear are the things that will wound my heart.'[39]

It was with a mind set in this key that he stumbled into his first romance.

---

* So I must die, and yet I have not seen
   Full twenty times the snow upon the roof
   Nor twenty times the swallows build their nests.

IV

LA DONNA CHE NON SI TROVA*
(1817—1818)

Avranno tuttavia qualche mediocre conforto da questo fantasma ch'essi chiamano Amore.†

ON the 11th of December 1817 important visitors were expected at *casa Leopardi*. Conte Monaldo and Contessa Adelaide were at the door to receive them; at their side stood Carlo, the tall younger son, and Paolina, a shy, plain girl of sixteen in her best Sunday frock. Behind, in the shadow, waited the timid, serious boy in a priest's gown, who was secretly in a fever of expectation. 'For more than a year,' he had written in his diary, 'having begun to feel the power of beauty, I had been longing to speak, as all other men do, to attractive women; a single smile of theirs, thrown to me by chance, had seemed to me strange and sweet and wonderfully flattering. But this desire, owing to my enforced solitude, had remained ungratified until now.' At last the carriage rolled up—a private coach, with two fine horses. Conte Lazzari came from Pesaro, and this city, although still provincial, was less far from the great world than Recanati. He stepped out (an elderly man, noted Giacomo, fat and phlegmatic) and gave his hand to the ladies: first to a little girl, Vittoria, who was to be placed in a convent school in Recanati, then to his wife, Contessa Geltrude. A Junoesque beauty; her voluptuous figure, her dark flashing eyes, her manner, more candid and effusive than that of the ladies of Recanati—these in an instant were enough

---

* The woman who can never be found.

† They will yet obtain some moderate comfort from that phantom to whom they give the name of Love.

Storia del genere umano.

to captivate Giacomo. Embraces and introductions followed. Timidly Giacomo kissed the lady's hand; her eyes glanced over his black gown and his deformed body, and compassion mingled with repulsion to infuse a special cordiality into her greeting. Giacomo fled to his room, shut himself up, and noted in his diary that 'the ladies of Pesaro differ, in a certain indescribable manner, from our ladies of the Marches'.

Two days, and three evenings—that was the length of the lady's visit. The whole of Giacomo's first romance was compressed into this narrow compass, and his 'love-diary', begun the day after the lady's departure, tells us all that happened. It was little enough. The first evening he did not speak to her at all. The second day he was able to say 'a few cold words' before dinner; but during dinner, 'silent as ever, I fixed my eyes upon her, receiving a cold and curious delight in gazing at a lovely face—a delight considerably greater than if I had been contemplating a fine picture!' That evening his brother and sister played cards with the lady, 'but I, greatly envying them, had to play with someone else'. An interminable game; all the time Giacomo was listening to the laughter at the other table—would he, he asked himself, always be excluded from all that was pleasant, all that was gay? But he struggled to be victorious at chess, so that he might win her praise. If only she would come! He won, and she did come, but, 'thinking of other things', she did not even notice his victory. She leaned over his shoulder, asked to be taught the game, learned quickly; but all the others followed her, they insisted on teaching her too—and Giacomo's pleasure was spoiled. Would he never be alone with her, would his longing 'to talk to a charming woman' never be fulfilled? He heard that she was to stay on for one evening more, and all through the next day he looked forward to the evening's game, 'and it never entered my head that I might be discontented afterwards'. At last the evening came, and he played with her; but all through the game, 'the more I was enjoying myself, the greater was my anguish, caused by my eagerness to enjoy fully the delight which soon, too soon, would be lost to me'. Poor Giacomo! How often in the future these fears were to come between him and all enjoyment! All through his life his happiest hours were haunted by the sense of their transience, and this evening was but a foretaste of future suffering.

E

And now his premonitions were well justified; soon, too soon, his
mother interrupted the game, insisting that it must come to an end,
and as for Giacomo, 'instead of feeling the satisfaction that I expected,
I came away restless and discontented. . . . The lady had been kind
to me, and I for the first time in my life had caused a beautiful
woman to laugh at my wit, and had been answered by kind words
and smiles. . . . Therefore seeking in my heart why I was so dis-
satisfied, I could find no explanation. I did not feel the regret that
often pierces one's heart after some pleasure, because one has not
made the best possible use of it. No, I felt that I had done and
obtained as much as I could expect. . . . Only my heart was touched,
and at supper, attentive to every word and act of hers, I found they
pleased and moved me more and more. And in short, the lady was
very dear to me. But when I left her, I realized that on the morrow
she would be gone—and that never should I see her again.'

That is all. No word of love was spoken; nor did the Contessa
ever realize that, to this tongue-tied boy who gave her a lesson in
chess, her visit had been a revelation. 'I lay in bed', he wrote, 'considering the feelings in my heart: vague disquietude, disconsolate
melancholy, some sweetness, much affection, and a desire for I know
not what—nor can I imagine anything that would satisfy it.' For
hours that night he remained awake, living again through the evening and the preceding days, 'and when sleep came I dreamed again,
as in a fever, of the game and of its play, and of her'. He woke
before dawn, and through his window on the court came the sounds
of the travellers' departure: 'First horses clattering, then the arrival
of the carriage, and people walking to and fro—and then, listening
with the utmost impatience, I hoped every minute that the lady
would come down, that I might hear her voice again for the last
time—and so I heard it.'

The Contessa had gone, and in his diary Giacomo noted each
successive wave of emotion that swept over him during the next few
days. This 'love-diary' is a remarkable document, and an astonishingly sincere one. Through his grief, which is genuine enough, there
rings a youthful note of satisfaction at being able to feel so intensely.
'So here I am, nineteen years old, and very much in love. And I see
that love is a very bitter thing, and I shall always be its slave.'

For the first day after his lady's departure he was very unhappy;

he felt a 'little bitter pain that attacks me whenever I remember these past days, and I see a great emptiness around me'. He found it impossible to look anyone in the face, 'for it seems to me that the sight of any other face would contaminate the purity of my thoughts and of the vivid and clear image that is in my mind all the time. . . . And to hear that person spoken of, shakes and torments me. . . . By comparison, everything else disgusts me, and I despise many things which I did not despise before, even study, to which my mind is entirely closed, and almost, though perhaps not entirely, to fame as well.'

A little later, however, he was able to observe his feelings with detachment. 'I am sure that time will swiftly cure me . . . but now, wishing to relieve my heart, and not being able or wishing to do so except by writing, I have made this record in order to examine minutely the workings of love, and thus to be able to renew the first entry into my heart of this sovereign passion.'

As the days passed, his feeling for Contessa Geltrude gave place almost entirely to interest in his own emotions. One night he found that her image no longer returned to him as freshly as before, while he could clearly visualize the inexpressive countenance of her husband, 'for which I was not looking'! 'Nevertheless', he wrote, 'I enjoyed that state of still, even melancholy and meditation; for it seemed to render my mind more noble and more indifferent to worldly matters and to the opinion and contempt of others, and my heart more sensitive, poetical and tender.' Three days later he was really anxious; he feared that his 'dear sorrow' was 'about to depart'; he had recovered his appetite, he felt inclined to return to his studies, he almost thought that he might be able to laugh again! Fortunately, however, someone mentioned the lady's name in his presence, and this brought back the melancholy that he missed. 'I do not see how I shall be able to renew my old love of study, for it seems to me that even when my present infirmity of mind has passed, the knowledge will yet remain with me that there *is* one thing more delightful than study, and that once I experienced it.'

Two more days went by, and the 'melancholy object' of his love appeared to him in a dream in so confused a form that he felt no emotion whatever in remembering it on waking. And on the same day he decided to discontinue his diary, 'for, having nothing more to say, I feel that I am wasting my time . . . and that I had better start making use of it again, since my passion no longer impedes me'. He pictured to himself how agreeable it would be, when he had become a great and famous figure in literature, to appear before his lady and to be received by her 'with pleasure and esteem'. But in the meantime he had the candour to write: 'I will not deny that I have assisted and cultivated these feelings of mine with great care, and that part of my sorrow in seeing them weaken comes from my desire to be capable of feeling and loving. But, hating every touch of false romanticism . . . I have never written anything that I have not truly and spontaneously felt.' And in his final conclusion, after all, satisfaction prevailed over grief: 'I have felt one of those affections without which one cannot be great.'[1]

Did someone in Recanati, after the lady had gone, laugh at him, or show that his secret had been guessed? We can only surmise. In the *Zibaldone* there is a single passage which may give a clue. 'I have always been disgusted by the trivial and vile and ridiculous things that are said and done by the people I live with. . . . But never have I felt so horrible and tormented a distaste, as when I felt love in me, or some lingering of love.'[2]

The last echo of the episode is to be found in his notebook three years later. 'In the transports of love, in speaking to the beloved, in the favours she gives you, you are seeking for happiness rather than experiencing it; your agitated heart still feels something lacking—something, you know not what, for which you hoped—a longing for a little, for a great deal more.'[3]

'Seeking for happiness rather than experiencing it'—with these words Leopardi speaks not only for himself, but for his epoch. It is easy to overestimate the influence of a great man's contemporaries; but certainly at this period of his life he was much affected by the 'Romantics'. How, indeed, at the age of nineteen, could he have escaped? The works of Mme de Staël, of Rousseau, and Chateaubriand, *Werther* and *Don Juan* (both translated into French), were all to be found in Leopardi's library—and in them he found an echo of his own sensibility, a justification of his own disenchantment. 'If all my dreams had turned into realities,' he read in Rousseau, 'they would not have sufficed me; I would have continued to imagine, to dream, to desire. There was in me an unaccountable void that nothing could fill, an impulse of the heart towards another kind of delight, for which I had not the capacity, but only the need.'

These words might have been Giacomo's own. He never attained reality in love, because he was not seeking for it: he preferred his own 'illusions'. Contessa Geltrude, in all the pages of his love-diary, is never revealed to us as a real human being, a living woman. We are told no word that she spoke, we are shown no single gesture, no turn of her head. She is, like all the women he was to love, only a vehicle for his own emotions. Like Rousseau at les Charmettes, Giacomo was capable of avoiding the presence of his beloved, if he found that his image of her became more vivid in her absence. 'I have often avoided for several days', he wrote, 'the object that had charmed me during a delicious dream. I knew that the dream would be destroyed, on approaching the reality. Nevertheless, I was always thinking of that object, but not considering it as it really was; I contemplated it in my imagination, as it had appeared in my dream.'[4]

Soon after Contessa Lazzari's departure—in his own phrase, 'while melancholy was still fresh'—Leopardi composed a Petrarchian lyric, *Il primo amore*; but the poem, owing to a certain artificiality and stiltedness, is neither as vivid nor as moving as the diary. It was not till nearly six years later, in 1823, that he turned this experience —the first, but the decisive one, since never in his romances was he to come any closer to fulfilment—into poetry. Then, in the ode entitled *Alla sua donna*, he wrote of '*la donna che non si trova*'—the woman who cannot be found. 'She is', he told his readers, 'one of those images, one of those phantoms of celestial and ineffable beauty, who come to our imagination between sleeping and waking, when we are little more than children. . . . The author does not know whether this lady—and in calling her so, he shows that he loves none but her—was ever born, or ever will be; he knows that she does not live on this earth, and we are not her contemporaries. He seeks her among the ideas of Plato, in the moon, in the planets, in the constellations of the stars.'[5]

Here is a note older and clearer than that of the Romantic movement; it is that of Plato himself, of the philosopher who taught 'that all the truth and meaning of earthly things is the reference they contain to a heavenly original'. It is the love of Dante for Beatrice, of Petrarca for Laura—for a symbol, not a woman. 'The history of our loves', says Santayana, 'is the record of our divine conversations, of our intercourse with heaven. . . . In one sense, all mortal loves are tragic, because never is the creature we think we possess the true and final object of our love; this love must ultimately pass beyond that particular apparition.'[6]

Equally symbolic, equally transient, were the objects of Leopardi's next two romances; indeed they were so like each other that his biographers have devoted many pages to guessing who they were. It is completely irrelevant. Both were of humble birth, both died in early youth; one, the 'Nerina' of his poems, was probably called Maria Belardinelli; the other, 'Silvia', was the coachman's daughter, Teresa Fattorini. Both, his brother Carlo related, were only seen at a distance by the two young men from the library, as the girls sat by the open window opposite, weaving and singing. 'Distant and imprisoned loves,' he calls them, in a phrase that might be Giacomo's own —sweeter, more lovely, because distant and imprisoned. Indeed, of all Giacomo's romances, these are the only ones on which, in later years, he dwelled in memory without bitterness. They were the inspiration of two of his loveliest poems, written nearly ten years later, *A Silvia* and *Le ricordanze*.

All that we know of these early romances, apart from what is contained in these poems, is to be found in the fragmentary notes in which Leopardi also set down his recollections of his childhood— *Ricordi d'infanzia e di adolescenza*. Here are his first thoughts 'about a girl of humble birth' (Nerina or Silvia or maybe another) 'whom I often saw and then began to dream of, who always used to greet me. After the dream, I thought of what we would say to each other— but the next day I saw her, and was not even greeted by her, and so was uneasy. "You fool, her thoughts were elsewhere—and anyway you do not care for her, have never said or will say a single word to her"—and yet, I should have liked her to greet me. . . .'[7] Does not this contain the very essence of vague, ineffectual, youthful love?

The next fragment describes a May evening. The poet was outside the town, by a little wood of low trees, and there 'I had my much-desired glimpse of *la Brini*. . . . She was looking back after her master, who had just gone by—then she ran away in a great hurry, in her red dress with a gay handkerchief on her head, and as she turned, I saw her looking towards me for a moment. But she was unstable as a bee, resting here and there, and jumping up to see the *pallone* game, but all with a sweet seriousness; . . . My thoughts that evening, and my disturbance looking out over the fields and the setting sun and the city turned to gold . . . and my spirit was lifted to a great height . . . and so I knew that love would make a hero of me and render me capable of great things, even of killing myself.' Some time later he saw the girl again, and she greeted him 'kindly, or so I imagined'; but he was not alone, and could not get rid of his companion. He hurried back at last to the spot where he had left her, but with little hope of seeing her again, when suddenly she reappeared. 'I dreamed of her that night, and it was heaven to speak to her while she listened with a smile, and then I asked her if I might kiss her hand, and she stretched it out to me, looking at me with a simple and candid air. And I kissed it, without daring to touch her, but with such delight that only then in my dream did I realize for the very first time what these satisfactions can consist of, and this so vividly that suddenly, waking up, I saw that the pleasure had indeed been exactly what it would have been in reality, and was astounded. And thus I discovered that it is true that the soul can melt into a kiss, and so lose sight of all the world.'[8]

Was *la Brini* the 'Nerina' of his later poem, or was it some other woman? We do not know: and indeed it is enough that he should make us feel that here are youth and youthful love, feeding on its own dreams—the only love ever known by Giacomo Leopardi.

About the 'Silvia' of his poem we know a few bare facts. Teresa Fattorini, the coachman's daughter, lived in the square outside *casa Leopardi*, which the poet afterwards made famous in his poem *Il sabato del villaggio*. The windows of the library look out upon it; from his writing-table Giacomo could hear Teresa's voice singing, and, looking up from his books, he would see her sitting by her window, weaving.

> Mirava il ciel sereno,
> Le vie dorate e gli orti,
> E quinci il mar da lungi, e quindi il monte.

Lingua mortal non dice
Quel ch'io sentiva in seno.*

Then one day—perhaps from his mother—he heard that Teresa was
ill, dying of consumption. At first his comments were cold and
egotistic enough. 'I knew her little and the interest I felt was that
which I take in everyone who dies young, as I know I shall do, too.'
Then her illness dragged on, and one day he saw her weeping, but
she would not say why. 'And as some people live long enough to
enjoy their fame while they are still alive, she owing to the length
of her illness, watched her parents console themselves for her death,
forgetful of her and indifferent to her pain. Poor child, she did not
even die in peace, but tormented by cruel suffering.' 'And so', he
quoted from *Werther*, 'this is the end of all my hopes, my dreams,
and my infinite desires.'[9] For her, as for himself, he lamented, not
the mere approach of death, but the forfeiture of unexperienced joys.
It was the same grief that he had felt in childhood at the party's end,
with 'the game unplayed and the chairs upset and the children
weeping'.

Of Nerina we know only that she was gayer than Silvia; she is
seen dressing for a party and dancing. When he wrote of her ten
years later, the poet was almost able to forget that he had never
exchanged more than a few greetings with her; he could persuade
himself that for a season he too had been happy and loved. But now
Nerina too was dead.

Se torna maggio, e ramoscelli e suoni
Van gli amanti recando alle fanciulle,
Dico: Nerina mia, per te non torna
Primavera giammai, non torna amore.†

* I gazed at the cloudless sky,
   Orchards and golden lanes,
   And there the far-off sea, and here the hills.
   No mortal voice can tell
   The thoughts that filled my heart.
                              A Silvia.

† When May returns, and lovers greet their lasses
   With gifts of flowering boughs and serenades,
   For you, Nerina, spring will not return.
   For you, Nerina, love returns no more.
                              Le ricordanze.

FRIENDSHIP AND PATRIOTISM
(1817—1819)

. . . risveglia i morti
*Poi che dormono i vivi.**

LEOPARDI'S romances had given him little happiness; they had been dreams, rather than realities—an attempt to escape from the squalid world of Recanati, to find a spiritual climate in which he could breathe more freely. First he had found a refuge in books, then in romance; now, in the same year in which he met Contessa Lazzari, he was to find his first friend, the Abate Pietro Giordani. Leopardi was nineteen, Giordani forty-three, and one of the leading figures in the group of patriots and writers—Vincenzo Monti, Lodovico de Breme, Silvio Pellico—who had made Milan the centre of Italian liberalism.

'A decent fellow,' Carducci called him, 'learned and eloquent, even if his eloquence is now a little out of date, perhaps a little *exalté*, perhaps a little emphatic—but a great upholder of Italian prestige, an admirable friend, and at that time a considerable authority among the young, as a writer.'[1] He was, moreover, by temperament and experience, peculiarly suited to understand and to sympathize with Giacomo. He too, in childhood, had taken refuge from unsympathetic parents—a weak father, a hard, avaricious, bigoted mother—in a precocious devotion to study; he too had suffered in youth from ill-health and over-sensitiveness. At the age of twenty-three he had entered a monastery, chiefly to get away from

* . . . arouse the dead,
   Since the living sleep.
   Ad Angelo Mai.

57

his family; but after three years he had come out again, having
acquired an intense and intolerant anti-clericalism which coloured
his opinions for the rest of his life, and to which he soon added an
almost equally strong anti-aristocratic bias, and a burning passion
for freedom. A loquacious, rhetorical, impulsive, generous, and
sometimes touchy man, he could be extremely good company—and
indeed Byron, in speaking of the literary men he had met in Italy,
remarked that Giordani was the only man among them whom he
ever wished to see twice.[2] Above all, he had the qualities of which
Giacomo's lonely and repressed nature was most in need: enthusiasm
and simple human warmth.

Leopardi had first heard of him at the age of fifteen, when a
cousin of his father's, Marchese Benedetto Mosca, spoke of Giordani
as 'the first writer of Italy'. At this time Leopardi's longing to get
into touch with the well-known Italian writers of the day was
becoming almost an obsession. They were his heroes; to be known
by them, to enter through them into the world of letters, was, he
believed, the only path to fame—indeed, for him, the only approach
to life. 'Love and patriotism', writes Zottoli, 'reached him through
literature—they were literature before they were life.' It was natural,
then, that when Giacomo had completed his translation of the
second book of the *Aeneid*, he should have sent copies to the three
leading literary men of his time: the poet Vincenzo Monti, whose
own translation of the *Iliad* had recently appeared, the Abate Angelo
Mai, to whom he had dedicated his *Fronto*, and the Abate Pietro
Giordani. All three copies were sent with humble and deferential
letters, which asked for no reply, but plainly revealed the high hopes
in which they had been sent off.

'If it is a crime in a nobody to write of his own accord to a great
man of letters, then I am greatly in fault. . . . Nor can I proffer
anything in my excuse, save an incomprehensible craving to make
myself known to my prince (for certainly I am your subject, as are
all lovers of literature), and the trembling that comes over me as I
write, which I should not feel in addressing a king. . . . I do not ask
you to read my book, but only not to reject it, and in accepting it,
to make clear to me that you are not offended by my daring.'[3]
Monti replied with a neatly-turned compliment, followed by the
remark that the young author's work still contained many defects,

and some of them not slight;[4] Mai, with a cordial, but conde-
scending, word of encouragement, advising the young man 'to
transfer himself to a stage more worthy' than that of Recanati.[5]
But Giordani's answer changed the whole course of the poet's life.
The Abate's first letter, indeed, though courteous, was formal; the
adulation expressed by Giacomo had been so fulsome that he feared
his correspondent was pulling his leg! But when he heard from
Leopardi's publisher how young the writer was, and read his work,
a second letter went off post-haste to the 'Signor Contino'. 'I like to
think', he prophesied, 'that in the twentieth century Conte Leopardi
(whom I already love) will be remembered among those who
restored to Italy the honour she has lost.'[6]

Leopardi was overwhelmed, and in his reply all reserves were
thrown aside. For the first time in his life he was writing to a man
who had offered him friendship and help, who was willing to
receive the pent-up confidences of many lonely years.

'That I should actually see and read Giordani's writing,' he began,
'that he should write to me, that I should hope to have him as my
future master—these are things I hardly dare to believe . . . since
the things one longs for most seem most incredible, when they have
come to pass. I should like you to believe without reserve all that I
write to you, now and in the future—for every word, I promise
you, will come straight from the heart.' Then followed an outburst
of longing for someone to guide him on the path of letters. 'I have
a great desire—perhaps an immoderate and insolent one—for fame;
but I cannot endure praise of any part of my work that does not
satisfy me. That my work has many defects, I knew before and
know still better now, because Monti has told me so. . . . But it is of
little use to say to a blind man, "You are out of your road", unless
you also tell him which way to turn.'[7]

Giordani answered him in the tone of an affectionate elder brother,
advising him not to overwork, and to struggle against his dislike of
his native city, and Giacomo dared to believe that, at last, he had
really found a friend.

'How often', he wrote, 'I have implored Heaven to let me find
a man who was not only kind but also eminent in talents and erudition, and whom I might ask to honour me with his friendship! But I
did not really believe that such a boon would be granted.' He assured

Giordani that he was not overworking: 'I do not study more than
six hours a day. . . . I read the Classics in three languages (Latin,
Greek, and Italian) in pocket-volumes, and study in the manner of
the Peripatetics.' But as to Recanati, he kept his own opinion. 'Who
would ever have thought that a Giordani would attempt to defend
Recanati? It is all very fine to say that Plutarch loved Cheronea,
Alfieri loved Asti. They loved these towns—they did not live there!
So shall I, too, love my birthplace when I have got away from it. . . .
"But here you may be among the first; in a larger town you would
hold no such position." This seems to me a miserable form of pride
unworthy of a noble soul. . . . Here, dear sir, all is dead, all is folly
and stupidity. . . . Literature is a word unknown. The names of
Parini, of Alfieri, of Monti, of Tasso and Ariosto need explanation.
. . . Do you believe that a fine mind would be valued here? As a
pearl in a dung-heap. . . . I am certainly not a great man; but I have
some friends in Milan, I order newspapers, books, there is something
of my own in print—all this no other citizen has ever done. . . . If one
wishes to read a book that one has not got, or even to glance at it,
one must order it from elsewhere without being able to look or
choose before buying, with a thousand difficulties in the way.* But is
not this the worst? To have no man of letters to speak to, to keep all
one's thoughts to oneself, never to be able to air and discuss one's
own opinions or to take an innocent pride in one's studies, never to
be able to ask for help or advice. Who assures me that I am not
constantly taking the wrong turning? No one. But apart from all
that—what is there in Recanati that is beautiful? What is there that
is worth seeing or learning? Nothing. Yet God has made this world
of ours so beautiful, man has created such loveliness within it, there
are so many kinds of men whom anyone who is not a fool must
long to see and know, the earth is so full of marvels—and must I
say at the age of eighteen, "In this hovel I will live, and die where I
was born"?'[8]

It is the eternal cry of youth—the desire to see, to hear, to feel,
to hold the whole of life within one's grasp—but never, perhaps, felt
with greater intensity. One is reminded of the Brontë sisters, equally

* In a letter of the same year Giacomo complained that a parcel of books from
Milan to Recanati had not arrived after fifty days, while usually 'It takes less than
a month'.

deprived of any external stimulus or encouragement, and burning with no less fierce an inner life.

Giacomo, however, at last, had found someone in whom he could confide. 'You are misinformed that the climate of this town is healthy. It is most changeable, damp, marshy—trying to the nerves. Add to this the obstinate, black melancholy which drowns me and which grows with great strides . . . when I cannot study. Well do I know, for I used to experience it, that gentle melancholy which gives birth to beauty, a melancholy sweeter than happiness, like twilight—while this is blackest night, a poison to destroy both body and soul. But how shall I free myself from it while I do nothing but think? . . . How can you speak of distractions? My only distraction in Recanati is study, my only distraction is what is killing me—all the rest is tedium.'*

Nevertheless, it is clear that he was not entirely unhappy. Giordani had given to his studies a fresh impetus, a new life. Soon he even dared to contradict his mentor. 'That one should necessarily write first in prose and then in verse—this I frankly tell you I do not agree with. . . . Since I have begun to distinguish what is beautiful, only the poets and no others have given me an intense wish to translate them and to make them my own. . . . Will you not allow me to read Homer, Virgil, Dante, and the other greatest? I do not know whether I could keep away from them, for in reading them I feel an inexpressible delight. And it has happened to me, too—being alone in my study with a free and placid mind, in an hour most friendly to the Muses, to take up Cicero, and to try, in reading him, to lift up my mind, but to be so tormented by the slowness and heaviness of that prose, that I could not go on, but instead took up a Horace. . . . And if you allow me to read these great works, how can you expect that I should enjoy them, and examine and analyse their beauty, without trying to imitate them? When I see the beauty of

---

* 'Noia,' the French ennui—a word constantly used by Leopardi, and almost impossible, as Byron observed, to translate into English.

> For ennui is a growth of English root
> Though nameless in our language: we retort
> The fact for words, and let the French translate
> That awful yawn which sleep cannot abate.
> *Don Juan.*

the country here, at this time of year in particular, I feel so transported out of myself that it would seem to me a mortal sin not to pay heed to it, and to let this ardour of youth pass, while I am waiting to become a great prose-writer.'[9]

During the first months of this friendship, however, Leopardi's health began to trouble him again. He told Giordani that it was more than six months since he had been able to do any real work, and sent him a most depressing account of his daily routine. 'I get up late in the morning, then immediately start off for a walk, and go on walking, without ever speaking or opening a book, until lunch-time . . . then walk again until supper. So I have been living for six months. In these last four days I have been feeling much better, but it is only a respite.'

Without books, Giacomo was thrown back more and more into his own thoughts. 'My other source of unhappiness is thought. I think you know, but hope you have never experienced, how thinking can torment and martyrize a man whose thoughts are unlike other people's. I mean when that man has no other distraction. . . . In short, solitude is not good for men who burn themselves up from within.'[10]

This was the melancholy that Chateaubriand, too, knew—'the melancholy which insinuates itself into the very core of our passions, when they, having no goal, burn themselves out in a lonely heart.' And in Leopardi it led to the state which, of all others, he most dreaded: tedium. 'I am sorry for you', he wrote to Giordani, 'in all your troubles and annoyances; they are what the Greeks called ἄθλους. Often this word comes to my lips, and I delight in it, even though if I were now to accomplish an ἄθλος, it would assuredly be my last. But surely this too is a terrible ἄθλος, to have all one's days and months swallowed up, as is happening to me. What Italian word could render it? *Travaglio* [travail] has its horror, but not its greatness and vastness. Yet I would not dare to say that the word cannot be translated into our language, so little do I trust my own knowledge of our great sovereign, omnipotent tongue.'[11] In later years the poet was to find the simpler word he required: *fatica*, labour.

In the autumn Giacomo was better, and again reading the Classics, 'Greek in the morning, Latin in the afternoon, Italian in the evenings', but with every month his dependence on his 'worthy and singular friend' (the phrase is his own) was increasing, and at the end of the year, directly after Contessa Lazzari's departure, he wrote to him: 'I need your presence now, more than you can imagine.'[12] The greater part of the next year was spent in waiting for Giordani's coming. He had promised to do so, very early in the friendship. 'I should not be sorry', he had written, 'to stay for a while in the Recanati that you find so tedious—to stay there for the sole purpose of interrupting your studies, of providing you with an ear and a heart open to your words, and of forcing you to take long frequent walks in the hills.' Giacomo had replied with unmeasured delight: 'I love you so much that I almost go mad at the thought that next year—if you have not been indulging me with a vain hope—I shall see you and talk to you!'[13] And in a later letter: 'If we see each other, I believe I shall be unable to say anything for the first few days, through not knowing where to begin. You will be lucky if I leave you any time for food and drink, in the intervals of assailing you with my endless talk.'[14]

But the months wore on, and Giordani did not come. In the following March Leopardi reminded him that a year had elapsed since the beginning of their friendship, 'which, unless our natures change completely, will only be dissolved by that which brings all things to an end',[15] and he added that he was anxiously awaiting the month of May, which had been chosen for Giordani's visit, 'and when I have had you here, I shall no longer be able to say that all my greatest desires have remained unfulfilled'. But when May came, the visit was put off until July. 'I am waiting for you most impatiently, eaten up by melancholy, filled with longings, bored, irritated, savouring days which are either bitter or tasteless.'[16]

A few weeks later Giordani had got as far as Bologna; but some of Giacomo's letters were lost, and the Abate, always quick to take offence, suggested that perhaps he would not be welcome after all, and had better go on to Rome by the Tuscan road, instead of by the Marches. But his susceptibilities were soothed by an imploring letter, and on the 10th of September he arrived.

In the history of the Leopardi family, the five days of Giordani's visit were momentous. They began badly. Giordani, having alighted at the inn, sent a note by hand to Giacomo, which was intercepted

and opened by his father, and in consequence the Count himself
hurried to the inn to greet the stranger. But unfortunately Giacomo,
who had meanwhile heard of his friend's arrival, was also on his way
there—and his father ran into him. It was the first time in Giacomo's
life that he had gone out alone, and he was severely rebuked for it.

During the following days, however, things went better, and the
two friends were allowed to talk to each other in peace. Conte
Monaldo had only heard of Giordani as a famous writer; otherwise,
far from allowing his sons to talk to him, he would never have
allowed the Abate inside the house. Later on he bitterly regretted
having done so, reproaching himself in particular for the unprece-
dented permission he had accorded to Giacomo to go with Giordani
for a day's excursion to Macerata, thirty miles away. In this one
day, according to the legend which subsequently grew up in the
Leopardi household, Giordani's diabolical influence corrupted Giacomo's mind and heart, destroyed his religious principles, and infected him with the dangerous Liberal views that were soon to
cause his father such deep concern. A lady of Recanati, Contessa
Ippolita Mazzagalli, went so far as to say that Giacomo, on returning
from Macerata, was already 'unrecognizable';[17] and Monaldo,
writing two years later to a friend, complained that 'on Giordani's
arrival both my sons changed their nature'.

'Until then', the Count wrote, 'they had never, literally never,
been out of my sight and their mother's. I left them freely with
Giordani, thinking to leave them in the arms of friendship, of
honour. I do not know—or at least, I had better ignore—a large
part . . . of their long conversations. Certainly the misfortune of
living in a small town was exaggerated; certainly their imagination
was inflamed, so that they came to believe themselves destined to
great enterprises, and to a wide stage. A post, or at least a visit, in
Milan or Rome was planned for Giacomo; a position as officer in
the troops in Piedmont, for my second son; and there was even some
talk of I know not what marriage for my daughter. When Giordani
left, he took with him the secrets of my children.'[18]

In all this the Count—for whom it is impossible not to feel some
sympathy—showed considerable acumen, for indeed all these plans
appear to have been made. And this was not the worst. 'He [Gior-
dani] suggested that Giacomo should correspond with many Italian
men of letters, dangerous and restless spirits. . . . They have openly

invited my son to share their views and to become one of the chief supporters of their plans. . . . Dear Advocate,' the Count concluded, 'I am far from blind. My sons are respectful to me, because they have been well brought up, but they give me no other satisfaction. They hate their *patria*'—[we must remember that, to Monaldo, this term meant only Recanati]—'which every honest man should love and serve, whatever it may be like, and as it has been allotted to him by Providence; they also hate their father's house, in which they feel themselves to be strangers and prisoners; and perhaps they hate even me, who, with a heart only too full of love for everyone, am depicted by their corrupted imaginations as an implacable tyrant. I envy the fate of any beggar who, when he brings home a crust of bread bathed in sweat, sees it received by the love and gratitude of his sons. I am consuming . . .'[19]

And here the draft of the letter, as preserved in *casa Leopardi*, breaks off, as if emotion had overcome the writer. Even twelve years later, Monaldo could not refer to Giordani without bitter resentment. 'That miserable apostate,' he called him, 'whose breath contaminates whoever dares to approach him.'

Did the Count really believe that, until then, Giacomo had shared all his opinions? Perhaps he had in mind that only three years before, in 1815, Giacomo (then a schoolboy of seventeen) had written an oration on *The Liberation of the Marches* which was a mere echo of his father's views. Its occasion had been the expulsion of the French from the Marches which followed upon the defeat, at Tolentino, of the troops of Joachim Murat and of the Italian volunteers whose hopes had been raised by the Proclamation of Rimini, in which Murat had offered a free Constitution to the whole Italian people. But the victory of the Papal and Austrian troops had soon brought these hopes to an end. In the words of a popular lampoon of the day:

> Fra Macerata e Tolentino
> È finito il re Gioacchino,
> Fra il Chienti ed il Potenza
> Finì' l'indipendenza.*

* Macerata and Tolentino
Saw the end of Gioacchino,
The Chienti and the Potenza
Saw the end of independence.
  Quoted by G. Mestica, *Studi Leopardiani*.

F

Among Murat's troops there had been a regiment of Italian volunteers led by Conte Andrea Broglio of Recanati, but neither of the
Leopardi brothers was among them, and Giacomo's comments on
these events had been quite as reactionary and prejudiced as Conte
Monaldo's own. He had expressed a childish abuse of the French
('every Frenchman is deserving of hatred') and a complacent satisfaction in the disunited condition of Italy, which offered 'the gay
and flattering spectacle of numerous capitals, thus rendering our land
attractive to the eyes of foreigners'. But in three years a young man
has plenty of time to change his opinions, and in these, a great deal
had happened. It is easier to awaken national sentiment than to
quench it, and—in spite of this initial defeat—the idea of freedom had
now taken hold in almost every Italian province. In Romagna and
the Marches, especially, the numbers of the *carbonari* were rapidly
increasing; the world, in their symbolism, was a forest, and 'to rid
the forest of its wolves', was to free a country from its tyrants. They
dreamed of an Italy wholly free—not only from France, but from
Austria and the Pope—and were determined, if necessary, to achieve
this independence by force.

On St. John's eve, 1817, an insurrection—the first in Italy—broke
out in Macerata, with the object of overthrowing the Papal government. 'When God, the All Highest, wishes to punish His people, He
places them under the government of fools'—so ran a proclamation
posted one night upon the walls of Recanati, and although the
Macerata insurrection was promptly and brutally suppressed, some
of the conspirators escaped death or hard labour and resumed their
secret plans.[20] Indeed it was suggested—though perhaps with insufficient foundation—that on the single day of Leopardi's visit to
Macerata, Giordani introduced him to some of them, and it is
certain that even the shuttered windows of Palazzo Leopardi had
not been able to keep out every breath of this new spirit. Already,
in Giacomo's mind, his *patria* was not limited by the city walls of
Recanati or the boundaries of the Marches; already he had written:
'My country is Italy, and I burn for love of her, thanking God that I
was born an Italian.' 'Today', so he wrote in a rough draft of a poem
found among his papers in Naples, 'today I have reached my twentieth year. What have I achieved? No great deed yet. . . . Oh, my
country, my country! I cannot shed my blood for you, for you do

not exist any more. . . . In what work, for whom, for what country, shall I give my labour, my sufferings, my blood?'[21]

It was in September of this year that Giordani came to stay at Recanati, and on the following 1st of January 1819, Leopardi published his first two patriotic *canti*: *All' Italia* and *Sopra il monumento di Dante*.

It is almost impossible for us to realize, at this distance in time, the effect that these poems (together with the ode *Ad Angelo Mai*, which was written soon after) produced upon the poet's contemporaries, and upon the next generation. The first two poems appear to us unreadably rhetorical and bombastic, and even Carducci admitted that the first part of *All' Italia* seems to be the work of 'one who on a summer's day comes out of a dark prison (seven years of philology), and at first is dazzled, hesitates and totters, then suddenly breaks away at a run'. Both poems contrast the country's past greatness and her present littleness, and culminate in an impassioned appeal to Italy to throw off her chains and return to the greatness she once knew. In both of them, as De Sanctis admits, the young poet has brought with him 'all the luggage of his classical reminiscences'—and the luggage is heavy. In *All' Italia* Leopardi sees himself as a second Simonides, evoking the valour of the Spartans at Thermopylae; in the ode *Sopra il monumento di Dante* he calls up the great poet's ghost, that he may see how low his country has now fallen. 'Leopardi's feelings', says De Sanctis, 'are genuine, and their warmth is sincere; but the setting, and the mechanism with which they are presented, are artificial.'[22] It is poetry still academic and immature, and of which the interest, for us, is historical, not literary. Leopardi has not yet entered his own world.

As soon as the two poems were completed, in October 1818, Leopardi sent them to Giordani, asking him to have them printed, and to obtain Vincenzo Monti's permission to dedicate them to him. Days and weeks passed, and no answer came from the Abate; Giacomo feared that the manuscript was lost. He sent another copy to the Abate Cancellieri, who undertook to correct the proofs and even to obtain the *imprimatur* of the Papal government; and at last, in January 1819, the little volume appeared. But when it reached Recanati its author had a shock, for not only was the cost of the printing much higher than he had expected, but there were so many mistakes in it that he said he could hardly recognize his poor verses 'all dressed up in rags', and in a moment of rage declared that he would hand over the lot to the grocer. Eventually, however, he decided to distribute the three hundred copies—for there were no more—among his own friends and relations, with the result that his father, as might have been expected, was considerably taken aback. Conte Monaldo's first emotion, indeed, seems to have been a puzzled anxiety. 'I am not competent to judge such matters,' he wrote to a friend of more Liberal tendencies, to whom he sent Giacomo's verses for his opinion, 'but I am not in sympathy with his admiration of Italy in her period of glory and of strife. I myself feel it necessary to obey, and see little difference between a sovereign born on this side, or the other, of the Alps.'[23] But when he saw more clearly where his son's words were leading, his doubts gave place to sheer fright. 'Our father', said his son Carlo, with youthful callousness, 'nearly went bald with terror.'[24]

Conte Monaldo's nervousness was not wholly unnatural. He had, after all, nearly been shot during the French occupation in 1801; he identified democratic ideals with the chaos he had witnessed there at that time, and the Papal rule, not only with the will of God, but with lawful security. And he could hardly fail to be aware that Northern Italy, at this moment, was full of men very unlike himself—men who felt no necessity whatever 'to obey', and who were determined to shake off every yoke as soon as possible. If their first enemy was Austria, their second was certainly the Papal government; they aimed at nothing less than complete freedom from any foreign rule.

It is difficult, indeed, to convey the intensity of the unrest and apprehension which prevailed, at this time, in the little towns of the Marches and the Romagna. The insurrection of 1817 at Macerata had been a first, premature explosion, but in the following year a Congress was held in the Palazzo Hercolani in Bologna, at which the duties were laid down of the members of the *Carboneria*, all of whom had taken a vow of 'eternal hatred against all monarchies', and had sworn 'to give their strength and their lives for the independence of Italy'. In every little town new lodges were springing up; their members—'Pagans wandering in the Forest'—were enrolled in secret midnight meetings, at which, on their knees and surrounded by a ring of naked daggers, they swore to keep the secrets of the Order, and to come to the aid of all other *carbonari*. Their vows ended with these words: 'If I break my oath, let my body be torn to pieces and burned, and my ashes be scattered to the winds.' There is no record of such a lodge at Recanati itself, but several of its citizens, as we have seen, were already *carbonari*—and among the plotters there was at least one young insurgent, Vito Fedeli, who later on gave his life for his cause, and another, called Pastori, who was mysteriously assassinated for having revealed the name of a fellow-member.[25]

For indeed one of the chief causes for disquiet in these little towns was that no man could trust his neighbour. The little groups of conspirators, if they included many genuine patriots, also held fanatics, fools, mere trouble-mongers, and an occasional spy. And the fanaticism on the other side was no less intense. The *Sanfedisti*, the members of an association originally founded by the Jesuits to defend the Catholic faith and uphold the temporal dominion of the Pope, had come to include all that was most reactionary in the country—men who had sworn 'to show no mercy to any man belonging to the infamous rabble of the Liberals, and to bear an undying hatred against any enemy of the true religion'. Sometimes members of the same family were on opposite sides. 'Two or three?' was the question asked of each other by strangers in the street—for the Austrian flag had two colours, and the badge of the *Carboneria* three—and so the inquirer would know whether he had met an enemy or a friend. Plots and counter-plots, secret passwords, wild dreams, wilder rumours—and at night, sudden shots in the street, sudden searches of suspect houses by armed guards, sudden arrests and banishments—such was the climate of these little towns. Can we wonder that Monaldo—a law-abiding, timid man, who believed that 'wars should be fought by soldiers, and citizens remain innocent spectators'—was alarmed, when he saw his own son embracing the ideals of such conspirators?

As for the poet's uncle in Rome, Marchese Antici, he did indeed write to congratulate his nephew on the literary success of the *Canzoni*, but pointed out at the same time that in the days of the past, whose glories the poet had sung, 'Italy was the prey of the Whites and the Blacks, the Guelfs and the Ghibellines' and the

various tyrants of each city, whereas now 'peace, lawfulness, and a
strong police force are the chief boons required by society'. How
much better it would be, he wrote, if Giacomo turned his undoubted
gifts to extolling the forces of Christendom! 'The victory is certain,
and the palm of immortality assured.'[26] He ended by promising
to try to dispose of some copies of Giacomo's poems, but pointed
out that their author could hardly hope to gain more than one *paolo*
for each.

At the same time, however, a copy of the poems had also gone off
to Giordani—and when his reply came, Leopardi could not complain of the faintness of his praise. 'Oh Giacomino, what a great man
you are already! . . . Your songs are running through the town like
wild-fire; everyone wants them, everyone is overwhelmed by them.
I have never, never seen any poetry or prose so much admired or
praised. They talk of you as a miracle. Oh, what a fool I was when
I advised you to write prose before you attempted verse; do you
remember? Do what you will; you are equal to any high enterprise.'[27]

This praise, for all the hyperbole of its expression, was completely
sincere. When, a few months later, Giordani heard from a friend in
Bologna that the *Canzoni* had not had much success there, he replied
with great indignation: 'That wretched young man [Giacomo] is
going to die; but if perchance he does not, remember what I tell you:
no one will speak in the same breath of any other genius in Italy. He
is immeasurably, frighteningly great.'[28] And, soon after: 'Give
him only ten years to live, and sanity, and pull him out of the horrible circumstances in which he is living, and you may call me the
greatest fool in Italy, if in 1830 it is not said that few Italians, in the
greatest centuries, deserve to be compared to Leopardi.'[29]

Giordani was right. And if to us these *Canzoni* seem hardly equal
to the great poems of the later years, we must remember the climate
in which they were written—and what they meant to the men by
whom a united Italy was made. With the exception of Monti's
Congresso d'Udine, these were the first Italian patriotic poems to
appear since Petrarch, the first to sound once again the name of
Italy. And if the Italy called up by Leopardi was still a rather shadowy
figure, 'that shadow', Carducci wrote, 'moved a whole generation'.[30] In 1848 the young men of Naples, then still under the

Bourbon rule, would visit Giacomo's tomb, muttering his stanzas under their breath; and when, a few months later, the Roman volunteers were passing through the Marches on their way to the battles of the Po, they paused at Recanati, as on a pilgrimage, to visit Leopardi's house, and his sister Paolina bade them God-speed.[31] 'To church with Manzoni, to war with Leopardi,'[32] cried the volunteers of '59.

Many years later, when the unity of Italy was already an accomplished fact, those songs still had power to stir the men who remembered it in the making. Carducci, in his old age, wrote of 'the trembling that came over me as I read those poems as a boy; and I find myself feeling it still'.[33] And the great *garibaldino*, Settembrini, wrote to De Sanctis: 'Do you remember, my friend, the days of our youth, when the Austrian police were at our heels, and we created in our books a world in which we found life and liberty? . . . All that world, that excitement, those unlimited plans, those dreams, were represented by Leopardi in those *Canzoni*. . . . The memory of the past awoke in us first shame, then faith, then action. . . . Those words were a real flame; we repeated them and they were repeated at their death by those who died for our country.'[34]

AN ATTEMPT AT FLIGHT
(1819)

*Nous ne vivons pas, mais nous espérons de vivre.**

GIORDANI had gone. In the first excitement after his visit,
Leopardi's poems had been written; a few months later they had
been published, and had received recognition. For the first time in
his life, the poet had felt himself in touch with the world. But here
in Recanati the days dragged on with the same dull monotony, the
same exasperating restraint. No one, except his brother Carlo, was
pleased by his achievement; few even were aware of it. Again the
universe dwindled to the four walls of the Leopardi library—but
no, this time Giacomo would not resign himself. He would find a
way out.

A month after Giordani's visit, Giacomo was writing to his
friend: 'Our plans go from bad to worse.' On Giordani's advice, it
appears, he had asked his uncle, Marchese Carlo Antici, and perhaps
some other relations, to plead with Conte Monaldo; but in vain, for
he complained to Giordani: 'We have been betrayed, mocked, and
treated as fools, rogues, or madmen, while our father laughs quietly
at us, as if we were children. . . . Pray continue to be fond of us, and
grant us what will cost you nothing, but we receive from no other
living soul—compassion.'[1]

Giacomo's next endeavour was to find some employment in
Rome, however modest, that would give him independence, and
he hoped for some help from Marchese Antici, whose wife's uncle,
Cardinal Mattei, had some influence in the Vatican. But un-

* 'We do not live; we only hope to do so.' Pascal, set down by Leopardi in his
day-book.

fortunately the only good post available, that of librarian to the
Vatican, had just been given to Monsignor Mai, and Marchese
Antici's help to his nephew confined itself to some good advice.
Literary men, he remarked, were generally both irritable and con-
ceited; Giacomo would find their company very inferior to that of
'the great dead'. 'A tranquil sojourn in your father's house', with
a course of studies in philosophy, theology, and law, would be
'much more suitable, than a distracting visit to Rome'. And moreover—for Uncle Carlo was not averse to plain speaking—Giacomo
would do well not only to fortify his health, but to improve his
manners, before he came to town. 'You have not only neglected
your body, but also the most important attraction of a pleasant and
interesting conversation, which would impress those who listen to
you.' He might begin, his uncle suggested, by making himself more
agreeable at home. 'Be cheerful, speak openly to them [his parents],
confide your perplexities to them. . . . Lay down for ever those
black looks, lift up that bent head; open the mouth which you keep
firmly shut whenever you are in the company of your family, or
indeed in the company of anyone who does not talk about literature.'[2] And he added that he himself had stopped going to dinner
in *casa Leopardi*, since he had observed that both Giacomo and
Carlo rejected every opportunity of conversation that was offered
to them in the family circle.

Advice such as this is seldom palatable, and to Giacomo it seemed
an insult. All that he cared for was somehow, anyhow, to get away
from Recanati—and this, he now believed, his relations had never
really meant to happen, even when they pretended to help him.
Of course, he burst out to Giordani, Cardinal Mattei could have
procured a post for him and for Carlo, if his family had really pressed
it; but he was convinced that they had not. 'They never will do it,
unless their hand is forced; they are glad to see us in our present
condition, and wish us to live and die in it. They are even sorry that
they allowed us to study, and say openly in our presence that now
they see the bad fruits of education, and will bring up our little
brother to be a carpenter.'[3]

It must be remembered that Giacomo, who was now nearly
twenty-one, had not only never left home alone, but had never
possessed any money. His father had fed, clothed, and educated

him, but an allowance was beyond the range of his ideas. Giacomo
was a *figlio di famiglia*, and this implied that while the head of the
family was still alive, his sons must turn to him for all that they
might need. Even nowadays, in some provincial families of the
South, this way of treating a grown-up son would not seem odd.
But to Giacomo it seemed so unbearable that he often preferred to do
without what he required, rather than ask his father for it. 'You must
know', he wrote to Giordani, 'that I have not got a penny to spend;
my father provides me with everything I ask for, and likes me to
turn to him. But, since I must choose between asking and doing
without, I prefer the latter, except for what is necessary for my
studies.'[4]

Meanwhile the winter months passed—long, cold months, when
Giacomo, not daring to venture out of doors, sat in the library hour
after hour, with a rug wrapped round his shivering knees and
another upon his shoulders. If he looked out into the little square, it
was empty, or he would see some friend of his mother's hurrying to
church—a sombre matron with a black shawl over her head, to
protect her from the bitter wind that was blowing the mist up the
valley. Giacomo looked out and shivered, and returned to his books.

At last the spring came; but he was not any nearer to freedom,
and gradually his very hopes had died. 'You may be certain', he
told Giordani, 'that I shall never get out of Recanati, until my
father's death—which I do not want to take place before mine. . . .
Neither your eloquence, nor that of Pericles and Demosthenes—no,
not the goddess Persuasion herself—could change my father's mind.
. . . What I ask, which is not to live in a grand manner, or even
comfortably, but only away from here, is far beyond my reach.'[5]

But when the summer came a return of his ophthalmia goaded
Giacomo into action. 'I am in such despair,' he told Giordani, 'that
I could eat the paper I am writing on. . . . Shall I never do anything
great?—not even now, when I am trampling round this cage like a
bear?'[6] He decided at last to try to break his bars.

The episode which ensued was perhaps the decisive one of
Leopardi's youth. It was his first independent effort, his first bid for
freedom—and it failed. His plan was to leave Recanati secretly and
go to Milan, where, with the help of Giordani and some other
friends, he hoped to find some occupation. He took no one into his

confidence, not even Giordani or Carlo, for fear of getting them into trouble.[7] But he wrote a letter, which has been called a little masterpiece of hypocrisy, to the same Liberal friend in Macerata to whom his father had sent his patriotic *Canzoni*, Conte Saverio Broglio d'Ajano,[8] asking him whether he could help him to get a passport for Lombardy and the Veneto, and clearly implied that the request was made with his father's approval and consent.

Interminably long must the days have appeared, while he was waiting for Conte Broglio's answer. Paolina and Carlo noticed his gloom and preoccupation, but could not guess the cause. But indeed Giacomo had become desperate, desperate enough—if we can believe his brother's subsequent account of the affair—to have collected some tools to break open the family safe.

While he was waiting he composed two long letters, which he intended to leave behind. The first was to his brother. 'I am leaving this place without having said a word to you, so that you should not be held responsible by anyone for my departure, and also because advice, which may be helpful to an undecided man, can only do harm to one who has already made up his mind. . . . Two main reasons have influenced me: one is the impossibility of studying [owing to the weakness of his eyes]; the other I will not express, but you will guess it easily enough. And this second reason, which, owing to my mental as well as my physical qualities, might well have brought me to the depths of despair, and has made me play with the thought of suicide, now impels me to throw myself, with my eyes closed, into the arms of fortune.' This second reason, it is easy to divine, was Giacomo's need for the society and love of women; a need frequently discussed by the two brothers, but by Giacomo never satisfied. Then followed a characteristic outburst: 'Oh, you are so much better than I! What am I? Entirely worthless. This I feel and see so clearly that it has strengthened my determination; I am running away from the thought of myself, which fills me with disgust. As long as I thought well of myself, I was more prudent; but now that I despise myself, my only resource is to surrender myself to fate. . . . Hand the enclosed letter to my father. Ask both him and my mother to forgive me. Do so with your whole heart, as I am doing now. It would have been better, humanly speaking, for them and for me, if I had never been born.'[9]

This letter shows the depths of despair that he had reached. To his father he wrote with greater restraint, but no less bitterness.

'My conduct until now is known to you; you know that in the whole of Italy you could not find a young man of my class who has shown a greater prudence, abstinence from youthful pleasures, obedience and submission to his parents, than I. Although you may have an indifferent opinion of the poor talents that heaven has granted me, you cannot completely disbelieve the writers and eminent men to whom I have become known, and of whose opinion of me you are not unaware. Nor can you fail to know that, even among those who share your general views, there are many who think that I might turn out well, were I given those opportunities which are indispensable for the success of a young man of even mediocre promise. . . . You considered me unworthy of a father's sacrifice, nor did you think that my present and future welfare deserved any alteration of your family plans. In the interest of something that I have never known, but you call home and family, you have required from your children the sacrifice, not only of their physical welfare, but of their natural desires, their youth, their whole life. You have been made aware of the wretchedness of my life by my terrible attacks of melancholy, and by the strange torments of my imagination; nor can you fail to know what is obvious: that for these troubles and for my ill-health, no remedy can be found in Recanati.

'Nevertheless you have permitted a man of my constitution to wear himself out for many years in fatal studies, or else to be engulfed by the deepest tedium. . . . It did not take me long to realize that your mind was proof against every imaginable argument, and that the extraordinary inflexibility of your nature, concealed by your constant dissimulation and apparent weakness, was such as to leave me no shadow of hope. All this convinced me that I must trust myself alone. . . . I would rather be unhappy than mediocre, rather suffer pain than boredom. . . . I find consolation in the thought that this is the last trouble I shall cause you. My dear *Signor Padre*,' he concluded, 'if I may still call you so, I beg you on my knees to forgive me, who am unlucky both in my nature and my circumstances. . . . If fortune is ever kind to me, my first thought will be to give back to you what necessity now obliges me to use. The last favour I ask of you is that if ever you should call up the memory of the son who always respected and loved you, you will not spurn that memory, nor curse him. If fate has not ordained that you should be able to be proud of him, do not deny him the pity that is granted even to criminals.'[10]

This letter, which would undoubtedly have caused Conte Monaldo not only pain but great surprise, was never delivered. Carlo put it away with Giacomo's letters, and it was not published until after his father's death. For, once again, fortune was against the young man's plans. Conte Broglio did indeed get the passport for him from the head of the Macerata police, Marchese Filippo Solari, but the latter recognized Giacomo's name, and, meaning no harm, wrote to Marchese Antici to wish his nephew a happy journey. So the secret was out. Monaldo, still saying nothing to Giacomo, hurriedly wrote to Solari for an explanation, and he, 'since nothing in the world is more respectable than paternal authority', told Broglio to send the passport straight to Monaldo. Broglio obeyed, writing: 'I have been fooled—*pazienza*—it is easy to fool a trusting old man.'

Meanwhile Giacomo was still waiting; but, instead of receiving the hoped-for letter, he was summoned into his father's presence, for a conversation of which the nature is revealed in his next letter to Giordani. 'I was going to escape from here, but I have been discovered. It did not please God that they should use force; they used supplication and grief. I no longer hope for anything.'

It is easy to guess the pressure that was put on him, and finally, on receiving Conte Monaldo's promise not to intercept his passport (which was, in fact, already lying in the old man's writing-desk), Giacomo, on his part, gave his word never to make use of it. 'I thought my father was speaking from his heart,' he wrote, 'and so I did what I have not done for many years; I trusted him. I have been deceived—but for the last time.'[11] Four days after receiving his son's promise, Conte Monaldo showed him the passport, and with it a letter written in Broglio's hand, but clearly at Conte Monaldo's own request. 'Give my affectionate greetings to your excellent son, for whom I enclose the requested passport, and offer him my wishes for a happy journey.'[12]

'My father must indeed think me a fool,' wrote Giacomo to Broglio, in a bitter letter of explanation, 'if he believes that so simple a trick can deceive me!' He asked Broglio's forgiveness for his own

deceitfulness, which he freely admitted; and in the rest of his letter
he attempted to justify it. 'My plan', he told him, 'was neither recent
nor sudden. I have not repented nor changed my mind. I have given
way for the present, not from compulsion or conviction, but
because my feelings were played upon and taken advantage of. . . .
I will not live in Recanati. If my father will give me the means of
going away, as he has promised, I shall be grateful and respectful,
like any other good son—if not, what was to have happened, and
has not, is only postponed.'

Bitterly he described the restrictions and frustrations of his daily
life at home, and the failure of all his attempts to get away. 'If my
father, in his abhorrence of anything great or even unusual, now
regrets that he allowed me to study, if he is sorry that Heaven did
not make me a mole . . . if he denies me what any father anywhere
would grant to a son with even a spark of talent, and insists on my
living and dying like his ancestors—is it rebellion in a son to refuse
submission to such a rule? I know for certain that he has declared that
none of us shall get away from here, so long as he is alive. And I want
him to live, but I want to live myself, too, while I am still young,
and not when I am old and of no more use to myself or anyone
else!'[13] And he ended by a threat, that has a puerile and unconvincing ring, that his father's behaviour might well oblige him to
'abandon the path of virtue'.* Meanwhile Conte Monaldo put away
in his cupboard the passport and the letters, adding to them a brief,
but not altogether frank, account of the episode. 'And thus', he
complacently concluded, 'the matter ended.'

It is at this point, I think, that something more must be said about
the poet's relationship with his father. That it was an unhappy one
can hardly be denied, but the story is far from being a straight-
forward one of paternal tyranny, and genius misunderstood. For
Conte Monaldo was a much more complex character than some of
Leopardi's biographers would have had us believe. He was a rigid
and old-fashioned provincial nobleman, bigoted and reactionary; he
was both obstinate and vacillating, each at the wrong time; he

* In the copy of the letter owned by the Broglio family in Macerata, some pious
reader has been moved to render this passage illegible.

mistrusted new ideas and new manners; he was under his wife's
thumb. But he also possessed some traits which do not fit into this
picture at all; he was subject to sudden inconsistencies and disarming
generosities. He attacked the clergy with vehemence and humour;
he took off his trousers to give them to a beggar; and pompous
though he was, he wryly observed that even in people of very
superior minds, a small corner is often left for childishness. Moreover, in spite of his ineptitude in practical affairs, he was no fool; he
wrote with wit and candour; he liked books; and—of this there can
be no doubt—he tenderly loved the sons who spoke of him so
harshly. If he also, in later years, failed to understand them, it must
be remembered that—in addition to the barriers of temperament,
and those which lie between each generation and the next—he was
bringing up his children at a particularly difficult time: one in which,
all over Europe, a transition was taking place from the old tradition of absolute paternal authority to the new *sensiblerie* of Rousseau,
and also from aristocratic to bourgeois manners, from formality to
familiarity. The struggle between Conte Monaldo and his children
reflected a general conflict of the age, intensified by the fact that one
of his sons, for his own misfortune and that of his parents, chanced
to be a genius. But even this Monaldo perceived and, according to
his lights, respected. He gave to Giacomo the first requisites of the
literary life: books, leisure, and encouragement. And he even, when
his sons were only fourteen and fifteen, applied to Rome for permission for them to read the books proscribed by the Church, for
the benefit of their studies.

For a man of Conte Monaldo's upbringing, this was a great deal,
and if he afterwards failed to understand Giacomo's ideas, it was his
own tragedy, even more than his son's. What rankled most bitterly
in Conte Monaldo's heart—as we have seen in his letter to Brighenti
—was the conviction that Giordani had stolen from him what in
truth he had long ceased to possess: his son's confidence. It is pathetic
to watch him, as the years went on, making awkward, loving over-
tures, in the hope of having it restored to him. So strong was his
desire for a greater mutual trust that he was even prepared to like
his son's writings—if only he might be shown them. 'Everyone
asks me for your things to read,' he wrote to Giacomo in 1828, 'and
I am ashamed not to have them.' He begged him to bring a copy

home with him, 'and we will make peace about your literary works, as to which you have always regarded me rather sourly, since my grumblings over your first two *Canti*. But I believe', he humbly concluded, 'that by now that criticism of mine is considered less severely by you, and that, even if you cannot applaud your father's intelligence, you will at least be fair to his most loving heart.'[14]

And indeed of his father's affection Giacomo, for all his annoyance, was always aware. Perhaps he would have been less exasperated if he himself, too, had not always continued to love him and to need his approval. Even when, in 1826, he published the *Operette Morali*, he wrote to Carlo that he was much distressed by the thought 'that *Babbo* and *Mamma* should have a poor opinion of me' and begged his brother to keep the book out of their sight, 'as there are certain ideas in it that might perhaps be displeasing to *Babbo*'.[15]

The truth was that, as is shown in some of Leopardi's later poems —in particular, the *Palinodia* and the *Batracomiomachia*—Giacomo Leopardi never completely freed himself from his father's influence. That he himself, at least sometimes, both knew and resented this is suggested by a passage in the *Pensieri* in which he remarked that there is hardly an instance in history of a great man whose father did not die while he was still a child. 'Paternal power', he wrote, 'brings with it a kind of slavery of the children . . . more stringent and more deeply felt than any law. . . . It is a sentimental bond which a man, so long as his father is alive, carries perpetually with him . . . a feeling of awe and of dependence, and of not being his own master—indeed of not being, so to speak, even a whole person, but only a part and member of another. . . . This feeling', he added, 'can hardly be combined, I will not say with great deeds, but even with any plans of greatness.'[16]

Certainly in 1819, when all his plans had been frustrated, the weight of his father's influence seemed intolerably heavy. Moreover his disappointment, coinciding with an attack of ophthalmia so severe that for a time he thought he was going blind, precipitated a grave spiritual crisis. With all his thoughts turned inward—and perhaps (or so his father always believed) under Giordani's influence— he lost the unquestioning faith of his boyhood—and with faith, hope vanished too. He refused to dress any longer as an *abbé*, and he declared to his father that, whatever profession he adopted, it would not be the Church. 'This total change in me . . .' he wrote later on, 'occurred in the course of one year, that is in 1819, when, being deprived of the use of my sight and of the constant distraction of reading, I became far more darkly aware of my unhappiness, and began to abandon hope.'[17]

In later years Leopardi always referred to this phase of his spiritual development as the time of his 'philosophic conversion'; but what really happened to him is extremely vague. To his friend Vincenzo Gioberti, nine years later, he spoke one day, very sadly, of this period as the one in which he had lost his faith, and apparently hinted at Giordani's influence; but when, after Leopardi's death, Gioberti reported this conversation in print, his account aroused such violent protests from Giordani that in later editions the passage was suppressed.[18] And a contemporary and biographer of Gioberti's merely records that Leopardi spoke of 'his sadness at the sight of the beauties of Nature, when he was first tormented by the uncertainties of doubt'.[19]

But was it really for his faith that the poet was grieving? Was it not rather that he identified its loss with that of all his other youthful 'illusions', and with the vital, creative power that he owed to them? 'At first', he wrote, 'my strong point was fantasy, and my verses were full of images. . . . I was most sensitive to emotion, but could not express it in verse. I had not meditated about life and had only one speculative notion, the common illusion that my own position was an exceptional one. . . . In short, my condition was in every way that of the Ancients.' But after the passing of boyhood, his fancy became less active; imagination gave place to reason. 'I began to become a philosopher, instead of the poet that I was before, and to *feel* the world's unhappiness, instead of only knowing about it— and this also owing to a certain physical languor, which took me farther away from the Ancients and brought me nearer to the Moderns. Then my fancy was greatly diminished, and although my faculty of invention was just then greatly increased, indeed almost then began, it principally took the form of prose or of sentimental poetry. And if I tried to make verses, the images came with the greatest effort. Indeed my imagination was almost dried up . . . as it is now, when I am as cold as a stone.'[20]

Certainly the first consequence of this change of heart was an

G

unhappiness duller and greyer than any he had yet known. For many months he retreated into a desolate and passive solitude, and this state of mind was reflected in his letters. In vain did Giordani proffer the hearty consolations of common sense. 'Your condition is not a happy one; but by an attempt to be philosophical, it can be endured. Imagine that you are a prisoner, but in a healthy, well-aired prison; with a good bed, good food, plenty of books—well, after all, it is not so bad as not knowing where to eat, nor where to sleep.'[21]

Giacomo's answer was that of a man on a very different plane. 'I am so bewildered by the nothingness that surrounds me that I hardly know how to find strength to answer you. If at this moment I were to go mad, my madness, I believe, would consist in remaining seated with staring eyes and wide-open mouth, my hands upon my knees, not laughing, nor crying, nor moving. I have no energy left to conceive any wish, not even for death. This is not because I fear death, but because I see no difference between it and this life of mine. . . . This is the first time that tedium not only oppresses and wearies me, but suffocates me and tears at me like a sharp pain; and I am so terrified by the vanity of all things that I cannot control myself, and yet know that my despair, too, is nothingness.'[22] And a short time later he was noting in his day-book: 'I was terrified by finding myself in the midst of nothingness, and myself nothing. I felt as if I were stifled, believing and feeling that everything is nothing, solid nothingness.'[23]

This was not a darkness that could be penetrated by sensible exhortations. Giordani himself realized it, and in his next letter he struck a simpler and gentler note. 'I don't know what to say to you —your trouble is now beyond speech, and, as you see, I can do nothing for you. But I can love and pity you; you must believe that my heart is wrung by your grief.'[24]

But Leopardi was now beyond the reach of plain human affection. That his moods of despair, on this occasion as on many others, were closely connected with his ill-health is undeniable. Not only did his weak eyes often cut him off from any escape into the world of books, but his lack of vitality and his sedentary habits debarred him from the other distractions normal to youth. To all sensitive and intelligent human beings a moment comes when they become aware that life is a dangerous and painful adventure, that ugliness and cruelty lurk behind every corner, and that only by shutting a door upon that knowledge, is it possible to proceed. This door, in Leopardi's mind, was never closed. Unknown to him were sheer animal exuberance and heedlessness, those gifts of physical well-being which sheathe our nerves with a deceptive sense of false security. Unknown was self-forgetfulness; unknown, too, the capacity for resignation. Nor did the enclosed and monotonous circumstances of his daily life afford him any distraction or retreat, save into his own past. 'Since my manner of life here', he wrote to Giordani in December, 'is still that of my childhood, I am clinging with both hands to the last traces and reflections of that blessed time when I still hoped for happiness, and in my hopes and dreams still enjoyed it. But it is gone, and will never again, surely never again, return. For I see with great terror that the whole of life came to an end at the same time as childhood for me, as for everyone who thinks and feels, so that the only people who truly live until their death are the many who remain children all their lives.'[25]

For indeed Leopardi did not even wish his sorrow to be lightened. 'I gave myself up entirely', he wrote, 'to the terrifying and barbarous joy of despair.'[26]

VII

THE POET

*Tien quelle rive altissima quiete.**

LEOPARDI had now reached his twenty-first year, and all that was ever going to happen to him, had already happened. He had known the rich, vague fantasies of childhood, the melancholy and rebelliousness of adolescence, the secluded, laborious concentration of the scholar, the love of 'the woman who is not to be found'. He had made a single friend; he had tried to escape from home, and had failed; he had lost the faith of his childhood; he had become acquainted with disease, deformity, and despair. All that still lay before him was to be merely a variation or an intensification of the same pattern. And in one other respect, too, the pattern always remained the same. It was always during his periods of despondency and apparent inactivity that his greatest poems—like seeds germinating in darkness—took shape. The frustration that darkened his twenty-first year was followed by the creation of the early *Idylls*; the apathy and hopelessness of his last year in Recanati by the great poems of 1829; the tortured exasperation of his two years in Naples by *La ginestra* and *Il tramonto della luna*.

The six early *Idylls* of 1819 would assure him, if he had written nothing else, an undisputed place among the great poets of Italy and of the world.[1] He himself gave them this name, and certainly they owe something to Theocritus and to Moschus, whose poems he had translated four years before; they are Greek in their lyric clarity, in their directness and economy of expression. But their setting is wholly Italian—and their accent, that of Leopardi alone.

What are these poems? They are sketches of familiar scenes: a

---

* Eternal stillness holds those shores. *La vita solitaria.*

84

moonlit night, a lonely hillside, an early morning after rain; they hold the quintessence of a child's dream, of a youthful memory, of the silence and space of infinity. Leopardi himself has described how they were written: 'I have never followed anything but an inspiration (or frenzy) during which, in the course of two minutes, I form the plan and arrangement of the whole composition. When this is done, I usually wait until another moment [of inspiration] returns, and when it does—which is usually not until some months later— I begin to compose, but with such slowness, that I cannot finish a poem, however short, in less than two or three weeks. This is my method, and if inspiration does not come of its own accord, water would pour out of a log more easily than a single verse from my brain.'[2]

What this lucid description does not hint at, however, is the long process of apprehension and assimilation that preceded the writing of the poem itself. Something of it may be seen in some passages in the *Zibaldone* and in a number of notes and jottings found among his papers in Naples—in particular, those written in the same year as the early *Idylls* and found among Leopardi's papers after his death, the *Ricordi d'infanzia e di adolescenza*.[3] These are some brief, incomplete, often unpunctuated, autobiographical notes set down with a vague intention of using them for a tale in the manner of *Werther*, but still so fragmentary that an emotion is barely hinted at, a scene faintly outlined, a sentence often left unfinished. Perhaps, however, they are the most self-revealing passages that Leopardi ever wrote. There is scarcely a line among them that was not used later on in his poems. But here, in the first faint etching—delicate as the skeleton of a leaf—they have the evocative power, the immediacy, of a scent carried by the breeze or the faint echo of a distant tune. Not poetry yet, but the breath of a wing.

Here are a few characteristic passages: 'A solitary thrush—the steep hillside and peasants going down it, almost immediately out of sight—another image of infinity.' Summer noons—'looking out of the window, under the shade of the overhanging roofs: the dog on the grass, children, the coachman's door ajar'.[4] And spring evenings: 'A peasant saying the *Ave Maria* and the *Requiem Aeternam* aloud to himself at the door of his hut, looking up to the moon which hung low over the trees.'[5] And here is a Theocritan dawn:

'Early morning rain—a rainbow at sunrise. The moon fallen as in my dream, the moon which peasants say turns the skin black; so I overheard a woman laughingly advise her friend to put her arms under her apron, as they both sat there in the moonlight. Silkworms, and two women talking of them: "How much can they be worth?" and the other: "Be quiet, I have spent such a lot on them, and if God wills . . ." '[6] Are not these women the sisters of Praxinoe and Gorgo?

Here is a longer, fuller scene: 'One evening when I was very melancholy I stood at my window over the square; two young men sitting on the deserted, grassy steps of the church, joking under the great lantern, knocking each other about; the first firefly I have seen this year appeared, one of them got up and went towards it, and inwardly I begged for mercy for the poor thing, but he threw it down, and went back—meanwhile the coachman's daughter rising from supper and leaning out of the window to wash a plate called out to the others indoors, "Tonight it really will rain—what a night it is! —black as your hat", and soon after, the light at the window was put out. . . . I heard a gentle voice, of a woman I did not know and could not see—"Natalino, come on, it's late." "For God's sake, it's not dawn yet", he replied etc. I heard a child, who must have been the woman's baby in her arms, babbling and stammering in a laughing, milky voice. . . . The merriment increased, "Isn't there some more wine at Girolamo's?" . . . and the woman laughing gently, "Oh, what madmen!" (Yet the wine was not for her, and her husband would use the family earnings for it) and now and again patiently and laughingly asked them to come away, but in vain etc. At last a voice, "Ah, here's the rain!" And a light spring rain, and all of them went in, and I heard the sound of doors and bolts.'[7]

Bare, fragmentary sentences, mere jottings—yet they hold the essence of the village life: the grassy church steps, the young men laughing and drinking, the baby babbling, the woman coaxing, the soft spring rain—and alone, at his window in the dark, the young man listening—savouring the life he had no part in, but which he would distil into poetry.

For no drop of these experiences went to waste. The early morning rain, the lonely thrush—these reappeared, several years later, in

La vita solitaria and *Il passero solitario*.[8] The lonely hillside, the infinite serenity, are the first glimpses of *l'Infinito*: the poet's vision of the golden city and fields at sunset, when he watched la Brini, became '*le vie dorate e gli orti*' of *A Silvia*. And 'the moon fallen as in my dream' inspired the enchanting fragment, which begins: '*Odi, Melisso*'.

> Egli ci ha tante stelle,
> Che picciol danno è cader l'una o l'altra
> Di loro, e mille rimaner. Ma sola
> Ha questa luna in ciel, che da nessuno
> Cader fu vista mai se non in sogno.*

This is perhaps the most Greek in form of all the early *Idylls*, though the exquisite *Alla luna*, too, might have been placed on the lips of one of Moschus' shepherds. The others are more Italian in feeling: *Il sogno* owes something to Petrarca, and *La vita solitaria*—though only in its form—to Parini. In these poems, as in Leopardi's notes, the setting is often indicated, rather than described—etched, not painted. But how clear, how still the scene!

> Dolce e chiara è la notte e senza vento,
> E queta sovra i tetti e in mezzo agli orti
> Posa la luna, e di lontan rivela
> Serena ogni montagna.†

These flawless four lines, which open *La sera del dì di festa*—Carducci's favourite among all the *Idylls*—afford a good illustration of the various stages of the process by which many of the poet's loveliest passages reached their final shape. In the *Discorso di un italiano intorno alla poesia romantica*, in 1818, he had translated a simile of Homer's:[9]

---

* There are so many stars
  That little harm is done if one should fall
  While thousands still remain. But in the sky
  One moon alone, which never yet by man
  Was seen to fall, save only in a dream.

† The night is soft and clear and no wind blows,
  The quiet moon stands over roofs and orchards
  Revealing from afar each peaceful hill.

Sì come quando graziosi in cielo
Rifulgon gli astri intorno della luna,
E l'aere è senza vento, e si discopre
Ogni cima de' monti ed ogni selva
Ed ogni torre. . . .*

Then, some months later, in his note-books, we find a brief record of a summer's night in Recanati. 'Sight of the night sky, with the moon above my house in cloudless serenity, as in Homer's simile.'[10] But it was not until the following year, when the whole poem was taking shape, that the literary comparison and the recollection of what he himself had seen were fused in his imagination, and at last found their perfect expression.

In the *Zibaldone* Leopardi admitted that his approach to creative writing was almost always through literature, rather than his own experience. 'I was not lacking in imagination, but I never thought of myself as a poet, until I had read the Greeks. . . . I did not lack enthusiasm, creative powers, and passion—but I did not believe myself eloquent, until I had read Cicero.' And he added that often a man's most fertile talents, which appear to be natural to him, 'are in reality only produced by reading and study'.[11] In his own case, this was so.

His interest in his own language, which had begun during his philological studies in his boyhood, was perhaps the only passion of his youth that never failed him.

. . . Il cor di tutte
Cose alfin sente sazietà, del sonno,
Della danza, del canto e dell' amore,
Piacer più cari che il parlar di lingua;
Ma sazietà di lingua il cor non sente. †

Certainly the pages of the *Zibaldone* bear eloquent witness to the fact that, for Leopardi himself this statement was true! Some men have an addiction to drink, some to drugs, some to one particular

---

* As when, gracious in the sky, the stars shine brightly around the moon, and no breath stirs, and every mountain-top and every wood and tower are disclosed.

† 'The heart at last tires of all things: of sleep, dance, song, and even love—pleasures sweeter than the gift of words,—but of words themselves, the heart is never tired.' From Leopardi's notes to the *Canzoni*, *Poesie e Prose*, vol. I, p. 152.

human being: Leopardi had an addiction to words.[12] He greatly admired the English language, considering it to be the 'freest in Europe',[13] but for the richness, harmony, and variety of his own[14] he had a respect and a passion—no other words are suitable— only equalled by his contempt for the failure of most Italians to make use of their store. 'In Italy today,' he wrote, 'very few know how to write, and many will not allow others to do so'—and with the latter, he declared, he was prepared 'to come to blows, as is the custom in England'.[15] Of his own achievements, however, he spoke with the modesty that accompanies knowledge. A whole life-time, he said, would not be enough for an Italian to master the subtle-ties of his own language, 'as perfect as it is rich, but long ago fallen into disuse . . . Before beginning to write a man must learn it per-fectly, must absorb it into himself, turn it into sap and blood, become its absolute master.'[16]

And this, indeed, is what Leopardi did. A great critic of our own time, Professor Momigliano, has referred to the 'sublime poverty' of his style.[17] He was referring, I think, not only to the poet's de-liberate restraint and economy of expression, but also to the actual size of his vocabulary—which is surprisingly small. But this 'poverty' was rather like a millionaire's whim to lead the simple life: it was founded upon riches. The years that he had spent in his philological studies, noting down innumerable words and phrases, tracing their origin and their development, had provided him with an unequalled store-house to draw upon; and it is fascinating to observe the process of rejection and exclusion by which his personal lexicon was formed. He had always maintained that the exclusion of archaisms, as prac-tised by some of his contemporaries and especially by the French, was an unnecessary and mistaken act of self-impoverishment, and there are a number of words which he always preferred to use in their old form. Indeed it was this deliberate use of archaisms, as well as the close web of classical reminiscence, which formed the very texture of his thought, that caused Tommaseo to observe mali-ciously that Leopardi's work was like a badly scraped palimpsest, in which, beneath the new writing, one can always perceive the old. But beside these archaisms there are a number of familiar, very simple words so frequently used by him, and so often linked to the same adjectives or verbs, that they have almost come to form a personal language. The night is almost always *placida* or *quieta*, the moon *candida* or *tacita*, *solinga* or *pellegrina*; the woods, too (*selve*, not *boschi*), are *tacite*; beauty is *fugace* or *fuggitiva*, and so is life (though sometimes, instead, *sudata*); fate is *acerbo* or *duro*; youth *l'età verde* or *il fior degli anni miei*, and life '*il viver mio*'.[18] Among the most frequent archaisms are *speme* or *spene* for *speranza* (generally linked to *tanta* or *cotanta*), *desìo* for *desiderio*, *dì* for *giorno*, *alma* for *anima*, *donzella* for *giovanetta*, *beltà* for *bellezza*, *il sembiante* for *faccia*; illusions are called *inganni*, *errori*, *larve*, *fole*; a bird is an *augello*, and a beast a *fera*; every sword becomes a *ferro* or a *brando*, and most houses an *ostello*. It is the conventional language of Petrarca and Tasso and subsequently of Metastasio, and yet, used by Leopardi's pen, the well-worn phrases undergo a strange alchemy: they are renewed, they become his own. 'The whole of Arcadia', wrote Flora, 'is freed; what was merely literature, becomes poetry.'[19] In the *Idylls* Leopardi has already left the emphasis and rhetoric of the patriotic *Canzoni* as far behind as the elaborate pedantry of his youthful works of erudition—'the marks', as he himself wrote, 'of *un' arte bambina*'.[20] His tone is so still, so restrained, as almost to seem the voice of a man talking to himself—a man more accustomed to converse with Nature and the creatures of his imagination, than with his fellow-men. This man called poetry '*un respiro dell' anima*'—a breath of the soul.[21]

Yet what deliberate and conscious art had gone to the forming of each quiet phrase, to the choice and placing of each syllable, and to the construction of each complicated internal rhythm and harmony, may be seen by any reader who chooses to compare the successive drafts of one of his poems. This is especially marked in his corrections to the first drafts of his three early patriotic poems, and, later on, of the six *canzoni-odi* and the poem *Alla sua donna*. Indeed it might almost be said that, during the composition of these poems (i.e. before the end of 1823), Leopardi's personal vocabulary was formed for good.[22] The process, as we have said, was one of infinitely painstaking experiment and elimination, from among a very wide choice of words. In the *Inno ai Patriarchi* alone, twelve hundred variants were tried and rejected, but many of these were absorbed into his vocabulary, to be used again later on.

What was his criterion? He would have agreed with Valéry's:

INNO AI PATRIARCHI

Lines 31–58

(At the top of the page Leopardi noted:
"The work of 17 days—July 1822".)

'*De deux mots, il faut choisir le moindre.*'* 'The last things', Leopardi wrote, 'that a man reaches, who wishes to express the movements of his heart, are simplicity and naturalness, the first, artificiality and affectation . . . as we see in children, when they begin to write.'[23] Often, especially in the earlier *Canzoni*, intensity of feeling led him to choose at first some turgid or over-elaborate adjective, and it was only after many experiments that it was at last toned down. Thus— to quote only a few instances among hundreds—in *Ad Angelo Mai* '*stanca e arida terra*' was first '*putrida, marcida*', and in the *Inno ai Patriarchi*, before writing '*pallida cura*', he tried '*torbida, rabida, squallida, livida*, and even *ferrea, scarna, barbara, rugida, putrida, macera, gelida, spietata, torba, torbida*'. So, too, before achieving the characteristic phrase, '*la fugace, ignuda felicità*' he tried in the place of '*ignuda*' '*moribonda e stanca, inerme, doma, vinta, smorta, sola, egra e franta, magra, sozza*'.[24] And to the word '*fugace*' for which he had first tried '*fugata*' he added a note: '*Fugata* does not please me, be- cause it [happiness] is not yet *flown*, but is being put to flight—and so I would like this passage to be understood.'

How deep a joy in the sheer handling and juggling with words, is revealed in such passages as these! '*Vagheggiare, bellissimo verbo*'[25] —so runs a note in the *Zibaldone*, and for that day there is no other, as if the rest of his waking hours had been spent in dwelling on it. This is not pedantry, but a passion. And how sharp, too, how relentless, his ear for any discord!

> Onde per mar delizioso, arcano
> Erra lo spirito umano,
> Quasi come a diporto
> Ardito notator per l'Oceano:
> Ma se un discorde accento
> Fere l'orecchio, in nulla
> Torna quel paradiso in un momento.†

Indefatigably, inexorably, each unnecessary ornament or flourish was pruned away, till the satisfying cadence, the perfect harmony, was

* Among two words, one must choose the lesser.

† Thus the spirit wanders across a secret sea of delight, like a daring swimmer sporting in the waves. But once a discordant note offends the ear, in a moment the paradise melts into thin air. *Sopra il ritratto di una bella donna.*

reached. To look at these autographs is to be made free of Leopardi's workshop—as, in the days of Cellini's Florence, a common citizen might wander about a great artist's *bottega* and watch the chiselling of a limb or the gilding of a leaf.

Yet it is not, of course, only the craftsman that we seek in Leopardi's poetry, nor is it the choice of words alone that gives to his work its peculiar radiance. Is it, then, his themes? I hardly think so. To say that he was the poet of human grief has been, for over a century, a commonplace. When, in 1830, the first collected edition of the *Canti* appeared in Florence, his friend Colletta complained that it was not possible to endure the poet's constant harping on the same subjects and 'the same eternal, and now unbearable, melancholy'.[26] In a sense he was right. Leopardi's themes are often well-worn, and moreover they are all in the same mode. Human solitude, the transience of human life and all its delights, the mercilessness of '*la nemica Natura*', the vanity and emptiness of existence—all these, as Croce has justly remarked, are not philosophical concepts, but states of mind, born of personal disillusionment and despair. From Homer to the author of Ecclesiastes, from Sophocles to the *Imitation of Christ*, these themes echo down the ages. Nor is it difficult to find the same note among the Italian poets. Tasso, Metastasio, and—nearer to Leopardi's own time—Ugo Foscolo, are among the first who come to mind. Yet in Leopardi's hands this common coin, this small change of European song, has turned to gold.

For what Leopardi creates for us is not a philosophy, but a climate. It is the climate of a world in which anguish and desire are seen, as it were, at one remove; they reach us only through the filtre of his imagination, through the veil of his memories. 'If I were to say', writes a great Italian critic, 'what constitutes Leopardi's poetic tone, I should say that it is a kind of privation; he takes from words every taste and colour and perfume of common intercourse.'[27] They are lit, not by 'the wild heat of the sun', but by the pale radiance of the moon.

Of all European poets, indeed, since Lucretius, Leopardi is the greatest poet of the skies. '*Era in mezzo del ciel la curva luna*'*—so begins the enchanting youthful poem, *Le rimembranze*, the first in which he speaks with his own voice. And among the early *Idylls*

* The sickle moon in the sky's zenith.

only two (*L'Infinito* and *Il sogno*) do not contain a passage describing the heavens. Of the other four poems, one is addressed to '*mia diletta luna*'; one—*La sera del dì di festa*—opens, as we have seen, on a cloudless summer night; *Lo spavento notturno* is a boy's dream of the moon falling into his lap; and the last, *La vita solitaria*, ends, too, in the moonlight,

> . . . al cui tranquillo raggio
> Danzan le lepri nelle selve.*

What was the irresistible attraction of this music of the spheres? Partly, no doubt, it was the desire for evasion. In contemplating the cool distances of the stellar spaces he could escape for a while from earthly turmoil and human sorrow. He continued to pursue those 'considerations on the plurality of the worlds and our own nothingness' which he had begun in his boyhood and which, later on, he developed in the *Copernicus* and the *Dialogue between the Earth and the Moon* of his *Operette Morali*. All his life long this attraction, this retreat into the impersonal spaces of the skies, haunted his imagination; always he sought from the moon—*solinga, eterna pellegrina*†—the answers to the secrets that the earth would not reveal. Above the hills of Recanati, the Pisan plain, the deep Neapolitan bay, he watched her—a lonely little hunchback, finding comfort in the skies. And when, on the slopes of Vesuvius, he described her setting, his own life was drawing to its close.

> Scende la luna; e si scolora il mondo.‡

Yet if it is true to speak of Leopardi as the poet of the sky, there is at least an equal significance in the degree to which his work remained rooted in the soil of his native hills. All his life he retained, in his own words, 'an infinite affection for the simplicity of customs and manners and speech and writing, and the indescribable sweetness diffused in the soul, not only by the sight, but by the thoughts and images of country life'.[28] It was the attraction that the simplicity and vigour of primitive life hold for the intellectual and the invalid, but it was

---

* In whose gentle light
Hares sport in the woods.
† Lonely, eternal pilgrim.
‡ The moon goes down, and colour leaves the world.

also an awareness that here, for those who had ears to hear, lay the
true springs of Italian poetry. 'Our true Theocritan idylls', he wrote,
'are not the eclogues of Sannazzaro, but rustic poems, like *La
Nencia, Cecco da Varlungo*, etc. . . . most lovely and similar to Theocritus in their beautiful roughness and admirable truth.'[29]

As early as 1818 he had been noting snatches of country songs, of
those *rispetti* which, to this day, are improvised and sung by country
lovers:

> Fàcciate alla finestra, Luciola,
> Decco che passa lo ragazzo tua
> E porta uno canestro pieno d'ova
> Mantato colle pampane dell' uva.*

And

> Io benedico chi t'ha fatto l'occhi,
> Chi te l'ha fatti tanto 'nnamorati.†

Country feelings, country songs—'How marvellously and sweetly
they flow upon my memory!' Their refrains echo through all his
poetry: the songs of artisans, of labourers, of carters, of peasants in
the fields, of Silvia at her loom.

> Sonavan le quiete
> Stanze, e le vie dintorno,
> Al tuo perpetuo canto.‡

Often, he wrote, he would fall asleep with some such verse
or air upon his lips, and would wake to find himself repeating the
same words or the same refrain, 'as if the soul, in falling asleep, had
put away these thoughts and images, as we lay down our clothes, in

---

* Lean out of the window, Luciola,
 Here is your sweetheart passing by
 Bearing a basket-full of eggs
 Wreathed with tendrils of the vine.

 † My blessing on the maker of your eyes,
 Who filled them with the tenderness of love.
Both these country songs are quoted by Leopardi in the *Zibaldone* (I, p. 43) as
'popular songs sung in my time in Recanati'.

 ‡ The quiet rooms and neighbouring lanes
 Rang with your ceaseless song.
                                        A Silvia.

some place very near at hand, so as to be able to find them again on waking'.[30]

Not only human voices, but almost everything in nature, held for him the echo of a song: the wind in the forest, the dew upon the grass, the distant croaking of frogs in the valley, the birds singing and a hen clucking after rain, the harness-bells and creaking wheels of a traveller's coach, the hammer and saw of a carpenter, working late at night in the silent village, and, from his father's garden, soft night murmurings, heard with the sweet nostalgia of later years:

> ... susurrando al vento
> I viali odorati.*

No country custom or superstition, too, seemed to him too trivial to be noted. Fireflies, he wrote in an essay, are believed to produce warts, if you catch them,[31] serpents and crosses are drawn on walls and street-corners because, being holy symbols, this will prevent the superstitious from defiling them.[32] And other, more lovely myths, too, were set down—to well up again, after some years, into poetry. 'On Ascension Day, no leaf stirs from the bough, and no bird from its nest.'[33] Years later those still lines became the 'altissima quiete' of La vita solitaria:

> ... quando il meriggio in ciel si volve ...
> Ed erba o foglia non si crolla al vento,
> E non onda incresparsi, e non cicala
> Strider, nè batter penna augello in ramo;
> Nè farfalla ronzar, nè voce o moto
> Da presso nè da lunge odi nè vedi.†

In this deliberate return to country myths and scenes, Leopardi— like his great contemporary Manzoni—was following the current of

---

* ... the fragrant avenues
  whispering in the wind.

† When the sky quivers in the blaze of noon
  And neither leaf nor grass stirs in the wind
  And no wave ripples nor cicada shrills
  Nor bird upon the bough can raise a wing,
  Nor hums the butterfly, nor can be seen
  Movement nearby nor far, nor voice be heard.

his time; he was sharing in the revolution which was bringing back literature from the palace to the farm, from the heroic to the quotidian. His lady is not a goddess, but a country girl on a summer's evening, bringing home an armful of fresh grass; his subjects, not kings or heroes, but an old woman gossiping on the church steps, and children shouting, and a tired labourer, bearing home his hoe. His scene is the village square, the hedgerow beneath the hill. But the square holds the whole pageant of human life, and beyond the hedgerow lies infinity.

The search for infinity: of all the notes that echo in Leopardi's poetry, that is the most frequent, the accent most peculiarly his own. 'There are men', he noted, 'who seek everywhere a relation between the infinite and mankind . . . and in short consider everything under the aspect of the infinite, and in relation to the movements of their soul'[34] To define that relation is not easy; he was constantly striving to seize it. 'The soul imagines what it cannot see, what is hidden by that tree, that hedge, that tower—and goes wandering in imaginary spaces, imagining what it would not, if its sight were unobstructed, for the real would exclude the imaginary.'[35] And again: 'Everything that recalls the idea of infinity is agreeable for that reason alone— as a long row or avenue of trees, of which we cannot see the end.'[36] Even the thought of the past can, in some degree, awaken the same sensation, for 'although it is not eternal and therefore not infinite, yet the conception of the space of many centuries produces an indefinite sensation, *dove l'anima si perde.*'*[37]

This is, perhaps, what gives to Leopardi's poetry the evanescent light that bathes it. 'Sad', he wrote, 'is the life of a man (and yet it is commonly so) who only hears and sees plain objects, that is, only those which meet our eyes and ears.'[38] In his poetry, as in his life, there is always a double plane: that of the immediate object before his eyes, and the remote, eternal emotion it evokes. Always, in the foreground, a barrier, a tower, a hedge—but beyond it, the vast spaces of infinity, in which grief and pain are lost.

> Sempre caro mi fu quest' ermo colle,
> E questa siepe, che da tanta parte
> Dell'ultimo orizzonte il guardo esclude.

* Where the soul is lost.

View from the
COLLE DELL' INFINITO
which inspired Leopardi's poem.

Ma sedendo e mirando, interminati
Spazi di là da quella, e sovrumani
Silenzi, e profondissima quiete
Io nel pensier mi fingo; ove per poco
Il cor non si spaura. E come il vento
Odo stormir tra queste piante, io quello
Infinito silenzio a questa voce
Vo comparando: e mi sovvien l'eterno
E le morte stagioni, e la presente
E viva, e il suon di lei. Così tra questa
Immensità s'annega il pensier mio;
E il naufragar m'è dolce in questo mare.*

* This lonely hill was ever dear to me
And this green hedge, that hides so large a part
Of the remote horizon from my view.
But as I sit and gaze, I conjure up
Unending spaces, silences unearthly,
And deepest peace, wherein the heart almost
Draws nigh to fear. And as I hear the wind
Stirring among the branches, I compare
That everlasting silence with this sound:
And then I call to mind eternity
And all the vanished seasons of the past,
And our own living age, with all its noise.
So in immensity my thought is drowned
And sweet it is to founder in this sea.

H

VIII

TWO WINTERS OF DISCONTENT
(1820—1822)

*Nous ne vivons que pour perdre et pour nous détacher.**

I

THERE is a degree of anguish which, like ecstasy, cannot
endure. Either—as with Cowper—it turns to madness, or,
even without any external cause, some slow healing comes to the
wound, some deadening to the nerves. In his *Idylls* Leopardi had sub-
limated his sorrow. But, as Benedetto Croce has observed, those
poems have a strangely evanescent, iridescent quality, almost as if the
poet were himself astonished at being able to catch the tenderness and
beauty as it flies. Soon, he knows, an icy numbness will creep over
him—dulling indeed his capacity for pain, but also paralysing his
imagination. The 'glory of the visible world' will fade; its beauty
and its agony will both be dimmed. This form of destruction or of
alleviation was to come to Leopardi in the two years that followed
the despair and the great lyrical harvest of 1819. But first he wrote
one other poem, *Ad Angelo Mai*, and engaged in one more tussle with
his father.

For Conte Monaldo was seriously alarmed. News filtered slowly
to Recanati, but the success of the *Canzoni* did at last reach his ears,
and at the same time he heard that Giacomo, his own son, was
being acclaimed as the leading poet of the *carbonari*. Could anything
be more disturbing? Moreover, this folly was not likely to stand
alone. He apprehended more, and his suspicions were justified.

Early in 1820 Giacomo had embarked on a correspondence with

* We only live to lose, and to learn detachment.
                    D'Alembert, quoted by Leopardi in his day-book.

98

a printer of Bologna, Pietro Brighenti, of whom he had heard from
Giordani, with the view to the publication of his third patriotic
poem, *Ad Angelo Mai*. Its subject was the recent discovery, in the
Vatican library, of the books of Cicero's *Republic*, which Monsignor
Mai had exhumed, annotated, and published—but this interesting
event was merely used by Leopardi as a pretext for the expression of
his patriotic sentiments. Written at the same time as some of the
Idylls, this poem shows a greater technical skill than either
of the two earlier patriotic *Canzoni*, and strikes a note that is
more genuinely Leopardi's own. His appeal to young Italy to rise
to action is also an attack upon the general mediocrity of the age.
'The crowd has risen, but the wise man has fallen to meet it, and all
the world is upon the same flat level. . . . All is vanity, all the shadow
of an illusion, the world a desert, and nothingness the one reality
among these shades.' Leopardi is now describing his own vision of
the world, as contrasted with his youthful dreams of the heroic age,
and to Carducci this poem seemed 'the clarion-call of the Risorgimento'.[1] But now, and in colder blood, it must be admitted that
much of both the enthusiasm and the indignation has an academic
ring.

In the same volume as this poem Leopardi intended to publish
two others: a youthful poetical exercise entitled *On a Woman Suffering from a Long and Mortal Disease*, and a composition *On the Death
of a Woman Murdered by the Hand and Skill of a Surgeon, at the Instiga-
tion of her Seducer*. Of the latter it may be said that its poetical value
fulfilled the promise of its title. Brighenti agreed to publish all three
poems, and, in order to increase the bulk of the slender volume,
suggested that the two earlier patriotic *Canzoni* should also be
included. But first, he required an advance of twenty *scudi*, and for
Giacomo this sum was unobtainable. He was, he pointed out, a
figlio di famiglia, and by the same post a further confirmation of this
statement reached the publisher. For Monaldo, in the interval, had
taken action. Suspecting, after the publication of the two earlier
poems, that his son might be seeking contact with 'dangerous and
restless minds', he had searched through Giacomo's papers, found
his first letter to Brighenti, and had at once written himself to the
printer to forbid him to reprint the ode *All' Italia*, and to ask for his
help.

'Why must this son of mine waste his time with such trifles, which will bring him neither consequence nor fame? Tell him that such *Canzoni* and other separate pieces produce only a temporary and evanescent glory! . . . Exhort him, urge him rather to some occupation worthy of a Christian gentleman, and you will have done me an inestimable favour; perhaps you will have given back to me a son's affection.'² But it was not by this road that Monaldo would find his way back to his son's heart. Brighenti immediately wrote to Giacomo: 'By now I expect you know that I have received a letter from your father . . . [from which] I understand that that gentleman does not approve of this publication, fearing that in these times the songs may be interpreted as belonging to some faction or other.'

Giacomo's indignation at this interference—and especially at being 'eternally instructed and supervised'—was all that one could expect. And when his irritation had faded a deeper despondency remained: never, he told himself, would he be able to make any use of his gifts. He told Brighenti that he had given up any thought of publishing his poems, and had indeed renounced any hope for the future. 'In twenty-one years—for I began to think and feel when I was still a child—I have run the whole gamut of wretchedness of a long life, and am now morally old. Even feeling and enthusiasm, which once accompanied and sustained me, have disappeared. It is time to die, time to yield to destiny.'³

To Giordani, three days later, he sent the bad news—'It seems that I have been scratching on paper in vain'—and he added a description of his overwhelming misery. 'Again and again I throw myself down and roll over on the ground, asking myself how much longer I must still live. My misery is assured for ever; how much longer must I bear it, how much longer? It almost seems impossible to me that you should still love me. Certainly, if you do, you are the only man to do so. . . . Where is there a more unhappy wretch than I? What pleasures have I enjoyed in this world? What hope remains to me? What is virtue? I can understand nothing any more. Farewell.'⁴

If all this seems, to the dispassionate reader, a little disproportionate, he must remember that Giacomo's writing was his *only* form of activity. To be cut off from writing was to be deprived of life itself. Moreover he seems to have imbibed, in the course of his classical studies, something of the conviction of the ancient Greeks that to be unlucky was a sign of wickedness, which had aroused the hatred of the gods. 'If we belonged to the ancient world,' he told Giordani, 'you would be afraid of me; seeing me so much cursed by fortune, you would think me the worst man on earth.'[5]

But the last word, for all this, had not been said. A few days later Brighenti wrote again, saying that Conte Monaldo had now consented to the publication of the three later poems, but not of the two earlier ones.

Giacomo replied, with schoolboyish irony: 'I am grateful to my father for allowing me to print my own poems. But he won't let me reprint the two Roman ones. Very well. He has asked for the titles of the three unprinted ones. Better still. He does not wish the first of them to be printed. Very well too—not of course in my opinion, but it is only right that in the matter of my writings his opinion should prevail, since I am and shall always remain an unreasonable boy.' In the same letter he gave a curious explanation of his father's willingness to allow the publication of the poem *Ad Angelo Mai*. 'The title is fortunately very innocent; it concerns a *Monsignore*. But my father does not imagine that there is someone in his house who is capable of using any subject to speak of what concerns him most, and that this innocent title conceals a poem full of horrible fanaticism.'[6]

The upshot of all this was that the poem was published early in July, and dedicated to a friend of Brighenti's, Conte Leonardo Trissino of Vicenza, with a preface in which Leopardi quoted Petrarch's lines: '*Ed io son un di quei che il pianger giova.*'* But the man to whom it was dedicated declared himself not only gratified, but also 'astonished and confounded'—perhaps for the reason that as soon as the little volume had appeared, it had been suppressed by the Austrian police, 'for being written in a Liberal spirit and for having a tendency to confirm the disaffected in their malevolent point of view'.

This was not altogether surprising. For Leopardi's printer, the Avvocato Brighenti, was a very odd man. Handsome, gifted, witty, he was a most popular figure in Bologna, and counted among his friends some of the leading Liberals of the day; and he was also a tender and devoted husband and father. Indeed, to supply his ailing

* And I am one of those whom weeping heals.

wife and daughters with all their needs, he had embarked, with optimism and zest but very little success, on one profession after another:
he had turned printer, publisher, journalist, book-seller, impresario.
But unfortunately all these activities concealed another one: he was
also a spy for the Austrian government, and regularly sent off, under
the name of Luigi Morandini, reports to the head of the Venetian
police.[7] Moreover, he played his cards so well that it was not until
the last years of his life that anyone even suspected his double rôle,
and he seems to have possessed a sufficient elasticity of mind not
only to profess, but to feel, a warm friendship for the very men he
was spying on. Certainly now, at the same time as he was writing
encouraging letters to the young poet, he attracted the attention of
an Austrian informer to Leopardi's latest *canzone*—and when it had
been read, no doubts subsisted in the mind of the Austrian government. 'This poem'—so the head of the Venetian police was informed
—'breathes forth the fatal spirit of Liberalism which seems to have
blinded some unhappy regions of our land. . . . This is one of those
evil little books which, being short and cheap, may be read by
everyone, especially as it bears an inappropriate and (at first sight)
unalarming title. My respectful opinion is therefore that this little
work should be suppressed.'[8]

Nor was this the only occasion on which Leopardi's works were
banned. Some years later, in Florence, the police forbade the reprint
of the *Canzoni* and the publication of one of the *Operette Morali*; in
Naples, in 1835, a new edition of Leopardi's works was suppressed—
and it is recorded that soon after his death, in Calabria, a barber was
fined a thousand ducats for being found guilty 'of possessing a forbidden book, entitled *Canti* of Giacomo Leopardi'.

It is strange to think that, in the very summer in which *Ad Angelo
Mai* appeared, Byron (who also shared the honour of being spied
upon by the Austrian police) was riding, only a few miles away,
through the Ravenna pine-woods with his band of 'fine savage,
three-legged leopards', the *Cacciatori Americani*, 'all armed and singing with all their might, "*Sem tutti soldat' per la libertà!*"'[9] Did he
ever read, one wonders, Leopardi's three *Canzoni*? Did he find there
'the very poetry of politics'?

But indeed, though Leopardi's opinions on freedom and national
independence were the same as Byron's, their affinity went no

further. Byron was capable of action even in the cause of a country not his own, while Leopardi's nationalistic sentiments always remained exclusively a passion of the mind. His hatred of the oppressor was that of Simonides, Dante, and Alfieri—not that of Berchet, Mazzini, or Garibaldi. Indeed, the great events that were occurring throughout Europe during his youth left him singularly calm; there is no reference either in his diary or his letters to the Mazzini movement, or even to the revolution in Naples and Palermo of 1820 and 1821. Even the death of Napoleon, by which Mazzini was so deeply moved, aroused no comment. His praise of liberty and independence, which became the inspiration of the men who fought for these ideals, was in him the detached opinion of a dreamer and idealist, who was also too sceptical to believe in the importance of changes of governments or revolutions. Vossler has compared his spirit to a sensitive seismographic instrument which has been placed underground; it does not register the daily storms or changes of the weather, but only the fundamental, deeper tension and tremblings of the earth—the oscillations of the *Zeitgeist*.

Moreover in this, too, Leopardi was, perhaps, his father's son. For one volunteer did go from Recanati to fight for Greece—the Count Andrea Broglio, who had also fought with Murat—and he was killed by a Turkish bullet, in 1828, at the siege of Anatolico. The news was sent to Giacomo, who was then living in Pisa, by his father in the following terms: 'Recanati has paid her tribute of folly to the madness of the age, and has stained with her blood the classic soil of Greece.' He added that the poor young man would probably be buried in Treia, where his family came from, 'so we shall have one madman the less to commemorate here'.[10] These remarks leave us in little doubt as to what Conte Monaldo's feelings would have been if indeed Giacomo, through Giordani, had ever met Byron, and had been infected by his ideas. But indeed Giacomo's answer was all that his father could have wished: 'I am very sorry for the Broglios, both father and son; I did not know that his fanaticism had driven him to endanger his life for a cause and a country not his own.'[11]

During this period Leopardi's family life was becoming more and more trying, and his relations with his father increasingly strained. In his presence he now maintained a gloomy silence, while fiddling with a small bone paper-knife, which he always carried in his pocket. As soon as possible he would fly to the refuge of the library, there feverishly to write letter after letter to everyone he knew, begging for employment in Rome, in Milan, in Bologna—anywhere, but Recanati!

He wrote to his aunt Ferdinanda Melchiorri, Monaldo's sister—a gentle, affectionate woman, of a temperament very similar to his own. But she could only send him her sympathy: 'I too have never known happiness. . . . You, dear Giacomo, are young: perhaps you can harden your heart.'[12] He wrote to Angelo Mai: 'All the hopes of my childhood have vanished; I almost even regret the time spent over my studies, since I now see myself in the same position as the scum of the ignorant or the idle.'[13] But the Abate—whose name has only been saved from total oblivion by being linked with those of Cicero and of Leopardi—replied with a stiff little note, telling him that a humble post of copyist was vacant at the Vatican.

He wrote to Vincenzo Monti's son-in-law, Giulio Perticari—and in this letter all his pride and reserve were thrown aside: 'Since my birth, I have never known any delight. For a few years I felt hope; for a long time past, not even that. And my life, both inner and outer, is such that most men would shudder with fear, at the mere thought of it. . . . My parents are irrevocably resolved not to let me leave home, unless I can find some employment to sustain me . . . and yet they themselves obstinately refuse to help me to obtain it. . . . Dear Count, it is of no importance that I should live, but since I cannot die (and if I could, I assure you I would not finish this letter) I ask for mercy . . . for help to endure, not life itself, but just the passing of the years.'[14] But Perticari merely sent back a Latin tag —*Macte nova virtute: sic itur ad astra**—and an invitation (which was refused) to Pesaro.

As for Conte Monaldo, a letter which he wrote to his brother-in-law, Marchese Antici, at this time, sufficiently shows the poor man's unawareness of what was going on in his house. 'My sons are reading the great book of life . . . and I hope that soon they will both of them come to hate some ideas which at first attracted them, and will place themselves on the side of wisdom. . . . Woe to them, and woe to me, if I had yielded to their imprudent desires and had sent them

* Assume new virtue; thus the stars are reached.

to the Capital! By now I should be lamenting their perversion....'[15]

So the months passed, each one bringing fresh faint hope, followed by renewed disappointment. Leopardi's acute misery had gradually given place to what he called resignation, but was more truly numbness. Only occasionally did he awake from it to his former intensity of feeling. 'A few evenings ago,' he wrote to Giordani, 'before going to bed, I opened my window, and seeing a clear sky, and moonlight, with a mild breeze blowing and dogs barking from afar, some of the old images awoke again in me, and I felt my heart come to life again—so that I began to cry out like a madman, imploring some mercy from Nature, whose voice I had heard, after so long a silence. And at that moment, remembering my past condition, to which I was certain of returning immediately afterwards, I was frozen with horror—being unable to understand how life can be endured without illusions or vivid affections, without imagination or enthusiasm. For a year ago' [when he was writing the *Idylls*] 'these things filled all my life, and made me happy in spite of my afflictions. But now I am parched and withered as a dry weed, so that no passion can enter into this poor soul, and even the sovereign and eternal power of love is destroyed.'[16]

A few months later, in June, a curious episode roused him. We have seen how much he depended upon the letters he received from Giordani, who had never ceased to advise the virtues of patience and resignation. But now, absorbed in a trouble of his own, Giordani suddenly changed his tone. 'I see', he wrote, 'that your troubles have no limits, no end, no remedy, no mitigation. I can only say to you that when it is God's will to send you death, you should accept it as a boon—and be convinced that in losing life, you are losing nothing.'[17] Leopardi's diary records that this letter arrived during one of his worst moods, 'when I was in despair at not being able to die'. Its effect was strangely salutary. 'Will you believe that this letter, far from detaching me more completely from life, caused me to feel affection again for what I had already given up? Thinking of my past hopes, and of the consolations and forecasts which had once been offered to me by my friend, and looking back at my writings and my studies, remembering my childhood with its thoughts and desires and fine prospects—my heart was so much moved that I no longer knew how to abandon hope, and death terrified me—not indeed in itself, but as bringing to an end all those fine expectations of the past.' He went on to a singularly frank analysis of why his friend's candid remarks had distressed him. 'I had thought of my wish for death as a heroic one,' he admitted. 'I certainly believed that my friends—few in number indeed, but at least those few— would prefer me to be alive, and would not abandon me to my despair, and that, at my death, they would be astonished and cast down, saying, "So all is ended? Oh, God, so many hopes, such greatness of soul, such talent, all without fruit!" . . . But to think that they would say instead, "Praise God, his sufferings are ended . . . may he rest in peace", this seemed to me like shutting down the tomb over my head, and this sudden and complete acceptance of my death, however reasonable, stifled me, with a sense of my complete annihilation.'[18] Giacomo, in fact, realized that his hold upon life was still far stronger than he had imagined, and passed on to give himself advice about better ways of consoling a friend in trouble. 'Do not deny his suffering,' he wrote, 'but remember that in the last recesses of his heart there still lingers a drop of illusion. Agree not with his words, but with his heart.' A few days later— when Giordani, in his turn, had written an unhappy letter—Leopardi put these principles into practice: he sent his friend not good advice, but affection. 'I consider love', he wrote, 'as the most beautiful thing on earth, and find nourishment in illusions. . . . I do not think that illusions are merely vain, but rather that they are, to a certain degree, substantial, and innate in each of us—and they form the whole of our life.'[19]

II

After the publication of his poem *Ad Angelo Mai*, Leopardi let more that a year pass without writing any verses. He was, however, far from idle, for in this year alone he filled 1,167 pages of his great day-book, the *Zibaldone*.[20] What is this book? Its name means a hotch-potch or compendium—and indeed it is a hotch-potch, part note-book and part diary, containing not only all the author's knowledge, but almost every thought that, during the fifteen years in which he kept it, passed through his mind. The first suggestion of keeping such a book seems to have been given him in his boyhood by Don Giuseppe Antonio Vogel, an Alsatian priest who, having fled from the French Revolution, had come to live in Recanati, and who maintained that 'every literary man should have a *written chaos* such as this: note-book containing *sottiseries, adversa, excerpta, pugillares, commentaria.** They are', he said, 'the store-house out of which fine literature of every kind may come, as the sun, moon, and stars issued out of chaos.'[21]

Leopardi's store-house came to consist of no less than 4,526 pages of notes, begun in July 1817 and continued until December 1832, jotted down day after day in a minute, neat, even script. Here, besides notes on philosophy, philology, archæology, religion, science, politics, art, and history, he set down pages of literary criticism, quotations that had struck him, fragments of popular songs and sayings that had caught his ear, and reflections which he subsequently developed in the *Operette Morali* and the *Pensieri*. And embedded in all this, like a fine vein of gold, we come upon sudden, exquisite fragments of verse:

> La speme che rinasce in un col giorno.† [22]

> Sentia del canto risuonar le valli
> D'agricoltori. . . .‡ [23]

> Vedendo meco viaggiar la luna. . . .§ [24]

The *Zibaldone* throws open the workshop of Leopardi's mind. He is writing and recollecting not for an audience, but for himself— 'improving himself, teaching himself, pitying himself, telling his own story'.[25] For, in addition to all the rest, the *Zibaldone* contains a great many autobiographical notes—confessions, pages of self-analysis, descriptions of personal habits, recollections of childhood, hopes, dreams, regrets. Here we may find odd little bits of observation, such as the story—mentioned as an example of the 'faculty of compassion'—of 'a dog in my house, who, from a balcony, used

---

* Pleasanteries, arguments, extracts, counter-propositions, commentaries.

† The hope that every dawn renews again.

‡ I heard the song of peasants
  Echoing down the valleys. . . .

§ Seeing the moon travelling by my side. . . .

to throw down some bread to a dog in the road'.[26] We may learn how he liked to eat alone and to walk alone, and to stand in the dark outside a lighted house, admiring a gay scene, 'which would mean nothing to me if I were looking at the same room from within'.[27] We may read how he preferred, when some good fortune befell him, not to divulge it, but 'to give my content into the custody of melancholy',[28] and how greatly he valued anniversaries, especially those of 'the day and hour in which I first felt the touch of a very dear passion',[29] and how he discovered, by his own experience, that a man who confessed his misfortunes, lost 'not only protection and love, but even simple affection'.[30] These passages, indeed (there are over four hundred of them), might form—with the *Ricordi d'infanzia* of 1819 and a few other fragments—the material for the *Story of a Soul* which Leopardi himself planned, and which would have been as moving a human document as has ever been set down on paper.

As to the rest—we may now disregard the philological notes, so greatly admired by his contemporaries, and most of the philosophical reflections, which he himself subsequently condensed and clarified in the *Operette Morali* or the *Pensieri*. But what a granary still remains! What a tribute to human scholarship, industry, and search for truth, and—for no man who was able to share his thoughts with his fellows could have kept such a diary as this—what a record of human solitude! The *Zibaldone* is Leopardi himself. Here we have—undigested, unrefined—the raw material of all that he ever wrote, and of such else besides that never reached its final form. We find here the kind of literary taste—*le grand goût, le goût véritable*, were Sainte-Beuve's phrases for it—that is only attainable by a man whose mind, for many years, has been formed by a knowledge and love of classical literature. 'In the most modern landscape', says Logan Pearsall-Smith, 'the peaks of Helicon and Parnassus must be seen, however far and faintly blue, on the horizon.'[31] In Leopardi's vision their outlines are always very clear: no medieval haze, no Romantic mist, is allowed to obscure them.

We find in these notes, too, his intense interest in his own language, his diligent toil at his craft, his passion for clarity, his undeviating addiction to truth. And we also find, to be honest, much that is repetitive, wearisome, and confused—some self-pity, some unconvincing irony, and a good deal of pseudo-philosophy. We find notes dictated by disillusionment, by tedium, by a sense of grievance, by despair. But in the midst of all this welter of thought and feeling suddenly comes what Keats called a 'trembling, delicate, and snail-horn perception of beauty', and we are drawn back into the poet's own world. Few men can have read the whole of the *Zibaldone*, but no one knows Leopardi who is not acquainted with it.

Much else besides was taking up Leopardi's time in 1821. He told Giordani that he had so many plans in mind, that to carry them out would require more than four lives. 'And though I realize . . . the vanity of all human affairs, I yet feel sad and anxious when I consider how much could be done, and how little I shall be able to do. . . . For this one life that Nature has given me is weighed down and enchained by poverty, and I see it slipping away between my fingers.'[32]

All this work was accomplished in spite of the oppression of constant pain. 'For a long time,' he wrote to Giordani during the summer, 'I have had reason to regret that my skull contains a brain, for I cannot think about anything, even for the shortest time, without a contraction and pain of the nerves.'[33] To go on working, unceasingly and alone, under these conditions, requires a truly heroic constancy. Yet it was in this summer that Leopardi wrote the enchanting poem that is sometimes considered the last of the early *Idylls*, *La vita solitaria*, and in the course of the next twelve months he composed five of the six long poems which Carducci called *Canzoni-Odi*, and which were published in Bologna, in 1824.[34] All of these poems show much technical progress, but none of them reaches the heights of Leopardi's greatest work. None has the delicate beauty of the early *Idylls*, nor the depth and serenity of the later ones. But all have phrases or passages of great beauty, and they reveal very completely the state of the poet's mind.[35]

Two of these poems, *Nelle nozze della sorella Paolina* and *A un vincitore nel pallone*, reveal Leopardi's incurable idealization of the days of Greece and Rome, his ineradicable conviction that then alone was man simple, strong, and free. 'He considered Brutus', wrote Sainte-Beuve, 'the last of the *Antichi*; but that is what he was himself —an *Antico* born too late.'[36] This is, of course, a typically romantic attitude to classicism—inspired by a similar discontent with the present, a similar nostalgia for what was past or unfamiliar, to the

romantic cult for the Middle Ages. For Leopardi the medieval world
held no appeal; he saw his image of an ideal world in the golden light
of a Greek temple, rather than in the twilight of a Gothic cathedral.
But his process of historical idealization was that of a true Romantic
of his time. 'A song in honour of the Roman Virginia, in which one
imagines seeing her ghost in a dream, and speaks tenderly to her
about her fate and the present evils of Italy'[37]—such was his draft
for the earlier of these two poems. It is, as he himself remarked, 'a
poem about a wedding, where no one speaks of a marriage-bed or a
virgin's girdle, of Venus or Hymene'.[38]

Two others of these poems—*Alla Primavera o Delle favole antiche*
and *Inno ai Patriarchi*—are equally characteristic. They are Leopardi's
farewell to the fables and 'illusions' of his boyhood. In the first he
returned to the days of his childhood, 'the fabulous years . . . when
each thing that we saw seemed to wish to speak to us', and when, in
the still midday hour, a shepherd-boy heard Pan's piping, and
nymphs bathed in the streams.

> Vissero i fiori e l'erbe,
> Vissero i boschi un dì.*

Would those days never return—would spring not bring back to him
'*la favola antica*'?

So great was the fascination that the midday hour, *l'ora meridiana*,
had always held for him, that at one moment he thought of calling
this poem *Delle favole antiche o meridiane*. 'The weariness, rest, and
silence', he wrote, 'that prevail during the midday hour, rendered
that time mysterious and sacred to the Ancients, like the hours of
the night—so that it was believed that it was especially at midday
that the gods, nymphs, and fauns, and the souls of the dead, might
be seen and heard by men.'[39]

The *Inno ai Patriarchi*, too, is ostensibly a hymn to pastoral and
patriarchal life, to the days when the world was young. 'It says',
Leopardi wrote, 'that the golden age is not a fable.' But what it
really reveals is the poet's longing, not for the world's golden age,
but for his own—and '*la fugace, ignuda felicità*'.†

* Once flowers came to life for me
And trees and plants.
Alla Primavera.

† Naked happiness on the wing.

Perhaps the most self-revealing, however, of this whole group of poems is the *Ultimo canto di Saffo*. 'Its intention'—so Leopardi himself explained—'is to represent the unhappiness of a delicate, tender, sensitive, noble, and loving soul, placed in a young and ugly body.'[40] Such direct representations of one's own feelings seldom produce a successful work of art; and this is not wholly an exception. 'The most difficult thing in the world', the poet himself recognized, 'is to arouse interest in an ugly person,' and he added that, in this case, he hoped to achieve it only in virtue of 'the great space of time between us and Sappho', and the extreme vagueness that surrounds the story of her misfortunes and her genius—a vagueness 'most favourable to poetry'.[41]

> . . . Arcano è tutto,
> Fuor che il nostro dolor.*

The words are placed on Sappho's lips, but the dull hopelessness and despair that pervade the poem are Leopardi's own.

> Alle sembianze il Padre,
> Alle amene sembianze eterno regno
> Diè nelle genti. . . .
> Virtù non luce in disadorno ammanto.†

Like the Greeks themselves, he felt any form of ugliness to be not only sad, but ignominious; believing that he was despised for his deformity, he had come to despise himself. Whether indeed all the humiliations he thought he suffered were real or imaginary, is irrelevant.[42] What is certain is that the self-contempt they aroused in him, drove him to the verge of suicide.[43] A constant preoccupation with this subject is reflected in the *Zibaldone*, and found expression in another of the *Canzoni*, *Bruto Minore*. In a *Comparison between Theophrastus and Brutus*, Leopardi had described Brutus as 'a man overcome by an inexorable and unbearable calamity . . . freed from all the illusions of life . . . and determined to punish himself for his own unhappiness'.[44] This was now the theme of his poem. It

---

* All, save our grief, is mystery.

† To appearances alone, to appearances of beauty, have the gods given eternal power over man. . . . Virtue shines not in forms that have no grace.

Ultimo canto di Saffo.

expressed his desolate conviction that suicide was not an *ultima ratio*,
but reason itself, a human right. 'To continue in this life, once we
have realized its emptiness and nothingness, and are deprived of the
illusions on which nature has founded it, is not possible.'[45]

Eleven years later, in a letter to a friend, he declared that his
opinions were still unchanged: 'My feelings towards fate have always
been and still are those that I expressed in *Bruto Minore*'—a belief
that suicide was both more courageous and nobler than either
'frivolous hopes of an uncertain and unknown future happiness', or
'a cowardly resignation'.[46] The death-wish that had begun to
haunt him as a boy, looking down into the depths of the well in his
father's garden, had been fostered and rationalized; it had become
one of the leitmotifs of his life.

III

It was in this same year—1821—that, according to some notes in his
unpublished papers, Leopardi was planning a work of another nature,
one which would take him back to the earliest 'illusion' of his boyhood: his faith. 'No good poetry has ever been written about
religion,' he wrote, 'except by Milton.' (We must remember that
he did not care for medieval verse, and presumably was unacquainted
with the English seventeenth-century mystics, or with St. John of
the Cross; but it is surely very odd that Dante should not even have
been mentioned.) And he went on to note the qualities that, to his
mind, religious verse should have: it 'must belong to the pre-
dominating religion', and it must be 'popular'—that is, it must have
its roots in popular beliefs, as the Homeric hymns were inspired
by the myths of Greece.[47] And he quoted the legend of the three
fountains that are believed to have sprung up in Rome, where the
head of St. Paul fell when he was beheaded, and the poetic superstition of the peasants of the Marches that on Ascension Day 'no leaf
stirs from the bough, and no bird from its nest'. Among other
subjects he was considering we find the apparitions of the Archangel
Michael on Monte Gargano, the great pilgrimage site of the Middle
Ages, and the story of Tobias and the Angel. 'Angels and their
invisible forms pervading all the world . . . secret action of spirits in
animating springs and clouds.'[48] And, in another note, 'Imitation

of Callimachus in telling the story of Mary, as he told that of Diana'.

In all this, how closely Leopardi was following the great tradition of his country and his race, by which one culture and creed have always succeeded another, without the later one destroying what came before! So, too, the nave of many a Christian church has been adorned by the columns of a pagan temple, and in the streets of Genzano flower-petals bestrew the path of Christian priests, which once carpeted the passage of the god of the woods.

Among these brief notes there are two longer ones, more directly Christian: the drafts of odes in honour of the Redeemer and of the Virgin Mary. In both these poems Leopardi appealed to the element in Christianity which must always have struck the deepest chord in his own heart: the divine compassion for human pain, the divine participation in human suffering. 'Have pity on us,' was his cry to the Redeemer, 'you who have tried this life of ours, who have tasted its nothingness. . . . Have pity on so much suffering, have pity on this poor creature of yours, whom you have redeemed!' And then the supplication took on a more personal note—the cry of the lost wanderer, of the man who has the Hound of Heaven at his heels. 'Now I am wandering, day after day, from hope to hope, forgetting you, although perpetually disillusioned. The day will come when every other hope has faded, save that of death, and then . . .'

Immediately afterwards came the ode to Mary: 'It is true that we are all sinners, but we do not enjoy our sin; we are so terribly unhappy! You who are already great and secure, have pity on so much misery.' And then were to follow 'Invocations to Mary on behalf of our poor Italy'.[49]

Here, indeed, is an echo of the Catholic liturgy, which had sounded so deeply, so continuously, through the days of his child-hood: '*Passio Christi, conforta me*', '*Intra tua vulnera absconde me*'.* Far as Leopardi's intellect had travelled from the faith that had been taught him, his emotions always remained essentially Christian. Deep in his soul was the Christian awareness of the inevitability of suffering: all roads leading to the Cross.

How, indeed, could it have been otherwise? For the first eighteen years of his life he had lived, day by day, the life of Catholic ritual.

* 'May Christ's Passion comfort me.' 'Let me hide within Thy wounds.'

I

In those sensitive, malleable years all his strongest, most vivid impressions had come from the Church's rites: he had watched in childish amazement and terror the midnight processions of the missionaries, and, later on, had himself partaken in the penitential processions of Holy Week:

> Notturno stuol, di Cristo appo 'l feretro
> Il dí che di sua morte il ciel si dole.*

His feasts and holidays, too, had been the feasts of the Church: the annual outing to one of his father's farms, San Leopardo, on the feast day of the Holy Cross; the consecration of a convent which had been suppressed under the Republican rule. 'The blessing', he noted then, 'on that spring day in the deserted courtyard, hearing the birds who had just come back to their nests in the roof—a fine, cloudless day—sunshine—the sound of bells—and at the first sound, my feelings stirred towards my Creator.'[50]

So deeply did all these memories sink into him, that even in his day-book his notes are dated not only with the day of the year but also with the feast-day of the Church—Holy Saturday, Ash Wednesday, the day of the coming of the House of Loreto, etc. And here is a letter to Paolina, when he was living in Bologna: 'You will already have kept the feast of the Madonna, and I was not there. I assure you I thought of it and was sorry.'[51] At that time perhaps it was rather the tie of home and of old familiar habit that was tugging at him, but it was also something more: 'Every man brought up in superstition finds it painful to detach himself from that first companion of his youth, finds it difficult to consider as a chimaera, what he used to think indubitable.'[52]

There was in him, with regard to religious matters, a duality of nature which remained for ever unresolved.[53] His unquiet nostalgia for faith was that of a man whose instincts tell him what his intellect refuses to confirm. For the true Leopardi was not a philosopher, but a poet, and poetry offers a reality of its own. '*Cette divination du spirituel dans le sensible, et qui s'expliquera elle-même dans le sensible, c'est bien là ce que nous appelons poésie.*'† It was such a divina-

---

* The nightly throng behind the bier of Christ
  Upon the night when Heaven weeps his death.

† 'This intuition of the spiritual through the perceptible, and which finds expression in what is perceptible—that is surely what we call poetry.'
                                        Maritain, *Frontières de la Poésie*.

tion that Leopardi felt on the spring morning on which his heart was 'stirred towards his Creator'; this is what he himself called 'a sense of the spirit'.

Deliberately and painfully, in his maturity, he cast off the illusions of his childhood in favour of 'naked truth'; he declared that it was nobler to 'regard intrepidly the desert of life', rejecting all illusory consolations. Contessa Adelaide had laboured in vain to destroy in her son all traces of spiritual pride. But his emotions continued to seek a confirmation of what his reason had abandoned—'the existence of an immeasurable Being wiser and more conscious than we are, and who watches over our fate', a belief that is 'more comforting than any other possible one'.[54] Later on, the Church condemned his *Operette Morali*, and Paolina herself sadly placed them among the 'forbidden books' of his father's library. But when Giacomo's friend De Sinner, who knew as much of his mind as any man in his later years, received the book, he wrote upon the fly-leaf the words of St. Augustine: '*Fecisti me Domine, et inquietus est cor meum donec requiescat in te.*'*[55] It is not easy for a man to destroy entirely what has once stirred his spirit, and most men have some hidden altar in their hearts, dedicated to the fallen gods.

* 'Thou hast made me, O Lord, and my heart is unquiet until it rests in Thee.'

IX

ROME
(1822—1823)

I timidi non hanno meno amor proprio che gli arroganti, anzi più . . . e perciò temono.*

I

ON the 17th of November 1822 two post-chaises were drawn up in front of the Palazzo Leopardi. Marchese Carlo Antici, Giacomo's uncle, was returning to Rome with all his family, after spending the summer in his native town. He and his children had climbed into the first carriage; another uncle, Don Girolamo, had entered the second one; the servants had brought down the luggage; all was ready for departure. But at this point there was a delay. Carlo and Paolina were standing in the doorway, Paolina weeping, Carlo on the verge of tears; Contessa Adelaide was walking up and down impatiently; the eyes of all were fixed on the marble staircase, down which the missing traveller would descend. At last the library door opened—and Giacomo appeared. Behind him was his father, dressed in his unfailing black—a little paler than usual, distinctly moved. He had relented at last, had yielded to the persuasions of the Antici family, and was sending Giacomo with them to Rome; but, at the last moment, he had drawn his son aside into the library for a final word of warning. Giacomo hurried down the staircase, kissed his mother's hand, embraced his brother and sister, then entered the second carriage. Carlo rushed forward for a word to his brother, a smile to his pretty cousin Marietta, with whom he was in love; but the carriages started, and a turn of the winding road to the plain hid

---

* The timid have not got any less *amour-propre* than the arrogant, indeed more . . . and therefore they are afraid.

Pensieri LVIII.

them from him. Poor Carlo returned into the empty house, saying mechanically to the first person he met, 'Yes, Giacomo has gone; I shall miss him'. Then a full realization of his future loneliness came over him, and he burst into passionate tears. Giacomo Leopardi had left Recanati at last.

The journey to Rome by the fertile Chienti valley, the high pass of the Apennines above Foligno, and the Umbrian foothills, took six days. It led Leopardi through some of the most beautiful country in Italy, but he has told us nothing about it. He took with him a pocket edition of Lucian, a volume of *Don Quixote*, and his own unfinished manuscript of *Il Martirio dei Santi Padri*; and even during the journey —his first glimpse of the world outside Recanati—he found time to work a little at the manuscript, and to read some Spanish and some Greek; but never, apparently, to look out of the carriage window.

All left him equally unmoved—the deep gorges of the mountain pass, the upland valleys of the Apennines, with their great squares of ploughland and of pasture, like the folds of a giant's counterpane; the sudden, intoxicatingly beautiful drop into Umbria, with Assisi close by on the hillside, and Perugia shimmering across the plain; the enchanting little hill-town of Spoleto where he spent the night; even the great expanse of the Roman Campagna, that first announces the wonder of the approach to Rome. 'He only remembers', wrote Bouché-Leclercq, 'that he suffered greatly during the journey, that at Spoleto he had to restrain some insolent jokers, and that even with his short-sighted eyes he distinctly saw the dome six miles away.'[1] The Spoleto incident occurred when he was writing a dutiful letter to his father, after supper, in the dining-room of the little inn, heedless of a noisy crowd of young men from the vicinity who were ready for any sport. They saw the little hunchback writing in a corner, and a sly young priest among them, who had found out that he was a poet, began to exercise his wit upon him. 'But as soon as I made a retort,' wrote Giacomo—and it is easy to imagine the contempt and bitterness in his voice, and the pain in his eyes—'he was quick to change his tone, and the whole company became as quiet and docile as sheep.'[2]

On the 23rd of November he arrived in Rome. For the last ten years his thoughts, his dreams, and his desires had all been directed towards this goal; it was there that he hoped to find the greatness of the past, the promise of the future. The intensity of his expectations was such that some disappointment was inevitable. In a man of a more resilient nature it might have been temporary; in Leopardi it was immediate and final. Within two days of his arrival he began writing to his brother that all his hopes had been destroyed. 'You must know, dear Carlo, that I am beside myself; not indeed with amazement, for if I saw the devil himself I should not be surprised, and I do not take any pleasure in the great things that I see; but because, although I *know* that they are marvellous, I do not feel it, and I assure you that these crowds and this grandeur have become wearisome to me from the first day. Therefore when I tell you that I am beside myself, do not think it is from amazement, nor pleasure, nor hope, nor anything else agreeable. . . . During the journey . . . there still remained to me that breath of hope, which, without being exciting or pleasurable, is yet sufficient to sustain life. But now that I have got here . . . I swear to you, my Carlo, that my patience and my self-confidence, which had come to seem to me invincible and indestructible, are now not only vanquished but destroyed.'[3]

That is the gist of the matter. In Recanati Leopardi had felt that no one was capable of appreciating his worth; in Rome he found that they were unaware of his very existence. The great world was too great for him, after all! 'As to ambition,' he wrote to his brother, 'you must convince yourself that in a large town it is quite impossible to satisfy it. Whatever qualities you may possess, beauty or wisdom or nobility or riches or youth, there is so much of them all in a great city that no one will pay any attention to them.' Characteristically, within a fortnight of leaving Recanati and arriving in Rome, he began to construct a theory as to why life in a small town is preferable to being in a great one. 'In a little town', he wrote to Carlo, 'we may be bored, but, after all, men there have some relation to each other and to the things around them, because the sphere of these relations is small and in proportion to the human scale. But in a large city a man lives without any relation at all to what surrounds him, because the sphere is so large that no individual can fill it or be aware of it, and so there is no point of contact between them. Therefore you may imagine how much greater and more terrible the tedium of a great city must be than that of a small one; for human indifference —that horrible feeling, or rather absence of feeling—must inevitably have its seat in great cities, that is, in very big societies. The only way to live in a large town is to make oneself a tiny circle of friends . . . that is to say, to build oneself a little city within the great one.'[4]

He had expected, on his arrival in Rome, to enter the society of great scholars like the Abate Cancellieri and Monsignor Mai, of famous artists like Canova; he had thought himself certain of their recognition and their friendship. He discovered that these great men were indifferent to his admiration, and he hastily tried to transform it into scorn. After visiting the Abate Cancellieri, who had praised his philological works, he described him as 'a fool, a stream of chatter, the most boring and exasperating man on earth. . . . He speaks of absurdly frivolous things with the greatest seriousness, and of important ones with the greatest coolness; he drowns you in flattery and praise, but in so cold a manner and with such indifference, that, as you listen to him, you feel that to be a remarkable man, is the most common thing on earth.'[5] He called on Monsignor Mai, and found him much more agreeable, but alas, equally agreeable to other people, too. 'He seems to wish to please everyone, and in the end, follows his own convenience.' He hoped to visit Canova, who was a friend of Giordani's, and heard that the great sculptor had died a month before his arrival. 'To attract other people's attention in a great city is a despairing enterprise; such towns are only made for monarchs.'[6]

In his uncle's house, the Palazzo Antici, in which he stayed during the whole of his time in Rome, he found an atmosphere as provincial as that which he had left behind in Recanati, and no less uncongenial. The excessive formality and constraint of Contessa Adelaide's régime had weighed heavily upon him at home; but now he complained that 'the incredible and inconceivable disorder of the daily life of this family will not allow me to feel myself anything but a stranger among them. . . . Here', he wrote, 'no one will put himself to any trouble for others; mother and children, husband and wife, are constantly and vehemently fighting over every mouthful of bread, every sip of wine, every tit-bit—refusing them to each other, taking them out of each other's mouths, accusing each other of greed. Each one of them irritates the other, and is exasperated by him in turn.'[7]

It was not in order to live in surroundings such as these that

Leopardi had come to Rome. 'Since I set foot in this town,' he told
his brother, 'no drop of pleasure has fallen on my spirit, except in
such moments as I read your letters.' Both he and Carlo, in planning
this Roman visit, had included among its advantages the opportunities which a large town would afford for facile love-affairs. For indeed in Recanati—according to a singularly frank passage in a letter
of Giacomo's to Conte Broglio d'Ajano—the chaste life which the
Leopardis required of both their sons had been one of the chief
causes of their restlessness and gloom. 'Does my father believe', he
wrote, 'that with a nature as ardent, a heart as sensitive as mine, I
have never felt those desires and affections which all young men in
the world feel and pursue? Does he not know that this has happened
to me even more often, and more violently, than to other men? . . .
Does he think that if I have lived until now a life which literally
would not be required of a monk of seventy . . . this is a consequence
of the coldness of my nature?'[8]

But when Giacomo at last arrived in Rome, he made the bitter
discovery that his own deformity and lack of enterprise were more
serious obstacles than his father's vigilance. 'Out walking, in church,
in the street, you do not find even a hag who will look at you. I
have walked round Rome many times in the company of good-
looking and well-dressed young men, and have passed with them
close to young women who have not even lifted their eyes; and one
could see that this was not from modesty but from indifference. . . .
It is as difficult to approach a woman in Rome as in Recanati,
indeed more so, owing to the extreme frivolity and dissipation of
these female animals, who, apart from this, do not inspire any
interest, are full of hypocrisy, and only enjoy going about and
amusing themselves.'[9] Again, a few months later, he told his
brother: 'The Roman women, both high and low, really make
one feel sick; the men provoke both anger and compassion.'[10]
One can hardly doubt that all these remarks were the fruit of some
personal discomfiture, nor is it difficult to guess its nature.

While he was still in Recanati he had already felt such fears, but
he had still been sustained by hope. Outside the narrow circle of his
native town, he thought, there must surely be a woman more
sensitive, more spiritual, more kind, who would turn from the
defects of his body to the tenderness of his heart, who would 'dare

to love him', after all. '*Nous ne vivons pas*,' he quoted from Pascal in his day-book, '*mais nous espérons de vivre.*' But after his first winter in Rome, in which no such woman came across his path, his hopes began to fade. Twice more, in the course of his life, they were again awakened, only each time to be extinguished before they were satisfied. 'The man of imagination, sentiment, and enthusiasm, who is deprived of physical beauty,' he grimly noted, 'feels at once and forever that all that is beautiful, all that he admires and sees and loves, does not belong to him. He experiences the same grief that one feels in imagining or seeing a beloved women in another man's arms. . . . He almost feels that beauty was not made for him, but only for others . . . and he experiences the same disgust and pain as a starving man, who watches others eating delicate and abundant food with relish, without any hope of ever being able to do so himself.'[11]

In this constant awareness of his deformity, Leopardi's sufferings remind us of those endured by Pope; like him, he might have spoken of 'that long disease, my life'. Nevertheless, even in his bitterest and most scornful moments, Leopardi reveals an essential nobility of nature. He retained an intellectual and spiritual integrity —the *revers de la médaille* of his scorn—which was singularly out of place in a social world where to be pliable was the first requisite for success. He would not alleviate his despair by accepting consolations that he believed to be false, or making terms with what he considered trivial and unworthy. 'When I arrived in Rome,' he wrote several years later, 'the necessity of living with other men, of exteriorizing myself, made me stupid, inept, and inwardly dead. I became entirely devoid and incapable of an inner life, without becoming any more adept at the external one. This was, perhaps, the most painful and mortifying time I have ever spent in my life, for . . . I lost almost all my self-confidence, as well as any hope of ever being a success in the world.'[12]

To one confidant alone, his brother, did he express, in a heart-broken cry, the intensity of his loneliness, and the need for affection that his appearance and his manner alike repelled: 'Love me, by God; I need love, love, love, fire, enthusiasm, life. The world does not seem made for me; I have found the devil even blacker than he was painted!'[13]

II

Yes, here he was in Rome—and still as solitary, as scornful, and as melancholy as he had been at Recanati. To what extent was this his own fault? Are we indeed to believe that the Rome to which he came—the Rome of Keats and Shelley, of Stendhal and Chateaubriand—was as sombre as he painted it?

The year was 1823; the period, that of the Papal Restoration—a time in which the stagnation of the last century had given place to a scene as varied and strange, as full of inconsistencies, of conflict, and of colour, as has ever been seen in the history of Europe. Nine years before, in 1814, after fifteen years of Napoleonic rule, Pius VII had returned from his exile at Fontainebleau, had immediately issued an edict abolishing the Napoleonic code and restoring all the confiscated properties of the Church, and had attempted, in every respect, to renew the Papal rule, as it had been in the days before the Empire. The Popes, like the Bourbons, had learned nothing and forgotten nothing. Cardinal Consalvi, however, the Secretary of State and the real ruler of Rome, interpreted these measures in a more liberal spirit. He abolished the much abused Papal privileges, reorganized the laws of the Papal States, and opened the doors of Rome to the travellers, artists, and scholars of the whole of Europe. Suave, charming, witty, the great Cardinal was himself the central figure of this brilliant society, and prided himself on not forgetting, among his labours as a reformer and statesman, the patronage due to the arts. He divided his time between the cares of State, the amenities of diplomatic life, and his own passion for archæology, music, art, and literature; he was even seen one evening at a party at the French Embassy, shedding tears of delight, while a young composer called Rossini sang some airs of Cimarosa's, accompanying himself upon the harpsichord.[14]

Nor was it only the foreign embassies that entertained the great artists and writers of the day. Fifteen years of Napoleonic rule had introduced a new breadth of ideas and manners into Roman society. Many foreign ladies had married into the great Roman families and to their *salons* there now came scholars such as Niebuhr, artists like Thorwaldsen, sightseers and writers like Stendhal. Stendhal, indeed, was in Rome at precisely the same time as Leopardi; but it was a very different city that he saw. 'The Roman wits are very lively. . . . The good Cardinal Hoeflin, in spite of his ninety-two years, is always in society—engaged, like Fontenelle, in turning witty phrases to pretty women. . . . Every evening you may meet the same people in a different drawing-room. The ices are excellent; the walls are adorned by eight or ten pictures by great masters. The liveliness of the conversation inclines one to appreciate their merit. Out of courtesy to the ruling sovereign, one says, when the occasion arises, a few words in favour of God. . . . I have not seen in the whole of Europe any drawing-rooms preferable to the Roman ones; it is impossible to gather together a hundred people, all indifferent to each other, who would give each other greater mutual pleasure; is not that the perfection of society?'[15]

The parties to which Stendhal went were those of the great cosmopolitan world—the balls in *casa Torlonia*, the amateur theatricals at Prince Demidoff's. But Leopardi—*farouche*, touchy, deformed, unmistakably belonging to the *noblesse de province*—was not asked to houses such as these. Nor would he have been happy there. On one occasion, he told his sister, he went to call on a Roman lady, and, while waiting in the hall, overheard her husband comment on his unwelcome arrival. He was shown in, and the lady was charming to him; but he swore never to enter her house again.[16]

'Where talent and wits are not valued,' he had written, even before leaving Recanati, 'the most brilliant man will be despised. . . . Everywhere and always one must use the local currency, and the man ill-provided with that, is poor.'[17] He discovered now that his own personal coin was no more current in Rome than in Recanati; and he was also, of course, in a more literal sense, extremely ill-provided with Roman *scudi* or even *paoli*. He was entirely dependent on his uncle for food, and on his father for pocket-money —and that this was scanty we may surmise from a letter towards the end of his visit, in which he told his father that he had only got fifteen *scudi* left, and anxiously asked him which of the servants it would be necessary to tip.[18] A less self-centred man might have found solace, if he could not be an actor, as a spectator of the Roman scene. But this Leopardi could not do. 'The Romans', he admitted, 'have built themselves palaces, roads, churches, and squares fit for giants, and wish to have their amusements on the same scale'; but the magnificence of these entertainments gave him no pleasure.

'You can only enjoy Rome, or any other large town,' he wrote, 'as a pure spectator, and a spectacle in which one cannot take part becomes tedious the moment after, however beautiful it may be.'[19] He could never endure to be merely one of the audience; the drama must be his own.

He saw the carnival processions pass on the Corso, but his only comment to his brother, after eight days of these festivities, was that he was 'deafened by the infernal row of the carnival, which I will not tell you about, because you can imagine it for yourself'. During those eight days the whole of the Corso was turned into an outdoor theatre or drawing-room; the pavement was strewn with sand, and every window and balcony was adorned by gay brocades and tapestries, above which were to be seen the exquisite gowns of masked Roman ladies on the balconies. Driving along in carriages hung with flowers, drawn by horses wearing scarlet harness, silver or gilded bells, and plumes of many colours, were students and noblemen, artists and prelates, who threw flowers up to the ladies on the balconies, and exchanged jests with the ladies of less repute who crowded the broad staircase of the Palazzo Ruspoli. Troops on horseback in brilliant uniforms, then a procession of senators with their court, finally the Governor with his attendants, all went by in turn—giving place to trains of allegorical coaches, on which, seated around tables adorned with coral decorations, the beauties and gallants of the city represented the gods of Olympus. So, for a whole week, the spectacle unrolled itself—each day more brilliant, more noisy, and more fantastic. Finally, on the last evening, every balcony, every window, every carriage was lit up by galaxies of tiny candles, myriads of little flickering lights that shimmered in the darkness. Each man in the crowd carried one too, and every riotous clown or harlequin tried to blow out his neighbour's, shouting 'abbasso il moccolo!' ('Down with the light!'). But when the great bell of Montecitorio rang out at midnight, every light was extinguished; the plays in the theatres, the music and dancing in the palaces, all came to an end. Silence and darkness once again fell over Rome; Lent had begun. 'And on the morrow . . . the ardent dancers, the voluptuous ladies who had assumed the parts of Venus and Pallas Athene, now dressed in deep mourning, veiled in heavy mantillas, hurried to church—to hear Mass, to listen to a holy preacher, or to strew with ashes the same locks which, only a few hours before, had been smothered with scented powder and kisses.'[20]

Such was the Roman Carnival—to Leopardi, only one more spectacle in which he himself could not take part. In the same month he attended another great sight, the magnificent memorial service in honour of Canova, who had been created a 'perpetual Prince' of the Academy of Fine Arts, and for whom this Academy performed 'the most magnificent obsequies celebrated in honour of an artist in the memory of man'. The church was adorned with reproductions of the sculptor's most famous works; the Mass was sung by David, the most famous tenor of the day; the funeral oration was spoken by the sculptor's friend, the Abate Missirini. The whole world was there: Cardinals, Senators, diplomats, princes, prelates, and a crowd of the Roman *popolino*, who had adored the great sculptor. No such funeral had been seen since the one celebrated three hundred years before in honour of Raphael. But all that we know of Leopardi's impressions is that, at a dinner-party a few nights later, at which 'an unknown prelate' was present, he spoke contemptuously of the worthlessness of the funeral oration—only to discover, towards the end of the evening, that the 'unknown prelate' was the orator himself![21] Truly, he was not 'made for the world!'

III

In spite, however, of this unfortunate incident, it was the society of scholars and archæologists, of prelates and writers, that first extended a welcome to Leopardi. The Abate Francesco Cancellieri, of whom he had written so scornfully after their first meeting, was kind to the young poet and invited him to his Sunday morning receptions, where, according to a contemporary, 'on a long sofa which took up a whole side of the drawing-room and in front of which another bench was placed, one saw Cardinals, prelates in their short cloaks, heads of religious orders in their flowing robes, foreigners living in Rome to satisfy their love of learning . . . all assembled to enjoy the pleasures of literary conversation.'[22] The Abate himself, although then seventy years of age, was still a distinguished figure; the most erudite classical scholar of the century, he was also a man of the world, a charmer and a wit, who had been known in his youth as *il bell' abate.* But the scholars by whom he was surrounded formed a society as tedious and narrow as it was learned. 'The discovery of a new temple column, of an inscription, of a medal, these were the events which were discussed with seriousness, with solemnity, often even with passion,' and a guest did not find the conversation enlivening. 'As the Roman men of learning live apart,' Stendhal observed, 'cut off from humour by their solitary life, as soon as a fact suits them, they consider it already proved.'[23]

Leopardi, too, perhaps, was *soustrait à la plaisanterie*, but he recognized pedantry when he met it. 'I have not yet been able to find a Roman literary man', he told his father, 'who by literature means anything but archæology. Philosophy, morals, politics, psychology, rhetoric, poetry, philology, are all unknown by the Romans and seem to them child's play compared with finding a piece of bronze or of stone belonging to Mark Anthony or Agrippa.'*[24]

This passionate competitive interest in archæology destroyed, he believed, any true appreciation of the other arts. 'I don't know what to say about literature,' he told his brother. 'Horror is heaped upon horror. The most sacred names are profaned, the most egregious pieces of stupidity exalted sky-high, the noblest spirits of the century are considered inferior to the pettiest Roman scribbler; philosophy is despised as a study fit for children.' What caused him the deepest indignation was to see the commercialization and vulgarization of the literary fame which had once seemed to him the summit of human attainment. 'This miserable bartering of fame, this coveting it, fighting for it, tearing it from mouth to mouth . . . this continual talking about literature . . . in ignorance, as if it were a sort of commerce; this constant planning, criticizing, promising, self-praising, exalting people and writings that deserve contempt—all this depresses me to such a degree that if I had not got the refuge of posterity, and the certainty that, in the course of time, everything does

---

* Stendhal, himself the most enthusiastic of sightseers, shared Leopardi's opinion. 'Mr. Nibby,' he wrote, 'one of the most sensible antiquarians in Rome, has already given four different names to the three different columns of Jupiter Statius in the Forum. . . . At each new name, this scholar declared that only a madman or a fool could fail to recognize, at first sight of these columns, the correctness of the new attribution. . . . I recognized the emotion which, in the countries of the South, kindles the faggots of the Inquisition.'

Promenades dans Rome, II, p. 40.

fall into its right place . . . I would send all literature to the devil a
thousand times over.'[25]

Gradually, however, as he realized that it was the only hope of
finding employment, he submitted to some slight external compromise. 'I have changed my garments,' he told Carlo, 'or rather I
have put on again those which I wore as a boy. Here in Rome I am
not a writer . . . but a scholar. . . . You cannot believe how useful
I find these crumbs of philology which I have pieced together again
in my mind from the occupations of my youth. Without them I
should be a man of no importance to these foreigners, who now
esteem me and honour me by their approval.'[26] Certainly it was
among the foreign scholars in Rome that Leopardi first received the
appreciation and encouragement that was denied him by his own
countrymen. 'I dined last night', he told Paolina, 'in the house of the
Dutch minister. The company was a choice one, and composed
entirely of foreigners. I may say that this is the first time that I have
been present at a conversation which was in good taste, witty, and
elegant, and so to speak comparable to a French conversation; indeed
we spoke French nearly all the time.'[27]

The most distinguished of the diplomats in Rome was Niebuhr,
the Prussian Minister to the Vatican, and one of the most eminent
scholars in Europe. The Chevalier Bunsen, who was then first secretary at his Legation, has left an account of how the elderly diplomat
set out to make the acquaintance of the young Italian philologist.
'One day Niebuhr came into the room where I was working, and
exclaimed: "I must go out at once, to look for a man who is the
greatest Italian philologist that I have ever come across. Look at this,
read his *Annotations to the Chronicles of Eusebius*—what penetra-
tion, what real scholarship! I have never met with anything like it
in this country before! I must go and see him." Two hours later he
came back. "I have found him with the greatest difficulty, in a garret
of Palazzo Antici. Instead of a mature scholar, I find a young man
of twenty-two or twenty-three, frail, delicate, who has never had a
competent teacher, and who has educated himself in his father's
library in Recanati by reading the Classics and the Early Christian
Fathers. I am told, moreover, that he is one of the first poets and
writers in the country; but there he is, disregarded and in the depths
of gloom. In him one sees the extent of the genius that is latent in

this nation."* And Bunsen's widow, in her *Memoir* of her husband, adds that, on returning to the Legation, Niebuhr exclaimed: 'At last I have seen an Italian who is worthy of Ancient Rome!'[28]

It is difficult for us, to whom Leopardi's philological studies now hold little interest, to realize that to his contemporaries they seemed almost the most remarkable of his achievements. Niebuhr considered him the most promising philologist in Italy, and told him that he was the only one on the right track.[29] Later on Sainte-Beuve and De Sinner were no less laudatory; and in Giordani's inscription for Leopardi's tomb, the philologist was praised, even before the philosopher and the poet. But Leopardi himself, once his boyhood was over, valued his 'crumbs of philology' chiefly for the friendships and hopes of employment that they brought him. 'No father could be kinder to me,' he said of Niebuhr, and to his brother he wrote: 'The Prussian Minister . . . has undertaken of his own accord to have printed in German whatever I have discovered or will discover in the libraries of Rome. In short, he has shown me so much interest that, on hearing that I should soon be leaving Rome, he has asked me whether I would not instead accept some employment.'[30]

It was, indeed, becoming urgent for Leopardi to find an occupation. The Roman editor De Romanis had suggested that he should undertake a translation of the complete works of Plato, and for a while he had considered the offer, but his father had urged him to refuse. The work, he said, was too ill-paid to be worth undertaking, and moreover, he feared that it would keep Giacomo away too long from Recanati, 'the town in which rest the ashes of our fathers'. So the translation of Plato was given up—to the impoverishment of Italian literature.

But now Leopardi's time in Rome was drawing to a close, and unless he could find a permanent post he would be obliged to go home. The most influential of his friends was the Prussian Minister, who went so far as to tell Cardinal Consalvi that he would consider

---

* Another, possibly apocryphal, account of this meeting is given us by the Italian lawyer, Pietro Capei, who says that on first seeing the great Prussian Minister, Leopardi was so overcome by shyness as to infect Niebuhr with it too, 'so that they remained for some time looking at each other, only able to stammer a few disconnected words'.

any favour awarded to the young man a personal parting courtesy to himself. (For Niebuhr was about to leave Italy.) And certainly, if his remarks had resulted in a meeting between the great Cardinal and the young poet, it might have changed the whole course of Leopardi's life; Consalvi might have recognized his genius, and have given him his powerful protection. But the Cardinal's first question was whether the young man was prepared, if not to enter the priest-hood, at least to wear the *mantelletta* (the little cape) of the members of the Papal court. Leopardi was now faced by a dilemma. 'I was terribly upset', he wrote to his brother, 'at having to decide *de agenda vita*, all in a few hours.' His objections to the *mantelletta*, which dated from the time of his first religious doubts, had certainly not been diminished by what he had seen of the Roman prelates; yet he could not fail to be aware that to accept it might be the first step on the road to Fortune. 'A prelate's career', he told Carlo, 'offers very great advantages, especially to a gentleman, for there is a great lack of them in that career, and the Secretary of State wishes certain posts to be filled by men of good family; so that one could hope to receive soon, or even immediately, a diplomatic post and then rapid advancement. . . . In short, it is almost certain that if I agreed to become a prelate, you would soon hear that your brother in his *mantelletta* was off to govern a province.'[31] (Here perhaps Giacomo was exaggerating a little.) He even got to the point of talking over the plan with his two uncles and of deciding that 'the great expense of the purple robes' could be met by a loan. But nevertheless, in the end, he could not bring himself to it; his months in Rome had only served to fortify his conviction that freedom and independence were worth more to him than any worldly advance-ment. He would not become a prelate.

On the very evening on which he reached his decision, he called on the Prussian Minister and explained his views, and together they com-posed a letter to the Cardinal, in which Leopardi asked for a more modest secular post, that of Chancellor to the Census in some pro-vincial town, while Niebuhr added his own personal recommenda-tion. But unfortunately Leopardi was unable to deliver his request to the Cardinal in person. After four useless expeditions to Monte Cavallo, under a burning sun, he only succeeded in giving it to the Cardinal's secretary, with very little hope of success. Nor did his

K

family do anything to assist him. '*Ma bene, ma bravo*,' was his uncle's only comment, on hearing of Niebuhr's efforts on Giacomo's behalf; and when asked for his own advice, he only added, '*Eh, vedete un pò*'.*[32] As for Conte Monaldo, he pointed out—with some truth—that Giacomo was likely to be sent to some little town no less provincial than Recanati, and would in addition have a very tedious job. 'Pray be persuaded, once for all,' he wrote to Carlo Antici, 'that the true and best employment for Giacomo is in his own library . . . because he needs comfort, freedom and care, and because no post will ever suit those to whom fate has allotted a nature like his, yours and mine.'[33]

And indeed nothing came of the plan. The Cardinal promised his aid, but by the end of that summer a complete reversal of fortune had overtaken him too. In August Leopardi wrote to Giordani from Recanati: 'The Pope has died—and with the Pope, the Secretary of State also vanishes—and his promise with him!'[34]

IV

So now both Leopardi's hopes had failed him; friendship and fame alike had eluded him once more. Yet, although doubly disillusioned, smarting from the wounds both to his pride and to his heart, it still seems strange that so great a poet should not have found some consolation, some solace, in the undying beauty of the scene before him. For Rome, in all the history of her greatness, was perhaps never more romantically lovely than in his day. The recent additions to the city—the great Piazza del Popolo, the gardens of the Pincian hill, the obelisks of the Trinità dei Monti and the Quirinal—had not impaired the beauty or destroyed the lonely grandeur of the ancient ruins. Cardinal Consalvi, indeed, had completed the excavation of Trajan's Forum and had freed the Arch of Titus and the great Aqueduct of Claudius from the buildings that surrounded them. But still the Colosseum, according to Shelley's description, was 'overgrown by the wild olive, the myrtle, and the fig tree, and threaded by little paths, which wind among its ruined stairs and immeasurable galleries'. Still, within the city walls, 'wide wild fields are enclosed . . . and there are grassy lawns and copses winding

*'Well, wait and see.'

among the ruins, and a great green hill, lonely and bare, which
overhangs the Tiber. The gardens of the modern palaces are like
wild woods of cedar, and cypress, and pine.'[35]

Surely these were scenes that might have delighted another poet
too—a poet whose imagination had first been stirred, in the Recanati
library, by dreams of ancient Rome. But none of Leopardi's visions
reached him from the outer world. 'In these places,' he told his
brother, 'a man's sensitive faculty is limited to his sight, and this is
the only one of a man's senses which is in no way reflected within
him.'[36] Imprisoned within the walls of his own self-preoccupation
—like a wasp under a tumbler, crawling half-way up the slippery
glass, and falling back again—he could see no landscape but that of
his own mind. Moreover, he was not wholly free from a provincial
anxiety never to seem overwhelmed, but always to appear 'more
inclined to despise than to admire'. Such a state of mind is apt to
recoil upon its possessor. When Paolina asked him for a description
of Rome, all that he could tell her was how much too big it was.
Everything in his mind was measured by the human scale alone.
'All the greatness of Rome serves no purpose but that of multiply-
ing distances and the number of stairs which one must climb to
find anyone. These enormous buildings, these interminable streets,
are so many spaces interspersed between men, instead of being spaces
to contain men.'[37]

Once, and once only, in all the pages of his letters, do we find a
passage in which one of the sights of Rome aroused in him a
spontaneous enthusiasm, a genuine emotion. It is his description of his visit to the tomb of Tasso, in the church beside the
convent of S. Onofrio on the Janiculum, where the older poet,
in his last years, had found a refuge from his wanderings and his
grief.

Of all the Italian poets, Tasso was the one with whom Leopardi
had always felt a true affinity of temperament. Dante, to his mind,
was a strong man, able to stand up against his fate; 'so much the
more admirable, no doubt, but the less lovable and pitiable'. But
Tasso seemed to him 'a man who has yielded to adversity. Even if
all his calamities were imaginary, his unhappiness most certainly
was real.'[38] And for real unhappiness Leopardi could not fail to
feel compassion.

'On Friday, the 15th of February 1823,' he wrote, 'I went to see the tomb of Tasso—and I wept there. This is the first and only *pleasure* that I have felt in Rome. The way there is long, and one chooses it for no other purpose than that of seeing the tomb; but would one not come all the way from America, to enjoy for two minutes the pleasure of tears? ... Many people feel indignant at seeing Tasso's ashes marked by nothing but a bare stone, a span-and-a-half in length and breadth, hidden away in the corner of a poor little church. But I would on no account find this dust placed under a mausoleum. You can conceive the variety of emotions that arise from considering the contrast between the grandeur of Tasso and the humility of his sepulchre. But you cannot form an idea of another contrast, that which strikes an eye accustomed to the infinite magnificence and vastness of Roman monuments, when one compares them with the smallness and nakedness of this tomb. There is a sad and fearful consolation in reflecting that this poverty suffices to interest and inspire posterity, while the superb mausoleums which Rome contains are observed with complete indifference about the persons for whom they were erected, of whom one does not even ask the name.'

The same letter even contains a passage revealing a shade of homesickness for the familiar, simple life of the provinces. 'Even the street which leads to this place' [S. Onofrio] 'prepares the spirit to be moved. ... It echoes with the creaking of looms, the song of women and artisans at their work. ... Even the expression and the manners of the people whom one meets in the streets have something, I know not what, that seem simpler and more human, and that expresses the character and habits of people whose life is founded upon reality and not upon falsehood—that is, who are living by work, and not by intrigue, imposture and deceit, like the greater part of this population.'[39]

The great city, by this time, had lost every attraction for him; he had found no employment, had won no friendship and no love. With every day that passed he felt a more intense desire for the company of the one friend who had never yet failed him: his brother. 'I am not suited to talking to those who do not understand me, much less to loving those who do not love me. ... I can assure you that every conversation, whether brilliant or stupid, has become detestable to me. Everything is dried-up except one's own heart—and that is never exercised. To the devil with all society!'[40]

At the end of April 1823, after a five months' visit to Rome, tired and disillusioned, Giacomo Leopardi went back to Recanati. 'In returning,' he wrote to his brother, 'I hope to find nothing but friendship and love.'[41]

X

THE 'OPERETTE MORALI'

*Gran conforto: un sogno in cambio del vero.**

AFTER his return from Rome, Leopardi spent two more years in Recanati. These years mark a change in the direction of his mental activity, a movement from poetry to prose, from the cultivation of 'illusions' to philosophy. His thoughts and his energies were given, not to his poems or his letters, but to a philosophical work which he described as 'the harvest of my life up to this time ... dearer to me than my own eyes';[1] his *Operette Morali*.

These are a series of twenty-four Essays and Dialogues, rather in the manner of Lucian, of which the first twenty were written in 1824.[2] 'What shall be done with this book?' asks one of the characters in the last dialogue, and his friend ironically replies: 'Burn it. Or if you do not wish to do so, then keep it as a book of poetic dreams, of melancholy inventions and caprices, or else as an expression of the author's unhappiness.'[3]

This is indeed an accurate description; but it is also precisely what the author himself did not intend. What he wished to create, as he told his publisher, was a complete exposition of his philosophy, and also to enrich the Italian language by adding to it a new literary form: a satire in the classical manner, which would contain 'the true Attic salt'. A few days before beginning the first of the *Operette* he wrote in a letter: 'Indifference and gaiety are the proper emotions, not only for a sage, but for anyone who has had any experience of human life, and the wit to profit by it.'[4] But indifference and gaiety could never be, for Leopardi, anything but efforts of the will, and Comedy was never his muse; there is little spontaneity in his wit or

* Great solace, a dream in exchange for truth.
Dialogo di Torquato Tasso e del suo Genio familiare.

134

lightness in his irony. We are often conscious instead of a laborious adherence to classical tradition, a self-conscious archaism which at times renders his style both artificial and involved.

Moreover, though the book does possess the organic unity of a humanly consistent, if entirely subjective, attitude to life, it hardly possesses the unity which Leopardi claimed for it, of a complete philosophic system.[5] For Leopardi is a philosopher only in the sense that the author of Ecclesiastes is one. On the problems of life he bestowed much thought, and he clothed that thought in fine language, but the conclusions which he reached cannot be said to possess any great novelty. The universe, he says, is an enigma and an insoluble one; human life, when weighed in the balance, is an unhappy affair, and the more highly developed a man is in feeling and in intelligence, the less fitted he is to live happily. Such happiness as men do enjoy is founded upon 'illusion'.

These generalizations come from a man who persisted in identifying happiness with the life of instinct, sensation, and action, from which both temperament and circumstance debarred him.[6] The world-weariness, the *noia*, from which he suffered was in his view the inevitable condition to which a noble mind is reduced by a clear-sighted apprehension of the truth. 'The man most subject to falling into indifference and insensibility', he wrote, 'is the sensitive man, full of enthusiasm and of mental activity. For such a man, just because of his unusual sensibility, exhausts life in a moment. And when he has done so, he remains profoundly disenchanted, for he has experienced everything deeply and intensely. He has not been content with the surface, has not sunk in step by step; no, he has gone straight to the depths, has embraced everything and rejected it all as unworthy and trivial. There is nothing more for him to see, to experience, or to hope.'[7] Human life, he says, is woven of grief and tedium, and man 'only finds rest from one of these passions by falling into the other'. Tedium invades all things. 'It is of the nature of air, which occupies all the spaces between natural objects. . . . So also the spaces in human life between pleasure and pain, are filled by tedium, which is also a passion, no less than suffering and delight.'[8]

He even exalted *noia* as 'the most sublime of human sentiments. . . . To be unable to be satisfied by earthly good—even, so to speak, by the whole world—to accuse life of insufficiency and nothingness

—that seems to me to be the chief sign of the greatness and nobility that exists in human nature. And therefore, tedium is little known by mediocre men, and not at all by other animals.'[9]

It is possible to trace, in some of the forms in which Leopardi's pessimism expressed itself, the *mal du siècle*; it was this all-pervading weariness and *Welt-schmerz* that led both Leopardi and the Romantic poets of France and Germany to a false idealization of past ages, in the belief that what they themselves had lost—the desire for experience, and the capacity to enjoy it—was then still fresh and unimpaired.[10] But the true roots of Leopardi's own pessimism go far deeper; he had carved for himself his own deep, narrow channel of pain. '*Sans avoir usé de rien, on est désabusé de tout*',* that note of disenchantment, that *taedium vitae*, is older than the Romantic movement; it is a disease to which the human spirit has always been liable. It is the *accidia* which St. Thomas Aquinas defined as 'a certain sadness which weighs down and oppresses man's spirit, so that he no longer cares to do anything; like acid things, which are also cold',[11] and which Bossuet called 'the gnawing of the inexorable tedium which lies at the very foundation of human life, since man has lost the taste for God'.[12]

This state was Leopardi's malady; it was not a process of the mind. 'His own tortured condition', wrote Benedetto Croce, 'had become for him a prison in which he was enclosed.' His resentment against life for all that it had denied him 'gradually took the form of a philosophic doctrine—a doctrine of evil, of suffering, of the vanity and nothingness of existence—which intrinsically . . . was nothing but a form of regret, of bitterness—a mummified emotion, a reasoned projection of his own unhappy state. . . . Philosophers who call themselves pessimists or optimists', Croce concluded, 'are valuable as philosophers only in the contribution which they bring, in their pessimism or optimism, to . . . logical or ethical inquiries, and to similar problems; only through these do they enter the history of thought, which is always a history of science and of criticism.'[13]

Judged by this standard, Leopardi does not take very high rank as a philosopher, but he occupies an interesting position in the history of European pessimism. *Die Welt als Wille und Vorstellung* was pub-

* Without having made use of anything, one is disillusioned with everything.
                                                          Chateaubriand.

lished ten years before the *Operette Morali*, and, although Leopardi had never read this work, the points of resemblance between his scheme of things and Schopenhauer's are striking; there is little difference between the German philosopher's conception of a universe governed by blind will and the Italian poet's idea of life as an irrational activity. Schopenhauer himself, after Leopardi's death, included the Italian pessimist among those who followed his own way of thought. 'No one in our time', he wrote in the preface to the third edition of his work, 'has explored this subject so deeply, and exhausted it so completely, as Leopardi. He is wholly filled and pervaded by it; the irony and misery of our existence, that is what he depicts on every page of his work, yet with such a multiplicity of forms and applications, with such a wealth of imagery, that far from ever provoking boredom, he each time reawakens one's interest and emotion.'

It is curious that Leopardi should have made so few references to Oriental philosophy; he either did not realize or did not care to state that he was resorting to ideas which had been at the foundation of Oriental philosophy for two thousand years more. Again and again we find him using words that might well have been used by Gautama himself in expounding the doctrine that life is necessarily *Dukka*: pain, unrest, and suffering. 'All that exists is evil, that everything exists is an evil, everything exists only to achieve evil, existence itself is an evil and destined to evil. There is no other good than non-existence.' Leopardi's illusion corresponds to Buddha's *samyojanas*, or delusions, his truth or reality is near to the Noble Truth of Buddhism or to the Brahm of the Hindus, and the idea of suicide which so greatly fascinated him is the Western equivalent of extinction in Nirvana or absorption in Brahma.

Nevertheless he offers a striking illustration of the fact that what the Oriental is able to accept in all sanity and placidity cannot be accepted by the Western mind, no matter what its bias may be. The Orientalism of Europeans is nearly always a pseudo-Orientalism. It is born of a cerebral activity which is different in kind from that of the East; in the pessimistic philosophies of Europe an unacknowledged belief in the value of life is nearly always lurking.

Throughout Leopardi's prose-writings there are passages revealing the constant conflict between his poetic enthusiasm and his philosophic creed. 'Either imagination will come to life again, and illusions will take form and substance in an energetic and active life, and the greatness and beauty of things will once again seem a reality and religion reacquire its credit—or the world will become a cage of despairing madmen, perhaps even a desert.'[14] And again: 'If in my writings I mention some stern and sad truths . . . I do not cease to deplore and oppose and discourage the study of that miserable, cold truth, which brings about either indifference and slothfulness, or else baseness of mind, iniquity and dishonesty of behaviour, and perversity of customs; while, on the contrary, I praise and exalt the opinions, even false, which generate acts and thoughts that are noble, vital, magnanimous . . . and the fancies, beautiful and gorgeous, though vain, that give worth to life.'[15]

In passages such as these Leopardi gave expression to the heroic, the Nietzschean element in his nature—to the love of adventure, danger, and glory—and in his *Dialogue between Plotinus and Porphyry* he made the former say: 'Give ear to Nature, rather than to Reason. I mean to that primitive Nature, who, although she has made us unhappy, has yet been much less hostile and malignant to us than we have been to ourselves—with our continual, unsatisfied curiosity, our speculations, our reasonings, our dreams, our wretched opinions and doctrines. . . .' And he added: 'There is no disgust with life, no despair, no sense of the nothingness of things, which can last for long. Little by little the taste for life is formed again, one fresh hope or another is conceived, human affairs resume their former semblance and appear worthy of our care—not indeed to the intellect, but, so to speak, to the sense of the spirit.'

This is the poet writing, and not the philosopher—and it is the poet who must be sought in the *Operette Morali*, as in all Leopardi's other works. How close, indeed, the connection of these Dialogues is, on the one hand, with his notes in the *Zibaldone*, and, on the other, with his *Canti* and the later *Pensieri*, may be seen by tracing any one of his favourite themes in its different stages. Some of the *Operette*—in particular the *Memorable Sayings of Filippo Ottonieri* and the essay *On Parini*—are composed almost wholly of extracts—rewritten, condensed and clarified—from the *Zibaldone*; and some of the others have an equally close connection with his poems.[16]

The only *Operette* which are not directly linked to the rest of Leopardi's work (and even in these, there are many echoes of ideas

or images also expressed elsewhere) are those which he himself
called 'poetic dreams and caprices'—the work of the man who used
to dream of 'a little house suspended in the air, held by a rope to a
star'. It is a fantastic world, between earth and sky, in which the
author is wandering—a world in which an Elf converses with a
Gnome, the Earth with the Moon, and Nature with an Icelander;
in which a poet wishes to become a bird, 'to savour their contentment and delight',[17] in which Tasso asks his Familiar Spirit to conjure up for him a vision of his Leonora,[18] and a great naturalist is
visited, at midnight, by his own mummies, come to life. Written by
another pen, these would be Gothic stories, but so deeply is their
author impregnated by the classic tradition that, whatever their subject matter, they take on the colour of Greek myths, and his characters
are like the figures of a Greek chorus.

Here is one of the most typical: Frederick Ruysch, the great
Dutch naturalist and anatomist of the seventeenth century, is standing at the door of his study, where lie the embalmed mummies of
his collection, 'whose complexion had kept its brightness, without
dryness or wrinkles . . . like men asleep, ready to speak upon
waking'.[19] He has been woken at midnight by the sound of voices:
his mummies have come to life, to tell him that, 'for a quarter of an
hour once a year, in every graveyard, in every tomb, at the bottom
of the sea, beneath the snow and the sand, under the open sky,
wherever they may be, the dead can speak at midnight'. The tidings
that they bring are reassuring to human fears: the moment of
death brings no greater pain than sleep; all that is felt is a gradual
languour, and at the last, a liberation. To these spirits the memory
of their past life is as shadowy and confused as a child's recollection of the womb; all that they fear is to be summoned back to life;
they fly 'from the vital flame'. For now they are, not happy, but
secure.

> . . . Come da morte
> Vivendo rifuggia, così rifugge
> Dalla fiamma vitale
> Nostra ignuda natura;
> Lieta no, ma sicura.*

* As once, in life, we fled from death, so now our naked nature flies from the
vital flame—not happy, but secure.

Coro dei Morti.

Their master cries, 'But how does a man know that he is dead?'
They do not answer. 'Children, don't you hear me? The quarter
of an hour must have passed. Let's touch them. They're dead again,
no fear; there's no danger of their frightening me once more. Let's
go back to bed.'[20]

In this dialogue, the *Chorus of the Dead* is a poem as gravely,
serenely beautiful as any Leopardi ever wrote. But its theme is a
total denial of all life's values, and the same theme, in varying tones,
echoes in the last two *Operette*, written eight years later; the dialogues
Between a Seller of Almanacks and a Passer-by and *Between Tristan and
a Friend*. The first of these is a brief Socratic fable.

' "Almanacks, new almanacks, new calendars!" "Will the new
year be happy?" inquires the passer-by. "Oh, assuredly, your
Excellency." "Happier than the last?" "Oh, much, much more."
"For how many of these years have you sold almanacks?" "For
twenty years." "And which of these twenty years would you wish
the coming year to resemble?" "I? I do not know." ' The obvious
conclusion is reached; there is no year of his life to which the seller
would wish to return, 'with all the pleasures and sorrows he knew
in it'; he only wants 'just another year, as God wills to send it,
without conditions'. 'The good life', comments his hearer, 'is not
life as we know it, but the life we do not know', and he buys a
calendar, 'the finest that you have got', for thirty *soldi*. 'Thank you,
your Excellency, farewell. Almanacks, fresh almanacks! New
calendars!'[21]

And so we come to *Tristan*—the last of Leopardi's dialogues, and
the saddest. Composed in the summer of 1832, shortly after the end
of his last romance, it contains a final rationalization of his own
wretchedness, an attempt to convince all men that they are doomed
to a misery as deep, as inescapable as his own. The controversial
part of the dialogue is marred by an artificial and elaborate irony,
but the last pages express, with a grave and moving restraint, the
death-wish that had haunted all his life.

'The fable of life', Leopardi wrote, was ended for him; he was ripe
for death. 'Books and studies, which I often marvel at myself for
having loved so dearly, plans of great deeds, hopes of fame and
immortality—all these are things at which it is too late even to
smile. . . . I no longer envy the foolish or the wise, the great or the

small, the weak or the powerful. I envy the dead, and with them only would I exchange. . . . The memory of the dreams of my youth, and the thought that I have lived in vain, no longer trouble me. . . . If on the one hand there were offered to me, unsullied, the fortune or the fame of Caesar or of Alexander, and on the other, death today —I would say, death today, and take no time in choosing.'[22]

MILAN AND BOLOGNA
(1823—1826)

*Qu'est-ce donc que le bonheur? Et si le bonheur n'est pas, qu'est-ce donc que la vie?**

I

D URING the years that Giacomo was working at the *Operette Morali* the atmosphere of *casa Leopardi* was no less 'opaque'— the expression is Conte Monaldo's own—than it had been before his visit to Rome. The *palazzo* was divided into two armed camps; one side fortified by the habit of absolute authority and by an elaborate system of spying, the other defending itself by petty deceits and evasions and whispered plots. One camp consisted of Conte Monaldo himself, his wife, his two uncles (both ecclesiastics), his old tutor, his chaplain, and a French emigrant priest named Don Pascal; these represented the old régime; they stood for clerical influence, parental domination, and political servitude. On the other side Giacomo, Carlo, Paolina, and now their younger brother Luigi, fought not only for happiness, but for a principle; that of freedom. A similar struggle was taking place in many other provincial families during these years. And these guerillas were not lacking in incident.

A fortnight before Giacomo's return—as he already knew from a letter of Carlo's—his younger brother Luigi (then twenty-one years old) had been caught by his parents in a midnight escapade. He had been in the habit of climbing out of his window at night, to take part in such dissipations as Recanati afforded. Before long, however,

---

* What then is happiness? And if there is no happiness, what then is life?
Leopardi to Jacopssen.

142

a rumour had reached Contessa Adelaide's ears, and late one night she visited Luigi's bedroom—to find it empty. 'Father', wrote Carlo, 'hurried out to surprise him, but not having found him, came home. Then I went in search, and then, and then—you can imagine the uncomfortable scene! Father was in a pitiable state of agitation, Mother in convulsions, Paolina sobbing in despair, we two on our knees—since I, too, am guilty, for not having revealed his secret, and for having "corrupted" him.' An 'uncomfortable scene', indeed! And it was not the last. 'This morning,' wrote Carlo the next day, 'after further similar scenes, forgiveness has been granted; but now I am expecting the subsequent inquisition—as you know is the custom here.'[1]

Such incidents did nothing to increase the amenities of family life; moreover, underneath this surface, with its trivial storms, ran far stronger currents of feeling. The heart of Paolina was at this time tormented by passions no less violent than those of Giacomo himself. Before Giacomo went to Rome, in 1821, her parents had planned for her a marriage with a man called Peroli of Sant' Angelo in Vado, a desolate village near Urbino—a suitor who was possessed of neither looks, amiability, nor intelligence, but who was rumoured to be well-off. And indeed the arrangements had got so far that, as we have seen, Giacomo had written an ode to his sister on her approaching marriage. On discovering, however, that the young man did not even possess a suitable fortune, the engagement was broken off. But very soon after there appeared upon the scene a young man named Ranieri Roccetti, not of noble birth, but amiable and good-looking, with 'fine eyes and a good and healthy mouth' and 'sufficient talent and cultivation'—and Paolina fell desperately in love with him. For a short time it appeared that an engagement might be possible, although the young man was already half-committed to a widow of Ancona, whose dowry and rank were inferior to Paolina's, but who was both younger and prettier. For Paolina, according to her own pathetic self-portrait, was distressingly lacking in personal attractions. 'My mother', she wrote, 'omitted to sacrifice to the Graces before bearing me. . . . I confess to you . . . that Paolina Leopardi is neither tall nor well developed, her complexion is not white nor her hair fair, and her nose—oh, her nose!'[2] But the consciousness of a lack of beauty does nothing to diminish the capacity for emotion, and poor Paolina was now solemnly, intensely, desperately in love. 'I want to laugh and to cry at once,' she told Marianna Brighenti, 'to love and to despair, but to love continually, and to be equally loved in return, to rise to the seventh heaven, and then to be hurled down again; and indeed, I have been cast down, my Nina—but I have never been raised to heaven.' Such intensity of emotion, in a very plain woman, might well alarm an ordinary young man; and there is every reason to believe that Roccetti, who disappeared soon afterwards to Bologna, was very seriously alarmed. For one day a great anxiety had seized Paolina: perhaps Ranieri's love was not equal to hers; perhaps, since her brother had written of him as 'a young man like *all* others', he did not love her alone! A scene ensued, and to her only confidante, Anna Brighenti, she wrote: 'He could not dispel my fears . . . I have remained with his image indelibly imprinted on my heart, and with the cruel pain of having failed to awaken in him the love which he so ardently, so violently inspired in me. . . . Nina, do not laugh at me. I am almost mad with pain, when certain chords are touched . . . now that all is over.'[3]

'Farewell to hope,' Paolina had written, 'farewell to dreams, fare-well to happiness'—but still she felt that married life with anyone at all would be preferable to living at home, and in her letters to her brother in Rome she implored him to help her. Giacomo did his best. Soon after his arrival in Rome he had met a certain Cavalier Marini, a widower of between forty-five and fifty years of age—in appearance neither young nor old, 'an amiable and generally smiling expression—bright eyes, healthy complexion, and ten times more lovable than Peroli'. His manners, moreover, were agreeable, and his character unexceptionable. 'His pleasures and his desires lie in the direction of sincere friendship, of domestic peace, and of deep affections.' He had loved his wife profoundly, 'although she was lame and ugly', and he mourned her death inconsolably. 'I myself have seen him weeping over her loss, two months and more after it occurred.'[4] Surely even Paolina would be satisfied by such a proof of sensibility? Moreover, the Cavaliere was religious, sociable, and 'prepared to procure all suitable pastimes' for his bride; he was also well-off, and not at all *exigeant* in the matter of her dowry. In short, the advantages were many: 'To live in a capital, by the side of a man who is rich, beloved, esteemed by his inferiors, kind, intelligent, prudent, interested in the welfare of his spouse, cordial, religious, and obliging'—could Paolina hope for more?

Her father thought not, and wrote to Marchese Antici, through whom the formal proposal had been made, to continue negotiations. As for Paolina, her delight at the prospect was so intense that Giacomo was alarmed by it. 'She must be more moderate in her transports,' he wrote to Carlo. 'I see that hope is tormenting her more than despair and sorrow. . . . The poor child has not yet "rendered up her arms to fortune", as Petrarch did.'[5] Paolina indeed was nearly beside herself, while Cavalier Marini shilly-shallied and wondered whether the dowry which he would receive with his bride would be sufficient to marry off his daughter. 'I cannot conceal from you', her brother told her, 'that your state of mind and the agitation you describe in your letter, fill me with compassion. . . . Hope is a very turbulent passion, since it necessarily brings in its train a great fear that it may not be realized. . . . I assure you, my Paolina, that if we do not acquire a little indifference towards ourselves, it is impossible, I do not say to be happy, but even to remain alive.'[6]

But these wise reflections were of small comfort to Paolina. The next few months were spent by her in an agony of uncertainty, which was only brought to an end by the news—after Giacomo had returned to Recanati—that Cavalier Marini had married someone else. Paolina's family then tried to renew her engagement with the unprepossessing Peroli, and even the wedding-day was decided. 'The 29th of November', wrote poor Paolina, 'is the day, and it looks as if it really will come off. . . . I was prepared to put up with more mockery and sarcastic remarks than have been paid me . . . but I remembered your teaching and armed myself with great courage.'[7] But when it came to the point, her family again failed to produce the 7,000 *scudi* for her dowry, and again Giacomo, with touching fraternal solicitude, tried to come to her assistance. 'Paolina is still here,' he wrote to Giordani, with an almost audible sigh. Could his friend do nothing about it? In Parma, perhaps, or in Piacenza? The dowry, he repeated, was 7,000 *scudi*. 'As to her person—both her appearance and her spiritual and mental capacities —I think one should be able to find someone who would be satisfied with them. Her age is twenty-two; she would not require too much youth in her bridegroom, nor too great nobility.'[8] It is a depressing epilogue.

In later years, like her brother, she took refuge from disappointment in despising what she had failed to obtain. 'These men,' she wrote to her friend Marianna, 'they are not worth the trouble we expend in sighing for them. Don't you see how they treat us, how they despise us? . . . Well, let us despise them; let us show them that we are not so wretched as they suppose. The world', she added, 'is not so fine, is it, as it was promised to us in books? We entered it full of confidence, hoping to find it a delicious place, certain of finding a heart that would love us . . . and then we find that this delightful world is a place full of thorns, full of enemies. And so farewell to hope, farewell to all the dreams of our early years!' She told her friend that when she died her wreath would not be of lilies, but of the virginal may. 'When its scent reaches you, remember your friend, who will die without having known in this world a single moment of real happiness.'[9]

Paolina was right. Her later years were as unhappy as her youth—except that, gradually, she ceased to be tormented by expectation or by hope. Up to the age of fifty, when her mother died, she was never allowed to go out, unless accompanied by a *duenna* and followed by a servant in livery. Her wish to see the world beyond Recanati was never realized until she was over sixty, when for the first time she went for a three days' expedition to Ancona. At the age of sixty-seven, she extended her travels as far as Naples to visit her brother's tomb, but she did not go to see the only man who could have told her about Giacomo's last years, Ranieri. As she grew older, the family traits became accentuated in her. Contessa Adelaide's avarice was reflected in her daughter's extreme reluctance to spend even one unnecessary *scudo* for the upkeep of her farms or for her food; a single egg (measured, it was said, with the same little hoop that had served her mother) constituted her midday meal, and sometimes her nephew's tutor, after dining in Palazzo Leopardi, was obliged to enter a *trattoria* to still the pangs of hunger.[10] But in other ways she showed something of her father's prodigality. She was generous to beggars and servants, she bought horses for the stables and books for the library; she had her bed gilded, and she took an especial delight in wearing bright-coloured clothes, in the latest fashion of Ancona. Her incurable romanticism expressed itself in reading an inordinate number of novels, in writing long emotional letters to female friends, and in the love she lavished, not on her nephews, but on a small dog to whom she gave the name of 'Lovely', and called '*mio figlietto*'.* Her piety became more and more extreme, and when, at the age of sixty-nine, she died in Pisa— where she was spending the winter—she left instructions that she was to be buried in her best clothes, with all her jewels, 'to make the great journey from earth to heaven in party clothes'.[11]

II

Spent entirely in *casa Leopardi*, the next two years of Leopardi's life were almost without incident. 'My health is good,' he wrote to a friend, 'I live here as in a hermitage; my books and my solitary walks take up all my time. My life is more monotonous than the movements of the stars, more colourless and insipid than a *libretto* of our opera.' On his return he had told Giordani that he felt as if he were going back into a tomb, but that he was not wholly sorry to do so. 'In truth, it was too late to try to adapt myself to life, never having had any taste of it. . . . I felt old, almost decrepit, before I had ever been young.'[12]

During this year one poem only came from his pen—*Alla sua donna*, but in the summer he wrote to a young Belgian, M. Jacopssen, whom he had met in Rome, a curiously revealing and intimate letter.

'Assuredly, my dear friend,' it begins, 'either we should not go on living, or we should continue to feel, to love, to hope. Sensibility would be the most precious of gifts, if one could only make use of it. . . . But now the art of how not to suffer is the only one I try to learn. . . . It is true that the habit of reflection often removes the capacity for action and even for enjoyment. An excess of the inner life always pushes a man towards the outer one, but at the same time it renders him incapable of dealing with it. He embraces everything, he would like to be perpetually fulfilled; yet all these things escape him, precisely because they are smaller than his capacity. He exacts

* 'My little son.'

of his own slightest deeds, words, gestures, movements, more grace and perfection than any man can attain.'[13] This passage—and the cry with which the letter closes: 'What then is happiness, my friend? And if there is no happiness, what then is life?'—is the final comment on Leopardi's visit to Rome.

During 1824 the writing of the *Operette Morali* absorbed all Leopardi's energies; his letters are few and uninteresting. But so long as he was working, he was fairly contented. It was only when, in the spring of 1825, this book was completed, that he again felt the full emptiness and purposelessness of his daily life. After a silence of many months, he sent a picture of it to Giordani: 'I have been studying day and night for as long as my health could bear. When it failed, I spent my time for several months on end in walking round and round my room; then I returned again to my work; and that has been my existence. As to the kind of studies I pursue, they are changed, even as I myself am changed from what I used to be. Everything that is emotional or rhetorical bores me, and seems to me foolish and childish. I am seeking for nothing but the truth, which once I hated. . . . And now I plainly see that when the passions are extinguished, no source of pleasure remains in study, except a vain curiosity, the satisfaction of which has yet some power to delight.' Leopardi had once again returned to a dreary detachment, very like his state of mind before his first visit to Rome. 'The more men appear to me like plants or stones, in the tedium they evoke in me, the more each day I hold to the thought that there *is* one man whose speech and company seems to me that of an equal, or (to speak less conceitedly) that of a human being. You', he informed Giordani, 'are that man—the only one (I swear it!) whose company would seem to me sweeter than a hopeless solitude. . . . I love you with all the strength of my frozen heart.'[14]

When he wrote this letter he saw no prospect of leaving Recanati, but only a few weeks later an opportunity arose. His Milanese publisher, Antonio Stella, who was planning a complete edition of Cicero, with Italian translations and notes by various writers, and who had already asked Leopardi to undertake this work, now wrote to him, proposing that he should come to Milan to get it started. Leopardi replied that he would be delighted, but had no money, whereupon Stella invited him to his own house. 'You may feel assured of finding in me a father rather than a friend, and in my family a good mother and affectionate brothers. Do not worry about expenses for your journey and your lodging; I will see to it all.'[15] Leopardi hastened to accept, promising his future host, in return, 'a heart which is sincere, honest, sensitive, and capable of true and tender friendship'.[16] His father's permission was easily obtained—apparently because Conte Monaldo thought that Milan, which was under strict police supervision, would be less dangerous than any other Italian town to a young man of Liberal tendencies. Doubtless remembering the trouble in the past, he added his own authorization to his son's application for a passport—but there his helpfulness, or his means, gave out, and Giacomo was obliged to apply to his great-uncle, Conte Ettore Leopardi, for some pocket-money for the journey.

On the 17th of July 1825 he set out. But hope too long deferred, and perhaps anxiety about how he was going to live by his pen alone, clouded his departure. He felt, he wrote, 'a feeling of blind and desperate resignation, as if I were going to die', and looking back out of the carriage window he saw poor Carlo—no less rebellious than he, and once again, left behind—running after him down the dusty road, to wave farewell once more.

The ten days spent by him in Bologna on his way are remarkable as being among the few in his life in which he found nothing but praise for his surroundings. Giordani and Brighenti were there to welcome him and for the first time in his life the poet found himself the centre of a sympathetic and admiring circle. 'In Bologna', he told his brother, 'everything is fine, materially and morally. . . . The men are wasps who have lost their sting. Believe me, I have come to agree with Giordani and Brighenti that kindness of heart does in truth exist here, is indeed very common, and that the human race is different from what you and I believed.'[17]

There is a touching *naïveté* in his delight at the hospitality of the Bolognesi. Here, in nine days, he wrote, he had made more friends than in five months of Rome. It was natural that his thoughts should turn to settling down in this town, 'where strangers can hardly rest for the constant kindness they receive, where men of ability are invited out to dinner nine times a week, and where—so Giordani assures me—I might live more happily than in any town of Italy, excepting Florence'. He could hardly bear to tear himself away from so pleasant a society, and when at last he did arrive in Milan, he vented his ill-humour upon his host. He wrote to Carlo that he was horrified by the bourgeois atmosphere of the house, which seemed to him 'the worst inn he had met upon his travels', and he added that he did not think he could bear to live in Milan for more than a week.

There, as previously in Rome, he could not endure the anonymity and indifference of a large town. In Milan, he complained, 'no one pays any attention to you, and everyone lives even more independently than in Rome. It is incredible, but true, that there is no social life except that provided by the *passeggio*,* or by the café. Unless a man has some business to transact, or is prepared to give himself up to dissipation, no life is possible but that of a solitary man of letters.' His own works, he found, were practically unknown, and of the Milanese men of letters whom he had longed to meet, he saw only Monti, and found him so deaf 'that I practically had to spit blood in order to make myself heard'.[18]

His desire to leave Milan was now increased by a letter from his uncle, Marchese Antici, telling him that the Chevalier Bunsen—now the Prussian *chargé d'affaires* in Rome—had been trying to find him a post in the Vatican, and that there was a good chance of his obtaining one, if he would send a suitable letter of application, addressed to the Pope himself. The letter, Marchese Antici added, should be written 'on fine paper in a large clear hand', and should contain 'a suave eloquence'. 'Speak with heartfelt effusion, show yourself zealous for all good principles and averse to the incredulous spirit of the times . . . say (be sure to do so) that, knowing how necessary it is to fight the detestable maxims of false philosophy with the true, you had planned to make all the works of Plato more widely known in the whole of Italy, but that, confined in Recanati'[19] etc., etc. So the advice goes on, for several pages—an instructive document as to the manner in which posts in the Vatican were obtained.

Giacomo sent Bunsen a letter on the lines recommended by his uncle. But meanwhile his wish to get away from Milan as quickly as possible was frustrated by his obligations to Stella. 'My hands', he

* The evening promenade.

wrote, 'are stuck in bird-lime; no sooner have I pulled one out, than
the other is caught again.' At last, however, by the end of September,
he did get a plan drawn up, and persuaded his publisher to agree
that he might now supervise the progress of the work from Bologna,
receiving a modest monthly salary of twelve *scudi*. On the 29th of
September he was back again in Bologna.

III

His plan was to spend the whole winter there, and he settled down
in *casa Badini*—in lodgings beside the Teatro del Corso, kept by an
ex-tenor called Aliprandi. A less suitable dwelling-place could hardly
have been found. The house was 'bursting with harmony', and as
Giacomo sat in his cold little bedroom of an evening, he was enabled, through the thin partition that separated him from the theatre,
'to hear the piece distinctly without moving from home'. Moreover, among his fellow-lodgers there was a buxom young soprano,
Madama Rosina Padovani, with the assurance and brio of a *prima
donna* and a pair of fine flashing eyes. Her arpeggios, too, echoed
over the house, but apparently her fine eyes were attractive enough
to earn the poet's forgiveness, for when she asked him for a ticket
to an evening-party of the *Accademia dei Felsinei*, at which he was
going to recite one of his own poems, he obediently applied for
one. But alas—these tickets were reserved for the wives of members
and for distinguished guests, and the awkward question came back:
was Signora Padovani distinguished?[20] Leopardi replied that she
was 'distinguished by a pair of eyes which seem fine to me, and a
figure which to me, and to some others, has seemed fine, too. But
that she is distinguished in any other way, I do not think or
believe.'[21] So Madama Rosina failed to get her invitation.

Meanwhile it was urgently necessary for the poet to find some
means of livelihood. Among the acquaintances he had made during
his first visit to Bologna were two rich, literary young men, to
whom he now gave Latin lessons, receiving from them eight *scudi*
a month, which, with Stella's twelve, just enabled him to make both
ends meet. But his father, as was to have been expected, did not
approve. 'Rather than accept a fixed salary from a mere merchant
of a printer,' he wrote, 'I should have thought it better to let him

pay you so much per page for each of your writings. And similarly, instead of receiving eight *scudi* per month from a Greek, I should have preferred receiving an unspecified gift from him. . . . These monthly emoluments seem to me distinctly humiliating.'[22] But Giacomo sensibly replied that it was more convenient to know where one stood at the end of each month, and that there was 'nothing ignominious about the functions of a tutor'.

Unfortunately, however, both pupils soon left Bologna, and poor Leopardi was left in such straits that he had to sell his watch. Sometimes he went out to dinner with friends, and on such occasions he was able to take with him some tasty sheep-cheeses from home, or a flask of oil, or a handful of figs—all sent to him by Conte Monaldo from home—partly from paternal affection, and partly in the hope that these products of the Marches, if appreciated in Bologna, might find a market there.

At this point, however, Giacomo had a small piece of good luck. At Paolina's request, he went to see a certain Angelina who had previously been a maid in *casa Leopardi*, and who was now settled in Bologna, and he found her not only 'still young and fresher than I am', but so glad to see him that she blushed 'like the rising moon' and at once invited him to dinner. Better still, she had married a cook, and a very prosperous one, 'who keeps a fine table' and even 'in habits and manners seems like a gentleman'. 'I shall eat very well,'[23] wrote poor Leopardi—and in return he sent to Angelina a sonnet written at her request, 'for a priest on saying his first Mass'. Alas, alas, the sonnet—the only one ever written to order by Leopardi—has disappeared; but it is pleasant to think that what he refused to many fine ladies was not denied to Angelina and her *tagliatelle*. We even find the poet following the various stages of Angelina's *accouchement* ('she has a few pains every day now'), and at last standing godfather to the baby, '*un maschio e très viable*'.* Thus the author of the *Operette Morali* wrote a sonnet for a young priest and opened to a baby the doors of Paradise—and all for the sake of Angelina. Here is a simple, domestic, kindly Leopardi—*le poète en pantoufles*. It is a pity to see him so seldom.

But indeed during this time in Bologna we frequently catch a glimpse of the man that Leopardi might have been, had a little more

* 'A male, and very promising.'

happiness been granted him. Somewhere in his nature there must have been, beneath the self-defensive scornfulness that renders his Roman letters so unsympathetic, an essential sweetness, to call forth the faithful devotion of such friends as Giordani and Ranieri, and now, in Bologna, of a whole circle of new friends. They all gladly put up, apparently, with his headaches, his constipation, his insomnia, and with his unceasing complaints about the cold, the heat, the light, and the noise. They sat with him in the dark, to rest his eyes; they endured the complete airlessness of the rooms in which he liked to sit, and of the carriages in which he chose to travel; they satisfied his perpetual craving for ices and sweets (Monaldo has recorded that he required a pound of sugar to sweeten only six cups of coffee). They even bore with some very unattractive personal habits—a scarf used also as a handkerchief, food spilt upon his clothes—and with his long, gloomy silences, only broken by the snapping of his fingers, the *crepitus digitorum* of the Romans, he would explain, and the loud sniff with which he would draw up a pinch of snuff, when one of the company made a particularly foolish remark.

What was it that made them all so long-suffering? All that they have told us—but in this all their accounts agree—is that he had 'a sweet, a heavenly smile'. But is it not always very difficult to say what renders another human being *attachant*? Whatever it was, Leopardi seems to have had it, and the ladies of Bologna felt the charm. Among the most devoted were the two young daughters of his publisher, Brighenti. Ninin was vivacious and gay, Marianna romantic and melancholy, with a fine voice; both were pretty and enthusiastic, both hung upon Leopardi's words, and both entered into an emotional, intimate correspondence with Paolina, which lasted for forty years. And meanwhile, on many a winter's evening, the poet was to be seen in *casa Brighenti*, sharing their Christmas dinner and their Paschal lamb, welcomed and admired and made much of.

And then there was *casa Tommasini*. The master of the house was one of the ablest doctors of the University of Bologna (the same who had attended Byron's daughter, Allegra), and it was as a patient that Giacomo had first met him. But soon the acquaintance became friendship—not only with the doctor himself, but with his cultivated, clever wife, Antonietta, and their delicate, romantic married daughter, Adelaide Maestri, who developed a sentimental friendship, almost an *amitié amoureuse*, for the sad, ailing young poet. In this house Giacomo found what he had never known at home—an atmosphere of unconstrained family affection, in which no one was obliged to take sides. Here he spent many an agreeable evening, delighting the ladies with his 'gentle manners and learned conversation', and reading aloud 'in verse and prose'. And at night, after he had left, the gentle Adelaide would write him little tender, sentimental notes, with half the sentences scratched out. But alas—for really it was very difficult to please Leopardi—there is a note in the *Zibaldone* at this time: 'Too many assiduous attentions, too many demonstrations of care, solicitude, and affection (as women often show), become very tiresome and unpleasing to their object, even when they come from most amiable persons', and beside this remark, in the Greek letters which he often used as a disguise, is his own grandmother's name, and also that of poor Adelaide![24]

Nevertheless his friendship with the whole family, even after he had left Bologna, endured for his whole life. They followed his literary successes with delight, and his disappointments and illnesses with a touching sympathy; they sent him presents of books and of snuff. And as the years passed, he too seems to have felt grateful for the support of these unquestioning friends, for he told Antonietta Tommasini that 'if all women thought and felt like you, and behaved according to these thoughts and feelings, the fate of Italy would be a very different one!'

All these new ties were very agreeable. But it was still necessary to find some permanent employment—and indeed he was still hoping for a favourable answer from Rome about the Secretaryship of the Academy of Fine Arts, for which he had applied in the summer. At first, since he had been recommended to the Cardinal Legate of Bologna by the Secretary of State himself, the prospects seemed good—so good, indeed, that his brother was already addressing him as 'dear Secretary'. But he himself did not allow his hopes to rise too high—and rightly. For the volume of his *Canzoni*, which had appeared two years before and had fallen, on the whole, very flat,[25] had now attracted the attention of the ecclesiastical authorities, and the Vatican was informed that Conte Leopardi had shown, 'although with some astuteness, sentiments favourable to the new

moral and political opinions', and moreover was 'an intimate friend
of persons well-known for their unwise views'. It would therefore
certainly not be desirable, the Cardinal wrote, to give Leopardi a
post in Bologna, 'far from the government's eye'; but, as he was
'still young and capable of being led into the right road', he might
perhaps be employed in the Vatican, 'while at the same time super-
vising and controlling his moral and political behaviour'.

This document was hardly likely to incline a young man towards
serving the Vatican. It is hardly surprising that Giacomo refused the
chair of classical rhetoric that was offered him in Rome; nor did he
accept a family benefice made vacant by the death of his great-uncle,
a post which would have brought him 150 *scudi* a year and the title of
Canon, but would have obliged him to assume the dress and duties
of an ecclesiastic. 'I could at once obtain for you', Conte Monaldo
wrote, 'a prelate's distinctions, and you would appear in society in
a more respected rank. . . . Besides, I do not see what repugnance can
be felt at wearing a dress which has been that of so many saints. . . .'
With transparent guile, he attempted to appeal to Giacomo's vanity,
telling him that he was now in a position to set a fashion in the world
of letters, instead of following one. 'What a triumph, my son, for
the cause of the saints . . . what a glory both for the Church and the
State, if the most erudite man in the province openly vaunted the
banner of the Church! You would be applauded on earth, and
gloriously rewarded in heaven.'[26]

Strangely enough, Giacomo did not at once reject this proposal.
On the contrary, he told his father that he 'did not feel disinclined
to accept it', though under two conditions: firstly, 'to be obliged
to wear no more habit or tonsure than is customary among the
priests here; which consists only of a black or blue suit, with a black
necktie', and secondly, 'to be dispensed from reading the Office,
even on condition of reciting an equal number of prayers'.[27] Conte
Monaldo replied that he thought the second dispensation might
be obtained, in view of Giacomo's eyesight, but that the other
would hardly be granted. A dark suit and black necktie, he wrote,
might do very well as a priest's country dress, but in society Giacomo would certainly have to wear the full dress of an Abbé,
'with cape, collar, tonsure, and priest's hat'. In short, 'you must
recognize and profess yourself an ecclesiastic'. At this point, indeed,

Conte Monaldo shows a greater moral integrity than his son. 'It would greatly please me that you should like the state of an ecclesiastic and therefore the garments that fit it. . . . But if that state does not suit you, and you are only considering it for this trifle of a benefice, I advise you not to take it. An honest man must behave in accordance with his principles, and one cannot receive a salary from a prince if one is ashamed to wear his uniform. It seems to me that God's blessing would not be on either you or me.'[28]

So the 150 *scudi* and the title of Canon were handed over to the youngest son, Pietruccio, to whom Giacomo sent a charming mock-solemn letter of congratulation, beginning '*Signor Canonico estimatissimo mio fratello*'* and ending 'I kiss your hand, and commend myself to your protection'.[29]

Meanwhile the winter wore on, and a few weeks later Leopardi also informed Chevalier Bunsen, who had found him a post at the University of Bonn, that his health would not permit him to accept it. The truth was that he did not wish to leave Bologna, even though its winter climate is one of the coldest in Italy. One shudders to think of the icy blast from the Apennines whistling after him under the arcades and pursuing him round Piazza San Petronio. Nor were his sufferings any less great indoors. The inflammation of the intestines and kidneys which troubled him made it impossible for him—or so he believed—either to sit by a fire, or to stay for long in bed. 'So from morning to night I find no rest, and do nothing but tremble and shake with cold, which sometimes makes me want to cry like a child.'[30] According to Brighenti, he attempted to find some warmth by wrapping up in a sort of sack lined with feathers—and would spend whole days at work without emerging from it, to appear in the end so covered with feathers that he looked like a wild man of the woods. 'I am awaiting,' he wrote, 'I am anxiously awaiting the reign of Ormus, the victory of Osiris over Typhon, the coming of the Redeemer, the triumph of the Paschal Lamb.'[31]

At last the spring returned, and with it came a time of what might almost be called happiness, for Giacomo at last tasted the sweets of popularity and—or so at least he fancied—of literary success. Among his new friends was Conte Carlo Pepoli, a lively,

* Reverend Canon, my most esteemed brother.

elegant, gifted young man of his own age, with pleasant manners
and strong patriotic feelings.[32] It was to him that Leopardi dedicated a poem in the manner of Parini—the first that he had written
for two years—and Pepoli, who was the vice-president of the
Accademia dei Felsinei, invited Leopardi to recite it at one of their
meetings, on Easter Monday. This Academy was one of the innumerable literary societies modelled on the famous Roman
academy, *L'Arcadia*, which in the eighteenth century had been the
centre of Italian literature, music, and painting. Almost every little
town, by the end of the eighteenth century, contained one or more
of these societies, dignified with elaborate and often incomprehensible names,[33] and existing chiefly, as Conte Monaldo candidly
remarked, as 'a little theatre in which a man can conveniently make
some show of his abilities, without the need of much scientific
capital'.[34] Here minor poets could recite minor (but very seldom
brief) verses; here amateur philosophers could give dissertations,
moralists express fine sentiments, musicians perform upon the
flute, the oboe, and the harp. And all this would take place in a gay
salone, adorned with stuccoes and frescoes, with gilt mirrors and
shining chandeliers, and in the presence of a highly select society of
nobles, prelates, and fine ladies—all conscious of being *la fine fleur*
of the aristocracy of the spirit—while, after the intellectual feast, a
rinfresco of sweet lemonade and chocolate, of dry biscuits and sponge
fingers would bring the party to a close.

Of such entertainments, Leopardi had written with great scorn.
The custom, he said, of reading one's own works aloud had become
'a plague, a public calamity. All men, when the opportunity comes
of reading their works, become like cruel children.'[35] But these
opinions did not prevent him from attending the *Accademia dei
Felsinei* on Easter Monday, and reading aloud his own poem, 'in the
presence of the Legate and the flower of the Bolognese nobility,
male and female'.[36]

He was not, on this occasion, the only performer. One fellow-
member read an oration on the peace of mind induced by scholarship, so boring that the despairing audience brought it to an end by
their applause; another read a sermon on matrimony; yet another,
a meditation on death and the tomb. Finally, just before Leopardi,
Conte Pepoli delighted the audience with several hundred insipid

verses entitled *La miosotide, fior della memoria*,* which told the sad
tale of a young man who, in picking some forget-me-nots for his
lady-love, fell out of a boat, was drowned, and died with the words
'Forget-me-not' upon his lips. A lamentable performance, one
would think, but Conte Pepoli had a fine beard and a graceful
manner, and he was much applauded.

Then came the turn of Conte Leopardi. After the dapper Pepoli,
his appearance was disappointing; it was that 'of a learned literary
man, in a black mood',[37] and he recited his poem, without any
oratorical devices, in so quiet and flat a voice that little of it could
be heard. Moreover what could be, was not enlivening. The poem
holds little that is lyrical, and much that is elaborate, artificial, and
dull, and its theme was singularly unsuited to its hearers. Happiness,
the poet said, is the goal of life; but since it is unattainable, all human
activity is nothing but a glorified form of idleness, at the end of which
'eternal tedium lies'. An audience whose real life was spent in an
idleness with which they were very well pleased, did not care for
this doctrine; and one of them, the poet Giovanni Marchetti, wrote
to a friend in Florence that Leopardi 'had not justified the fame he
had acquired'.

Fortunately, however, the poet was unaware of all this. 'I am
told that my verses made a great effect,' he wrote to Carlo, 'and that
everyone, both male and female, wants to read them.'[38] He felt,
as he told his father, that he had now entered 'the great world'.
'*Oh qu'heureux que tu es!*'† cried poor Paolina, in the French she had
learned at Recanati, and Carlo's warm congratulations had a wistful
note: 'Success is a thing that greatly resembles happiness.'[39]

IV

It was not a pleasure that Giacomo had known before, and it was to
be followed by an experience still more unfamiliar. Among the distinguished members of his audience was the Contessa Teresa Carniani
Malvezzi, herself a well-known poetess, whose *salon* was famous in
Bologna. By birth a Florentine, she could boast that she had been

---

* The forget-me-not, flower of remembrance.
† Oh, how fortunate you are!

taught geometry as a child and she had followed it up, after her marriage, with the study of the Classics, of philosophy, and of modern languages with Mezzofanti. Her own poetical works—alas, only too numerous!—included a translation of *The Rape of the Lock*. Whatever the merit of her poems, however, she appears to have been an intelligent and gifted woman, who was admired and liked by the ablest literary men of her day. Monti and Pindemonte, Strocchi and Paolo Costa, all frequented her *salon*; learned academies, in which she bore the name of *Ipsinoe Cidonia*, vied for her presence; and Monti even addressed to her a charade and an octave of highly flattering, if mediocre, verses. Beauty she never possessed, and at the age of thirty-nine, when Leopardi first met her, her chief charm was the ease of her conversation, and a versatility, a readiness of response, which seemed to him as rare as they were agreeable. Like Madame de Sévigné, she might have said, '*Jeunesse et printemps ce n'est que vert, et toujours vert; mais nous, les gens de l'automne, nous sommes de toutes les couleurs.*'*

For Leopardi, who had never before met a woman capable of understanding what he said to her, the praise of this amiable bluestocking was a bewildering and intoxicating pleasure. 'I have entered upon a relationship', he wrote to his brother in May, 'with a lady in society, which forms a large part of my existence. She is not young, but she is of a grace and a wit which—believe me, who thought this impossible until now—takes the place of youth, and creates a wonderful illusion. In the first days that I met her I lived in a sort of delirium and fever.' The acquaintance ripened rapidly. Almost every evening, the poet visited her from the hour of the Angelus until past midnight, 'and it seems to me one moment only'.[40]

The lady's husband, however, was more conscious of the passing of the hours. 'Last night', so the Contessa wrote to Leopardi, 'I got a fine scolding for having been so indiscreet as to keep you till midnight. My better half is annoyed by any visits that are frequent and long.' Nevertheless she made an appointment for another evening, promising him the treat 'of examining a little poem of mine—if it does not displease you'.[41] And Leopardi, who would not have

* 'Youth and spring are green, always green; but we who belong to the autumn, we are of every colour.'

allowed even Virgil or Dante to read aloud their poems to him, listened to *La Cacciata del Tiranno Gualtiero*, in the soft accents of the Contessa Teresa; and when the poem was over they 'never lacked a subject of conversation'. 'She esteems me very highly; when I read her some of my work, she often weeps bitterly, without affectation. The praise of other people has no reality for me; hers enters my blood, remains in my soul.'

Nevertheless, he denied that he was in love with her. 'We have never spoken of love except as a joke, but we live together in a tender and sensitive friendship, having an interest and confidence in each other which is like love without disquietude. . . . We confide to each other all our secrets, we criticize each other, we tell each other all our thoughts. This acquaintance forms and will form a *marked period* in my life, because it has cured me of disillusion. It has convinced me that the pleasures I disbelieved in do indeed exist in this base world, and that I am still capable of stable illusions.'[42]

So Giacomo spent his evenings, and on his way home after midnight, along the dark arcades of Bologna, dreamed of the beauties of spiritual friendship, of mutual admiration, and of the melting glance of two fine eyes, '*la più degna del ciel cosa mortale*'.* For this at least we should be grateful to Contessa Malvezzi: for the first time in his life, Leopardi knew 'a love without disquietude'.

All through the summer the romance continued; but in the autumn he was obliged to return to Recanati. The Contessa had promised to write to him, but the months passed, and brought no letters from her. Finally, five months after his departure, a parcel arrived, addressed in the lady's hand; eagerly he opened it—only to find her translation of *The Fragments of Cicero's Republic*, unaccompanied by even a line. But Leopardi, usually so quick to take offence, on this occasion was long-suffering. 'At last', he wrote in gentle mockery, 'a book has reached me from you, which shows me that you have remembered me once, at least, since my departure; and the address in your handwriting assures me that the book is not a posthumous work, that it comes to me as a gift, not a legacy. The many letters which you meant to write, and had promised me, have turned into one address.' Nevertheless he sent her his approval of her

* Of all mortal things, the most worthy of heaven.
            Al Conte Carlo Pepoli.

book, 'in which I admire the sobriety and good judgment of the preface, the purity of the style and language, and the many difficulties that you have overcome'. It was too late, he assured her, for her to answer him, for by the following week he would be in Bologna again. 'Nor will I ask you for your news, because I hope soon to be able to tell you all that you will wish to know, and to ask of you all that I wish to hear. Meanwhile, love me, as you certainly do, and believe me *your most faithful friend, or servant, or both,** or what you like, Giacomo Leopardi.'[43]

He returned to Bologna on the 26th of October, and hurried off to see the Contessa. What occurred in the interview we do not know. By one account, little worthy of credence, the impassioned poet flung himself at the lady's feet—and she summoned a footman to give *il signor conte* a glass of water. It is certain, however, that after this he did not call on her again. But, in the spring, before his departure for Florence, he sent her the following letter: '*Contessa mia*, The last time I had the pleasure of seeing you, you told me so clearly that my conversation *en tête-à-tête* was tedious to you, that you left me no excuse for continuing my calls. Do not believe that I am offended. If I were to complain of anything, it would be that your words and behaviour, although clear enough, have not been still clearer and more frank. Now, after such a long interval, I should like to bid you farewell, but dare not do so without your permission. I implore you to grant it, wishing intensely to repeat to you that I am—as you well know—your true and cordial friend.'[44]

We are not told what the Contessa replied; but we know that if Leopardi did call on her, it was his last visit. His friends, as was inevitable in so small a society, had followed the episode with some amusement—except Giordani, whose touchy jealousy had been aroused. 'Have you news of Leopardi?' he asked Brighenti. 'I should like you to clear up a matter which seems to me unbelievable. Is it true that he went often to the Malvezzi's, who calls herself a lady of letters? Is it true that she gave him to understand that she could not endure the frequence and length of his visits? How is it possible that Giacomo should have gone twice to such a woman?'[45] Even Papadopoli, from Venice, added to the chorus, in a letter to Leopardi himself: 'Tell me if that Contessa has stopped her tittle-tattle; it

* The words italicized are in English in the original.

M

would be better for you to stop seeing her altogether.'[46] And
Leopardi, once again wounded in his weakest spot, believing that he
had become a laughing-stock, flung chivalry to the winds: 'How can
it come into your head that I should go on seeing that —— of a
Malvezzi? May my nose fall off if, after hearing her gossip about me,
I went back there again, or ever will. . . . The other day, running
into her, I turned my face towards the wall, so as not to see her.'[47]
Once again, love had turned to scorn.

That the Contessa may have chattered about her conquest is more
than likely, but that she herself was unaware of the extent of
Leopardi's resentment is plainly shown by a note she sent him when,
three years later, he returned to Bologna for a few days. 'How
could you be in Bologna, and not honour me with a single call?'
And she declared that she would never cease 'to honour your very
high merits, praying that fate may give you all the satisfaction due
to a man who is a sublime ornament to Italy and to letters'.[48]

But Giacomo sent no graceful compliment in exchange; and his
final comment, in a letter to a friend, is not that of a lover: 'I have
seen the Malvezzi's poem. Poor woman!'

XII

FLORENCE AND PISA
(1826—1827)

Ho scritto alcuni versi all' antica. . . .*

I

GIACOMO'S visits to Milan and Bologna had occupied fifteen months, and during this time he had supported himself entirely. But suddenly, just before his return to Recanati, Conte Monaldo, with a furtive and uncertain gesture, tendered him an olive-branch. 'It is now fifteen months', he wrote, 'that you have been away from home, and have travelled and supported yourself without my help. You know my feelings, and can deduce the pain it has given me not to be able to provide for your needs, or even for your pleasures; even if you have not needed this help of mine, I have felt both the need and the desire to prove to you my very tender affection. But these really disastrous times, and most of all your mother—who, as you know, keeps me not on a diet but in complete starvation—having obliged me to a course of action condemned alike by my feelings, by justice, and almost by propriety. Nevertheless, I am still alive, and still remember that I am master of my own house. If you are in need of nothing, so much the better, but if you require some money for the journey, or to pay some little debt, or for any other purpose, whisper it in the ear of your father and friend.' In this case, Monaldo added, Giacomo must send his letter to another address, which he gave him. 'You will understand why.'[1]

Such was the life in the Palazzo Leopardi! To draw closer to his

* I have written some verses in the old manner.

Leopardi to Paolina.

163

son, Conte Monaldo was obliged to deceive his wife—but, in the same breath, he could still assert that he was 'master of his own house'. His pathetic effort was unavailing; Giacomo responded with no more than a formal expression of filial gratitude. The gulf between the two generations had become too wide to be bridged.

Three weeks later, on the 11th of November 1826, Leopardi returned to Recanati—and this time not unwillingly. A few days after his return we find him noting in his day-book: 'I remember that while I was away from my family, although I was surrounded by well-disposed persons and had no enemies, I lived in a constant state of apprehension or timidity.' He felt himself to be 'alone in the midst of enemies—that is, in the hands of hostile nature' ('*in mano alla nemica natura*'). But when he came home, he recovered 'a lively sense of security, courage, and peace of mind'.[2]

It did not last long. His first object had been to avoid the bitter cold of another winter in Bologna, but the climate of his native town was hardly less rigorous. In December he wrote to Brighenti: 'I spend my morning in working, my evenings in shivering and swearing',[3] and he added ten days later that, although perhaps he was physically a little less cold than in Bologna, 'my spirit feels a deathly chill, and every hour seems to me a thousand, till I can get away again'.[4]

This statement is hardly astonishing, when we consider what it was that he encountered, as soon as he left the four walls of Palazzo Leopardi. At the street-corner the boys of the town would be waiting for him, like a merciless pack of little wolves. 'Hunchback!' they would cry. 'Little hunchback of Monte Morello!' And then they would run after him, pelting him with snowballs and sometimes even with stones, and singing a doggerel rhyme, made up by their ringleader, the curate's nephew:

> Gobbus esto
> Fammi un canestro
> Fammelo cupo
> Gobbo fottuto.*

* 'You are a hunchback—
   make me a basket—
   make me a deep one—
   bastard of a hunchback.'

On one dark evening he came out of the *palazzo* to find his chief tormentor loitering there alone, and went up to him: 'How do you dare to call me *gobbo*? Now I'm going to revenge myself; these are *my* snowballs.' And out of his pocket he drew a handful of round white sweets. But the terrified boy—looking up at his misshapen benefactor—took to his heels, shouting at the top of his voice: 'Father, father, the hunchback has given me these balls!'[5]

It is hardly surprising that—according to the account of one of the village girls in her old age—it was the poet's custom, when he ventured out, to slink along under the eaves of the roof, hoping to avoid his tormentors. When he met the long crocodile of seminarists, who mockingly raised their hats to him, two by two, he would flatten himself up against the wall, his hat in his hand and his head held low, and would thus remain motionless, without looking up at them, until they had passed. One day, his hat was blown off by the wind, and he was obliged to go home through the town with his cape wrapped round his head, followed by a booing and jeering crowd of boys, and muttering to himself under the cloak, 'Yokels! Cowards!' And there is another, hardly credible, story of a whip-slash across the face, inflicted on the poet in the street by a tall, brutal young cousin.

True or false, these stories undoubtedly reflected the general attitude of his fellow-citizens, resentful of his learning and his superior airs. To them he was 'the hermit', the wiseacre', 'the philosopher' —a horrid little freak of Nature, who thought himself great. '*Vedo le mura e gli archi.*'* . . . 'What's he talking about?' they asked of an evening in the *farmacia Bonacci*: 'No walls or arches here! What a presumptuous little monstrosity!'[6]

Small wonder that, at the end of the winter, Leopardi was writing to Brighenti that he was 'a little sad, because complete and absolute solitude has had its usual effect',[7] and that in April he wrote to another friend, Francesco Puccinotti, 'I am counting the hours until I can leave this swinish city, where I know not whether the men are greater fools or knaves'.[8]

During the winter he had been compiling—for his Milanese publisher, Antonio Stella—an anthology of Italian prose, the *Crestomazia*

* I see the arches and the walls . . .

All' Italia.

italiana, which was to contain selections from the prose-writings of eighty Italian authors, and to fill about six hundred pages—every word of which had to be copied in his own hand. And a further sidelight upon his diligence is afforded us by an anecdote told by his friend Puccinotti. 'Do you know how Leopardi learned German and English? I was with him one day in his library, when he was writing his dialogues. . . . At the end of every page, putting down his pen, he stretched out his hand to an English grammar which lay beside him, and read and learned a verb from it. When he had learned it, he looked back at the page of his dialogue, to see if the ink were now dry. In answer to my inquiries he said, "I never use sand; while what I have written is drying, I learn English; and I have done the same thing with German". '9

At last, in April, the cold weather was over, and Leopardi was able to set forth again—first to Bologna, where he stayed for nearly two months, and then, at last, to the town which, of all others, he most wished to visit: Florence.

The capital of Tuscany was, indeed, at this time the centre of a most active intellectual Renaissance. Two remarkable men had brought it about: a Tuscan aristocrat, Marchese Gino Capponi, and a merchant of Swiss origin and literary tastes, Gian-Pietro Vieusseux, who, having settled in Florence, had founded there a reading-room, the *Gabinetto Scientifico Letterario Vieusseux*, on the model of those he had seen in London and Paris. Here his subscribers found, not only every European and American periodical worth reading, but also, on several evenings a week, some agreeable company and lively conversation. 'How delightful it is,' cried one of the guests, 'on a winter's night, to stay in a warm room in the company of so many able men, all speaking gently of letters and the arts!'10

Sooner or later, most of the independent writers and thinkers in Italy, and many able travellers, found their way to the *salon* of the kindly, genial, 'Sor Pietro', whose candour was never lacking in shrewdness, and whose warm cordiality and inexhaustible patience somehow succeeded in conciliating men of the most various opinions and temperaments. A stout, white-bearded little man with a shining bald head and eyes reddened by over-reading, he seemed to Stendhal like a hawk—and there was, indeed, something hawk-like in his swiftness in detecting and pouncing on any genuine spark of talent, and in drawing out any awkward or obscure young writer. 'I never knew any man', said Guerrazzi, 'who possessed, as Vieusseux did, the feel of the men and times in which he lives.'[11] Literary men and politicians, artists and historians and professional patriots, refugees from the tyranny of neighbouring governments, distinguished foreigners like Stendhal, Michelet, Fauriel, Von Platen—all flocked to his *soirées littéraires*, while outside, by the column in Piazza S. Trinita, uneasy Austrian agents waited about, industriously noting down the names of everyone who went into 'that dark and terrible conventicle'.

It was here that Marchese Gino Capponi, the booming-voiced, noble-featured Tuscan aristocrat, who looked and sounded like one of the Priors of medieval Florence, but who had been to England, was a friend of Foscolo's, and thought the *Edinburgh Review* 'the finest paper that has ever been published', launched the plan of a Tuscan liberal review, *L'Antologia*. Its purpose was to provide not only Tuscany, but the whole of Italy, with a free and independent mouthpiece, and to arouse in its readers a more lively sense of their national character and destiny.[12] That such a paper could be founded at all was due to the policy of sleepy tolerance and *laisser faire* of the Tuscan granddukes—'*un gouvernement assoupissant*',* said Stendhal. But its Liberal tendencies were at once perceived by both of Tuscany's neighbours—Austria and the Papal States—and, in spite of Capponi's declaration that the paper would always maintain 'a noble urbanity' of tone, and only mention religious matters 'with the greatest veneration and always in general terms', eventually caused its suppression.[13] For twelve years, however, it did contain, largely thanks to Vieusseux, a great deal that was vigorous (though not always lively) in Italian thought. Here first appeared the articles of an unknown young Genoese patriot, whose work was signed with the pseudonym '*un italiano*'—Giuseppe Mazzini; here, too, the work of an equally obscure young Dalmatian historian, the brilliant, intransigent, touchy Niccolò Tommaseo. And it was in the *Antologia* that three of Leopardi's *Operette Morali* were first published.[14]

Sor Pietro's penetrating eye, indeed, had not missed the first writings of the young poet of Recanati, in spite of the smallness of

* A soporific government.

their circulation and the seclusion of their author's life. As early as 1823 he had heard his praises sung by Giordani—indeed in terms of such hyperbole that he was nearly put off by it[15]—and had suggested that Leopardi should become the *Antologia's* correspondent for the Papal States—and this offer he repeated three years later, after seeing the manuscript of the *Operette Morali*. Would Leopardi play the role, he suggested, of a '*hermite des Apennins*', who from his hermitage would attack all that was amiss in Tuscany—its government, its customs, its educational system, its censorship, and even the *Antologia* itself?[16] This appears a task well suited to Leopardi's pen, and indeed the picture of himself seems to have pleased him, for he playfully signed a letter to Brighenti as 'Frate Jacopo da Monte Morello'.

Nevertheless, he again refused the offer. 'In order to attack our customs and institutions', he wrote, 'that good hermit should have lived, before retiring to his hermitage, in the world. . . . That is not my situation. My life, first of necessity and against my will, then by my own choice, has been and always will be solitary, even in the midst of company; in which I am (to use an English term) more *absent* than a blind or dead man. This vice of mine is incorrigible.' The consequence, he said, was 'that men are in my eyes what they are in nature, a very small part of the universe, and that my relations with them, and theirs to each other, do not interest me at all'. So Vieusseux had to content himself with publishing the three *Operette*, and with welcoming the poet, when at last he came to Florence, at one of his literary evenings—thus enabling Brighenti, whose activities as a spy had extended even to Florence, to inform the Venetian police that Conte Leopardi, too, attended Vieusseux's 'centre of Liberalism'—though, he added, as one of its most moderate members.

On his first appearance Leopardi made no striking impression on the Florentines. 'His expression', noted a fellow-guest, 'is mild, his manners gentle and courteous, but his body is defective, owing to the height of the shoulders. He speaks very little, is pale, and seems to be melancholy.' But Vieusseux himself was immediately attracted by him, and showed him a protective paternal kindliness. He found him lodgings,[17] he offered him work, he introduced him to most of the literary men of Florence. They were all cordial, they came to call. But the poet was neither well nor cheerful enough to enjoy their company. He was suffering from acute toothache, but was too apprehensive to go to the dentist, and his eyes were again troubling him, so that he could not go out 'until after dark, like the bats'. He refused all invitations; he did not go sightseeing; he even missed—to his great regret, for he took a childlike delight in such *feste*—the celebrations on St. John's day, when horse- and chariot-races were run in the streets, and there was a display of fireworks over the river.[18]

Moreover, he was exceedingly hard up. He implored Stella not to delay his monthly allowance, because he found himself 'in such straits as I have never known before in my life', and this is confirmed by the Florentine historian Niccolini, who has recorded that, 'but for his friends, there were more occasions on which he would have gone supperless, than supped'.

But indeed it was precisely in the company of these 'friends' that Leopardi was most disconsolate; for he had come to Florence, as to Rome, with too high expectations. All his life he had had a mental image of an ideal society composed of men of taste and breeding, who were also able and scholarly—a world in which, at last, he would feel himself at home. And now that he had found it—he was still an outsider, still alone. For in Florence, most unfortunately, he had landed among a group of men who had passionately embraced a number of convictions which Conte Monaldo's son could never share. They believed in the amelioration of the human lot by scientific discovery, by education, by legislative reform; they valued literature as a means to moral or patriotic ends; they demanded the abolition of slavery and of capital punishment; they believed in the young, and in the future of Italy.

It was, perhaps, after listening to some of these opinions that Stendhal wrote that the Liberals of Florence reminded him of 'certain English peers', and added: '*Si la candeur anglaise peut exister quelque part ici, c'est au sein d'une famille florentine qui habite à la campagne.*'*

But a Nordic ingenuousness was not a quality that Leopardi prized very highly; he preferred clear-sightedness. His pessimism was rooted

* 'If British ingenuousness can exist anywhere here, it is in the bosom of a Florentine family, living in the country.' Stendhal, *Rome, Naples et Florence*, p. 213.

in an unshakeable conviction of the congenital wretchedness of the human race, unalterable by any changes in circumstances or régime; and the ideas of these worthy Florentine gentlemen seemed to him curiously half-baked. Moreover, both as a poet and a scholar, he rebelled against treating literature merely as a means to an end. One of his most characteristic letters, written to Giordani in the following summer, clearly expresses his feelings: 'I am beginning to be disgusted', he wrote, 'by the supreme contempt professed here for the whole of art and literature, especially as I cannot be convinced that the summit of human knowledge lies in politics and statistics. On the contrary . . . I am often inclined to smile at this whirlwind of political and legislative calculation and construction, and humbly inquire whether the happiness of nations can be attained, without the happiness of individuals.'[19]

The sadness of mankind, he wrote, was caused by human nature, not by circumstance; what men needed was not panaceas, but comfort, and 'for this I value the pursuit of beauty, and our affections, dreams, and illusions'. This is the poet speaking, the man who once wrote to Giordani, in almost the same words as Keats, 'I find nothing in life desirable but the joys of the heart, and the contemplation of beauty'. In the busy, worthy beehive of Florence there was no place for him.

A further confirmation of his spiritual isolation reached him after the appearance, during the summer, of his *Operette Morali*.[20] His Florentine friends were civil, and one reviewer—Giuseppe Montani, a friend and disciple of Giordani—accorded to the essays a review of fulsome praise in the style of the Abate, declaring that henceforth he would not dare to approach their author, save hat in hand.[21] But Giordani's own eulogy was refused by the *Antologia*, and with the rest of the Florentine public the *Operette* fell very flat. Colletta declared them to be 'very inferior to their author', and Gino Capponi told Vieusseux that, although he had them on his desk, he had not yet found time to read them.

Moreover, Vieusseux's circle contained one real enemy of Leopardi's, the passionately Catholic, vigorous, sensual, arrogant Niccolò Tommaseo. Some years before, in 1825, the two men had had a passage of arms over some notes for an edition of Cicero which Tommaseo had prepared for Antonio Stella, and which Leopardi considered oratorical and unscholarly. This Tommaseo never forgave. When Leopardi's *Crestomazia* appeared, he noted in his diary that it was 'a meagre piece of work, revealing a false and narrow talent'.[22] And some of his later attacks on Leopardi are so savage as to suggest not only a divergence of opinion, but an instinctive physical repulsion, no less primitive and brutal than that which caused the little boys of Recanati to throw stones at the '*gobbetto di Monte Morello*'. Here is a typical passage: '*On vit sortir du sein des flots . . . un petit comte, qui chantait comme une grenouille de Cephisse, et disait en chantant: "Il n'y a pas de Dieu, parce que je suis bossu, je suis bossu parce qu'il n'y a pas de Dieu."*'*

Even after Leopardi's death, his savage opponent was not moved to pity. 'I never told you my rhyme about him,' Tommaseo wrote to Capponi barely a month later:

> Natura con un pugno lo sgobbò:
> 'Canta', gli disse irata; ed ei cantò.†

Can one wonder, after reading such passages as these, that Leopardi was no less morbidly obsessed with his deformity in Florence than he had been in Recanati? 'He could not bear his physical afflictions,' wrote Capponi, 'which were indeed very great. No one can imagine the sufferings he endured and those he created for himself, nor how many impediments, both to his work and his affections, entered into his soul.'[23] But how could it have been otherwise? 'A man', Leopardi bitterly wrote, 'who has a physical or moral defect, is always being given its name: *il sordo, lo zoppo, il gobbo, il matto*.‡ Indeed such persons are seldom called by any other name. . . . The reason', he added, 'is that this gives the speaker a sense of superiority: his self-love is flattered.' And he proceeded to describe how he had seen 'a deformed man, a man of the people', talking with others 'who never called him by anything but the name of his deformity, so that

---

* 'One saw rising from the waters a little Count, who was croaking like a frog in the river of Cephisus, and saying as he croaked: "There is no God because I am a hunchback; I am a hunchback because there is no God."'

† A blow from Nature made him a hunchback.
'Sing!' she commanded in anger; and he sang.

Tommaseo e Capponi, *Carteggio inedito*, I, p. 571.

‡ The deaf man, the lame man, the hunchback, the madman.

I never succeeded in hearing his real name. And if I have any knowledge of the human heart, I plainly see that each one of them, as he called this man by that name, felt an inner joy and a malignant satisfaction.'[24]

To Tommaseo the publication of the *Operette Morali* afforded one more opportunity of attacking his opponent. Though obliged to admit the excellence of the style of the essays, he referred to their author as both 'profane and pedantic', and deplored his 'cold and arrogant mediocrity'. 'What I cannot bear', he said, when Vieusseux protested against the word 'arrogant', 'is his coldness. . . . His entirely negative principles, which are not founded on reason, but only on some partial observations, diffuse both in their images and their style a revolting chill, a deplorable bitterness.'[25]

There can be little doubt that such attacks as these greatly increased Leopardi's sense of mental isolation, and that they were rendered still more bitter by the overwhelming, immediate success which attended the publication, in the same year, of Manzoni's great novel *I Promessi Sposi*.

It was during this summer, too, that Leopardi met Manzoni him-self—the only other man in Italy of his calibre, the only one whom he would have liked to call his friend. But this meeting, too, was a failure. It took place, like all other literary events in Florence, in the *gabinetto Vieusseux*, but Leopardi hardly had a chance to speak to the great novelist at all. For Giordani, too, was present, and, with his unfailing tactlessness and vehemence he attacked the guest, as soon as he had entered the room. 'Can it really be true that you believe in miracles?' he asked, without a word of greeting, and on receiving no answer beyond a mild, 'Well, it's a large question', he stumped off round the room, staring belligerently at the other guests through his *lorgnon*, and then returned to resume the attack. The next day his host wrote to Capponi: 'Manzoni seemed much pleased with the meeting, and much less timid than is said . . . but Giordani spoiled everything by the intemperance of his language on religious matters, and Leopardi himself was shocked by it.'[26]

But indeed, even if the two great writers had been able to speak to each other in peace, it is doubtful whether they would have become friends; their differences were not only of opinion, but of tempera-ment. Manzoni, for all his natural reserve, had the convictions and the ardour of an apostle; when the conversation turned to religious matters, his shyness left him, and he spoke with enthusiasm and force. But Leopardi had no good news to impart; and it was in a low, quiet voice, almost as if talking to himself, that he would express his most destructive, his saddest opinions. It was on this occasion, or at a subsequent party of Vieusseux's, that he was seen, sitting alone and observant in a corner, while a whole crowd of admirers and disciples thronged round Manzoni. 'What do you think of the great man?' the poet was asked. 'I think very well of him,' was the quiet reply, 'and I am delighted that the Florentines have not forgotten their old courtesy, nor that they themselves were once marvellous cultivators of the arts.'[27]

But Manzoni, on his side, was less generous—or less perceptive. He greatly praised the style of the *Operette Morali*, but he made little effort to become acquainted with their author, and all that we know of his attitude to Leopardi are two unfortunate remarks. He once said to a friend, almost in the same words as Tommaseo, that Leopardi's religious opinions were merely: 'I am hunchbacked and ill, therefore there is no God.' And, on another occasion, Manzoni confessed to De Sanctis that he did not understand how Leopardi could be considered a poet!

So Leopardi retreated again into solitude. Alone, in his hot and airless little rooms, training his inflamed eyes to decipher the tiny notes of his *Zibaldone*, he tried to order them into a book which he characteristically proposed to call *An Encyclopædia of Useless Knowledge*. But his eyesight failed him once again, driving him into another period of inactivity—and into the deep gloom which it always caused. He was worn out—too blind to work, too exhausted and discouraged to see anyone, or to bolster up his courage by any fine attitude. 'I am tired of life,' he wrote, 'tired of the philosophic indifference which is the only remedy to suffering and tedium, but which at the end becomes tedious itself. I have no other plan, no other hope, than death. In truth, it was not worth taking so much trouble to attain this end.'[28]

II

The winter was approaching. The mist which rises from the Arno and the bitter *tramontana* which blows down from the Apennines, would not allow Leopardi to remain in Florence; but he was determined not to return to Recanati. Papadopoli invited him to Venice, the Tommasinis to Parma; but both the long journeys alarmed him, so that he decided to move for the winter to the milder climate of Pisa, and settled down in lodgings there, in Via della Faggiuola. The terms offered him were generous: for eleven *monete* a month he had a room with light, linen, and service; breakfast, with 'coffee, chocolate, and good biscuits'; dinner in his room, at any time he pleased (and the times were often very odd); a fire in the *scaldino* all day, and his bed warmed at night—and, besides, his clothes were washed and ironed, and his boots cleaned. These were good terms, even for those days; and in a letter to Vieusseux he made use of an expression we have seldom heard from his lips: 'I am contented.'

His father, however, who had set his heart on his returning home for the winter, was deeply disappointed. 'If in the fine weather you must leave us so as to be in touch with men of letters, and in bad weather must stay away, to avoid our severe climate, the only season left to us for living together is Paradise and Eternity.'

This same letter contained a touching appeal: he begged for the return of his son's affection and trust. Giacomo's letters, he said, had become 'as painfully stilted as a boy's Latin verses, almost as if your heart found some stumbling-block in coming close to mine. . . . But', the poor Count pleaded, 'it longs for nothing but to be seen clearly by yours—once only, in a single flash, and that would be enough.'[29]

The pain underlying these phrases was so evident that it penetrated even Giacomo's self-absorption, and he sent his father the answer for which Conte Monaldo had been waiting for many years. 'You wish I could see into your heart for a single moment. . . . Let me protest to you with all possible sincerity, before God, that I love you as tenderly as it is possible for any son to love his father, that I clearly realize your love for me, and that I feel for your kindness and tenderness a gratitude as deep and lively as human gratitude can

be; that I would gladly shed my blood for you. . . . And if you sometimes wish for greater trust or greater tokens of intimacy, believe
that the lack of them only arises from the habits formed in my
childhood.'[30]

But, in spite of all this, Leopardi did not return to Recanati. He
was, indeed, delighted with his winter in Pisa, and wrote an enthusiastic account of the city. 'The appearance of Pisa pleases me far
more than that of Florence; the Lung' Arno is so beautiful a sight,
so wide, magnificent, gay, and smiling that one falls in love with it.
I have never seen anything like it in Florence, Milan, or Rome; and
indeed, I do not know whether in the whole of Europe many other
sights can be found to equal it. It is a pleasure to walk there in
winter, because the air is almost always spring-like; and in certain
hours of the day that part of the town is full of people on foot and
driving in carriages. One hears ten or twenty languages spoken,
while brilliant sunshine lights up the gilding of the cafés, the shops
full of *galanterie*, and the windows of the palaces and houses, which
are all of fine architecture. . . . As for the rest, Pisa is a mixture of a
big town and a little one, of town and country, a romantic combination, such as I have never seen elsewhere.'[31]

Pisa, indeed, by all accounts, must have been one of the pleasantest
cities of Italy at this period. Only five years before Leopardi's arrival
a strange little group of Englishmen, already of some renown, had
taken an equal delight in the mildness of the climate and the beauty
of the surrounding country. Shelley had spent his days walking in
the great forest that skirts the shore at Migliarino, listening to 'the
solemn music in the pine-tops', and known to the peasants of the
district as *l'inglese malinconico*. Byron had been installed in the *piano
nobile* of the Palazzo Lanfranchi, with his mistress and her brother,
his bulldog Moretto, and a cage containing four white geese; while
Leigh Hunt, his Marianne, and their gaggle of spoiled children, 'as
dirty and mischievous as Yahoos', had occupied the ground floor,
and 'a wild but kind-hearted seaman, Mr. Trelawney', had visited
them all in turn.

What would Leopardi have made of this eccentric company?
We have seen that in Rome he was more at his ease with foreigners
than with his own compatriots; but these foreigners were very
different from the scholars and diplomats of Rome. It is to be feared

that the son of Conte Monaldo would never have penetrated beneath the extreme oddness of their appearance and behaviour: Byron, in a ridiculous little jacket of Gordon tartan, with a blue velvet cap and very loose nankeen trousers, taking a dramatic part in his servants' quarrels or practising pistol-shooting in a remote *podere*; Shelley, with his long wild locks blown by the wind, reading the plays of Calderon aloud to any casual visitor; Trelawney, dark and sinister, insisting on playing the pirate, and given to planning mad expeditions in unsafe little sailing-boats.

No—Leopardi would never even have attempted to form a friendship with such strange foreigners as these. For here lies one of the most profound differences between the Latin and the Anglo-Saxon character, and one of the greatest barriers to their mutual understanding: the sense of what is due to the conventions and to decorum. Genius, in Latin peoples, is seldom linked to oddity. The genuine unself-consciousness of a Shelley, the deliberate unconventionality of a Byron, are both equally unknown—and both would be considered equally silly. We may doubt whether even Shelley's angelic charm and beauty could have overcome so profound a prejudice—although in him, more than in any of his contemporaries, Leopardi might have found a personification of those poetic 'illusions' whose passing he deplored. Moreover, though Shelley might have been prepared to forgive a great deal to the man whose brain had conceived the serene loveliness of the early *Idylls*, Byron and Leopardi would certainly have disliked each other. Leopardi greatly admired Byron's creative powers, but he has left it on record that he could find no real emotion in his poems, of which he said that they came from the imagination, not from the heart.[32] To him, Byron would have seemed merely a *poseur*: flamboyant, worldly, and above all, flippant. Like Trelawney, Leopardi might have suspected Byron of not taking him seriously—and Byron, on his side, would certainly have thought the Italian poet provincial, gloomy, and inexcusably dull.

But these meetings were not to be. On the 13th of August 1822, Shelley's funeral pyre had lit up the Tuscan shore; a few weeks later Byron and his menagerie had left by land for Genoa, Hunt and Trelawney following in two small sailing-boats. By the time Leopardi arrived, even the interest aroused by the vagaries of the mad English had died down, and Pisa had fallen back into its accustomed peace.

During the winter Leopardi lived there very quietly, refusing even to go to the carnival parties of the grand dukes. He did, however, visit the university, to listen to a lecture on penal law delivered by the celebrated jurist Carmignani, and was introduced to the applauding students as one of the greatest poets of Italy. His diary also gives an account of an evening spent at a meeting of the famous Pisan *Accademia dei Lunatici*, of which Lady Mountcashell was president, where the poet Guadagnoli 'recited some burlesque verses on his own life, rendering the style and the subject yet more ridiculous by appropriate mimicry and gestures'. This entertainment, however, caused no amusement to Leopardi. To him the sight of a young man 'laughing at himself, at his own youth, at his own misfortunes, exposing himself to ridicule for the entertainment of others', seemed 'the saddest of all forms of despair'. Such a view can hardly have added to the gaiety of the evening—and one of his fellow-guests has noted for us that, in all his acquaintance with Leopardi, he cannot remember ever to have seen him smile.

In his *Operette Morali*, and later on in his satirical poems, the *Palinodia* and the *Paralipomeni*, he showed a sardonic pleasure in human folly; but the gentle, kindly human laughter which Cowper, for instance, knew in the intervals between his periods of despair, was unknown to Leopardi. 'A very common thing', he grimly noted, 'in the most melancholy and despairing madmen, is a stupid and empty laughter, which comes only from the lips. They will take you by the hand with a deep look, and on leaving you, will say good-bye with a smile that seems more despairing and madder than despair and madness itself.'[33]

The months of this winter in Pisa, however, if not exactly gay, were certainly among the least unhappy ones of Leopardi's life. 'I am well,' he wrote to Paolina, 'am eating with appetite, and have a room looking out westwards over a great orchard—with so wide an opening that one can see far towards the horizon.'[34]

The fields and lanes of Pisa reminded him—now that distance had bathed them in a golden light—of those of Recanati. 'There is here', he wrote, 'a delightful path which I call "the path of memories", and I walk there when I want to dream with my eyes open.'[35] In

N

the foreground of these dreams there was now, once again, a young girl: Teresa Lucignani, the sister-in-law of his landlord, a child of barely fifteen, with blue eyes and large curls, which she put into curl-papers every night. Many years later, when she was a garrulous old woman of ninety-two, in the Pisa workhouse, she told an enterprising journalist what she remembered about the little hunch-backed poet who had spent six months with them.

She did not find him attractive. He was misshapen, she said, and frail, and his personal habits were far from pleasing. He was fussy about his food, he let his chocolate dribble on his chin, he very seldom changed his shirt—though, when he went out, he was 'most elegant' in a fine blue frock-coat, *alla Mazzini*. To Teresa he was unfailingly kind: he insisted on her calling him Giacomo, instead of *signor Conte*; he showed her a book with pictures in it, and even tried to give her lessons. 'If I had wanted to,' she said, 'I might even have become a governess or a teacher!' But the girl was shy; she would not let him teach her, and when he came and sat beside her, she moved away. 'People said', the old woman cackled, 'that he was in love with me!' When he came home, he had a special way of ringing the bell, and when she leaned out of the window, he would look up, laughing—'You should have seen how he laughed!'[36]

It is unnecessary to ask whether he really was in love with Teresa. He was in love with her image, as with other gay, vital images of youth; he warmed his cold hands at their fire. Anything more we may wish to know is told in a note, written soon after leaving Pisa, in which he described the feelings that may be aroused in a man by a girl of sixteen. 'She has in her face,' he wrote, 'in her movements, in her voice, something—I know not what—almost divine. . . . This pure, fresh, vital flower of youth, this untouched hope marked on her face and in her gestures, or which, as you watch her, you think you see there; this air of complete unawareness of evil, misfortune, or suffering—in a word, this flower, this very first flower of life—all these things, without making you fall in love or even really awakening your interest, yet make so lovely, so deep, so indescribable an impression, that you never tire of looking at that face. . . .'[37]

It was in the same spring that, for the first time in five years (if we except the academic Epistle to Carlo Pepoli) Leopardi began to write poetry again, and poetry that had the accents of his early *Idylls*.

'I have written some verses this April,' he told Paolina, 'as in the old days, and with the same feelings I had then.'[38] This was Teresa Lucignani's gift: the 'sense of the spirit' stirring again within him, at the sight of two childlike eyes and the sound of a girl's voice, and the softness of mild spring days, walking in green meadows by the Pisan sea. In six April days he wrote *Il Risorgimento*—the story of his heart's reawakening.

> Meco ritorna a vivere
> La piaggia, il bosco, il monte;
> Parla al mio core il fonte,
> Meco favella il mar.*

The spring passed, and when the summer came, the poet returned to Florence. There, as he sat again in his darkened room during the long, hot summer days, the memories of Pisa mingled with those of Recanati. Teresa's laughing eyes—'*ridenti e fuggitivi*'†—became Silvia's, and her voice, too—was it Silvia's or Nerina's?—or was it the voice of youth itself, of spring and joy and love? '*Era il maggio odoroso....*' In these weeks Leopardi wrote what is perhaps the most perfect and serene of all his lyrics, *A Silvia*—the poem in which the tormented longings of his youth turned to pure melody. 'I know', wrote Tasso in his old age, 'that in poetry certain amorous concepts [*concetti amorosi*] are almost like a poison in rare foods. I shall purge this poison.' So, too, Leopardi. In *A Silvia* all the poison has been purged; every ornament, of feeling or of expression, has been discarded; the words of common speech have acquired a new, a disembodied flavour. The song on Silvia's lips might be the song of the Spirits to Persephone as she rose from the kingdom of the dead; the light that shines upon her loom is the pearly light of the first dawn of the world.

> * Again the shore, the woods,
>   The hills return to life.
>   The fountains and the sea
>   Hold converse with my heart.
> † Laughing and fleeting glances.

XIII

REMEMBRANCE
(1828—1830)

Il rimembrar delle passate cose,
*Ancor che triste, e che l'affanno duri.**

I

JUST before returning to Florence Leopardi had received bad news from home: his younger brother Luigi, at the age of twenty-four, had died of galloping consumption. Conte Monaldo's letters at this time show a touching intensity of feeling, and of attachment to the son who, though absent, was still left to him. 'When we were all of us in the greatest distress here,' the Count wrote, 'I was thinking of you, and saying to everyone, "Our poor Giacomo is thinking of us now, and of our feast at S. Leopardo, and does not know that these festive days have become for us, and soon will be for him, days of grief and mourning". . . .' His only consolation lay in the recollection of the piety of Luigi's deathbed, and urgent were his appeals to Giacomo to turn to the same source of consolation. 'We have all partaken of the Holy Sacrament; and I do not doubt that you, too, will give this token of love to your dear brother, who loved you so fondly and is praying for you. My Giacomo, let us save our souls; all the rest is vanity. I implore you with a father's heart to read the second chapter of Saint Thomas à Kempis, Book I. Read it for love of me.'[1]

Was Giacomo lying when, in reply, he told his father that he, too, had partaken of the Sacrament 'with the intention you know

* Remembrance of the things that are no more
Though it be sad, and still the grief endures.
Alla luna.

180

of?[2] Most of his biographers have thought so. But can we really be so sure? He would not have been the first unhappy man to find a brief comfort in a return—transient, but not necessarily hypocritical—to the practice of rites no longer consciously believed in. Certainly his grief for his gentle, unintellectual brother was genuine enough. 'My sorrow', he wrote, 'is so great that I cannot wholly grasp it. I am only aware that you need comfort more than anything, and it is the thought of your state, and that of my mother and brothers, that makes me weep so bitterly.'[3] His sorrow was so deep that he fell ill, but with the secretiveness that was growing upon him, he told none of his friends what had happened, and in a letter to his father he said that he was not wearing mourning, 'in order to avoid the innumerable questions it would arouse, which, from people who are indifferent to me, would be unbearable in my grief'.[4]

Leopardi's first impulse, on hearing the bad news, had been to go home, by such slow stages as would enable him to bear the fatigue of the journey. But when he had got to Florence, his health broke down again. Colletta wrote to Capponi that he seemed 'more dead than a corpse. Everything harms him: wind, air, light, every sort of food, rest or movement, work or idleness.'[5] And Leopardi himself wrote to Antonietta Tommasini: 'The doctors tell that all my organs are sound; but *none* of them can function without great difficulty, owing to an extreme, unheard-of sensibility which, in the past two years, has increased every day. Almost every action and sensation causes me pain.'[6] So great was his weariness that, at one moment, he again played with the thought of suicide, or at least hinted at it, in a letter to Adelaide Maestri: 'I feel a great desire to bring so many complaints to an end for good, and thus become still more completely immobile.'[7] Both Adelaide and her mother took immediate alarm, and it was not until Leopardi had sent them a long and affectionate letter of reassurance, that their fears were soothed. 'I swear to you, that the infinite love I feel for my friends and relations will keep me in this world as long as fate shall ordain; so let us never again speak of this matter. Meanwhile I cannot tell you how deeply I am touched by the affection shown by your dear words. I do not need esteem, or glory, or anything like that, but I do need love.'[8]

His health and spirits, however, remained at a very low ebb.

Incessant headaches and inflamed eyes prevented him from either thinking or writing, and the effort of transcribing extracts for an anthology of Italian poetry which he had begun for Stella in Pisa, was beyond him. 'Even to write a letter about it', he wrote, 'throws me into convulsions and a sort of fever.' He was unable to complete the *Encyclopaedia of Useless Knowledge* and therefore felt, as he himself scrupulously wrote to Stella, that he could not go on accepting the publisher's monthly allowance. All he asked was that it should be continued until November, when he intended to go home.

Several other offers of work had also to be rejected. The Chevalier Bunsen wrote, offering him the chair of Dantesque studies in the University of Bonn. 'But how', he wrote to Puccinotti, 'could I abandon my family in Italy, and how could I endure the German climate?' Vieusseux asked him to write a review of Niebuhr's *Roman History*, and an article on the Homeric question—a subject that had always interested him. Notes in the *Zibaldone* show that he at once began to work upon it, but he was too ill to go on, and, once again, inactivity brought on an attack of spleen, in which everything he laid eyes on seemed unpleasing. He complained to Giordani that the streets of Florence were nothing but muddy lanes, that the Florentine ladies were all 'silly, ignorant, and proud', that he saw no one but Vieusseux and his circle, and that, when these failed him, 'as often happens', he felt as if he were living in a desert. And on their side the Florentines seem to have felt some natural impatience at his eternal complaints. Colletta confessed to Capponi that he really 'did not know what to do, to cheer him up', and that he was beginning to believe 'that unhappiness was as necessary to Leopardi as dissipation to Giordani or gaiety to Poerio'.[9] 'His excuse', Capponi remarked, 'is being a hunchback—but is it not perhaps a *piccolezza** not to know how to live with a hump?' And he added that Leopardi 'would have learned to do so—for in his soul and his talents there was something great—if Giordani and other literary men of his kind had not weighed down his genius with a philosophy of wretchedness'.[10]

In this comment there was some truth, though a more sensitive man might have worded it less harshly. But there was little in the Tuscan temperament akin either to Leopardi's *sensiblerie*† or to his

* A pettiness.   † Acute sensibility.

gloom. Stendhal, who came to Florence at about this time, declared that the Tuscans were 'the most civilized people on earth', and much admired their extraordinary reasonableness. But he also observed their complete absence of what he called *l'air exaltable*;* even the women, he complained, never lost their common sense. 'Those sharp and piercing eyes seem more inclined to judge, than to love you.'[11]

During this autumn, however, Leopardi did meet in Florence one man who—if the circumstances of their life had been favourable—might have become a real friend: a young Piedmontese priest called Vincenzo Gioberti. Though fresh from the training of the theological college in which he had distinguished himself by his brilliance, this grave, austere young priest had yet preserved a remarkable independence of mind. There seems, indeed, to have been a real spiritual affinity between the two men. Even though on many religious and philosophical points they did not agree, they both approached them on a very different plane from the utilitarian and practical spirit of the Tuscan reformers. In Gioberti's mind, as in Leopardi's, philosophy was closely linked to poetry, to an intuitive perception of a realm beyond the visible world. 'Poetry', Gioberti wrote, 'links us to another life, lifts us up to the contemplation—barely foreshadowed and *per enigma*—of a better order of things.'[12] He told Leopardi that he considered his poems 'the finest lyrics that have been written in Italy since Petrarca's', and that the last sentence of his essay on Parini was 'engraved in my heart, to fortify me against the sufferings of life'.

For a few weeks they saw each other constantly, and when, on the 10th of November, Leopardi left Florence to return to Recanati, Gioberti travelled with him. It appears that on the journey the poet opened his heart to his companion and told him of the suffering that had attended the loss of his faith.[13] Had the two men continued to see each other often, the last years of the poet's life might have taken on a different colour. After they had parted, Gioberti wrote to him: 'Your affection is so dear to me, and mine for you is so great and sincere, joined to my admiration for your rare parts, that to be with you and talk with you again would be one of the greatest pleasures I could have in life.'[14] But the pleasure was never renewed, for Gioberti never returned to Recanati or Florence, and

* Any appearance of enthusiasm.

Leopardi never saw him again. Once again alone, he settled down to face the long winter in Recanati.

II

The next sixteen months of Leopardi's life were the last that he was to spend in his native town. Could he but have known this, what misery would he not have been spared! 'I shall remain here, I know not for how long,' he wrote to Giovanni Rosini. 'Perhaps for ever. I consider that my life has come to an end.'[15] To Adelaide Maestri, on the last day of the year, he wrote: 'As to Recanati, my answer is that I will go, escape, fly away from here as soon as possible—but when will that be? That is what I cannot tell you. Meanwhile be sure that my intention is not to stay here, where I see no one but my own family, and where I should die of rage, tedium, and melancholy—if these were evils that one died of.'[16] His letters during this time had one object only: escape. He implored his friends in every town in Italy to find him 'an honourable literary occupation'; but at the same time he told them that he was capable of neither 'reading, writing, nor thinking'.

During the first months after his return he went for long solitary walks—his head down, his hands behind his back—taking the paths most sheltered from the wind, and in which he was least likely to meet other *Recanatesi*. But after a while his morbid dread of meeting any acquaintances became so great that he ceased to go out at all, and limited his exercise to pacing up and down a room. He even insisted on taking his meals alone—a habit contracted in Bologna. 'To eat alone', he had then noted in the *Zibaldone*, 'τὸ μονοφαγεῖν, was considered infamous by the Greeks and Romans, and was called *inhumanum*; and the name of μονοφάγος was used as an insult, like that of thief. I would have deserved this infamy.'[17] He returned several times to the subject, defending his preference both on the score of health and of seemliness—since, he said, the enjoyment of physical pleasures forms a spectacle which is disgusting to others, and it is therefore undesirable to expose ourselves at such times to the mocking and envious eyes of our servants—'importunate lackeys,' he wrote, borrowing from Rousseau, 'who eavesdrop on our conversation, criticize our behaviour, count our every mouthful with a

PALAZZO LEOPARDI AND THE SQUARE OF *IL SABATO DEL VILLAGGIO.*

(The Square is the one where Leopardi was baptised. The large house on the left is Palazzo Leopardi; the little house opposite, Silvia's.)

covetous eye, and take a delight in keeping us waiting for our drinks'.[18] All this, of course, was merely a rationalization of his extreme boredom during family meals; but he now cut down even his solitary repasts to one a day—which, as his father pointed out, caused his stomach to be 'depleted before the meal, and oppressed after it'.[19]

With such a régime, it is not surprising that Leopardi's health did not improve. Moreover, his loneliness was greatly increased by the absence of his brother Carlo, who had quarrelled with his family over his marriage. For some time the whole Leopardi family had been trying to find a suitable wife for Carlo—that is, a young woman with a sufficient dowry, who would yet be willing to live in Recanati. Giacomo had written to all his friends about it, and had himself even found one well-born young lady in Ravenna, a daughter of the Pasolini family—but with only 10,000 *scudi* to her name. Another *parti*, in Modena, had the opposite defect: her dowry of 50,000 *zecchini* was considered disproportionate to the bridegroom's fortune, while yet other similar proposals had fallen through in Faenza and Milan. But meanwhile Carlo had been following his own inclinations, which had led him to a penniless but attractive cousin, Paolina Mazzagalli. The immediate and unwise opposition of Contessa Adelaide fanned the flame; an uncle on the girl's side of the family, Monsignore Mazzagalli, encouraged the match; all the relations took violent sides, and made Giacomo their confidant. Finally a visit of Conte Monaldo's to Rome gave the lovers their opportunity; early one morning they were married in secret, and Carlo went away to live with his bride's family. Conte Monaldo declared that he forgave his son 'with the heart of a loving father and of a Christian', but his forgiveness confined itself to these words, and for twelve years his daughter-in-law was not allowed to set foot in his house.[20] So now Giacomo was deprived of even his brother's company—the brother whom he loved, he said, with a dream-like affection—*amor di sogno*.[21]

It is at this point that Carlo, too, passes out of our story. During Giacomo's last years in Naples very few letters were exchanged by the brothers and the old link seemed broken. Many years later, when Carlo was asked for his reminiscences of Giacomo, he could give very few. But, he said, 'he was a brother to whom it was an honour to belong. I cannot say it without a grief so great, as to fill a whole lifetime.'[22] Certainly with Giacomo's death the last spark of all the dreams and hopes that the brothers had shared seems to have been extinguished in Carlo, too. The rest of his long life was spent in an apathetic obscurity and a sordid miserliness, lending money at a high interest to his fellow-citizens, by whom he was well hated.[23] It was said of him that he had all his brother's faults, without any of his talents. And when, on the day of his death, his funeral procession wound its way down the streets of Recanati, his fellow-citizens—on learning that he had not left, in his will, a penny for the poor—threw stones at the coffin, and even broke the glass that covered it, to pull out the dead man's whiskers and to spit into his face.[24] Giacomo was not the only Leopardi to hate his fellow-citizens, and to be hated by them in return.

But meanwhile the poet was still at home, and still alone. Indeed his sense of his own solitude was becoming almost an obsession. He wrote to Vieusseux that he was 'stifled by a melancholy that is little less than madness', and said that tears streamed down his face 'when I remember you, and the time spent in your company'.[25] To Puccinotti, who was then in Macerata, he sent an invitation in terms only suitable to a man in solitary confinement: 'Let me hear the voice of a human being and of a friend.'[26]

For indeed Leopardi was beginning to realize, as he noted in his day-book, the peculiar dangers of too much solitude, especially when combined with inactivity, for a man of his temperament. 'The more', he wrote, 'I was freed from external occupation and effort, and from any practical anxiety—even from the necessity of asking for what I needed, so that I spent whole days without opening my mouth—the less was my spirit at rest. Constant fears and anxieties . . . a continual travail of the imagination, unpleasant premonitions, disgusting fantasies, imaginary pains. . . . Persons of a vivid imagination', he concluded, 'who try to escape from action and society into solitude, make a great mistake. To find peace, they need, more than others, to escape from themselves, and therefore require external distractions and occupations—even with tedium. They must be bored, in order to be at peace.'[27]

But not even this peace was available—at least for the poet—in Recanati. For sixteen long months, unable to escape from himself and his obsessions, Leopardi sank into a deeper dejection than he had ever known. Even his relations, as they watched him, were sadly obliged to admit that nowhere was he quite so unhappy as at home. 'Ours is a horrible situation,' wrote Paolina to Marianna Brighenti, after her brother had gone away again, 'for with all our intense desire to see him again and our conviction that only in his family can he find the tenderness and care that his condition requires, we yet cannot wish for it, since we have always before our eyes the spectacle of his terrible discontent, of his despair!'[28]

An acute return of his ophthalmia again cut him off from his books; he was able to do no work, and the *Encyclopaedia of Useless Knowledge* lay on his desk uncompleted. He did, however, draw up a long list of projected works, which included an autobiographical novel, to be called *The Story of a Soul*, and a new kind of '*Galateo*', or book of etiquette, which was to teach 'the respect that is necessary in conversation and civilized life, in order to avoid offending some of men's passions'—a document which might well have been painfully instructive.

He also proposed to write a treatise on the passions. 'The science of the intellect and of ideas', he wrote, 'has been much cultivated in the last two centuries, and is now adult; but that of the feelings, which is at least equally important, has made no progress since Aristotle, and is still in its infancy.' And finally the poet was planning a work on a theme on which he might well call himself an expert: *The Art of being Unhappy*.[29]

None of these plans, unhappily, bore any fruit. But in these long fallow months of inactivity and dejection, Leopardi's poetic genius was stirring again, and during the summer of 1829—at the very time when he was telling Bunsen that he could neither think nor write—he composed the exquisite later *Idylls*: *Il passero solitario*, *Le ricordanze*, *La quiete dopo la tempesta*, and *Il sabato del villaggio*, and these were followed, in the course of the next winter, by the *Canto notturno di un pastore errante dell' Asia*.

Il passero solitario—no sparrow, but a rock-thrush, *cyadonus montanus*—was placed by Leopardi himself, in the Neapolitan edition of the *Canti*, immediately before the early *Idylls*, and indeed its inspiration dates from the same period; but the art that has gone to its composition is more elaborate, more mature. The little thrush's song, on the summit of a lonely tower, becomes a symbol for all the fleeting joy, the fading brilliance, of spring and youth.

> . . . alla campagna
> Cantando vai finchè non more il giorno;
> Ed erra l'armonia per questa valle.*

Leopardi's three next poems—*La quiete dopo la tempesta, Il sabato del villaggio*, and *Le ricordanze*—all belong to a similar mood. They hold not so much the memories, as the myth, of Leopardi's life; they spring from the rich under-soil of his 'fabulous years'. 'If I knew', he had written, 'how to depict and awaken in others the sights and feelings of my childhood, I would think myself a divine poet.'[30] And now, after long years of suffering and disillusionment and wandering, he had returned to these sources, to the sky of his childhood, and the familiar sights and sounds of his father's house. 'Analyse carefully', he wrote, 'your most poetical sensations and dreams, those which draw you most completely out of yourself, and out of the real world; you will find that they, and the pleasure drawn from them, consist wholly or principally in memories.'[31] In these later *Idylls*, as in those written at Recanati ten years before, Leopardi attained the summit of his achievement; here he translated the pain of his own experience into terms of universal pathos. These poems are 'clear, cool, and transparent in the clarity of their form, like spring nights in Pisa, like mornings of early autumn in the hills of the Marches; they achieve a perfect balance between feeling and imagination'.[32]

In *Le ricordanze* Leopardi has returned to his own youth; to the summer nights, when he would sit in silence on the grass and listen to the distant croaking of the frogs in the valley below—

> E la lucciola errava appo le siepi
> E in su l'aiuole, susurrando al vento
> I viali odorati, ed i cipressi
> Là nella selva; e sotto al patrio tetto
> Sonavan voci alterne, e le tranquille
> Opre de' servi. E che pensieri immensi,
> Che dolci sogni mi spirò la vista
> Di quel lontano mar, quei monti azzurri,

---

* Singing to the fields until the day is done
  And the strain wanders through the valley.

Che di qua scopro, e che varcare un giorno
Io mi pensava, arcani mondi, arcana
Felicità fingendo al viver mio.*

And then Nerina herself came back into his thoughts, Nerina—
dolcezza mia—who was youth itself, and tenderness and love.

. . . Passasti. Ad altri
Il passar per la terra oggi è sortito,
E l'abitar questi odorati colli.
Ma rapida passasti; e come un sogno
Fu la tua vita.†

His next two poems, *La quiete dopo la tempesta* and *Il sabato del villaggio*, are coloured by the same tone. They present idyllic scenes —the village's return to life after a storm, and the joy of a young girl adorning herself for the coming holiday, while the old crones, sitting on the stairs at their spinning-wheels, tell stories of past days and of their own happy youth. This last is a scene that Giacomo, looking out upon the little square beneath the library windows, must have watched upon many a summer's evening; and the traveller to Recanati today may see it still.

The four poems of which we have written were all composed during the summer of 1829; but the last, and perhaps the greatest, of the poems belonging to this period, the *Canto notturno di un pastore errante dell' Asia*, was not completed until eight months later. The intervening months were spent by him, as we have said, in the

* . . . the fireflies danced
Among the hedges and the flowers,
In fragrant avenues and cypress woods
The night-wind murmured; in my father's house
The servants' voices rose in antiphon
About their quiet tasks. What lofty thoughts,
What beckoning dreams, the sight of that far sea,
Those distant azure hills, awoke in me,—
Those distant hills that once I hoped to scale,
Picturing lands unknown, unknown delights.

† You have gone by. Today the fates ordain
That other men should wander o'er the world
And find a home among these fragrant hills.
Swiftly you slipped away, and all your life
Was but a dream.

enforced inactivity that, as he himself well knew, always drove him into deep dejection.

> E un fastidio m'ingombra
> La mente, ed uno spron quasi mi punge
> Si che, sedendo, più che mai son lunge
> Da trovar pace o loco.*

But in these long months of isolation and anguish he conceived a poem in which the nostalgic melodies of *A Silvia* and *Le ricordanze* gave place to a graver, cooler note—almost to the detachment of an observer contemplating our world and its sorrows from another planet. The landscape of the *Canto notturno di un pastore errante dell' Asia* is a lunar world, pale and bare and leafless; the wind that blows across it is one of tedium and emptiness; yet the total effect is one of infinite serenity, as of tidings brought to us by a survivor, or a visiting ghost. Two themes, recurrent and interlaced, run through the poem: the turmoil, anguish, and hopelessness of human life, and the eternal and immutable revolutions of the stars.[33] Already in the opening lines—with Leopardi's magical gift for stating his theme in his first few words, for immediately evoking the world of his own vision— we are caught up into the skies:

> Che fai tu, luna, in ciel? dimmi, che fai,
> Silenziosa luna?†

The shepherd of the title is an Eastern nomad, resting at night beneath the stars after the long wanderings of the day. In a note to this poem Leopardi quoted a passage by a French traveller in the East, who described some of those shepherds 'spending the night seated on a stone watching the moon, and improvising words of great sadness to tunes no less mournful.'[34] It was in the mouth of one of these

---

* And a disgust oppresses
  My soul; a kind of goad pricks me, that so
  As there I rest, I am more far than ever
  From peace and from repose.

† What dost thou, Moon, what dost thou in the sky?
  Tell me, thou silent moon.

  Canto notturno, trans. by R. C. Trevelyan.

shepherds that the poet placed his eternal, unanswerable questions
about the nature of the universe and the destiny of man. The moon's
life, he said, like the nomad's, is one of wandering. Perhaps she,
'*solinga, eterna pellegrina*',* can explain the mysteries the shepherd
cannot fathom. Surely, beyond human life, there must be some other
mystery? Surely she can reveal it, she can tell

> Che sia questo morir, questo supremo
> Scolorar del sembiante,
> E perir dalla terra, e venir meno
> Ad ogni usata, amante compagnia.
> E tu certo comprendi
> Il perchè delle cose, e vedi il frutto
> Del mattin, della sera,
> Del tacito, infinito andar del tempo.†

The shepherd with his flock travels across the great plains, and at
night, looking up at the sky, he asks:

> A che tante facelle?
> Che fa l'aria infinita, e quel profondo
> Infinito seren? che vuol dir questa
> Solitudine immensa? ed io che sono?‡

No answer comes—no answer from the moon, and from his own
spirit, too, no knowledge—only the old lament:

* Lonely, eternal pilgrim.

† What means this dying, this last fading out
Of colour from the cheek, this perishing
From earth, this mournful last forsaking
Of all familiar dear companionship?
Ah surely you at least must understand
The why and wherefore, you who always see
The morning's promise and the evening's peace,
And the unending passing of the days.

‡ Why all these flickering lights?
Why breathes this air? what stirs
This boundless firmament?
What does this lonely vastness mean,
And I, ah what am I?

Questo io conosco e sento,
Che degli eterni giri,
Che dell' esser mio frale,
Qualche bene o contento
Avrà fors'altri; a me la vita è male.*

Meanwhile another long winter in Recanati was dragging by, and still there seemed no prospect of escape. Leopardi was offered the chair of natural history in the University of Parma, but refused it on the score of his ignorance of the subject. His Florentine friends, who had been shocked, a few months before, by a rumour of his death, got Colletta to suggest that he should at once return to Florence, and, while waiting for a post, accept a monthly pension, which he would pay back, when he was again able to write. This, Colletta wrote, his fellow-author, the historian Botta, had not been ashamed to do. But Leopardi would not hear of it. 'I confess that I cannot bring myself to publish my beggardom in this manner. If Botta had had to do so, in order to feed himself, I am not yet in such straits; and if I were, I do not know whether I should choose to beg or to starve.'[35]

The pride shown in this letter was certainly genuine, but it was also still sustained by a faint hope. In 1828, before leaving Florence, Leopardi had sent in his *Operette Morali* to compete for a quinquennial prize of five thousand *scudi*, offered by the famous *Accademia della Crusca*, and the assignation of the prize was to be early in 1830. Both Capponi and Niccolini were on the examining committee, and the poet's only serious rival was Botta, who had submitted a voluminous *History of Italy*. During the last months of waiting Leopardi alternated between hope and fear. At one moment he was seized with panic that Manzoni, even though he was not competing, would be awarded the prize for his *Promessi Sposi*. In spite of what he had said earlier in the year, he now sent to Colletta a desperate appeal: 'In order to get out of this Tartarus, my despair would now cause me to lay down my old pride, and embrace any suggestion, accept any offer.'[36]

* This I both know and feel:
The world's eternal course
And my poor fragile self
To some may spell content:
But life for me is woe.

The examiners met at last, and their reports were read; among the thirty-nine works submitted, eleven were to be put to the vote of the Academicians, with Botta's *History* and Leopardi's *Operette* heading the list. But when the final vote took place, the tide had turned against Leopardi. Some of the members took exception to the anti-religious tone of the *Operette*, and said that they did not deserve to be called *morali*; others did not like the fantastic tone of the first essay, the *Storia del genere umano*. In the end safe mediocrity won the day: thirteen votes were awarded to Botta, and only one to Leopardi.[37]

So yet another door was closed. It was now, in March 1830, that Leopardi reached a desperate resolution: to take the small sum he had earned by his previous writings and to set forth 'to look for health or die, but never, never again return to Recanati'. 'I will make no distinction between professions,' he wrote to Vieusseux, 'any that can be reconciled with my ill-health will suit me; I fear no humiliations. . . . I have nothing left to lose. Tell me in all sincerity whether you think that I could earn enough to support life by giving lessons or literary entertainments at home [in Florence]. I mean literary lessons of any kind, even the humblest, in language, grammar, and the like.'[38]

But while this letter was in the post, one from his Florentine friends was already on its way to Recanati—a letter which showed their deep affection and concern. It was written by General Colletta, and contained what is surely one of the most generous and tactful offers ever made to a man of letters:

'It is now open to you, my friend, to come and live among us, to care for your health, and give pleasure to your friends. You once told me that eighteen *francesconi* a month were enough for you to live on; well, you shall have eighteen *francesconi*, for a period of one year, beginning if you like from this April. I shall hand over to you, every month, in advance, the above-mentioned sum, but I shall have no office or duty besides that of handing over the money. Nothing will come out of my purse. The giver does not know to whom his gift is destined—and you, who are receiving it, do no know from whom it comes. It shall be a loan, if it pleases you to return the sum received; or it shall be less than a loan, if the opportunity of returning it shall fail. No one knows whom to ask for the

money, and you do not know to whom to return it. No obligation
is imposed on you. May it be the good fortune of Italy that, with
the return of your health, you will be able to write works worthy
of your genius! But this hope of mine confers no obligation upon you.'
And the letter ended: 'Answer at once, come soon; we are awaiting
you with open arms. Do not try to guess the giver, or the ways and
means; you would probably be mistaken. Believe all that I have
written, literally.'[39]

So generous a proposal could receive but one answer. 'I can only
tell you', said Leopardi, 'that your letter—after sixteen months of
horrible darkness, after a life from which God deliver my worst
enemies—has now come to me like a ray of light, more blessed
than the first dawning of twilight in the polar regions.'[40]

On the 29th of April 1830, Giacomo's carriage was again at the
door of Palazzo Leopardi; his mother and Paolina embraced him
tenderly. But Conte Monaldo was not there; he wrote, after his
son's death, that he had only had a hurried last glimpse of him
('almost by stealth') on the night before he left, but had not had the
heart to embrace him, or to come downstairs to bid him farewell.[41]
And indeed, it was their last parting: Giacomo Leopardi had left
Recanati for ever.

XIV

RANIERI
(1830—1832)

Viviamo, Porfirio mio, e confortiamoci insieme.*

I

IN the autumn of 1830, a few months after Leopardi's return to Tuscany, a handsome young Neapolitan, who had been exiled from the Kingdom of Naples on account of his Liberal opinions, arrived in Florence after a long journey in Switzerland, England, and France. He was tall and fair, with an effusive manner, a romantic and amorous disposition, a generosity rather greater than his means, and somewhat more enthusiasm than intelligence. His name was Antonio Ranieri.

His acquaintance with Leopardi had begun three years before in Florence, and as soon as he arrived there he hastened to call upon the poet—only to find him 'very ill indeed and inconsolable'. To his romantic sensibility this state was an added attraction, and soon, according to his own account, he came to prefer the melancholy of Leopardi's conversation to the charms of the Florentine ladies. He spent all his days and nights with his friend, sleeping on a sofa in the adjoining room, and, finally, in November, after a brief visit to Rome,[1] he gave up his own flat altogether and moved into rooms adjoining Leopardi's. His own account of the incident that led to this decision must be quoted:

'Leopardi's incurable sadness increased every day, and one evening, when I thought it had reached its height, I could no longer restrain myself from inquiring, in gentle tones, what its cause could

---

* Let us live, my Porphyry, and find comfort together.
Dialogo di Plotino e di Porfirio.

195

be. "Cease", he replied, "from the vain enterprise of comforting a
man in despair." ' Ranieri, however, was not easily discouraged,
and he discovered that Leopardi was living in terror lest, when the
subsidy from Colletta came to an end, he should be obliged to return
to the 'detested sepulchre' of Recanati. The unhappy poet added
that doubtless his Florentine friends were expecting him to do some
writing in return for their help, and to dedicate his works to them,
but that he was incapable of fulfilling the first of these wishes, and
unwilling to gratify the second. 'In these seven years', wrote
Ranieri, 'I have never seen Leopardi weep. But that evening, by the
faint light of his shaded lamp, I saw that he was crying: and, indes-
cribably moved by those words and tears, I said what a man would
only say at the age I was then: "Leopardi, you shall not return to
Recanati! What little I have will suffice for two as well as for one;
moreover, let it be as a gift from you to me, not as from me to you!
Never shall we separate again!" This promise', he added, 'was kept
with a rare fidelity; but I cannot deny that for me, and for my
angelic Paolina [Ranieri's sister] it became the cause of long, incurable, and incomprehensible sorrows.'[2]

Such was the beginning of a friendship which, remaining unbroken for seven years, was terminated only by Leopardi's death,
and which has given rise to a tedious and unpleasant controversy.
It is not my intention to examine it in detail, but its fundamental
point—Ranieri's character and the nature of his relation with
Leopardi—cannot be disregarded. During Leopardi's lifetime, and
immediately after his death, it was generally believed that Ranieri's
friendship and generosity had been the poet's chief consolation and
support in his last years. The two men, as the following chapters
will show, were inseparable, and Ranieri allowed it to be supposed
that not only his companionship and his devoted care, but also his
purse, had been at Giacomo's disposal. But when, many years after
Leopardi's death, his letters were published, two things became
evident: firstly, that throughout the last seven years of his life he
had received regular, although scanty, sums of money from his
family, and so had not been dependent upon Ranieri's charity, and
secondly, that his irritable dislike of every place in which he lived
for any length of time had led him to make some very unflattering
remarks about Naples and the Neapolitans. Ranieri, who was then

nearly eighty years old, responded with the publication of his *Seven Years of Companionship with Giacomo Leopardi*, an unpleasant and inaccurate book, which is both over-emphatic and sentimental. In it Ranieri, while making much of his own devotion and of the sacrifices demanded of him and his sister Paolina, depicts his friend not only as an exacting and querulous invalid (which may well, at least in part, have been true) but also as hypocritical and un-grateful.[3]

These senile outpourings make one wonder why Leopardi chose Ranieri for his friend. Of the sincerity of his feelings there can be no doubt, nor that it was this friendship alone that made the last years of his life worth living. But Ranieri, as he reveals himself to us with his own pen, is vain, trivial, and only moderately intelligent. One explanation of the attachment, perhaps, is that the Ranieri of the book was not the Ranieri Leopardi knew. Enthusiasm, hyper-sensibility, and romanticism are qualities which, with the passing of time, are apt either to fade, or to degenerate into caricatures of them-selves. But in this good-looking young man of twenty-four, who offered a devotion as unlimited as his admiration, they must have seemed to Leopardi like the breath of life itself. Even Ranieri's obvious faults—his vanity and loquacity, his occasional silliness—must in his eyes have been compensated by his warmth and vitality; they may even have seemed rather endearing. Moreover, we must remember that his uncritical devotion was offered to Leopardi at a time when, for all the practical kindness of his Tuscan friends, he knew himself to be separated from them by unbridgeable differences of temperament and opinion; when he had left his family for ever; when he was ill, penniless, and alone. In Ranieri's unfailing admira-tion and support, as in Giordani's during his youth, he found reassur-ance and peace; he could afford to throw off his armour of mistrust and doubt, and to show the deep craving for affection that lay beneath.

Ranieri's kindness first took practical form in correcting Leopardi's proofs, at a time when the poet's eyesight was again very weak. On his arrival in Florence in June, Leopardi had announced a new edi-tion of his poems, which was to include the verses recently composed in Pisa and Recanati, and in September he informed Paolina that she need not trouble to collect subscribers for him in his birthplace, as he already had nearly six hundred. Moreover, shortly afterwards, he wrote to his brother Pierfrancesco that 'for various reasons' he would accept no payment from any subscribers in Recanati.[4]

The book was ready in November, and was entrusted to the Florentine publisher Piatti, after some bargaining, for the sum of eighty *zecchini*. It appeared in the April of 1831, preceded by two lines of Petrarca's:

> La mia favola breve è già compita,
> E fornito il mio tempo a mezzo gli anni,*

and by a tragic letter of dedication to his 'Tuscan friends'.

'Dear friends of mine, it is to you that I dedicate this book, in which I have attempted, as one often does in poetry, to sublimate my sorrow—a book with which (I cannot say it without tears) I am bidding farewell to study and to letters. I hoped that my dear studies would sustain my old age, I believed that with the loss of all the other pleasures, all the joys of childhood and of youth, I had yet obtained one boon which no power, no calamity could steal away. But, before I had reached my twentieth year, that single boon was in great part snatched from me by an infirmity of my nerves and health, which, while it removes all value from my life, yet gives me no hope of death; and two years before I was thirty, this work of destruction was completed, and, as I now believe, for ever. You well know that I have not even been able to read these very pages, and that to correct them, I have had to make use of the eyes and hands of others. I will complain no more, my dear friends; the greatness of my sorrow is not compatible with lamentation. I have lost everything; nothing is left of me but a useless block that feels and suffers. Yet now, even now, my friends, I have acquired your friendship, and your company; they take the place of my studies, of every hope and every delight, and would almost compensate for my sufferings, if these ailments of mine allowed me to enjoy them as much as I desire, and if I did not know that Fate will soon deprive me of these also, obliging me to waste the years that may still remain to me, abandoned by every comfort of civilization, in a place where the dead are happier than the living. But your love will

---

* My brief fable has reached its end—
My time is spent halfway through life.

remain with me, and will endure even when my body, which has already ceased to live, has turned to ashes. Farewell. Your Leopardi.'[5]

The last part of this letter betrays the fear Leopardi had already confided to Ranieri: that his Florentine friends, when they realized that he was no longer able to write, would cut off his allowance. The premonition was justified. For some time Leopardi's friendship with Colletta had been suffering an eclipse. The warm-hearted, but vain and garrulous Neapolitan had hoped for the poet's help in correcting his *History of Naples*, but now he complained that his chapters were returned to him with no more than a couple of minor alterations; and, when the *Canti* appeared, he was offended because a copy was not sent to him, and perhaps because the dedication was not addressed to him alone. Moreover he was himself in straits over money, and seriously ill. Whichever of these causes was the decisive one, it is certain that on the 10th of April 1831, when he sent to Leopardi the twelfth instalment of his allowance, he not only wrote that it would be the last, but clearly indicated that it was he alone, and not a whole group of friends, who had supported the poet during the past year. For comfort he only added the pious hope: 'May Italy value your works as much as they deserve, and enrich you!'[6] Thus he deprived Leopardi not only of a stable income, however small, but also of one more illusion.

In this same spring a most unwelcome honour was awarded to Leopardi by his native city. The new King of France, Philippe Egalité, had proclaimed himself the defender of all the oppressed peoples of Europe—an unfortunate statement, since it was followed by insurrections in every country under foreign rule. Poland, Belgium, and Italy led the way, the Italian insurrections breaking out in the Duchies of Modena and Parma, in the Romagna and the Marches. At Osimo Cardinal Benvenuti, who had been sent by the Pope to placate the revolutionaries, was instead arrested by them, under the horrified eyes of Conte Monaldo; the Papal troops threw down their arms, or passed over to the ranks of the insurgents; and a proclamation announced 'the end, *de facto et de jure*, of the temporal power of the Pope', and the convocation of a 'National Assembly' in Bologna, to which every city in the Marches was to send a deputy. Whereupon, on the 19th of March 1831, the town

councillors of Recanati—'after imploring Divine help'—elected as
their representative, in spite of his father's demurs, Conte Giacomo
Leopardi.

The Revolutionary Committee's official letter informed the poet
that he had been elected unanimously, 'as the most worthy representative that could be desired, in view of the ample equipment of
his learning, and the evidence of his past heroism'.[7] Poor Conte
Monaldo, who thus unexpectedly found himself forming part of a
revolutionary committee, was one of the signatories, and his feelings
were divided between paternal pride and congenital prudence; but
the latter sentiment prevailed, and he added a private letter, begging
his son not to accept a post 'which might in future compromise
himself and his family'.[8]

He need not have been anxious. Giacomo's 'heroism' in the past
had lain only in the publication of his poems, and his disinclination
to take part in the present activities was extreme. To his father he
wrote: 'My chief desire is that my town and my province should
now forget all about me and my family; be assured that they could
not do us a greater favour.'[9] But his official answer to the committee was facilitated by the fact that in the meantime, the insurrection had been suppressed, and Austrian troops had again taken
possession of Bologna. 'The altered circumstances', Leopardi wrote,
not without humour, 'have rendered it impossible to carry out the
plans, with regard to myself, of the Illustrious Members, but they
have not destroyed my gratitude for the confidence that they have
shown me, nor my ardent wish to serve my native town at any cost,
whenever the times render it possible, and my assistance does not
seem to be, as in this case, entirely out of place.'[10]

For indeed the insurrection—like so many other uprisings in Italy,
irresponsibly sponsored by foreign governments, and then deserted
by them—began as comic opera, and ended in tragedy. Austrian
troops crossed the Po, and occupied the Marches and the Romagna;
the leaders of the insurrection were banished or executed; and at
Modena the Italian patriot Ciro Menotti, on his way to the gallows,
left a last bitter word of counsel to his wife: 'Tell the Italians never
to trust in foreigners.'

II

During the summer of 1831 Leopardi and Ranieri remained together in Florence, but on the 1st of October—so suddenly that they did not find time to bid farewell to some of their Florentine friends—they set forth together, to spend the winter in Rome. For the journey Ranieri hired—'at great expense, all incurred by me', as he is at pains to tell us—'a very spacious carriage, with many excellent mules. I reserved the whole coupé, so that I might sometimes be able to breathe, for Leopardi insisted on the carriage being so completely closed that it was impossible ever to renew the used-up and foul air within.'[11] The journey took five days, but, in spite of these travelling conditions, apparently did not injure Leopardi's health, and, after a short time in unsatisfactory lodgings, the two friends settled down in a small flat in via Condotti.

Ranieri, in his account of this time, maintained that the move to Rome had been made entirely for the sake of Leopardi's health, which could not have stood another winter in Florence. If this was so, the winter may be considered a failure, for certainly neither Leopardi's health nor his spirits benefited by the change. He complained that the region where they lived was 'the foreigners' quarter, where one pays four times as much, is served like a dog, and robbed every day';[12] he observed that to walk half a mile in Rome is ten times more tiring than to cover four times the distance in Florence or Bologna;[13] he refused to visit any of the great sights of the city. As for company, he kept away from *casa Antici* as much as he could, and only occasionally visited his cousin Giuseppe Melchiorri or the ever-kind Chevalier Bunsen. In November, moreover, he had a severe attack of bronchitis, which lasted all the winter. To his brother Carlo he wrote that he considered these months as a time of 'most bitter exile'; and added, with an air of mystery: 'Absolve me, I pray, from laying before you a long romance, much sorrow, and many tears.'[14]

For indeed the real reason for the move to Rome appears to have been an entirely different one; it was caused by Ranieri's uncontrollable desire to be near his mistress, a beautiful actress named Maddalena Pelzet, who was then acting in the Roman Teatro Valle. The story of the first year of Leopardi's and Ranieri's friendship is

closely interwoven with the varying fortunes of Ranieri's infatuation. His 'Lenina' was beautiful, gifted, and passionate, but she did
not, apparently, reserve her favours for him alone, and the romantic
young man was devoured by a torturing jealousy of his mistress's
other admirers, as well as of her husband. He raved and he ranted, he
threatened suicide, he confided his sorrows, in the style of the young
Werther, to other ladies only too ready to console him, and to his
melancholy new friend. Indeed it would appear that it was only
Leopardi's devotion and common sense that saved Ranieri from
either killing himself or running away with his Lenina.

It was Leopardi, too, who now assumed the ungrateful task of
writing to an old friend of Ranieri's, Carlo Troya, to beg him to
intercede with Ranieri's father, who apparently had cut off his son's
allowance. Ranieri, Leopardi wrote, was in grave financial straits,
'and I am sharing them, for we two have become so completely
one, that I can hardly even imagine how I could exist without him'.
The whole letter plainly shows how completely Leopardi now considered his life and Ranieri's to be bound up together. 'Of this
union,' he wrote, 'the closest that it is possible to have, I will not
say more, so as not to go on for ever.'[15] And in a second letter he
wrote that he had done his best to persuade Ranieri to return to his
father, and was prepared—'to save him and myself the pain of
separation'—to accompany him to Naples himself.[16] 'The affection', he concluded, 'that binds me to Filippo* is such that our
destinies are no longer separable.'

So close an association, described in such romantic terms, could
hardly fail, in the gossipy provincial world of Florence, to awaken
some comment. We may gather its nature from a letter of Fanny
Targioni's. 'I do not doubt', she wrote to Ranieri, 'that Leopardi is
good company and shows you great friendship, for he is very kind,
and he must certainly be a comfort to you, being so well-educated
and enjoying (as is right) your whole confidence.' But, she added,
she feared that Ranieri's refusal to return to Naples, so as not to
leave his friend, would end in a break with his father. 'The intensity
of your feelings may blind you, but consider that your birth and

---

* In the correspondence with Troya, Ranieri, who was still in the black books
of the Neapolitan police, is always referred to as 'Filippo', while Troya's own
letters were signed 'Cleophas'.

breeding require a comfortable and independent existence, and that unfortunately—if you do not make some sacrifices—your father can deprive you of it.' And she concluded: 'I should be greatly distressed if your mutual passion led you into some great trouble.'[17]

Are we to conclude, from an expression such as this, and from the highly emotional tone of Leopardi's and Ranieri's own correspondence, that their relationship was homosexual? I do not think so. It is true that some of the unpublished letters in the *carte Ranieri* in Naples imply that the young Neapolitan—though his affairs with women were also numerous and ardent—was ambivalent.[18] But Leopardi's own remarks about homosexuality—in spite of his cult of 'the Ancients'—are quite uncompromising.[19] As to the tone of the letters, it is necessary to remember the extreme romanticism of expression that was then permitted by convention to friends of the same sex. Some of Foscolo's letters to his men-friends (to take only one other instance) are no less prodigal of endearments and passionate protestations than Leopardi's and Ranieri's. Certainly Leopardi showed himself more at ease, more spontaneously himself, with a few men friends than with any woman. But need we seek any more complicated explanation than the recollection of what his youth had been? In childhood, an intense need for affection chilled and thwarted by his mother; in adolescence, a growing awareness of his deformity —were not these enough to cloud, for ever, his relations with women? Self-mistrust, fear of ridicule, desire for the unattainable— these were the emotions that, from the day of his first glimpse of Contessa Lazzari, he had felt in their presence.

Yet affection, from one source or another, he had to have. 'I need love, love, love, fire, enthusiasm, life.' Is it strange that he should have sought it, instead, from his men-friends?—and, moreover, in the case of both Giordani and Ranieri, from men who were singularly uninhibited, frankly and eloquently emotional, enthusiastic, warm. What a change from the régime of Contessa Adelaide! With these men he could afford to lay down, at last, his guard. These friendships were the fulfilment of a chilled, starved nature craving for warmth, of an unutterably lonely man needing kindness.

Yet here, too, the outside world intervened. Giordani was disapproved of by his parents, Ranieri not much liked by his Tuscan friends. Leopardi took refuge in the last defence of the vulnerable:

secretiveness. And this, as the years passed, grew into a veritable obsession, extending itself even to matters of quite trivial importance. Even in writing to Giordani about a projected trip to Naples he said: 'Please keep this a secret. . . . My affairs are of very little interest to anyone, but my liking for sharing them with others is even less.'[20]

It may well have been this increasing touchiness and secretiveness, coupled with his desire to protect his new friendship, which caused his entirely disproportionate exasperation when, in the course of this winter, he ran into some of his fellow-townsmen from Recanati in Rome. 'It is not the least of my troubles here', he wrote to his brother, 'that I can almost fancy myself at home again—such a large number of Recanatesi swine . . . are to be found in this city.'[21] One of these unfortunate fellow-townsmen made so bold as to ask Leopardi in, to visit his shop; another, a hairdresser who had come to cut Ranieri's hair, pestered him with gossip about Recanati and impertinent questions as to why he 'had Conte Monaldo's son with him'. 'With me?' Ranieri replied (or so runs his own account). 'I don't know what you mean. We are two friends who have taken an apartment together.' Unfortunately, however, Leopardi had overheard the conversation, and as soon as the man was gone he burst into the room. 'I feel like a madman,' he cried, 'at the mere thought of my affairs being bandied about by people,' and he then, according to Ranieri, solemnly warned his friend that he considered himself free to invent any lie, any fable he pleased, in self-defence against such pryings.[22]

Another link with Recanati, a few months later, was more seriously annoying. In December Conte Monaldo published, in Pesaro, a volume entitled *Little Dialogues on Current Affairs in the year 1831*—a profoundly reactionary work, which one of the Florentine Liberals, Montanari, described as 'anti-social, anti-Italian, and anti-Christian',[23] but which had an immediate and sensational success. It was translated into German, French, and Dutch, it was read in every Florentine and Roman *salon*—and not unnaturally, since the rumour soon spread that the author's name was Leopardi —it was everywhere attributed to Giacomo himself.[24] 'Ah, the author of the *Little Dialogues*,' he would hear murmured as he entered a Roman *salon*—and it is not surprising that he was much annoyed. He waited for four months, and then wrote to his father: 'It is said in public that I am the author, that I have changed my opinions, that I have been converted, that Monti did the same, that all honest men come to this; . . . Everyone speaks of what some call my conversion, and others my apostasy.'²⁵ His honour, he said, now required that he should publicly declare that he had never changed his opinions. 'I believe that you will approve my resolution.' He asked Vieusseux to publish a denial of his authorship in the *Antologia*, 'in such a manner that it cannot fail to catch the eye', and he requested his cousin to do the same in the *Diario di Roma*, adding: 'I really cannot stand it any longer. I will not appear with the stain of having written that infamous, most infamous and wretched book.'²⁶

Throughout the winter, Leopardi had told his friends in Florence that, at the latest, he would return there in March; and although, when this month came, the cold weather was not yet over and he was far from well, he started back on the 17th of March—with barely enough money in his pocket to last him for a week after his return—and again settled down with Ranieri in the same flat they had had before.

A few days later Leopardi received a welcome piece of news; he heard that he had been elected a member of the *Accademia della Crusca*. This honour gave him especial pleasure because he believed that he owed it to the loyal support of his friends, 'particularly Gino Capponi and Niccolini'. But in this poor Leopardi was mistaken; neither of the two men had taken part in the election.

This spring also brought a great disappointment. In the previous summer Vieusseux introduced to Leopardi a young Swiss philologist, Louis De Sinner, who had heard of the poet's work and wished to make his acquaintance. He was both astounded by Leopardi's erudition and charmed by his turn of mind, and Leopardi, on his side, felt that he was again receiving from a foreign scholar an appreciation more generous than he had ever been granted by his fellow-countrymen. 'You cannot know', he wrote to Paolina, 'what a comfort this event has been to me; for several days it has taken me back to the ideas of my first youth [his philological studies], which I had come to consider completely wasted.' After only a fortnight's acquaintance, he handed over to De Sinner all his philological manuscripts, with the highest hopes. 'He will edit them, complete them, and get them published in Germany. He promises me riches and a great name.'[27]

But once again Leopardi's hopes were disappointed. De Sinner did, indeed, continue to write him hopeful and effusive letters. 'If ever', he assured him, 'I have spent some happy hours in my life, they were those spent with you. Their memory will never be effaced.'[28] He took the *Canti* and the *Operette*, as well as the philological manuscripts, with him to France and Germany, and caused some of them to be translated, while an article on Leopardi's work, with a translation of the *Canto del gallo silvestre* and of *Il sogno*, appeared in the German review *Hesperus*. But the publication of Leopardi's philological works as a whole proved to be impossible, since the German scholars to whom De Sinner sent them thought them too immature. And not one penny reached the poet's purse.[29]

Moreover, the article in *Hesperus*, which appeared in the spring of 1832, afforded Leopardi less satisfaction than annoyance. Like many other pessimists, he was extremely touchy about any suggestion that the colour of his thoughts might have been affected by his health, and, most unfortunately, a passage in the article contained precisely this insinuation.

'Whatever my troubles may have been,' he wrote indignantly to De Sinner, 'that have been thought suitable to be displayed and perhaps also slightly exaggerated in this periodical, I have had enough courage not to try to lighten their burden, either by frivolous expectations of an uncertain and unknown future happiness, or by a cowardly resignation. . . . Before dying, I wish to protest against this invention of weakness and vulgarity, and beg my readers to try to controvert my remarks and my arguments, rather than to accuse my ill-health.'[30]

ASPASIA

*Amor, di nostra vita ultimo inganno.**

IN the summer of 1830, shortly after returning to Florence, Leopardi had written to his sister: 'Unbelievable news! My blue suit has been turned in the latest fashion, with long lapels; it looks new again, and suits me very well.' Dressed in his blue suit, and with a new self-confidence, Leopardi was going out in Florentine society. Carlotta de' Medici Lenzoni invited him to join the writers who met once a week in her *salon*, a model of provincial intellectualism; Charlotte Buonaparte, the widow of Prince Louis Napoleon,[1] asked him to her parties in Palazzo Serristori, where she was living with her cousin Juliette de Villeneuve. Charlotte was not pretty—indeed she was very slightly deformed, like the poet himself—but she was intelligent, fastidious, and melancholy; she talked to Leopardi about the Classics, and she asked him to write a compliment in her album. 'I should have liked to say it to you in Greek,' the poet wrote, 'but since that is only permitted on condition of furnishing a translation, I had better say quite simply in French, that you are made to charm the spirit and the heart.'[2]

How much happier Leopardi might have been, could he indeed have been charmed by a woman of this sort—a woman intelligent enough to appreciate his genius, and vulnerable enough to be kind. But it was invariably creatures of an entirely different type who attracted him, and now, once again, he began to fall in love with one who was young, pretty, and lively, but to whom his gifts seemed valuable only for the prestige attached to them, to whom

---

* Love, last illusion of our life.
                                        Ad Angelo Mai.

manly vigour was all-important. In Italy, even at the present time, a man's physique is more frankly assessed than in the countries of the North; not only good looks and vigour, but a certain *allure*, a certain self-confidence and ease, are essential, in order to please. It is not only women, but often also other men, who require these qualities—though not everyone would express contempt for the lack of them quite as brutally as Tommaseo. But even Capponi, who considered himself Leopardi's friend, habitually wrote of him (and no doubt also spoke) as '*il gobbo*'. The lettered society of Florence was not so very different from Recanati, after all!

Moreover, Leopardi's own deformity, as he well knew, was a peculiarly unfortunate one: it aroused not only contempt, but ridicule. A hunchback (provided that he be a man, since in a woman the same deformity brings ill-luck) may be accorded a good-humoured tolerance. He may sell you a lucky number in a lottery, or, if you succeed in rubbing shoulders with him in the street, he may bring you unexpected good news or good fortune. But, like the Court jester of the Middle Ages, he is not a *man*. Certainly no commonplace little coquette would dream of loving such a creature. All this Leopardi knew, yet it was with a woman of this mind—a woman essentially frivolous, sensual, and insensitive—that he fell in love.

How must he have appeared to her, at their first meeting? 'His stature', says Ranieri, 'was mediocre, slight and bent, his complexion pale; his head was large, with a broad square forehead, languid blue eyes, a sharp nose and fine-drawn features. His voice was low and very faint, and he had an indescribable heavenly smile.'[3] The picture is not unprepossessing, but it is scarcely that of a conqueror of women. Except in the company of a few intimate friends, the 'heavenly smile' that Ranieri saw was hidden beneath a mask of reserve and contempt; the 'fine-drawn features' were pinched with suffering; the low voice spoke very seldom, and then without eloquence. Only an exceptionally kind and perceptive woman would have taken the trouble to discover the qualities of such a lover—and Fanny Targioni, although not heartless, had no exceptional qualities. The wife of Antonio Targioni Tozzetti, a famous Florentine doctor and botanist, she was not the accomplished siren whom some of Leopardi's earlier biographers have depicted; she was merely a *femme moyenne sensuelle*—devoted to her children, generous to her lovers, kindly to her friends, not unkind, it appears, even to her husband—attractive, amorous, lively, pretentious and commonplace.

Leopardi was introduced to her by the poet and patriot Alessandro Poerio, who, in a letter to Ranieri, remarked that Florentine gossip attributed to the lady no less than four lovers, 'but I believe that two of them at least are imaginary'; and in any case, he added, 'she is now all literature and gentility'.[4] Aspasia was the name Leopardi chose to give her, but there is no reason to believe that she had the intelligence of her Greek prototype. Pretty, young, surrounded by a circle of admirers, she did not object to increasing their number. But she greatly preferred the handsome young Ranieri to his melancholy companion; Leopardi, to her, was merely 'il mio gobbetto'.*

Yet even a hunchback could have his uses. Fanny collected autographs, and soon we find Leopardi writing to his literary friends for letters for the album of 'a lady, who is both beautiful and amiable, is indeed beauty and amiability itself'.[5] Paolina was told to send her brother all the literary letters he had left behind at Recanati, and soon he was able to enrich his lady's album with many signatures—and to feel, perhaps, that he was not entirely unwelcome.

Then spring came, and with it an afternoon that he has made memorable. Calling at her house, he came upon Fanny on the sofa, surrounded by flowers, with her children playing about her. In that moment, he wrote, 'a new heaven and a new earth, almost a divine light, appeared to him'.† From that day he loved her—nor was it long before the whole of the little provincial society was in possession of his secret—of which they saw none of the pathos, but only the absurdity. 'Do you know that your friend Leopardi is rather queer?' wrote Juliette de Villeneuve to Giordani. 'While he was here, he used to go every evening to pay his court to the Sacrati, who laughs at him.' Marchesa Orinzia Sacrati, in her youth, had been beautiful, cultured, charming, and intriguing, and the mistress of a celebrated *salon* in Rome. But now her youth was gone; 'a

* My little hunchback.

† Apparve
Novo ciel, nova terra, e quasi un raggio
Divino al pensier mio.
This scene is described in Leopardi's poem *Aspasia*, written two years later.

P

fat little old woman in a yellow wig, who was always to be found spinning silk, never rising from her seat', she consoled herself for the passing of love by promoting the affairs of others, and it was at her house that Leopardi was ever hoping to meet his Aspasia.

Did he realize, one wonders, that he was being laughed at? Perhaps he did—perhaps it was after those evenings that he would hurry home to his rooms in Via del Fosso, and there, safe from those mocking echoes, would indulge, as Ranieri has related, in 'vain and unrestrained soliloquies of love, which went far beyond the limits fit for the dignity of so great a man'. Indeed, it was at this time that a malicious story was told which, according to Carducci, was still current in Florence long after Leopardi's death. The poet, it was said, used sometimes to dress up a boy—a relation of Fanny's who resembled her greatly—in a woman's shawl, and would then spend many hours 'gazing at him, and saying to him what he did not dare to say to his Aspasia'.[6] The story is probably—indeed almost certainly—untrue, but that it should have been invented is significant.

It is not easy for successful Don Juans like Ranieri to understand a predicament so far outside their own experience; yet Ranieri does seem to have realized that the sad, sickly little man who had become his friend was under the sway of a passion no less violent than his own, although so different in its manifestations. 'This man', he wrote, 'took the flower of his virginity untouched to the grave, and for that very reason loved twice, although without hope, as no other man has ever loved before. . . . Almost all his loves', he added, 'were one-sided, and unnoticed by the person he loved. They became all the more intense and ardent.'[7] The first of these infatuations had been the one for Geltrude Lazzari; the second and the last, for Fanny Targioni. But now the self-consciousness, the tongue-tied shyness of adolescence, had turned into the deeper, more humiliating self-distrust of a man whose consciousness of his deformity had become an obsession, and whose passions had never yet found a normal fulfilment.

> Sempre in quell' alma
> Era del gran desio stato più forte
> Un sovrano timor.*

* Always, in that soul, an overmastering fear had prevailed over great desire.
                                                              Consalvo.

So Leopardi himself described the conflict within him—a conflict which was never resolved.[8] Certainly, at the time of his first visit to Rome, he would gladly have exchanged all his poetic gifts, all his erudition, for the robust self-assurance and easy conquests of his brother Carlo. 'Whether it be spring or autumn,' he wrote to him wistfully, 'I really do not know what finer occupation there can be than making love—and assuredly it is ten times better to speak to a pretty girl than to roam, as I am doing, round the Belvedere Apollo or the Capitoline Venus.'[9] And in the same breath—in a pathetic attempt to emulate the cheap cynicism of other young men, to appear a man of the world in his cousin's eyes—he was expressing most unconvincing sentiments of contempt for the whole female sex. 'I should be insulting your common sense', he told Giuseppe Melchiorri, 'in reminding you that women are not worth our love and our suffering. . . . We must hold for an absolute axiom that there neither is nor can be a woman who deserves to be seriously loved.'[10]

So he wavered between desire and apprehension, between contempt and awe: not the first young man to do so, but more intense and humourless, more self-absorbed and fastidious, than others—and far more tragically handicapped. And always, beneath all this, lay a deeper and less easily defined disquiet—the fear that what he was really craving was something, in its very essence, unattainable —'another kind of delight'. 'The first feeling that beauty in the other sex arouses in a man', he wrote in his notebook at the age of twenty-five, 'is fear. . . . And this fear arises from the fact that it seems to him impossible to go on existing without the object of his desire, and at the same time equally impossible to possess it as he would wish; for even physical possession (though at that moment far from his thoughts) would never fully satisfy him or fulfil his desire. . . . And the violence of his longing fills him with terror.'[11]

Thus it was that, with every lost opportunity, every fancied snub, Leopardi's first adolescent attitude to love hardened and became crystallized. What he feared was not merely a rebuff; perhaps his real dread was rather of success—and of finding, then, the deeper dissatisfaction he had always foreseen, the 'unaccountable void that nothing can fill'. Geltrude Lazzari, Teresa Malvezzi, and now Fanny Targioni, what were they for him but shadows on a wall,

—paper silhouettes of his 'heavenly original', *la donna che non si trova*.

Nowhere is this attitude more clearly revealed than in the poem which Leopardi wrote at the height of his love for Fanny Targioni, *Il pensiero dominante*. This poem is not addressed to his lady, but to his abstract idea of love—his obsessive 'dominating thought'.

> Dominator di mia profonda mente;
> Terribile, ma caro
> Dono del ciel. . . .*

For this, he wrote, he thirsted during the dusty emptiness of social intercourse, as a wayfarer on a stony mountain seeks a green meadow. Only in his obsession could he feel himself like the gods; only then could he experience the sense of supreme power, of super-human exaltation, that comes even to unrequited lovers; only then, fully realize the triviality of all the rest of life. Its dangers—even death, the 'supreme necessity'—lost their power to alarm; all human opinions, ambitions, pride, became of small account.

> Avarizia, superbia, odio, disdegno,
> Studio d'onor, di regno,
> Che sono altro che voglie
> Al paragon di lui? Solo un affetto
> Vive tra noi; quest'uno,
> Prepotente signore,
> Dieder l'eterne leggi all'uman core.†

For more than a year Leopardi thus lived upon two planes: sometimes sitting, in his new blue suit, in the penumbra of Fanny Targioni's drawing-room—a silent, incongruous figure among the somewhat flashy young men, the florid ladies, who assured the success of her evening parties; sometimes a god-like lover, dwelling

---

* Sovereign of my inmost mind,
  Awful but cherished boon of heaven. . . .

† Pride, Avarice, Hate and Scorn,
  The itch for Fame and Power,
  Beside this thought, are merely fitful whims;
  One passion reigns alone—
  Fate to the human heart a single Tyrant gave.
  Il pensiero dominante.

alone in the *pays des chimères*. But then Ranieri, to further his own love-affair, insisted on carrying him off to Rome, and Leopardi discovered that, though he had found little happiness by Fanny's side, to be cut off from her was unendurable. His talk of 'bitter exile', his detestation of everything in Rome, his return to Florence early in March before the cold weather was really over—all are explained by his desire to get back to his Aspasia.

During the long winter of his absence even the consolation of letters was denied him. All that he received was a formal greeting, sent in a long letter to Ranieri, in which Fanny plainly showed how little she thought about Leopardi at all; her concern was all for Ranieri. And indeed the only letter that the poet dared to send her in the course of the winter could hardly have enlightened her as to his feelings.

'I have not written to you before,' he began, 'so as not to be tedious to you, since I know how busy you are, but I do not want my silence to seem forgetfulness—although perhaps you know that to forget you is no easy matter. You said to me one day that you often do not answer letters from your closest friends, but only those from other people—because the former would not be offended, like the latter, by your silence. Do me the honour of treating me as one of your greatest friends, and if you are very busy, or if writing tires you, do not answer me. I greatly desire your news, but shall be content to have it from Ranieri or Gozzani.'

This sentence hints at a strange feature of this unhappy infatuation. Aware that he himself had not the power to attract a pretty, spoiled young woman, Leopardi was willing to take any place, however humble, among those who were competing for her affections. Little by little he must have come to realize her lively interest in his friend, and he seems to have succeeded in reconciling friendship and love in an affection which included both Fanny and Ranieri. The latter, indeed, was still passionately absorbed in his infatuation for his pretty, inconsistent mistress, Maddalena Pelzet, and did not return Fanny's feelings, but he seems to have carried on a love-affair, or at least a flirtation, with her all the same. So Giacomo and Fanny were soon united by a new bond, a wish to free their friend from his entanglement with 'Lenina'.

But to return to Giacomo's letter. 'I do not believe', he continued, 'that you expect any news from me. . . . Still less can I give you any literary tidings. I must confess to you that I am in great danger of forgetting the alphabet, from having lost the habit of either reading or writing. My friends are horrified, and they, for their part, are right to pursue fame or the welfare of mankind, but I, who do not presume to improve humanity, and do not aspire to fame, am not wrong either to spend my days lying upon a sofa, without moving an eyelid. And I find a great deal of sense in the habits of Turks and other Orientals, who are satisfied to sit cross-legged all day, vacantly contemplating this ridiculous existence of ours.'

Poor Fanny, we feel, must have been a little bored by all this and Leopardi, too, may have become aware of its inappropriateness, for all at once he changed his tone, and his heart was revealed.

'But I am wrong to write these things to you, who are beautiful and privileged by nature to shine and to triumph over human destiny. I know that you, too, are inclined to melancholy, as all sweet and gifted spirits always have been and will be. But in all sincerity, and in spite of my genuine philosophy of despair, I believe that for you melancholy is unsuitable, so that, although natural, it is not altogether reasonable. At least that is what I wish. Good-bye, dear Fanny,' he concluded, 'give my love to the little girls. If you will deign to command me, remember that for me, as for everyone else who knows you, it is a happiness and an honour to serve you. Your Leopardi.'[12]

At last the winter ended, and he could return to his 'dear and blessed Tuscany'. During the next few months both he and Ranieri continued to visit *casa Targioni*, but when the hot weather came, Ranieri's departure to Bologna and Fanny's to Leghorn left Leopardi alone. Florence in midsummer becomes a deserted city. Its inhabitants, if they have not been able to escape to the seaside or the neighbouring hills, take refuge from the heat behind closed shutters. During the long hours of the afternoon no one dares venture out into the glare of the Lungarno, between the dazzling river and the torrid heat of the sun-baked *palazzi*. Even in the dark, cool avenues of the Cascine no sound breaks the stillness, but the strident crackling of the cicadas; the air is heavy with the scent of limes and hazy with white dust. Then, in the tension of that summer heat, every nerve is quivering; every sense becomes more alive than usual, every feeling more intense—and in his room, alone, the poet dreamed of his Aspasia.

At last a letter came from her—a brief, flat little note, which he forwarded to Ranieri, and, when he answered, he did not dare to speak of his own love, but only of his friend's. For Ranieri had gone to Bologna to visit his mistress, who was acting there, and Leopardi had to tell Fanny that Ranieri was 'still absorbed in that love of his, which is making him unhappy in more ways than one. But all the same,' the poet added, 'love and death are the most beautiful things in the world, and certainly the only ones worthy of our desire. . . . Good-bye, most lovely and charming Fanny. I hardly dare to ask for your commands, knowing that I am good for nothing. But if will and desire have some value, as one is told, you should indeed consider me fit to obey you.'[13]

> Due cose belle ha il mondo
> Amore e morte.*

That is the theme of the two poems—*Amore e Morte* and *Consalvo* —which Leopardi wrote at this time, and which reveal a great deal more about his feelings than is expressed in his letters. In the first, Love and Death appear as the twin protagonists of a Leopardian myth, in which Love stands for the creative principle of life, Death for the powers of destruction; but at the end of the poem the figure of Death—ardently invoked by the poet—has suffered a shadowy identification with the beloved woman herself; and thus, in seeking death, the lover also finds fulfilment. The other poem of this period, *Consalvo*, is a less fortunate composition; it is, indeed, the most sugary and lithographic of Leopardi's poems, a work of which the only merit, as Carducci was the first to point out, is as a human document; 'as a work of art it has none'.[14] Consalvo is Leopardi himself, an unhappy lover in whom fear has always been stronger than desire. He reaches the last day of his life without having received a single sign of love, and at last, on his death-bed, asks a last gift—a kiss. His wish is granted and his ecstasy is complete; his whole life has found a meaning. '*Felice io fui, sovra tutti i felici.*'†

---

* The world has two fine things: they are death and love.

† Happy was I, the happiest man on earth.

Fanny read these 'varnished phrases' (the expression is Carducci's)
when they were published four years later, and wrote complacently
to Ranieri: 'Please give many messages from me to the excellent
Leopardi, whose poems have delighted me, especially *Consalvo*.'[15]

One other poem, though written two years later, was inspired by
Leopardi's love for Fanny—*Aspasia*. Here he described his first
glimpse of his lady, her unawareness of his love, the humiliating
time of his subjection—and his final liberation. Both in *Consalvo*
and in *Aspasia* all the stage property of the most lachrimose romanticism is brought out: kisses on children's lips, the scent of flowers,
the last embrace of a dying man. Yet even in *Consalvo*, which is the
poem most tainted by this kind of sentiment, Leopardi's anguish and
sincerity find their way through the conventionality of the images
evoked. Almost in spite of the poet, some deep reality pervades the
stage: behind the lay figures we see the ghosts of Fanny and Leopardi.

At the end of the summer Fanny returned to Florence, but Ranieri
was still absent in Naples, and although he still continued to write
to her, he was more deeply involved than ever in his affair with
'Lenina'. It was now that Fanny and Giacomo joined forces in an
attempt to free their friend from this entanglement—and indeed
Ranieri's state of mind might well cause them anxiety. 'I am ill,'
he wrote to his mistress, 'because I cannot live away from you. . . .
Exhausted and broken by so many sufferings, and conquered by the
most terrible passion that could ever be kindled in a man's heart . . .
if I ardently desire to descend into the grave, it is because the grave
is the only boon that will be granted me.'[16] Lenina, on her part,
was weakening; she was seriously considering leaving her husband
and children, and wrote to her elderly friend and admirer, the
Florentine playwright Gian Battista Niccolini, asking for his advice.
Her husband, she said, was so unreasonable that he would not leave
her in peace unless she gave up 'Tonino' [Ranieri], but 'Tonino goes
on saying that he cannot live without me, and that he would rather
die than lose me'. What was she to do? 'Tell me whether I dare
abandon myself entirely in Ranieri's arms, whether this young man
is worthy of my love, and whether I shall be able to live in peace
with him for the rest of my life.'[17]

It was not unnatural that Leopardi, confronted by such a danger
for his friend, should have preferred to see him return to Fanny. He

may even have found a bitter satisfaction—not out of keeping with the romanticism of the period—in sacrificing his own passion on the altar of friendship. But Lenina—either influenced by Niccolini, or merely following the dictates of her own prudence or inclination—at last gave Ranieri his *congé*, and Leopardi received a letter in which despair was mingled with dark threats of suicide.

'My Ranieri,' he replied, 'I could hardly believe my eyes in reading your letter of the 6th. Such vileness in a human and feminine soul is never credible until after the event, as in this case. I feel it is useless to express my pity for you, for the most eloquent words would be hopelessly inexpressive of the truth.'[18] It is clear from his letters that he was frequently seeing Fanny, and sharing his news of Ranieri with her. 'Fanny and I', he said, 'are trembling for you.' But at the beginning of January Lenina came back to Florence, and Leopardi wrote to warn his friend, who was also about to return there: 'I trust in your manliness to incur no danger from seeing this wretched person, who was always unworthy of you, and now is most unworthy.'[19]

Ranieri, however, delayed—perhaps, in spite of his 'manliness', not anxious to meet his recent mistress, perhaps aware that his three-cornered relationship with Fanny and Giacomo was causing some amusement to the provincial society of Florence. To a letter in which he hinted at this, Giacomo replied in a fine romantic vein: 'My poor Ranieri! If men laugh at you because of me, I am consoled by the thought that they are certainly also laughing at me because of you. . . . The world always mocks at those things which, if it did not mock, it would be forced to admire, and, like the fox, criticizes what it envies.'[20] Poor Leopardi! His situation, when stripped of its glamour, was not an enviable one. Was Fanny at least kind to him, we wonder? Did he taste the sweets of friendship, if not of love? But the end was rapidly approaching. On the 22nd of January 1833 he wrote to Ranieri: 'Fanny, with whom I am always speaking of you, begs me to give you her warm greetings.' Then, a week later: 'Fanny is more than ever yours, and always sends you messages. She has begun to favour me with her caresses so that I may forward her cause with you—to which *sum paratus*.'[21]

With this curious sentence every reference to Fanny ceases. We can only guess at what happened next. Did Ranieri, on his return to

Florence, tell Leopardi—in order to persuade him to move to
Naples—that Fanny had only been amusing herself with him? Or
did Fanny herself, in compassion or impatience, tell the unhappy
poet plainly that it was Ranieri whom she loved? We do not know.
We only know that the break was final.[22]

So now, once again, he was alone. His loneliness and humiliation,
his sense of betrayal, his renewed self-mistrust, the profound weariness that engulfed him, all find expression in the most concise,
poignant, and nakedly self-revealing of his poems: *A se stesso*.

> Or poserai per sempre,
> Stanco mio cor. Perì l'inganno estremo,
> Ch'eterno io mi credei. Perì. Ben sento,
> In noi di cari inganni,
> Non che la speme, il desiderio è spento.
> Posa per sempre. Assai
> Palpitasti. Non val cosa nessuna
> I moti tuoi, nè di sospiri è degna
> La terra. Amaro e noia
> La vita, altro mai nulla; e fango è il mondo.
> T'acqueta omai. Dispera
> L'ultima volta. Al gener nostro il fato
> Non donò che il morire. Omai disprezza
> Te, la natura, il brutto
> Poter che, ascoso, a comun danno impera,
> E l'infinita vanità del tutto.*

> * To Himself.

Rest now for evermore,
My weary heart. Dead is the last deceit
I thought unending. Dead. At last, I know,
Not hope alone, but all desire has fled
For dear deceits. Tremble no more, be still.
For nothing here is worth
Your flutterings now and nothing worth your sighs.
Bitter is life and dull, and that is all;
Earth's but a clod. Be still, cease to despair.
One boon alone by Fate
To men is granted: Death.
Henceforth thyself despise,
Nature despise, the brutish evil power
That stealthily ordains the common doom,
And all the endless vanity of things.

Fourteen years earlier, before he had ever left Recanati, a presentiment of great suffering had come to him. 'I have not yet seen the world, but when I do see it and come into touch with men, I shall certainly have to hide away within myself. . . . What I fear are the things that will wound my heart.' Now the pain that he had feared had come—and when it passed away, it took with it what was most vital in him. There is a point beyond which men do not continue to suffer. After the destruction of this 'last illusion' Leopardi lived on for four more years; he added a considerable amount to his work, both in poetry and prose. But he wrote no more love-poems, and he brought to an end the great day-book in which, for seven years, he had jotted down all his thoughts. Some vital spring was broken —'not hope alone, but all desire had fled'.

The despair of *A se stesso* is not the rationalized, intellectual pessimism of the *Operette Morali*. Once again Leopardi lays before us 'the hidden and mysterious cruelty of human destiny', but this time he employs no argument, points no moral. No, we hear something simpler and more moving: a human cry of pain.

The degree of importance which Fanny, for her part, attached to the whole episode may be guessed from her subsequent letters to Ranieri, when the two friends were living together in Naples. She frequently sent cordial greetings to 'the good Leopardi', 'our poor Leopardi', but on one occasion she wrote: 'How is he getting on? I am in disgrace with him, am I not? and *the great love* [the italics are Fanny's] has turned to hate. This has happened to me often.'[23]

After Leopardi's death, some of his friends persistently asked Fanny who Aspasia was; but she begged Ranieri to provide an answer. 'For pity's sake, tell me if you know it, and save me from a series of unnecessary and tiresome letters.'[24] She received a very clear reply. 'You', Ranieri wrote, 'are Aspasia, and you know it. . . . Nevertheless, when asked, I have always said that I do not know, because I am uncertain whether you are pleased or not, and I only want to do as you wish, as seems to me to be required of my delicacy.'[25]

But even after so plain an answer Fanny—whether sincerely or disingenuously—refused to be convinced. 'If I did not know how fond you are of teasing and angering me, I would say you are unkind in trying to depress me by your answer about Aspasia. You know better than anyone else whether I ever gave the slightest encouragement to that poor man, and whether it is in my character to amuse myself with an afflicted man, and a decent one like him. When you spoke to me about him *at that time*' [the italics are Fanny's, and presumably she is referring to the period of her three-cornered relationship with the two friends] 'I used to be angry, and would not even believe certain things to be true, as I still refuse to believe them now—and the affection I used to feel for him will continue, even though he is no longer alive. So pray be kind to me, don't talk any more nonsense, and spare me a heavy heart, by dispelling the thought that, even without intending it, I may have given a poor opinion of myself to so afflicted a man.' And she ended: 'I hope it is not necessary for me to add, after this, that I should consider it the greatest breach of friendship, if you told anyone else what you have just told me. It would cause a quarrel between us, for ever.'[26]

Moreover, there is—if the story is to be believed—an even more depressing postscript. In Fanny Targioni's old age, Matilde Serao—then a romantic young girl—asked the old lady how it had been possible for her not to love so great a poet? Fanny's answer was very brief: 'My dear, he stank.'[27]

Among Leopardi's papers in Naples, unpublished until long after his death, were found some notes for an ode to the stealthy, unconquerable power of evil, 'whom some call fate, nature, or God', but to whom he gave the name of Arimane. 'Oh god of evil,' he cried, 'why have you given to life an occasional semblance of pleasure, of love? Was it to torment us with desire, with self-comparison, with regrets for our youth?' In vain, he wrote, did the human race strive towards perfection; it was Arimane who would always prevail, since her weapons were boldness and deceit. And it was from this power that the poet implored—'since I have been your chief advocate, the apostle of your religion'—a single boon. 'Grant that I may not survive my seventh lustre. . . . I do not ask for what the world calls gifts; not for riches nor love, the only things worth living for. I beg for what is believed to be the greatest of evils, death. *Non posso, non posso più della vita.'*[28]

* I cannot, cannot bear life any longer.

XVI

HOPE DEFERRED
(1832—1833)

*Se ci contentiamo di vivere ancora . . . non è che per una illusione della speranza.**

ARLY one morning in September 1832 a good-looking,
effusive young stranger descended from the stage-coach which,
on its way through the Marches, paused to change horses at Recanati.
From the small boys who ran up to him, turning cartwheels and
begging for pennies, he inquired the way to *casa Leopardi*, but before
he had got very far, he encountered Conte Monaldo himself, on his
way to early Mass. The Count, as usual, was dressed from head to
foot in black, 'wearing a hat with a very broad brim, knee-breeches,
and shoes with great buckles of white metal. . . . He carried under
his arm a sort of large breviary.' On being accosted by a complete
stranger, he showed some surprise: 'But', says Ranieri, 'I, being
young and quick, freed him from his embarrassment in a moment,
saying: "*Signor Conte*, I am a great friend of your son Giacomo's
and I feel for him an inexpressible love and admiration. Passing
through Recanati, I have taken the opportunity of this halt to glance
at the house in which he was born."' Neither by his manner nor
his speech does the young man appear to have impressed the Count
favourably, for his only reply was that he was at this moment on
his way to Mass. 'A courteous, but cold and brief dialogue' ensued,
and ended with Ranieri's expressing once more his delight 'at
having met the father of so great a man'.[1] Whereupon he took his
departure, while the sombre, dignified, and slightly absurd figure

---

* If we are satisfied to go on living . . . it is only thanks to a mirage of hope.
Zibaldone, 1 July 1827.

of Conte Monaldo, his breviary under his arm, passed into the little church—and that is the last that we shall see of him.

Ranieri was on his way to Naples—drawn there by a filial piety which had been sharpened by an urgent need for money. A recent decree having granted permission for political exiles to return to the kingdom of Naples, his father had declared that unless he did so his allowance would cease, and this threat could not be disregarded, for both friends were in severe financial straits. On returning to Florence Leopardi had attempted to secure himself a livelihood by launching a weekly paper, which was to be entitled *Lo Spettatore*. He even got so far as to apply for the government's permission, and to draw up a 'preamble', in which the paper's plans were enounced in a characteristically negative form: it was not to be either 'literary, philosophical, political, or historical', nor would it concern itself with 'fashions, arts and crafts, inventions or discoveries'; it would not attempt to achieve any increase of industry, or any improvement of the social order. In short, its main purpose appeared to be to avoid the aims of the *Antologia*; it would merely try to please its readers. But the government did not grant its approval, and the plan was given up.

Next, with great reluctance, Giacomo turned to his father, with a request for a small monthly allowance. For seven years, he reminded him, he had made every effort to support himself, but now all his hopes had failed. 'Literature in Europe has come to an end; some of the publishers are bankrupt, others are becoming so. . . . It would be ridiculous to count on selling any literary work profitably in Italy.' As for himself, he had reached the end of his endurance; his only longing was for death. 'God be my witness to the truth of these words. He knows what ardent prayers I have made (even offering up *tridui* and *novene*) to obtain this boon. . . . If death lay at my command, I again call God to witness that I would not have written this letter, for life anywhere is an abominable torment to me.' But since live he must, and since to live in Recanati ('as I think even you were convinced by the last bitter experiment') was 'more than my greatest capacity for suffering can endure', he could not but ask his father's help. 'Twelve *scudi* a month would be enough. With twelve *scudi*, indeed, one cannot live comfortably in Florence, which is the cheapest town in Italy; but I do not aspire to live in comfort. I shall make such sacrifices that twelve *scudi* will suffice me.'[2]

Conte Monaldo, in reply, sent a gift of twenty-four *scudi* for the next two months, but only after some delay, during which Giacomo was again obliged to apply to him, confessing that he had made out a draft, of which the payment was overdue. 'I am in a cold sweat. . . . I implore you, if my honour is dear to you . . .'[3] But now the Count wrote that he could not promise his son a regular allowance without his wife's consent. Let him apply to *la mamma*—and to her, after a delay which reveals how distasteful the step was to him, Giacomo did appeal, with the arguments he thought most likely to convince her. 'To cause you this annoyance is a thousand times more painful to me than to you. But pray consider that, if I came home permanently, I should be a great expense and a great and constant inconvenience, with my strange habits and my melancholy.'[4] This sentence surely tells us all that we need to know about the relationship of this man and his mother. And the allowance—twelve wretched *scudi* a month—was granted.

Meanwhile Ranieri was still in Naples, trying to extract an allowance from *his* father, and Leopardi was waiting in Florence, alone and dejected. These were the months that saw his infatuation with Fanny Targioni draw to its bitter end, and his profound unhappiness was further increased by a severe attack of ophthalmia. 'He obstinately refuses to do anything about his eyes,' Fanny wrote to Ranieri (for at that time Leopardi was still seeing her) 'and I don't think he even keeps them clean. For this, too, your return would be useful.'[5] Meanwhile, Leopardi himself believed, as he had done once before, that he was losing his sight, and was so terrified of any ray of light that he spent his days not only in a darkened room, but in bed, with the bed-curtains drawn—unable to read or even, owing to his violent headaches, to be read aloud to, and often not getting up until dusk, and going back to bed before the dawn.[6]

His loneliness at this time is painful to contemplate. His intense preoccupation, during the past year, with Fanny and Ranieri, as well as differences of opinion, had gradually estranged him from many of his Florentine acquaintances. Colletta was now dead, several others of the circle had been banished, the *Antologia* itself had been suppressed, and even Giordani, after loudly praising the tolerance of the Tuscan police, had been exiled at twenty-four hours' notice. Giordani and Leopardi, moreover, had been on less happy terms in recent years. Perhaps the older man's irascible jealousy, which amounted almost to a disease, had been aroused by the poet's new attachments, perhaps the two men had merely grown away from each other. Certainly, after Leopardi's death, Giordani did not hesitate to accuse him of both selfishness and ingratitude. 'When he began to be well known, he ceased to write to me. In his writings he has spoken of many others, but not a word about me. Apparently his heart was not as great as his genius.'[7] The note of grievance is unmistakable—but the accusation is certainly unjustified: if, in later years, one of the two men cooled, it was Giordani himself. In 1828, presumably in answer to a letter of reproaches, Leopardi was writing to him, 'In this year you have got to know me better than in the past, you have realized that I am a nobody, and this I had often told you. But you must not therefore diminish your kindness to me, which was founded on the qualities of my heart, on the old and tender love I swore to you in the first flower of my youth, and have always felt for you, and shall feel until my death. You must know . . . that, except for my family, you are the only man whose affection has seemed to me such that I could turn to it for shelter—a pillar "against which my weary life can rest".'[8] And four years later, in 1832, he wrote to him calling him 'the greatest spirit I know, and to me the dearest'.[9]

At the time when this letter was written—during the last months of his infatuation for Fanny Targioni, and when Ranieri was away, Leopardi was once again overwhelmed by an intense desire for death. In a letter to Giordani, he told him about the death of a young friend, the son of Carlotta Lenzoni, in the following terms: 'Poor Enrico, as others say, or as I say, most fortunate Enrico, ended his short life on the sixth of last month. Study, drink, smoking, and love-making quickly wore him out and brought him to his death after two months of painless illness. . . . I shall never think of his fate without infinite envy.'[10]

It was at about this time, too, that Leopardi composed an inscription for a bust of Raphael: '*Felice per l'amore fortunato in cui arse —Felicissimo per la morte conseguita nel fiore degli anni.*'*

* Happy in the fortunate love which enflamed him. Most happy in his death, in the flower of his youth.

Q

In his desperate loneliness, all Leopardi's craving for affection was concentrated upon Ranieri. Even making full allowance for the romantic phraseology of the time and for the convention which permitted a very great warmth of expression between friends of the same sex, the poet's letters to Ranieri during this winter are surprising and painful reading. They are, perhaps, the letters he could not, dared not, write to Fanny. Scribbled on odd scraps of paper, in a hand that betrays both his blindness and his emotion, they plainly show that his longing for his friend's daily presence and support had become almost an obsession. In January he wrote three letters a week; in February and March, almost daily. He addressed Ranieri as 'my heart', 'my soul', 'my only hope'; he told him that he would give his eyes to comfort him, that he could not live without him; he sent him 'a million kisses'. Then came the news of Lenina's break with Ranieri, and Leopardi's first thought was one of terror lest this new turn of events might 'work against the union of our destinies, which we have thought and dreamed of for so long'. 'But, my Ranieri,' he concluded, 'you will never abandon me, never cool in your love. I do not want you to sacrifice yourself for me; on the contrary, I ardently wish you to consider, first and foremost, your own well-being. But whatever you decide, you will arrange matters in such a way that we can live for each other, or at least that I can live for you, my last and only hope. Good-bye, my soul, I strain you close to my heart, which in every possible and impossible event will remain yours eternally.'

A fortnight later three of his friend's letters were delayed. 'Will you believe that I have been a whole week without news of you? I will not add anything more, will not even ask you to imagine my state, for who in the world can imagine the nature of this death-like week? Oh, my Ranieri, my Ranieri, a boon too great, such as your friendship is, must be paid for by uncommon pain.' The letters followed each other at two days' interval, becoming briefer as Leopardi's eyesight deteriorated, but no less high-pitched in tone. 'Remember, my Ranieri, that you alone—the only thing left in the world that has any value for me—render bearable in my eyes the time I still have to live.' Ranieri must have written hinting at a further delay, for now Leopardi, in spite of his ill-health, was prepared to set out for Naples. 'What, if you cannot get away, shall I not come to you? Shall we not be united all the same, and soon? I am threatened with the loss of my sight and cannot write; but listen, Ranieri, in memory of all the time we have spent together, remember that I must, by God, embrace you again before I die.' February came, and Ranieri was still in Naples. 'I need not repeat to you that I am always and in every way at your beck and call: a meagre consolation, but the only one left to us. My soul, my poor Ranieri, calm yourself for my sake. Surely some time I shall be allowed to comfort you. Farewell with a thousand kisses, an unending farewell.' The letters become still shorter; one was no more than this: 'My soul, my eyes will only allow me to greet you. I have your letters of the 9th and 12th, which console me for every ill. Farewell.'

As the weeks passed the notes became little more than a cry of longing and of pain. 'My Ranieri, I long for you as for the Messiah. Whether or not I can do without you, you well know. I send you a thousand kisses.' A week later: 'Believe, my Ranieri, that this scrap which I am writing, represents the very most I am capable of. My father and brother write complaining that they receive no answers to their letters, that they had no news of me for three months, and I do not even finish reading their letters. All day I cry out for you.'

At last Ranieri announced his return; but still the days wore on and he did not appear. On the 16th of March Leopardi told him that 'the well-beaten mattresses have been waiting in your room for months'. On the 2nd of April he asked: 'Will this still find you in Naples? I warn you that I can live without you no longer. I am possessed by a morbid impatience to see you again, and feel sure that if you delay any more, I shall die of melancholy before seeing you. Farewell, farewell.'[11]

Ranieri, on his side, was in a difficult position. Much as he might wish to return to his friend, he could not do so until he had secured an allowance from his father, and he was also held in Naples by his passionate devotion to his sister Paolina. But when, according to his own account, he told Paolina that he had left in Florence a friend who was dangerously ill and who needed his care, she generously cried out: 'Go and fetch him, bring him here, and I promise you that I will nurse him like a sister of charity.' 'And Papa?' asked Ranieri, not unnaturally wondering what his father would say to this new addition to the household. 'And Papa . . . well, we shall see.'¹² And so, in the middle of April, Ranieri set out for Florence.

By this time Leopardi's eyesight was better, but his spirits had not improved, and when Ranieri arrived in Rome, he found the following note: 'God grant that I may see you before I die; it now seems to me hardly likely, although certainly not through your fault. Farewell, ὦ πολύ ἐπιχαλούμενε,* farewell with all my heart.'¹³

Ranieri characteristically took this literally, and lost no time in informing Giacomo's relations that the poet was dying, while he himself set off post-haste for Florence. On arriving there, according to his own account, at dawn on the 20th of April, he found the poet at death's door, 'but God again granted me the grace to save him'. The truth, however, appears to have been somewhat less dramatic, for only a few days later Vieusseux was able to reassure Paolina Leopardi, who had written to him in agonizing anxiety,¹⁴ by telling her that 'our dearest Giacomo is in such good health that he was able to spend the evening, on the day before yesterday, in my *salon* until midnight'.¹⁵ And shortly afterwards a note came from Giacomo himself, saying that he was sorry to have caused her so much distress. 'God knows', he concluded, 'that I cannot, cannot write. But rest assured, I cannot die either. My organism (so my excellent doctor affirms) has not enough strength left to contract a mortal illness.'¹⁶ 'But what consolation', comments Paolina, 'is that to me, when from those few lines it is so plain that he is anything but well, anything but happy?'¹⁷

* Oh much-beloved.

XVII

TO NAPLES
(1833—1835)

*Incolume il desio, la speme estinta.**

ON Ranieri's return to Florence he at once announced to Leopardi his determination to take him as soon as possible to Naples; the mildness of the climate, he assured him, could not fail to benefit his health, and the gaiety of the Neapolitans to cheer his spirits. They would take a small flat and live there together, with the angelic 'Paolina' to look after them; they would begin 'a new life'. Leopardi was only too ready to be convinced. Like most valetudinarians, he was always prepared to believe in the value of any change, and he had little enough to leave behind in Florence. This was the time of his final break with Fanny, the summer in which he wrote *A se stesso* and the *Dialogue between Tristan and a Friend*. As soon as the midsummer heat had passed, he was ready to start; and on the 2nd of September 1833 the two friends set out.

Once again they made the journey slowly, in a tightly sealed carriage; and when they got to Rome they paused there for three weeks, so that it was not until the first of October that they arrived in Naples. Leopardi's first impressions were favourable: 'The mildness of the climate, the beauty of the city, and the amiable and welcoming disposition of its inhabitants are very pleasing to me.'[1]

The amiable welcome, however, had not come from Ranieri's father. Though he had now granted his son permission to live with his friend, he himself showed no inclination to invite a guest who

---

* Desire unspent, but hope for ever gone.
                                        Il tramonto della luna.

229

was both (as he believed) a consumptive and an atheist, and it was
only through the kindness of a Greek friend that some lodgings were
found in Palazzo Boerio, not far from the city's main street, Toledo.
But these rooms were soon given up, for their landlady was so
horrified by Leopardi's sickly appearance that she raised the rent in
the hope of getting rid of him, while he on his side maintained
(though Ranieri declared it to have been only a nightmare) that
thieves, living in the same house, had broken into his room one
night.[2] Eventually, however, the two friends settled down in
Palazzo Cammarota, in Via Nuova S. Maria Ognibene. Here, on
the slopes of the Vomero, they enjoyed a fine view of the bay,
contemplating 'the smoke of Vesuvius by day, and the burning lava
by night', and here—served by an old man-servant of Ranieri's,
Pasquale Ignarra, 'a very fine cook'—they lived for nearly eighteen
months.

At this time both friends believed that they would only stay for a
short time in Naples. They were planning to go to Paris, where
they would find the support of De Sinner, or to Prussia, where
Niebuhr said he would assist them. But what they were going to
live on in either place, once they got there, was not clear—nor how
Leopardi's health could stand the strain of a long journey. From
some letters of Fanny Targioni's at this time (for she was still corresponding with Ranieri) it is plain that at least some of Ranieri's
friends considered the poet's presence to be nothing but a burden.
'I think a journey to Paris would distract you, but how can you
undertake it, with the eternal and legitimate companion you have
given yourself? Now don't be angry. I appreciate and value this
friendship of yours for Leopardi more than I can say, but I can see
that he is going to be a great stumbling-block in the road of your
life, and that you have made it too unbreakable a bond. The health
and way of life of Leopardi is too unlike that of your vigour and
your youth!'[3]

Ranieri, however, with his usual optimism, was convinced that
the journey would be possible, and that once they got to Paris a
means of livelihood would turn up. It is pathetic, indeed, to see, in
Leopardi's letters at this time, how his natural pessimism and prudence were temporarily dispelled by Ranieri's facile hopefulness.
'My health', he wrote to De Sinner, 'does not frighten me any more.

I have become convinced in Naples that my ailments are affected as little by the South, as by the North; the difficulty lies rather in our means—but more for the journey than for a livelihood, since, once I had arrived, I imagine it would not be difficult to find a way to live [in Paris] as cheaply as I do in Italy.' Leopardi went on to ask whether an edition of the Italian Classics, selected and annotated by himself, would be successful in France. 'I should have the efficacious help of my friend Ranieri, to whom I am dictating this, and who has joined his destiny to mine.'[4] But De Sinner replied that a foreigner's only hope of earning a living in Paris was to become a regular contributor to a review, and that this was by no means an easy post to obtain.[5]

Discouraged by this reply, the friends set about making other plans, but all of them failed. In Leopardi's correspondence he was constantly declaring himself on the point of departure; but his next letter would contain fresh reasons for delay. The truth was that neither of the two friends had enough money to travel. The story of their life in Naples, as revealed by both Leopardi and Ranieri, is one of grinding poverty and anxiety,[6] and Leopardi's efforts to supplement their income were as varied as they were unsuccessful. He thought of opening a private school; he had a scheme of launching a literary review; he planned a collection of translations from foreign authors; but all these plans fell through. He received fifteen *zecchini* from his Florentine publisher for a new edition of the *Operette Morali*, but the whole sum was needed to pay his debts.[7] In July 1835 he got so far as to sign a contract with a Neapolitan printer, Saverio Starita, for a complete edition of his works, in six volumes; but the paper and the print were both, in the poet's opinion, 'infamous', and after the appearance of the first two volumes the censorship banned the rest of the edition, thus providing the printer with an excellent excuse for deferring any payment to the wretched author. He, meanwhile, had reached such a pitch of exasperation that he appeared one day in Ranieri's room armed with a stick, crying, 'I'm going out to beat someone!'[8] Ranieri succeeded in calming him down and took him out for a walk, but the poet's opinion of the Neapolitans was now formed. 'Their perfidy', he wrote to his father, 'is something unknown to anyone who does not know Naples.'[9] His only wish was 'to get away from these *lazzaroni* and *pulcinelli** both noble and plebeian, all thieves and b——s, all thoroughly deserving of the Spanish rule and of the gallows!'[10] This was the sentence which, when it met Ranieri's eyes at the time of the publication of the first two volumes of Leopardi's letters, was taken by him as a personal insult. 'When I heard', he wrote in 1853 to a lady of Recanati, 'that I had been called "deserving of the Spanish rule and of the gallows" I was plunged into a state of silent stupefaction, such as the Classics ascribe to the inhabitants of the Inferno.'[11] But his silence, as we have seen, was soon broken.

Meanwhile, day by day, Leopardi's financial troubles became more serious. On one occasion he was even pestered by the tax-collector for a small sum, in return for his exemption from military service, failing which (the picture can hardly be visualized) the poet might be called up for police duty.[12] He made out a draft for twelve *louis d'or* in Bunsen's name, he borrowed forty *ducati* from a certain Dr. Manni, promising to dedicate his translations to him in return, and finally, once again, he was obliged to turn to his father. The latter had, indeed, continued to send him a monthly allowance, but so small that Marchese Antici told him he considered it 'an insult to distributive justice'.[13] But later on it was this same uncle who delayed in honouring a draft that Giacomo had drawn in his name, and the poet, at the end of his resources, sent his father a desperate letter of appeal:

'You think I have spent these last seven years in a bed of roses, but it has rather been one of reeds.'[14] His need, he said, was so great that he had sometimes even gone short of bread, and his uncle's refusal to honour his bill would render him liable to arrest. 'None of you has ever in his life found himself—nor, thank God, ever will —in such terrible straits as those I have known very often, without any fault of my own.' Even his mother's heart, he wrote, would be softened 'when she sees the clothes in which I appear before her'; she would then deplore his uncle's 'hostile refusal'.[15] And indeed Ranieri's description of the poet's appearance at this time confirms this account. His only overcoat, the blue one which had been turned for Fanny's benefit, was seven years old; his socks were so threadbare and so much darned by Paolina Ranieri that her brother declared that Leopardi ought to write a poem about them. Even the

* Loafers and punchinellos.

wool in his mattresses was so thin that he could hardly get to sleep.

In all this, one can hardly fail to be struck by the fact that every attempt to earn some money was made by the invalid of the pair; never is it suggested that the young and able-bodied Ranieri, a qualified member of the Neapolitan Bar, should try to supplement his father's allowance! But in fairness it must also be said that to care for Leopardi left little time for any other occupation. Not only did he require constant nursing, but both Ranieri and Paolina read aloud to him, in turn, for the greater part of the day and the night, and as his sight failed still more he was obliged to dictate not only his letters but his writings. Almost all his works of this period are in Ranieri's hand, and it must be added that—partly owing to the low, indistinct voice of the speaker, and partly to the imperfect literacy of the transcriber—a number of minor errors thus found their way into the manuscripts.[16]

In May 1835 the two friends left the Palazzo Cammarota and moved to a new apartment in a higher and less crowded part of the town, Capodimonte, where Leopardi's health improved. Ranieri's sister Paolina was at last allowed to go and live with them, 'bringing with her', Ranieri wrote, 'peace and happiness'. . . . 'If', he went on, 'affection, charity, innocence, serenity, and consequent cheerfulness could become personified, that creature would be my angelic Paolina. . . . In Leopardi's eyes I saw a faint spark of happiness, such as I had not seen in him since the wretched state in which I found him on my return to Florence.'[17]

Leopardi does, indeed, seem to have been much attached to Paolina Ranieri—saying (but our only authority is still Ranieri) that only her presence made up to him for the lack of his own Paolina, at home. And she certainly nursed him with tenderness and devotion. But in other respects the household cannot be described as a happy one. Both Leopardi's and Ranieri's letters, as well as Ranieri's book, supply a painfully clear picture of the exasperation and weariness which at times overcame—to borrow Fanny's expression—both the 'eternal and legitimate companions'. Even in these days the differences in temperament between the Italians of the north and those of the south are very marked— and greater still is the difference between them in manner of life.

Ranieri and his sister were always kind, but their sensibility, like the vitality which had first attracted Leopardi, was that of the south—a sensibility that expressed itself in facile tears and pity and eloquent speeches—but did not help them to understand that their friend sometimes craved for quiet and privacy. Ranieri, moreover, was intensely and possessively jealous; in one passage of the *Sodalizio* he remarks on Leopardi's 'inexplicable desire to go out alone', and comments that this could only have been caused by his wish for 'certain free confabulations', with some men of whom Ranieri happened to disapprove. And when one of these acquaintances came to call, Ranieri would ostentatiously leave the room. Then Leopardi in a fit of exasperation would write home that he really did not think he could bear to stay on in 'this half-barbarian and half-African place, where I live completely isolated from everyone'.[18] Perhaps he even thought a little wistfully of his books and his quiet hours of work, in the peace of the Recanati library.

It is, however, impossible not to feel some sympathy, too, for Leopardi's hosts, for certainly he was neither an easy guest nor a docile patient. He was suffering greatly from insomnia, indigestion and breathlessness, and these ailments produced not only great irritability, but a neurasthenic refusal to heed the orders of the good Dr. Mannella, whom Ranieri had called in on his behalf. Mannella ordered the poet to give up all sweet dishes and especially all ices, but he had an unconquerable craving for them; he would sugar his coffee and lemonade until they resembled a syrup, and often, on days when he was feeling stronger, would steal out of the house, like a schoolboy, to buy himself the ices that he was not allowed at home. Sometimes, too, his host would find under his pillow a little *cache* of forbidden foods.

But at other times his regard for the doctor's orders was carried to the opposite extreme, equally characteristic of the neurasthenic.[19] If the doctor told him that his room was too dark, Leopardi would fling open the shutter and put his head out into the blazing Neapolitan sun; if the doctor protested, he shut himself up in total darkness. If advised exercise, he exhausted himself by a long walk up-hill; if warned against fatigue, he never set foot to the ground. If recommended to eat meat, he would live upon that alone, until another doctor told him to eat less, when he at once became a vegetarian.

Among the *carte Ranieri* there is a list in the poet's own hand of no less than forty dishes—of macaroni and cheese, rice puddings, potato soufflés, etc.—which appears to include all the food he thought he could eat with impunity. He was very fussy, too, about his bread. At Capodimonte 'there was a fine bakery, kept by an excellent Genoese woman, whom everyone called Madama Giro-lama; where certain long sticks of bread were baked in the Genoese fashion, and these he liked so much that he refused to eat any other bread'.[20] Certain sweet cakes, too, could only come from one special confectioner—Vito Pinto—and, moreover, the poet refused to eat any ices but his, and immortalized their maker's talents in verse.* Indeed, Ranieri expressed his conviction that perhaps the chief reason why Leopardi opposed the doctor's orders to move to the country, even when the cholera was raging, was that he could not bear to leave Vito's ices.

Even more trying to his hosts, however, were the poet's peculiar hours. For many years, as we have seen, he had preferred to sleep by day and sit up all night; and now poor Pasquale had to provide breakfast at four or five o'clock in the afternoon, and dinner at midnight. Moreover, he insisted on company, and Ranieri and his sister took it in turns to talk or read aloud to him, all through the night, or to write at his dictation, until they were reminded of the torture by which certain peoples of the East destroyed their prisoners: *captivos insomniis occidebant.*†[21]

Poverty and constant ill-health—both extending indefinitely into the future, without any reasonable hope of relief—these are trials which put any friendship to the test. It is easy to emphasize the more unpleasant aspects of Ranieri's friendship with Leopardi: the kudos which he gained from this association, the vanity and emo-tionalism with which he wrote about it in his old age. It is certainly true that Leopardi's tortured nerves sometimes betrayed him into irritable complaints—and also that Ranieri, when he was over eighty, responded with a lack of both dignity and restraint. The fact remains that during the last seven years of Leopardi's life Ranieri's devotion and unceasing care never failed him; from Ranieri, and

---

* *Quella grand' arte il cui barone è Vito*, the 'great art' being the making of ices.
† They killed their prisoners by depriving them of sleep.

from him alone, the poet received constant companionship, admiration, and love. To such a friendship, whatever its imperfections, our respect is due.

In spite of all irritations and flaws, this first summer at Capodimonte was perhaps the happiest period of Leopardi's time in Naples. His health was better and he was even able to enjoy the company of a few friends—among them the ardent Liberal poet, Alessandro Poerio (though he feared that Tommaseo might have poisoned his mind against him), the German historian Schulz, and, later on, the young German poet, August von Platen. He, at the first meeting, thought Leopardi's appearance 'absolutely horrible', but soon, like many others, he was conquered by the sweetness of his manner and the charm of his conversation. He continued, however, to be distressed by the poet's ill-health and by 'his manner of living, turning day into night',[22] and among the *carte Ranieri* there is a little card which he must have left on the two friends one morning:

> A.P. saluta
> Giacomo Leopardi
> che s'alza tanto tardi
> e Antonio Sempre-fuori
> dottissimi signori.*

Sometimes, even, Leopardi was able to go to the theatre, 'where', Ranieri wrote, 'I can still see him, leaning on his right elbow on the edge of the box, shading his eyes from the glare, and enjoying the famous *Socrate Immaginario* of the Abate Galiani, put to music by Paisiello and sung by Lablache'.[23] The theatres of Naples were then the best in Italy, and it is possible that Leopardi may have seen the first performance of *Il Trovatore*, which was given at the San Carlo during this year. But most of all he enjoyed the spectacle of Naples itself. He had always taken a childlike pleasure in watching any popular *festa* or animated scene, and now a similar delight to the one he had felt in watching the evening promenade on the Pisa Lungarno was awakened in him by the infinitely varied and lively spectacle of the Neapolitan streets.

---

* A.P. greets—Giacomo Leopardi—who always rises so late—and Antonio Always-Out, most learned gentlemen. *Carte Ranieri*, Ba. XV, 561 in Biblioteca Nazionale, Naples.

His first lodgings in Naples were near Toledo, which one English traveller called 'the loveliest street in the world', and another, 'the most depraved', and which caused Sainte-Beuve to remark that, as he walked along it, he was brought to doubt the perfectibility of human nature.[24] Here barefoot monks and richly-robed prelates, soldiers and fine ladies, misshapen beggars and prostitutes, fisher-men and sailors, artists and foreign milords, eyed and jostled and vied with each other in an unending carnival procession, a perpetual merry-go-round. Here the whole life of the city was led (as indeed it still is today) in the open street: everywhere vendors were crying their wares, *maccheronari* stirring their great cauldrons of macaroni, pastry-cooks handing out their crisp, hot *sfogliatelle* (puff-pastry), carriages and coaches, their horses adorned with great scarlet feathers and bells, parading up and down, horsemen and officers in full uni-form prancing by, money-changers rattling their coins, barbers plying their razors, letter-writers composing eloquent epistles of love, business, or hate. From the adjoining street of Santa Brigida came the aromas and cries of the fish-market—an inferno of bargains conducted in yells and shouts, of live eels still squirming in gutters, of glancing and darting fish in buckets—all lit up, at dusk, from the balconies by the sudden flare of fireworks and rockets and Bengal lights. All this vigour and violence and clamour had a strange attraction for Leopardi. 'Naples attracted him', Ranieri wrote, 'as a star attracts a planet.'

Sometimes, when he was well enough, he would slip out of the house alone, and would let himself be carried along in the noisy, jostling crowd. Twice the Chevalier Bunsen, driving by in his am-bassadorial carriage, had a glimpse of him on the quay at Santa

For *Il Trovatore*, on page 236, read *Lucia di Lammermoor*.

sack of the mendicant friars, while the fish-women screamed and bargained and tore each other's hair.

> Che dirò delle triglie e delle alici?
> Qual puoi bramar felicità più vera
> Che far d'ostriche scempio infra gli amici?
> Sallo Santa Lucia, quando la sera

Poste le mense, al lume delle stelle,
Vede accorrer le genti a schiera a schiera,
E di frutta di mare empier la pelle.*

Here, in summer, the seller of blazing red water-melons cried, 'O *fuoco, o fuoco, chiamate e' pumpieri,*† and in the winter the chestnut-seller held out his scalding chestnuts. Here, at the day's end, the rag-and-bone picker, the *muzzonaro,* raked the road for cigarette-ends and rags and bones, by the light of his little lantern, calling out his melancholy little refrain:

Munnezzariello
Senza malizia
Solo sporchizia
Saccio levà.‡

The bagpipe-player, *lo zampognaro,* played on his pipes, a ragged girl sang the latest song from Piedigrotta, *Te voglio bene assaie,*§ while, a few feet away, a half-naked boy capered for halfpence—'as happy as the South Sea savages', Stendhal wrote, 'before the missionaries came there'. The *pazzariello*—the wine-vendor—summoning his clients by the beat of a drum, handed round his flask of new wine from mouth to mouth; a fortune-teller spun his wheel, an old woman sold lottery-tickets, and a strolling singer, the *cantastorie,* told for the thousandth time the love of Pulcinella and Colombina, or the heroic deeds of *Orlando innamorato.*

This was the part of the crowd where Leopardi was most often to be seen. He even, if we are to believe Ranieri, did not disdain to buy tickets for the lottery, or would suggest lucky numbers to eager

---

* What shall I say of mullets and anchovies? What truer happiness can a man desire, than to guzzle oysters among his friends? Santa Lucia knows it, when at night, after the tables are laid beneath the stars, she sees people running up in a dense crowd, to fill their bellies with sea-fruit.
   I nuovi credenti.
† Fire! Fire! Call the firemen.
‡ Rag-and-bone-picker
   Meaning no harm,
   'Tis nothing but rubbish
   I've under my arm.
§ I love you very dearly.

members of the crowd—for did not a hunchback bring good luck?[25]
But above all he liked to listen to the epic tales of Orlando and Rinaldo, told with dramatic pathos and Gargantuan laughter. Always
these heroes had fascinated him; in the *Zibaldone* he had compared
their characters, as if they had been living men, with those of Hector
and Achilles. And now he could hear their stories sung, as the tales
of Troy were told, and stand spellbound among listeners no less
enthralled, no less quickly moved to tears and laughter, than Homer's
hearers. 'They take sides', he wrote, 'with the heroes with such
ardour that, after the story, as they talk it over among themselves,
they argue and come to blows, and sometimes even kill each
other.'[26]

It is not difficult, I think, to understand the fascination that such
scenes as these held for Leopardi. 'A stranger here'—not only in
Naples, but in life itself—he watched this apotheosis of human vigour
and activity with the peculiar vision, both sharper and more detached
than an ordinary man's, that is generally only granted to a foreigner
—and yet, at the same time, he could almost fancy himself a part of
it. Anonymous, obscure, unnoticed, one more little hunchback in
the crowd, he could enjoy a vicarious sense of colour and of life.

Sometimes, too, Ranieri, setting out anxiously in search of him,
would find him sitting in a small café in the Largo della Carità,
eating one after another of Vito's unparalleled ices:

> . . . al romorio
> De' crepitanti pasticcini, al grido
> Militar, di gelati e di bevande
> Ordinator, fra le percosse tazze
> E i branditi cucchiai. . . .*

The lines are not good ones, but how strange to find the subject
treated at all by Leopardi's pen!

Sometimes, too, but much less often, he would go to the grander
Caffè d'Italia, in Piazza San Ferdinando, the meeting-place of the
Neapolitan writers and artists. But he hardly ever spoke to any of
them. They would watch him crouching alone at a corner table, his

---

* Among the crackle of little cakes, and soldiers shouting as they ordered drinks
and ices, and brandished spoons clattering midst the cups.
                                                        Palinodia.

large head sunk into his high shoulders, his reddened eyes half-closed, sipping one syrupy cup of coffee after another, without speaking or looking up. '*O ranavuottolo*', they called him—the little toad.

The Neapolitan intellectuals did not like him, and he did not like them. He was as little in sympathy with their proselytizing Catholicism as he had been with the humanitarian Liberalism of the *gabinetto Vieusseux*. '*I nuovi credenti*' was his name for them—the New Believers—and it was under this name that he satirized them in a bitter, unpleasant little poem in *terza rima* (only published after his death) in which he described these apostles of virtue and reform as too stupid even to be unhappy:

> Racquetatevi, amici. A voi non tocca
> Dell' umana miseria alcuna parte,
> Che misera non è la gente sciocca.*

They, on their side, thoroughly disapproved of Leopardi's philosophy, and did not care much for his verses. Among the new works in the edition of *I Canti* published in Naples in 1835 was a long poem entitled *Palinodia* and dedicated to Gino Capponi—*candido Gino*—a political and social satire which attacked all the most cherished ideals and aims of Capponi and his friends, and, to a large extent, also those of the Neapolitan school. But the poem is not one of Leopardi's most fortunate works; its subject is not one that lends itself to poetical treatment, and the verses are often mechanical and flat, the irony ponderous and bitter. Moreover, not unnaturally, the whole work caused considerable annoyance both in Florence and Naples. A review in the chief Neapolitan periodical, *Il Progresso*, compared Leopardi's poems most unfavourably with the *Inni Sacri* of his cousin Terenzio Mamiani—a poet who has long since retired into well-deserved obscurity—and another critic wrote that Leopardi's new works 'could only greatly detract from the author's previous reputation'.[27] Even Leopardi's own friends were tepid. 'Your *Palinodia*', De Sinner wrote to him, 'is precisely the same thing in verse as your *Tristan and a Friend* in prose. I prefer the latter.'[28]

---

* Be tranquil, friends,
  Naught touches you of human wretchedness,
  Grief spares the fool.
      I nuovi credenti.

Nevertheless, Leopardi continued in this vein. During the winter he began another long satirical poem in *ottava rima*, *I Paralipomeni della Batracomiomachia*, and this he went on with during the following year—dictating its stanzas to Ranieri, when his eyesight failed him—and only finished it a few days before his death.[29] This work was a continuation of the Greek *Battle of Mice and Frogs*, which Leopardi had translated in his youth; but while the Greek poem is a parody of the Homeric battles of the *Iliad*, the Italian one is a satire on the Neapolitan revolution of 1820. The mice are the Neapolitans, the frogs the Papal subjects, and the crabs the Austrians. The *Paralipomeni* contains a few descriptive passages of great beauty, but its laughter, like that of the *Palinodia*, has a spiteful ring, and its gloom is that of disgust, rather than of despair. We are made conscious, once again, that irony was not Leopardi's weapon.

The Neapolitan edition of *I Canti*, however, did contain several other new works which must be mentioned: the three poems referring to his love for Fanny Targioni—*Aspasia*, *Consalvo*, and *A se stesso*—and also two others composed in Naples, the odes *Sopra un bassorilievo antico sepolcrale* and *Sopra il ritratto di una bella donna, scolpito nel monumento sepolcrale della medesima*. Both these poems, of which the first has some lines faintly reminiscent of the *Ode to a Grecian Urn*, reveal, in spite of the beauty of single lines or phrases, the deep spiritual lassitude that had overcome the poet. Both are variations on a familiar theme—the rapid passing, the inexorable end, of life—but they are now lamentations without passion, almost without grief.

> Morte ti chiama: al cominciar del giorno
> L'ultimo istante.*

As fugitive as human beauty is the passion it inspires; as the body turns into dust, so, too, crumbles the dream.

It would, however, be entirely misleading to suggest that Leopardi's poems had no admirers in Naples. Not only was his work appreciated by such personal friends as Poerio and Von Platen, but it was beginning to be known by the young, and among his most

---

* Death calls to you: even as day dawns
  The last encounter.
> *Sopra un bassorilievo antico sepolcrale.*

R

fervent disciples were the pupils of Marchese Basilio Puoti's famous school of literature. One day the poet went to visit them; De Sanctis, who was then one of the pupils, has left us an account of the occasion. 'When the day came', he wrote, 'our expectations were very great. The Marchese was correcting a passage of Cornelius Nepos, which we had translated, but we could not attend: we were watching the door. At last he entered, Conte Giacomo Leopardi! . . . All our eyes were upon him. The Colossus of our imagination seemed, at first sight, meanness itself; not only a man like other men, but inferior to others. In that emaciated, expressionless countenance all the life was concentrated in the sweetness of his smile.'

After listening to the boys' orations, Leopardi addressed them, making some statements that were in contradiction with Marchese Puoti's teachings. He said, 'to the great surprise of us all', that to make use of the word *onde* with the infinitive 'was not, to his mind, a mortal sin', and that, in both speech and writing, propriety was more important than elegance. 'If one of us had dared to say such a thing, he [Puoti] would have lost his temper; but the Count spoke so sweetly and modestly, that he did not answer a word.'[30]

Several of the other students were so much charmed by the poet that they went to Ranieri's house, to see him again; but De Sanctis was too shy to join them. 'I never saw again the man who had made so profound an impression on my spirit.' But when, in the following autumn, he came back to school, the new edition of the *Canti* had just appeared: 'I was mad about it, and had the book always in my hand.' The boy had been taking lessons in declamation, and had often been called upon to show his talents in reciting Dante's famous *Canto* about Conte Ugolino—but, he wrote, '*Consalvo* made me forget Conte Ugolino. . . . I went about declaiming it through the streets, as if I were drunk—like Columbus in the streets of Madrid, when he was thinking of a new world. I recited it on all possible occasions, moving even myself to tears . . . only I remember that, out of delicacy towards the young ladies present, where the poet said "kiss" I changed the word to "look".'[31]

The impression made on the schoolboy was never effaced. When, a few years later, De Sanctis began to hold a course in literature himself, Leopardi was the first of the modern poets whom he taught his pupils to admire. He may, indeed, claim to be the first critic who assigned to Leopardi his true place in Italian literature; and all that he wrote about him is worth reading. In those early days, however, his enthusiasm was wholly uncritical. 'We recited all the *Canti*', he wrote, 'with equal admiration; our taste was not yet sufficiently discriminating to make distinctions—and besides, we would have thought it irreverent.'³² And, when the lesson was over, the students and their young master would sometimes set off together to what was then the suburban village of Pozzuoli, on a pilgrimage to Leopardi's tomb. 'The villagers would look at us with wondering eyes, thinking we were going to fulfil a vow.'

XVIII

THE SETTING OF THE MOON
(1836—1837)

Così d'affanno e di temenza è sciolto.*

I

WE have now come to the last two years of Leopardi's life. At the end of 1835, in one of the few letters he was still able to write, he said to his sister, 'Dear Pilla, I am overcome with melancholy, when I think what a long time I have spent without seeing you all', and he promised that, on his return, she should have stories and talks enough to make her happy for many evenings.[1] And to his father, early in the following year, he repeated that he hoped to be with him before the spring was over, adding that this long time of absence had only increased the love he felt for them all.[2] But in April he went with Ranieri to spend a few days in a little village above Torre del Greco, some twelve miles from Naples, which had been lent to them by Ranieri's brother-in-law, the advocate Antonio Ferrigni, and they liked the place so well that they remained there for nearly three months.

Here, we may hope, the poet found some peace. The little white villa where he lived—then hardly more than a whitewashed peasant's house—stood on the slopes of Vesuvius, far above the clamour of the fishing villages on the bay. To this day it is called, from the title of the great poem he wrote there, the *Villa della Ginestra*, and the traveller who makes a sentimental pilgrimage there, can still only reach it by the same rough footpath up which Leopardi rode on a donkey. Then, as now, the house stood in the midst of vineyards in which, as is the custom in that part of the country, the long tendrils of the vines are looped from one fruit-tree to another, from pear to

* Thus freed alike from anguish and from fear.

Coro dei Morti.

VILLA DELLA GINESTRA

almond, from apricot to plum—and the poet must have looked
down over their deep green to the blue distances of the bay. But
above the house, where a fine group of stone-pines now stands,
there was then no vegetation and no shade, but only, in the stony
desolation left behind by the passage of a stream of lava, a sea of
golden, scented broom—*la ginestra*.

Only twenty years before his visit, one of the most violent erup-
tions of Vesuvius ever known had brought desolation to the whole
of that hillside:

> . . . d'alto piombando,
> Dall' utero tonante
> Scagliata al ciel profondo,
> Di ceneri e di pomici e di sassi
> Notte e ruina, infusa
> Di bollenti ruscelli. . . .*

Leopardi would spend hours listening to the stories of an old man
who had witnessed the terrible scene, and who, as he told his tale,
would still look uneasily over his shoulder towards the menacing
mountain which had destroyed, in a single night, his family and his
fields.

> . . . E il villanello intento
> Ai vigneti, che a stento in questi campi
> Nutre la morta zolla e incenerita,
> Ancor leva lo sguardo
> Sospettoso alla vetta
> Fatal, che nulla mai fatta più mite
> Ancor siede tremenda. . . .†

---

* . . . from that thundering womb
  Hurled to the heights of heaven,
  There swooped down from above
  A blackness like the night, a destroying cloud
  Of cinders, pumice, rocks,
  With boiling torrents mingled. . . .

† . . . And the poor husbandman
  Tending his vines, whom hardly in these fields
  The dead incinerated soil can nourish,
  Still with suspicious glance
  Peers at the fatal summit,
  Which grown no whit more kindly than of old
  Still stands there terribly. . . .

La ginestra, trans. by R. C. Trevelyan.

Sometimes, after listening to these tales, Leopardi would get Ranieri to take him to Pompeii and Herculaneum, and would wander meditatively among the ruins. And sometimes, too, on a cloudless day, the fancy would take him to walk up to the higher slopes of the mountain, where, sitting by the open door of a farmhouse and looking down upon the bay, he would listen to the songs of a young girl who sang at her weaving and whose name was Silvia. Perhaps then, freed by sheer lassitude of body and spirit from the acute suffering of the recent tormented years, he returned to the 'gentle melancholy' of the days when, at Recanati, he first heard another Silvia singing at her loom.

In June he returned to Naples, but in August, taking alarm from a menace of cholera, he persuaded Ranieri to go back with him to Torre del Greco, where they remained until the following February. During this period he insisted on Ranieri's being thoroughly disinfected when he returned from his visits to Naples (a precaution which seems less excessive to us now than it apparently did to Ranieri), and he refused to go back to Capodimonte until he was assured that the epidemic was over. To his father he wrote, in October, that he need feel no anxiety on his account, since he was taking every possible precaution, and was 'in excellent air and good company'.[3]

As the winter wore on, however, his satisfaction with both the air and the company decreased. The Ferrigni family, too, had taken refuge from the epidemic in the country, and though Leopardi was kind to one of their small daughters, Calliopina, he was not on equally good terms with his host's brother, a canon of the Church. Moreover, as usual, the poet was a trying guest. He required a constant supply of ices, but said that those of Torre del Greco were greatly inferior to Vito's; he insisted on sending all the way to Naples for some of Madama Girolama's bread, and he also bitterly complained—with some reason, since the walls of the little house were exceedingly thin—of the cold and damp. Indeed he wrote to his father that never in his life had he felt the cold so intensely, not even in Bologna. Every day, he said, brought with it 'six mortal dangers'.[4] Early in December his right leg swelled up to twice its normal size and also became discoloured; and in February he had an attack of bronchitis with fever. It was only after his return to town and a fortnight in bed, that he became convalescent again. Ranieri offers the explanation that 'no man has ever hated the country as much as Leopardi, after having described it so inimitably'.[5]

The intensity of his weariness, and of his sense of failure may be measured by a letter he wrote to a young pupil of De Sinner's, Charles Lebreton. The young man, who was an *élève de rhétorique au Collège Royal Henri IV*, had written to the poet, saying that, although he was not yet acquainted with the 'language of Tasso and of Leopardi', he had read his works in translation with infinite delight: 'You are the poet for all men of feeling.' He added, however, that the praise of obscure schoolboys could certainly have no value for so great a man.[6] 'No, monsieur,' Leopardi replied, 'if I wished for praise, yours would not be at all indifferent to me: it is for souls like yours, for tender and sensitive hearts, that poets write —and that I, too, would have written, *if I were a poet*. My good friend De Sinner has depicted me to you in too favourable a light. . . . Pray tell him that, in spite of the fine title of *Opere* that my bookseller has chosen to give to my collection, I have never achieved any real work. I have only made attempts, always believing them to be preludes—but my career has gone no further.'[7]

This, surely, is one of the saddest letters that Leopardi ever wrote. The man who in his youth had felt 'an immoderate, perhaps insolent, desire for fame', who in his maturity had believed that he could be 'a divine poet', had now come to this. He could write that all his work had been only a series of preludes, could say of himself: 'If I were a poet.'

Yet still he went on working. It was during his first spring and summer on the slopes of Vesuvius that he produced the two greatest poems of his later years, *Il tramonto della luna* and *La ginestra*. The first, *The Setting of the Moon*, is Leopardi's last elegy; its closing lines, indeed, were dictated to Ranieri only a few hours before his death. The poem owes its inspiration to the still, cloudless nights of the previous May and June, when the poet would sit in the vineyard before the house, and look down towards the bay,

> . . . e sulla mesta landa
> In purissimo azzurro
> Veggo dall' alto fiammeggiar le stelle. . . .*

> *. . . and looking up I watch
> Over the mournful waste
> The stars in purest azure blazing bright. . . .
> *La ginestra*, trans. by R. C. Trevelyan.

The theme is not a new one: it is an elegy of the passing of youth, with its illusions and its hopes. The poet compares the vanishing of joy and colour from a man's life, as his end draws near, to the slow fading of a landscape, at the setting of the moon:

> Scende la luna; e si scolora il mondo.

In the work of every great poet there are a few lines so happy, so characteristic, that—even if quoted out of their texture—they bear an unmistakable signature. They are the essence of his poetry, the attar of his roses. In such lines *Il tramonto della luna* is singularly rich:

> Sovra campagne inargentate ed acque.*

> . . . l'ombre e le speranze
> Dei dilettosi inganni.†

> Incolume il desio, la speme estinta.‡

Leopardi's art has reached its full maturity.

The other great poem of this period, *La ginestra*—which some critics consider the greatest of Leopardi's works—also owed its inspiration to Torre del Greco, and to a sight which lay daily before his eyes: the golden broom which bloomed on the bare mountain-side, scenting the desert air:

> . . . e quasi
> I danni altrui commiserando, al cielo
> Di dolcissimo odor mandi un profumo,
> Che il deserto consola.§

This plant became to Leopardi a symbol of the unconquerable vitality, but also of the fragility and impotence of man, before the relentless forces of Nature. 'If, of all Leopardi's works, this poem alone survived,' wrote a critic of our own time, 'it would suffice to

---

* Over silvery fields and waters.

† . . . the promise and the shade
  Of fond illusions.

‡ Desire unspent, but hope forever gone.

§ And as though pitying others' misery
  Fillest the air with a sweet scent, whose breath
  Comforts the wilderness. . . .

XXXIII.

Il tramonto della luna.

Quale in notte solinga,
Sovra campagne inargentate ed acque,
Là 've zefiro aleggia,
E mille vaghi aspetti
E ingannevoli obbietti
Fingon l'ombre lontane
Infra l'onde tranquille
E rami e siepi e collinette e ville;
Giunta al confin del cielo,
Dietro Apennino od Alpe, o del Tirreno
Nell'infinito seno
Scende la luna; e si scolora il mondo;
Spariscon l'ombre, ed una

IL TRAMONTO DELLA LUNA

(The beginning of the last poem written in Leopardi's own hand)

give us the measure of his mind and of his art.'[8] It is not an easy
poem and it is an unequal one, some of its passages being marred by a
faintly prosaic didacticism; its architectural structure is extremely
complex, its rhythm slow and grave. But in its finest passages it
attains a stark, noble serenity. In a sense, moreover, it is Leopardi's
last testament: a hymn to truth and love. Man, he says, is doomed, as
surely as the fragile flower on the hillside, to swift and total destruction; but his arrogance has always refused to accept his fate. Yet
if—renouncing his foolish dreams of greatness, joy and immortality
—he would dare to face the truth, to 'regard intrepidly the desert of
life', a true nobility might yet be his.

> Nobil natura è quella
> Che a sollevar s'ardisce
> Gli occhi mortali incontra
> Al comun fato, e che con franca lingua,
> Nulla al ver detraendo,
> Confessa il mal che ci fu dato in sorte. . . .*

'*Quand l'univers l'écraserait,*' wrote Pascal, '*l'homme serait encore plus
noble que ce qui le tue.*'† So Leopardi too believed, and declared that
from the lowest depths of despair a new human solidarity and
kindliness might arise, a justice and a piety such as could never grow
in the thin soil of illusion. Two realities alone can rise above the
cruelty of fate: a brotherly love based upon the acceptance of pain
and sorrow, and an uncompromising courage that dares to face the
truth, and in that 'firm foundation of unyielding despair', finds rest
at last.

II

In Leopardi's life, as in that of many other poets, there is a poignant
contrast between the elevation of his thought and the unending
petites misères of his daily existence. On the one hand, the slopes of

* Noble the man who in the teeth of doom
  Dares lift mere mortal eyes
  And with unbridled tongue proclaim—
  Withholding nothing of the naked truth—
  The misery of man's lot.

† Should the universe shatter him, Man would still be nobler than his destroyer.

Parnassus; on the other, the petty friction with Ranieri, the letters home for money, the querulousness and scornfulness, and, above all, the tragic, progressive failing of the worn-out body: eyes, digestion, kidneys, lungs, heart, all performing their functions more and more grudgingly. And, looming ever closer, the dark shadow of death—half-desired, half-feared.

What were the causes of Leopardi's increasing sufferings in his last years, and what, in the end, did he die of? A great deal has been written on this subject, and various different theories have been put forth.[9] All the doctors agree, however, that the poet suffered from not one, but several ailments, and that all were intensified by his neurasthenia, which began very early. His own recollections of his childhood described, as we have seen, not only waves of fear and insecurity, and an intense hyper-sensitiveness, but swift alternations of mood, and sudden wild high spirits, 'especially in times of anguish'. And his father's account of his adolescence recorded typical examples of preoccupation and anxiety, such as to affect even his physical functions. At one time, Conte Monaldo wrote, 'he gave so much thought to his breathing that he could no longer do so freely'; at another he found, for the same reason, great difficulty in urinating.[10] When told by the doctor that sunshine would benefit him, he insisted on spending whole hours hatless, in the midday sun; when told to bathe his eyes in cold water, he took off his shirt, seized two buckets of water, and 'continued to throw two torrents at his eyes for an hour'.[11] This trying behaviour is almost identical with that described by Ranieri in Naples, nearly twenty years later. His state of nerves affected, too, his digestive functions, manifesting itself in a chronic constipation and a mucous-membranous colitis, and also probably accounted for his acute headaches, and, at least in part, for the weakness of his eyes. Moreover, he was a typical allergic, suffering from frequent colds, from asthma, and—after 1828—from chronic bronchitis. Though some of his biographers have tried to prove that he was not impotent, the plain fact is that we do not know.[12] What we do know is that his state of mind, to the day of his death, remained that of an adolescent whose love has never been fulfilled, and to this state we owe some of the most beautiful poems ever written.

Finally, and above all, there is the question of his deformity. His doctors in Rome and Florence, observing that he sometimes spat blood, believed him to be consumptive. But it is now believed that it was rather the increasing constriction caused by the deformity of his thorax which gradually came to affect both his lungs and his heart, and eventually caused a condition of chronic congestive heart-failure. This was the chief cause of his sufferings in his last years, and it manifested itself in 1835, at Torre del Greco, in a swelling of the legs (which Ranieri's doctor called dropsy) and in extreme breath-lessness, which Leopardi himself called 'nervous asthma'—saying to Ranieri and Paolina, with a wry smile, that all asthmatics were long-lived, and that they would probably have forty more years of nursing him! But here he was mistaken. After his return to Naples there was a short improvement, but in May he was worse again; his insomnia and breathlessness increased; and it was a total collapse of the heart—the typical death of the hunchback—that at last, in his thirty-ninth year, brought his life to an end.

The story of his last days is one of great poignancy. Hardly had the friends returned to Naples, than the cholera broke out again, this time with increased severity. The population was panic-stricken; terrible rumours spread through the town, tales of whole families who had perished in a single day. Long processions of penitents, of monks and priests and all the religious confraternities, flocked to the churches or carried holy images through the streets, imploring the mercy of Providence. But, before long, fear of contagion put an end to these assemblies, too. The schools were shut, the shops deserted, the well-to-do citizens fled to the country. Only the terrified poor remained, huddled together in the dirty, airless houses and squalid alleys of the slums. Whole streets and squares, in which the disease had been particularly virulent, were marked at each end with a Cross, and a 'Lord have mercy upon us'. Even the masked and black-robed members of the *Misericordia*, who came to take away the dead, would not enter there, but stood at the entrance, crying their grim refrain: '*Chi ha morti, li cavi!*'* No one else came out of those deserted regions; the living remained beside the dying, soon sharing in their fate. The only sound to be heard was the ominous tinkle of the little bell of the priest who bore the Last Sacrament to the dying—and soon that too was forbidden. The dead, heaped upon

* Bring out your dead!

one another, were given secret burial at night, their bodies being destroyed by quick-lime in the 'cholera cemetery', while the legend of their ever-increasing number passed from mouth to mouth among the terrified survivors.[13]

Leopardi, according to Ranieri, was deeply affected by the prevailing terror, and his fears must have been intensified by the fate of his friend, August von Platen. The young German poet had fled to Syracuse, but before the epidemic had arrived there, died from the effects of sheer panic. Only the state of Leopardi's health prevented him and Ranieri from escaping once more to the refuge of Torre del Greco. For several weeks they hesitated and delayed, still further unnerved by the vacillations of their doctor, and weighing the certain fatigue of the journey against the risks that surrounded them in Naples. There is little doubt that at this time Leopardi was miserably oscillating between two states of mind, the fear of death and the longing for it. For many years these two conflicting, but not really contradictory, sentiments had simultaneously possessed him, and now, although a deepening lassitude of body and spirit induced an ever-increasing desire for release, he could not but recoil in horror from the terrifying spectre that was stalking through the Neapolitan streets. 'Do you know', he said one day in terror to Paolina Ranieri, 'that something very strange is happening to me? . . . When I think of my approaching destruction, I seem to see myself lying in a ditch, with a crowd of ribald fools dancing upon my belly.'[14] For now he well knew that the end could not be far off. On the 22nd of December 1836, six months before his death, he wrote to De Sinner: 'I feel an ardent and intense desire to embrace you once again, but where and how will it be satisfied? I fear only κατ' ἀσφοδελὸν λειμῶνα.'*

After his return to Naples his health, which had shown a slight temporary improvement, continued to deteriorate. His right eye was menaced with cataract, and on the 27th of May he wrote to his father: 'I have been attacked for the first time by a real asthma, which prevents me from walking, lying down, or sleeping.' The letter ends with these words: 'If I escape the cholera, I shall make every effort, as soon as my health permits, in any weather or season, to see you again, for now I too feel hurried, being convinced . . . that the end

* In the fields of asphodel.

to my life which God has ordained, is not far off. My daily and incurable physical sufferings have at length reached such a pitch, that further they cannot go. I hope that when at last the feeble resistance offered to them by my dying body has been overcome, they will lead me to the eternal rest which I call for unceasingly—not indeed from heroism, but from the intensity of the pain I endure. I thank you and my mother tenderly for the ten *scudi*, I kiss the hands of both of you, I embrace my brothers, and I beg you all to commend me to God, so that, after having seen you once again, a quick death may bring an end to my physical sufferings, for which there is no other cure. Your most loving son, Giacomo.'[15]

His death came eighteen days later. On the 13th of June, in a long letter to Conte Monaldo, Ranieri explained that Giacomo had been prevented from returning to Recanati by the illness 'of which Giacomo, in his letter, spoke very vaguely, partly in order not to distress you, partly because I thought it better that he himself should ignore some of the truth'. Dr. Mannella's diagnosis, he went on to say, was dropsy, or rather a pericardic effusion. The doctor had added that the disease was one 'for which science could do but little, but nature might do much'. He had ordered an immediate return to the drier air of Torre del Greco, and another consultant had confirmed his advice, adding that he would like the patient to take some ass's milk. 'You may be sure', Ranieri concluded, 'that everything that is humanly possible has been, is, and shall be done for your son, the only friend that Providence has granted me.'[16]

On that day Paolina Ranieri bought for Leopardi two large packets of almond comfits, which he ate up in a few hours. A German friend who came to see him described him as extraordinarily serene and gentle, with something childlike and candid in his expression; as if, he wrote, some dim reflection of the dawn of his childhood were mingling with another approaching dawn.[17]

It was Ranieri's feast-day, St. Antonio, and after supper the two friends sat for a long time on their balcony, beneath the starry summer sky, with the clamour of the street faintly rising from below. It was then that, after a few commonplaces on the unworthy manner in which some priests and monks traded on human credulity, Leopardi suddenly burst out: 'Why is it that Leibnitz, Newton, Columbus, Petrarca, Tasso, could all believe in the Catholic Faith,

and we cannot find any satisfaction in the Church's doctrines?'
'Of course it would be better to believe,' Ranieri glibly replied, 'but
if faith is repugnant to our reason, what fault is it of ours?' 'It was
not repugnant', said Leopardi, 'to the reason of those great men.'[18]
A silence fell. What melancholy nostalgia for the lost faith of his
childhood, what unquenched yearning for infinity, lingered in
the air? 'Now I am wandering, day after day, from hope to hope,
forgetting you. . . .' So he had addressed the Redeemer in his youth,
and had gone on: 'The day will come when every hope has faded
save that of death, and then . . .'

The draft of the ode broke off, uncompleted; the last conversation, too, reached no conclusion. The talk came back again to
commonplaces, to future plans. Leopardi seemed very hopeful; he
spoke of the move to Torre del Greco, and even planned some
donkey-rides and excursions to Nisida and to Capri, where he
wished to see the ruins of Tiberius' villa.

The next day was the one on which they intended to move back to
the country. Leopardi woke up feeling well, and drank a large cup
of sweet chocolate which Paolina had prepared for him. It was then
that—in a faint voice which Ranieri could hardly catch—he dictated
to his friend the poignant last six lines of *Il tramonto della luna*:

> Ma la vita mortal, poi che la bella
> Giovinezza sparì, non si colora
> D'altra luce giammai, nè d'altra aurora.
> Vedova è insino al fine; ed alla notte
> Che l'altre etadi oscura,
> Segno poser gli Dei la sepoltura.*

By midday the carriage was already at the door, but, as they were
sitting at luncheon Leopardi turned to Ranieri to say that he felt
his asthma growing worse and would like to see the doctor. Ranieri
replied that he would fetch him himself. 'It was one of the worst
days of mortality from cholera, and it did not seem to me a time to
send messengers.' 'I believe,' he added, 'that, in spite of all my efforts,

---

* But mortal life, once golden youth has flown
   Glows with no other light, reflects no second dawn.
   Bereft until the end; to mark the final term
   Set to our later, overshadowed years
   The gods have set a sign for us, the tomb.

some small part of my deep emotion must have transpired in my expression, for, getting up, Leopardi made fun of it, and smiling and grasping my hand, he reminded me of the long life enjoyed by all asthmatics.'

Ranieri was not long in finding the doctor and bringing him to the house. 'But now everything was changed. Accustomed, by long and painful habit, to frequent warnings of death, our beloved patient could no longer distinguish the true from the false. . . . He was cheered by our arrival, and smiled at us, and argued gently with Mannella—although with a voice fainter and more broken than usual—about his nervous disease, his certainty of diminishing it with food, his distaste for ass's milk, the miraculous effect of excursions into the country, and his intention of soon getting up to go there. . . . . But Mannella, skilfully taking me aside, told me to send for a priest at once, since there was no time for anything else. I sent a messenger immediately, and again at frequent intervals, to the monastery of barefoot Augustine friars which was near by.

'In the meantime we all of us remained beside Leopardi, Paolina supporting his head and drying the sweat that ran down from that wide forehead of his, while I, seeing him overtaken by an evil and dark stupor, strove to arouse him with smelling-salts of various kinds. He opened his eyes wider than usual, and looked straighter than ever into mine, then: "I can't see you any more," he said, as with a sigh—and ceased to breathe. His pulse and heart were no longer beating and at that moment Padre Felice di Sant' Agostino, a barefoot friar, came into the room, while I, beside myself, was calling in a loud voice to him who had been my father, my brother, and my friend, and who—although he still seemed to see me—did not answer.'[19]

Ranieri, indeed, could not bring himself to believe that Leopardi was dead, and implored the friar to 'accompany the passing of this great soul' with the prayers for the dying. Only after a violent argument with the friar was he finally convinced of his loss, whereupon he knelt down with his sister and the doctor, while Padre Felice recited the prayers for the dead. This done, the friar wrote out the poet's death certificate: 'To the priest of the parish is certified the sudden passing to a better life of Giacomo Leopardi of Recanati, for whom I have offered the last prayers for the dead.

This was my duty and no more. Padre Felice di Sant' Agostino, *Agostiniano scalzo.*'*

Five years before his death, on almost the last page of the *Zibaldone*, Leopardi had written: 'There are two truths which most men will never believe: one, that they know nothing, and the other, that they are nothing. And there is a third, which proceeds from the second—that there is nothing to hope for after death.'[20] This conviction, and with it a pride in rejecting 'all the vain hopes with which men comfort children and themselves, all foolish consolations',† remained with him to the end.

Fame, religion, love—from none of these had Leopardi been able to derive happiness or even consolation. 'Life', he had written, 'is a thing of so little moment that a man, thinking of himself, should not be greatly concerned either to retain it or to leave it.'[21] Friendship alone had not failed him—a friendship which, if it had not brought happiness unalloyed, had been a most poignant reality. In the last lines of his *Dialogue between Porphyry and Plotinus*, clearly written with the thought of himself and Ranieri in his mind, there is a Platonic beauty and restraint. 'Let us live, my Porphyry, and find comfort together; let us not refuse to bear the part that destiny has assigned to us, of the evils of our race. Let us give each other companionship and encouragement, each bringing help and succour to the other, so that we may accomplish as best we can this heavy task of living, which doubtless will be brief. Nor when death comes shall we lament, nor in our last hour shall friends and companions fail us, but cheer shall be in the thought that, when we are no more, they will remember us, and love us still.'[22]

III

Ranieri—in letters in which a genuine grief transpires even through the emotional rhetoric in which it is embedded—sent off the news: to the Leopardis in Recanati, to Fanny Targioni and Gino Capponi

---

* Barefoot friar of the Augustinian Order.

† Ogni vana speranza onde consola
   Sè coi fanciulli il mondo,
   Ogni conforto stolto. . . .
                        Amore e Morte.

in Florence, to Giordani in Parma, to De Sinner in Paris. One of the first letters was for Fanny. 'The grief I feel has never been felt by man before, for there never was, nor will be again, a friendship equal to that which bound me to my adored Leopardi. . . . I often catch myself seeing and hearing him close to me, and speaking to him (I am not romancing) as to a real living man.'[23] In reply Fanny told him that she was 'annihilated' by the news; but it is plain that such distress as she felt was not for Leopardi himself, but only for Ranieri, to whom she offered 'a heart into which you could pour all your grief'.[24]

We do not know what Capponi's answer was. But his final verdict on the poet, in his old age, was kinder than in the days when he had glibly written that it is a *piccolezza* not to know how to live with a hump. 'Leopardi', he wrote, 'was the greatest genius of his age, he felt goodness and beauty with an innate elevation. . . . In Naples I learned—from someone who could know it better than anyone else—that the most unhappy man of our age was even more wretched than I used to think him.'[25]

Giordani's final comment, too, rose above the jealousy and pettiness that had clouded the last years of their friendship. 'My grief for Leopardi', he wrote, 'is in my very bones, and will endure. We should not grieve that his sufferings are over; but that for forty years he was compelled to wish to die—that is an incurable grief.'[26]

Of all the tributes of Leopardi's friends, the most perceptive came from Gioberti. 'I knew him intimately,' he wrote, 'and I believe that a naturally purer, nobler, and more generous soul never lived on this earth. His errors were the fatal consequences of his period and of the circumstances of his life, but of few men can it be said with so much likelihood of truth, that his soul was innocent.'[27]

As for the Leopardis, they received the news upon an unfortunate day. Giacomo's youngest brother, Pier Francesco, had fallen in love with the cook's daughter and had run away with her, even promising to marry her—and his family's alarm was so great that they had gone to the lengths of sending the police after him. It was just as he was being brought home by the *carabinieri* that the news of Giacomo's death reached Recanati, and 'did not produce much effect until a few days later'.[28] Paolina alone felt an overwhelming and immediate grief. 'If only one *could* die of sorrow!' she wrote to

Marianna Brighenti. 'I had treasured up for so long so many things to tell him, and so many to ask; I was always dreaming of the moment when I should welcome him home. . . . And now I am left alone.'[29]

Alone she was, indeed. Conte Monaldo ordered ten yearly Masses to be said for his son on the day of his death, but then he shut himself away in his sorrow; neither Giacomo nor his other dead son, Luigi, might be mentioned in his presence. And Paolina wrote, some years later, that she was obliged to conceal her brother's works, as they came out, 'so as not to cause pain to Papa'.[30] She herself bought and anxiously read everything that appeared, but, especially when his letters were published—not without bewilderment and grief. 'Many many things have been published in the works of our Giacomo which I would have suppressed. Shuddering and weeping, I have read again and again sentences of his that I would have liked to wipe out in blood. . . . But now all the world will know that my brother has lost his faith! What a horrible, lacerating thought! Yet, when we were small, we played together with the *altarino*—and he was so religious, so full of scruples! How true it is that too much knowledge corrupts! Let us pray God that these volumes never come into my father's hands; he would die of grief.'[31]

Ranieri's statement to Conte Monaldo, in the letter in which he told him of his son's death, that Giacomo had died 'furnished with all the sweet comforts of our holy religion',[32] had brought to the Leopardis the only consolation to which they were open. But when Ranieri's book appeared, it did not confirm this statement, and a letter published in 1846 by a Jesuit Father, Padre Scarpa, who claimed that he could number 'among the joys of his apostolic career' that of having 'reconciled to the Church the great genius of Giacomo Leopardi', was even more disconcerting, since it contained statements so grossly inaccurate that even poor Paolina could not accept them.[33] Yet still, remembering the prayers that had been said by her brother's death-bed, she clung to a faint hope. 'Good-bye, dear Giacomo,' she wrote, in the family register of Recanati. 'Shall we not meet again in Paradise?'

Ranieri lived on to a ripe old age in Naples—giving vent to some of his emotionalism in a devotion to his sister which came to be almost a religious cult. He printed *I Paralipomeni* at his own expense (but with a good many mistakes); he put up the tombstone to Leopardi in San Vitale; he published, in 1845, two volumes of his friend's *Works*, which included his last poems, three of the *Operette Morali*, and various minor unpublished prose works, 'according to the author's intention'. But many of the poet's other papers he managed to keep concealed from the public for over fifty years, and he spent the later years of his life in a violent and vehement controversy with anyone who dared to throw a doubt on the disinterestedness of his friendship—saying, in his own defence, many things that it would have been better to have left unsaid. At his death, in 1888, he declared that for fifty-four years he had never been separated from his friend—'for seven years from the living man, and for forty-seven from his remains'.[34]

The relentless ill-fortune that attended Leopardi throughout his life, and some of his writings after his death, was no kinder in the disposal of his bones. On the day of his death the cholera was still raging, and the police regulations ordered that all corpses should be thrown into the common cemetery, to be destroyed by quick-lime. But Ranieri, determined to save his friend's body from this fate, acted with great energy and promptitude. He procured a doctor's certificate that Leopardi had not died of cholera, and by this means succeeded in obtaining a tacit permission to bury the poet elsewhere; he summoned an embalmer, to retard the decomposition of the corpse, and a sculptor, to take a death-mask; he bribed, with 'a fine basket of mullet and cuttlefish', the parish priest of San Vitale Fuorigrotta, in the suburb of Pozzuoli;[35] he borrowed two carriages from friends; and after dark, on the evening after his death, Leopardi's corpse was duly conveyed, with the help of Ranieri's brothers, towards San Vitale. On the way, however, a macabre incident occurred: the coffin was held up by the customs of Piedigrotta, and the corpse was found to contain two incisions (made by the doctor and the embalmer), whereupon the customs officers promptly suspected that the dead man had been murdered. Only after they had been provided with the certificates both of the doctor and of Padre Felice, was the little procession allowed to proceed to San Vitale, where Ranieri at last buried his friend in the church's crypt. Unfortunately, however, this was extremely damp, and seven years

later, in 1844, the coffin—first opened by Paolina Ranieri, so that her
brother might contemplate for two hours 'the skeleton of the man
whom he loved and admired above all on earth'—was moved up to
the sacristy of the church, and there a memorial stone was erected
by Ranieri. He engraved upon it not the Cross alone, but an owl, as
a symbol of Athene's wisdom, and above it two boughs, one of
laurel for the poet, and one of oak 'for the philosopher and benefactor of mankind'. But to the laborious inscription composed by
Giordani[36] Leopardi himself would certainly have preferred the
grim epitaph he had placed at the end of his *Memorable Sayings
of Filippo Ottonieri*:

OSSA
DI FILIPPO OTTONIERI
NATO ALLE OPERE VIRTUOSE
E ALLA GLORIA
VISSUTO OZIOSO E DISUTILE
E MORTO SENZA FAMA
NON IGNARO DELLA NATURA
NÈ DELLA FORTUNA
SUA*

But the unhappy poet's body had not yet found rest. On the 21st
of July 1900, Leopardi's tomb—which had been declared a 'national
monument' by the Italian government three years before—was
moved to a new porch before the church, and on this occasion the
coffin was opened once again. It was then discovered that it had
rotted, that the lid had fallen in, and that the bones, which had also
mouldered, were mingled with the rotting wood. It was impossible
even to find the skull. Of the mortal remains of Leopardi nothing
distinguishable was left.[37]

Following upon this, in 1908, a Philippine monk, Padre Gio-
vacchino Taglialatela, published a book, in which he not only asserted
that the whole funeral, as described by Ranieri, had been a *macabre*

* Bones
Of Filippo Ottonieri
Born for Noble Deeds
And for Glory
Lived in Idleness and Futility
And Died without Renown
Not Unaware of his Nature
And of his Fate.

DEATH-MASK OF LEOPARDI

farce, inasmuch as the coffin had only contained a bundle of Leopardi's old clothes (the poet's body having been buried in the
common cemetery), but also stated that before dying the poet had
received the Last Sacrament, referring, in support of this statement,
to Padre Scarpa's letter.[38] These assertions were completely refuted
by Gioberti.

The church of San Vitale, which at the time of Leopardi's burial
stood in a quiet suburban village, gradually came to be surrounded
by houses which formed one of the most crowded, overbuilt,
and squalid quarters of Naples. The dust from the little square blew
up over Leopardi's tomb; the squeaking of trams mingled with the
voices of street-sellers crying their wares and the shouts of children
dancing to barrel-organs. Such was, for a century, the resting-place
of the poet who had dreamed of '*sovrumani silenzi e profondissima
quiete*'.

Various plans were made for moving his remains to a more
peaceful spot; at one time it was proposed to take them back to
Recanati; at another to lay them in the church of Santa Croce in
Florence. Both plans, it need hardly be said, were violently opposed
by Ranieri. But finally, on the 2nd of February 1939, the casket containing the little that is left of the poet's bones was transferred to a
more suitable site. They lie—beneath the same stone that covered
them at San Vitale—on the side of the great cliff above Mergellina,
close to a little circular structure of Roman masonry which, for centuries, has been popularly known as the tomb of Virgil. Here Leopardi himself, remembering this tradition, used to come to look out
over the same classic earth and sea; and here at last he lies—one of the
most unhappy men, and greatest poets, who ever lived. The tall,
overshadowing cliff, planted with broom and oleander, looks out
across the bay to the slopes of Vesuvius and the '*campagne inargentate
ed acque*', and a small grove of cypresses and laurels guards his tomb.

> Sola nel mondo eterna, a cui si volve
> Ogni creata cosa,
> In te, morte, si posa
> Nostra ignuda natura;
> Lieta no, ma sicura
> Dall' antico dolor.[39]

BIBLIOGRAPHY

FOR a complete bibliography of Leopardi the reader is referred to the *Bibliografia Leopardiana* by G. Mazzatinti and M. Menghini, Florence, 1932 (vol. I, up to 1898; vol. II, 1898–1930). More recent publications are listed in the 'Bibliography of Leopardi' by Carlo Corti in *Problemi ed orientamenti critici e di lingua e di letteratura italiana* (Milano, 1948). English readers will find a shorter bibliography at the end of G. L. Bickersteth's *Poems of Leopardi* (Cambridge University Press, 1923).

The three chief collections of Leopardi's autograph manuscripts are in the Biblioteca Nazionale of Naples (*Carte Napoletane*), in the Biblioteca Nazionale of Florence (*Carte Sinneriane*), and in the Library of Palazzo Leopardi in Recanati (*Carte Recanatesi*). There are also some manuscripts of lesser importance in the Biblioteca Leopardiana Municipale in Recanati, in the Biblioteca Palatina of Parma, the Biblioteca Comunale of Livorno, the Biblioteca Marciana of Venice, the Biblioteca Estense, and in the Archives of the Commune of Visso, and thirty-five letters may be seen in the Cambridge University Library.

By far the most important of these collections is the *Carte Napoletane*, of which a full account is given by the present Librarian of the Biblioteca Nazionale, Dottoressa Guerriera Guerrieri, in *Autografi e carteggi napoletani* (Roma, 1939). These papers—which include the *carte Ranieri*, Ranieri's personal papers and letters—have had a curious history. After Leopardi's death Ranieri refused to hand over his papers to his father—most fortunately, since Conte Monaldo would hardly have allowed *La ginestra*, and still less the *Pensieri* and large parts of the *Zibaldone*, to see the light; Ranieri also refused the papers to Vieusseux and to Giordani—even though, a month before his death, Leopardi had written to Antonietta Tommasini: 'Giordani and you are the owners of all my poor things, published and unpublished'. Thus for fifty-one years a considerable number of Leopardi's manuscripts—including the whole of the *Zibaldone*—were hidden away, unpublished and unread. After Ranieri's death, in 1888, Leopardi's manuscripts were expropriated by the Italian State in the public interest and were handed over for publication to a Commission presided over by Carducci, which in 1898–1900 published the *Zibaldone (Pensieri di varia filosofia e di bella letteratura di Giacomo Leopardi*, 7 vols., Firenze), and in 1906 a selection of other unpublished notes, diaries, poems, etc., under the title *Scritti vari inediti di G. Leopardi dalle carte napolitane*. Ranieri's own papers, however, including a number of letters of great interest addressed to Leopardi, still remained unpublished, in the hands of his two maid-servants, and it was not until the death of the last of these, in 1923, that all these papers, too, came into the possession of the Biblioteca Nazionale of Naples. Moreover, it is only within the last few years that all these papers have been arranged and catalogued by Dottoressa Guerrieri and Prof. Piermarini, bringing to light a number of new letters, notes, drafts, translations, and *puerilia*.

In addition, the Biblioteca Nazionale now contains a full and invaluable catalogue of *all* Leopardi's manuscripts and letters, wherever situated. It is only to be regretted that this catalogue has not yet been printed, so that the student can only refer to it in Naples.

The masterly official edition of Leopardi's *Epistolario*, prepared by Prof. Francesco Moroncini, has now been enriched by three more volumes also edited by him, and by a final seventh volume (after his death, in 1941) edited by Prof. Giovanni Ferretti. This should be supplemented by the *Lettere scritte a G. Leopardi dai suoi parenti*, edited by G. Piergili (Firenze, 1878), and by the *Carteggio inedito di vari con Giacomo Leopardi*, ed. by G. and R. Bresciano (Torino, 1932).

A complete edition of Leopardi's *Opere*, in five volumes, with an invaluable analytical index to each section, has been edited by Prof. Francesco Flora (Mondadori, Milano 1940), and another selected edition, in three volumes, with numerous illustrations, has been made by Prof. Giuseppe De Robertis (Rizzoli, Milano, 1937).

For Leopardi's life I have drawn specifically on the works enumerated at the beginning of the notes to each chapter. I must, however, acknowledge a general indebtedness to the following works: G. Chiarini, *Vita di G. Leopardi* (Firenze, 1903); G. Mestica, *Studi Leopardiani* (Firenze, 1905); G. A. Levi, *Giacomo Leopardi* (Messina, 1931); A. Bouché-Leclercq, *Giacomo Leopardi, sa vie et ses œuvres* (Paris, 1874); A. Zottoli, *Storia di un' anima* (Bari, 1927); and to the two most recent biographies of the poet: M. Saponaro, *Leopardi* (Milano, 1952), and G. Ferretti, *Leopardi* (Bologna, 1945).

The *Autobiografia di Monaldo Leopardi*, edited by A. Avoli (Recanati, 1891), is both indispensable and entertaining.

Among the vast array of critical studies and interpretations of Leopardi, the works of De Sanctis and Carducci are still indispensable. See, in particular: Francesco De Sanctis, *Storia della letteratura italiana*, vol. II (Naples, 1885), and all the essays collected in *Studio su Giacomo Leopardi*, edited by R. Bonari (Naples, 1885), and in *Nuovi saggi critici* (Naples, 1890); and Giosuè Carducci, *Degli spiriti e delle forme nella poesia di G.L.* (*Opere*, vol. XVI), *Jaufré Rudel* (*Opere*, vol. X), and *Le tre canzoni patriotiche di G.L.* (*Opere*, vol. XVI). Sainte-Beuve's essay on Leopardi in *Portraits Contemporains*, vol. IV (Paris, 1863) is still admirable.

Among more recent critical works, no student can afford to miss Prof. Flora's illuminating introduction to his edition of the *Opere*, Prof. De Robertis's perceptive *Saggio su Leopardi* (Firenze, 1944), Benedetto Croce's essay on Leopardi in *Poesia e Non-Poesia* (Bari, 1923), Karl Vossler's *Leopardi* (München, 1923), Prof. Attilio Momigliano's essay in *Cinque Saggi* (Firenze, 1950), and Leone Piccioni's *Lettura Leopardiana* (Firenze, 1952).

For the *Operette Morali* the best edition is: *Operette Morali di G.L., con proemio e note di Giovanni Gentile* (Bologna, 1918).

For the *Canti*, Prof. Francesco Moroncini's scholarly and precise edition (Bologna, Cappelli, 1927, 2 vols.) is invaluable, since it contains the corrected autographs of most of the poems, and all the variants in the various manuscripts, as well as in the editions printed during the poet's lifetime.

The English reader unacquainted with the Italian language is referred to G. L. Bickersteth's translations, already listed, to John Heath Stubbs's *Poems from Leopardi* (John Lehmann, 1946), and to

James Thomson's translation of the *Operette Morali* (Routledge, 1905).

The text of all Leopardi's letters in this book is taken from Professor Moroncini's edition of the *Epistolario*; that of any of his other works, from Professor Flora's edition of the *Opere*. All references are to these two works.

NOTES

CHAPTER ONE

GENS LEOPARDA

The *Autobiografia di Monaldo Leopardi*, already referred to, gives a vivid picture of the background of the Leopardi family, and a self-portrait of the author. Unless otherwise specified, everything in this chapter written by Conte Monaldo is taken from this work. A lively portrait of the Count is to be found in Alfredo Panzini's *Piccole Storie del mondo grande* (Milano, 1901) and there are a number of anecdotes, as well as some unpublished passages from Conte Monaldo's *Diary*, in the following books by C. Antona-Traversi: *Documenti e notizie intorno alla famiglia Leopardi* (Firenze, 1888), *Notizie e aneddoti sconosciuti intorno alla famiglia L.* (Roma, 1885), *I genitori di G.L. Scaramucce e battaglie* (Recanati, 1891), *Paolina Leopardi* (Città di Castello, 1898), and *Studi su G.L.* (Napoli, 1885).

1. Antona-Traversi, *Documenti e notizie*, etc., pp. 265–379.
2. Antona-Traversi, op. cit., p. 322.
3. M. L. Patrizi, *Saggio Psicoantropologico su G.L. e la sua famiglia*.
4. Monaldo Leopardi, *Istoria Gentilizia della famiglia Leopardi*, in Antona-Traversi, *Documenti e Notizie*, etc., p. 374.
5. Monaldo Leopardi, ibid.
6. Antona-Traversi, *Studi*, etc., p. 48.
7. Will of Conte Monaldo, 5 June 1847, in Antona-Traversi, *Documenti*, etc., p. 192. Several years before his Will, however, in 1836, Conte Monaldo wrote a letter to his wife, to be opened only after his death, which throws a good deal of light both on his own character and on his relations with her. He felt bound, he said, to tell her of some debts 'which rest only upon my honesty and good faith', of which he had not told her during his lifetime, 'because I had no means of paying them with my own money, and you had no obligation to pay them with yours. . . . You know that for many years I have lived in a real state of poverty, in proportion to my rank; you have never let me lack any necessity, preferring rather to deprive yourself; but there has never been any margin.' The

debts are mostly small, and a tribute to Monaldo's honesty and kindness of heart. 'I have a scruple that I may owe 60 *scudi* to Sig. Girolamo Riccardi of Castefidardo, for I fear that I may have damaged him by some careless-ness of mine when his lands were sold. Anyway, I wish them to be paid to him, a few at a time, as is possible. And if I don't really owe them, let it count as charity, since he is poor.' (Published by Antona-Traversi for Nozze Arcoleo Vignati, Roma, 1889.)

8. Paolina Leopardi, *Lettere a Marianna ed Anna Brighenti*, edited by E. Costa (Parma, 1888).

9. Antona-Traversi, *Studi*, pp. 54 and 79.

10. Ibid., p. 79.

11. Antona-Traversi, *Paolina Leopardi*, pp. 41–2.

12. *Zibaldone*, I, 25 November 1820.

13. Antona-Traversi, *Documenti*, etc., p. 93, and *Studi*, pp. 50 and 53.

14. Teresa Teja Leopardi, *Note biografiche*, p. 76.

15. *Epistolario*, II, 22 January 1823.

16. Ibid., III, p. 196, note 4.

17. Ibid., II, 29 November 1822.

18. Ibid., 20 December 1822.

19. Monaldo Leopardi, '*Memorie inedite*', in Antona-Traversi, *Documenti*, etc., pp. 95 and 110.

20. Antona-Traversi, op. cit., p. 54. This prayer was followed by another one, in which Contessa Adelaide asked that her own soul, too, might fear sin more than death. Ferretti, *Leopardi, Studi biografici*, p. 124, note. 3.

21. F. Zamboni, *Roma nel mille* (Firenze, 1875), p. 408.

CHAPTER TWO

THE MAKING OF A POET

The most revealing glimpses into Leopardi's childhood are to be found in his own *Ricordi d' infanzia e di adolescenza* (*Poesie e Prose*, I, pp. 673–86), in his letters, and in his *Zibaldone*. Numerous anecdotes, possibly inaccur-ate but entertaining, may be found in the *Note biografiche sopra Leopardi e la sua famiglia* (Milano, 1882) by Contessa Teresa Teja Leopardi, the second wife of Giacomo's brother Carlo, and in Antona-Traversi's works. All the quotations in this chapter from Paolina Leopardi's letters are from her *Lettere a Marianna ed Anna Brighenti* (Parma, 1888).

1. Antona-Traversi, *Studi su Giacomo Leopardi*, p. 235.
2. Antona-Traversi, *Documenti e notizie*, p. 25.
3. Antona-Traversi, *Studi*, p. 56.
4. Teresa Teja Leopardi, *Note biografiche*, etc., pp. 26–30.
5. Antona-Traversi, *Paolina Leopardi*, p. 5.
6. Monaldo Leopardi, *Memorie Inedite*, in Antona-Traversi, *Documenti*.
7. *Epistolario*, II, 12 April 1820. To Pietro Brighenti.
8. Monaldo Leopardi, *Cenni biografici di G.L.*, written to Ranieri after Giacomo's death. *Carteggio*, p. 481.
9. Antona-Traversi, *Documenti*, etc., pp. 79–87.
10. Will of Conte Monaldo, in Antona-Traversi, *Documenti*.
11. *Zibaldone*, II, p. 255, 1 August 1823.
12. *Epistolario*, II. To Carlo, 25 November [1822].
13. *Zibaldone*, I, p. 310, 25 November 1820.
14. *Ibid.*, I, p. 1484, 11 June 1822.
15. *Ricordi d'infanzia e di adolescenza*, in *Poesie e Prose*, I, p. 679.
16. *Zibaldone*, II, p. 495, 25 September 1822.
17. Monaldo Leopardi, *Cenni biografici di G.L.*, in *Carteggio*, p. 478.
18. *Ibid.*
19. From the chapter *Dei terrori notturni* in Leopardi's *Saggio sopra gli errori popolari degli antichi*, written at the age of seventeen.
20. *Ibid.*
21. *Ibid.*
22. *Zibaldone*, I, 6 August 1822.
23. *Zibaldone*, II, p. 1058, 9 December 1826.
24. Monaldo Leopardi, *Cenni biografici*, etc., *Carteggio*, p. 478.
25. O dotto figlio di più dotto Padre
    Segui il cammin che a somigliar t'invita
    Quegli al sapere, alla pietà la Madre.
26. Antona-Traversi, *Paolina Leopardi*, p. 26.
27. Leopardi, *Vita del Poggio*, in *Poesie e Prose*, I, p. 690.
28. Leopardi, *Ricordi d' infanzia*, etc. *Ibid.*, p. 674.
29. *Ibid.*, p. 673.
30. *Ibid.*
31. The letter, which appears never to have been delivered, since it is still in *casa Leopardi* with the seal (a large pig) unbroken, is remarkable for some scatological jokes, and also for the precocious ease of its style.
32. Teresa Teja Leopardi, *Note biografiche*, pp. 366–7.
33. *La dimenticanza*, written in 1816.
34. Paolina Leopardi, *Lettere a Marianna e Anna Brighenti*, p. 8.
35. *Ibid.*, pp. 40–1.

36. *Zibaldone*, I, p. 251, 1 October 1820.
37. *Ricordi*, etc., in *Poesie e Prose*, p. 679.
38. *Zibaldone*, I, p. 265, 16 October 1823.
39. *Ricordi*, etc.
40. Ibid.
41. *Discorso di un italiano intorno alla poesia romantica, Poesia e Prose*, II, p. 480.
42. Ibid., p. 479.
43. Ibid., p. 480.
44. *Zibaldone*, I, p. 94.
45. *Elogio degli uccelli, Poesie e Prose*, I, p. 965.
46. *Zibaldone*, I, p. 120.
47. *Alla vita abbozzata di Silvio Sarno, Poesie e Prose*, I, p. 689.
48. *Zibaldone*, I, p. 413.
49. Ibid., p. 472, 11 February 1821.
50. *Ricordi*, etc.

CHAPTER THREE

IN CONTE MONALDO'S LIBRARY

1. De Sanctis, '*La prima canzone di G.L.*', in *Nuovi Saggi Critici*.
2. Conte Monaldo's pride in his library appears also in his Will, in which he laid down that the 14,000 volumes of which it was then composed (in 1847) should never be removed from the rooms in which he had placed them, and should be at the disposal of the citizens of Recanati for at least three mornings a week. Antona-Traversi, *Documenti*, etc., p. 210.
3. *Epistolario*, I. To Giordani, 30 April 1817.
4. *Zibaldone*, II, p. 105.
5. *Saggi degli studi fatti dai Fratelli Leopardi negli anni* 1808–1812, published by Antona-Traversi, per nozze Arcoleo-Vignati (Roma, 1889).
6. Monaldo Leopardi, *Cenni biografici*, in *Carteggio*, p. 479.
7. *Prose e Poesie*, II, p. 1106.
8. Piergili, *Nuovi documenti intorno alla vita e gli scritti di G.L.*, listing the documents in the Leopardi library at Recanati.
9. G. De Robertis, *Saggio su Leopardi*, p. 11.
10. De Sanctis, op. cit.

11. Giordani, *Delle 'Operette Morali' di G.L.*, in *Scritti*, IV, p. 152.

12. This work was quoted by an eminent German scholar, Creuzer. '*Lui qui a travaillé toute sa vie sur Plotin,*' wrote Sainte-Beuve, '*il trouve quelque chose d'utile dans l'œuvre d'un jeune homme de seize ans.*' Sainte-Beuve, *Leopardi*, in *Portraits Contemporains*, IV.

13. Monaldo Leopardi, *Cenni biografici*.

14. *Epistolario*, I. To Giordani, 30 April 1817.

15. Antona-Traversi, *Studi*, p. 99.

16. *Ricordi d' infanzia e di adolescenza*.

17. *Epistolario*, I. To Giordani, 30 April 1817.

18. From Leopardi's preface to his translation of the second book of the *Aeneid*, in *Lo Spettatore*. Mestica, *Scritti letterari*, II, p. 112.

19. Ibid.

20. *Epistolario*, I. To Giordani, 21 March 1817.

21. The *Idylls* of Moschus and the *Batracomiomachia* were published in 1815, the *Canto* of the *Odyssey* and two other fragments 'from the Greek' in 1816; the second book of the *Aeneid*, though composed in 1816, only in 1817, and Hesiod's *Titanomachia* in June 1817.

22. Preface in *Lo Spettatore* to Leopardi's translation of the *Odyssey*. 'May they answer me honestly', he begged, 'and spare me useless labour, if this effort cannot sincerely be praised.' *Poesie e Prose*, I, p. 524.

23. *Epistolario*, I. To Antonio Stella, 24 January 1817.

24. Ibid. To Giordani, 30 May 1817.

25. Preface to the *Inno a Nettuno* in *Lo Spettatore*. 'I am keeping this work', he wrote later on, 'rather as a work of ingenuity than of imagination or poetry. For while translators generally attempt to seem original, I —being original—tried to seem a translator.'

26. These verses so completely took in contemporary scholars that the Custodian of the Vatican Library was accused of having given Leopardi the manuscript, and 'swore that he would find out who had stolen it from his shelves without his knowledge'. *Epistolario*, I. To Giordani, 14 July 1817.

27. *Zibaldone* I, p. 46.

28. Ibid., II, p. 1230, 30 November [1828].

29. Ibid., p. 1233. 'Those words', he wrote many years later, 'will always cause me pain. Nevertheless I believe that there is no man, whatever sort of life he may have led, who would not say the same thing of himself.'

30. *Epistolario*, I. To Giordani, 2 March 1818.

31. Mestica, *Studi leopardiani*, pp. 269–70.

32. Monaldo Leopardi, *Cenni biografici*.

33. A. Avoli, Appendix to Monaldo's Autobiography, pp. 278–9, note 1.

34. Ibid, p. 279.

35. *Zibaldone*, I, p. 110.

36. This poem, for which Leopardi always had a particular affection, and to which he referred in *Le ricordanze*, was written in the autumn of 1816, and a fragment from it—beginning '*Spento il diurno raggio*'—was included by him in the Neapolitan edition of *I Canti*.

37. *Epistolario*, I. To Giordani, 2 March 1818.

38. *Zibaldone*, I, p. 56.

39. *Epistolario*, I. To Giordani, 2 March 1818.

CHAPTER FOUR

LA DONNA CHE NON SI TROVA

The story of Leopardi's first romance is told in his *Memorie del primo amore* (*Poesie e Prose*, I, pp. 657–82), first published in the *Scritti vari inediti dalle carte napolitane* (1906) with the title *Diario d' Amore*. This romance also inspired his first love-poem, *Il primo amore*, and, in 1823, the poem *Alla sua donna* (first published in the *Canzoni* in 1824). Concerning his other youthful dreams and romances, the little we can glean is derived from his own *Ricordi d' infanzia e di adolesenza* (*Poesie e Prose*, I, pp.673–86) written in 1819 and first published in the *Scritti vari inediti*; and from his poems, *Le ricordanze* and *A Silvia*, written ten years later, in 1829.

See also De Sanctis, *La Nerina di G.L.*, in *Nuovi saggi critici*; N. Serban, *Leopardi sentimental* (Paris, 1913); G. Mestica, *Gli amori di G.L.*, in *Studi Leopardiani* (Firenze, 1905); E. Boghen-Conigliani, *La donna nella vita e nelle opere di G.L.* (Firenze, 1898).

1. *Memorie del primo amore*, *Poesie e Prose*, pp. 657–73.

2. *Zibaldone*, I, pp. 88–9.

3. Ibid., p. 160, 27 June 1820.

4. *Epistolario*, III. To A. Jacopssen, 23 June 1823. 'Is this folly?' he added. 'Am I romantic? You shall judge.'

5. From Leopardi's notes to the *Canzoni*, printed in Bologna. *Alla sua donna* was composed in six days, in September 1823.

7. G. Santayana, *Interpretations of Poetry and Religion* (London, 1901)

CHAPTER FIVE

FRIENDSHIP AND PATRIOTISM

Leopardi's correspondence with Giordani, in the first and second volumes of the *Epistolario*, provides us with a detailed account of this period of his life. For Leopardi's patriotic poems see Carducci, '*Le tre canzoni patriotiche di G.L.*', in *Opere*, vol. XVI, *Poesia e Storia*, and also De Sanctis's '*La Prima Canzone di Giacomo Leopardi*', in *Nuovi Saggi Critici*, and, among more recent critics, Leone Piccioni, '*Il primo Leopardi delle Dieci Canzoni*', in *Lettura Leopardiana* (Firenze, 1952). The impression made on his contemporaries is shown in Sainte-Beuve's *Portraits Contemporains*, vol. IV, in Marc Monnier's *L'Italie est-elle la terre des morts?* (Paris, 1860) and in Settembrini, *Lezioni di letteratura italiana* (Napoli, 1872).

1. Carducci, '*Le tre canzoni patriotiche di G.L.*', in *Opere*, XVI, p. 191. Already in Stendhal's days, however, Giordani's eloquence was wearisome to some tastes. '*Pour parler comme ces messieurs,*' he wrote of Giordani and Perticari [Monti's son-in-law], '*je dirai que leurs proses me semblent des océans de paroles et des déserts d'idées.*' *Rome, Naples, et Florence*, p. 185.

2. Byron, *Letters and Journals*, edited by Prothero, V, p. 435. Giordani, after a long conversation with Byron in Venice, returned the compliment. 'I found nothing in him of the arrogance of a man who had become famous so young; nothing of English pride; nothing of the contempt which he constantly shows to some people.' Giordani, *Opere*, vol. IV.

3. *Epistolario*, I. To Vincenzo Monti, 21 February 1817.

4. Ibid. Vincenzo Monti to Leopardi, 8 March 1817.

5. Ibid. Monsignor Mai to Leopardi, 8 March 1817.

6. Ibid. Giordani to Leopardi, 12 March 1817.

7. Ibid., 21 March 1817. In a later letter, too—after the publication of his *Inno a Nettuno*—he repeated the same complaint: 'My things are printed, but I never know what is said about them—whether they are liked or not, whether they are thought mediocre or bad—so that, for me, a book that has been published is as if it were still a manuscript—except that in manuscript it has no mistakes, and the print is swarming with them.' To Giordani, 30 May 1817.

8. Ibid. To Giordani, 30 April 1817.

9. Ibid.

10. Ibid. To Giordani, 8 August 1817.

11. Ibid.
12. Ibid., 22 December 1817.
13. Ibid. Giordani to G.L., 30 May 1817.
14. Ibid., 8 August 1817.
15. Ibid., 2 March 1818.
16. Ibid., 14 August 1818.
17. *Epistolario*, edited by Prospero Viani, vol. III, p. 481.
18. From a letter to Pietro Brighenti, 3 April 1820, published by Avoli in his appendix to Conte Monaldo's *Autobiografia*, pp. 298–9.
19. Ibid.
20. Domenico Spadoni, *Una trama e un tentativo rivoluzionario*. After this insurrection, thirty-one conspirators were given severe sentences, among which there were eleven death-sentences, and eleven of hard labour for life.
21. *Argomenti di elegie, Poesie e Prose*, I, p. 381.
22. De Sanctis, '*Le poesie e Canzoni di G.L.*', in *Nuovi saggi critici*.
23. G. Mestica, *Studi Leopardiani*, p. 576, quoting a letter from Monaldo to Conte Broglio D'Ajano, 9 February 1819.
24. *Epistolario*, edited by Prospero Viani, vol. III, p. 485.
25. Dito, *Massoneria, Carboneria ed altre Società Segrete*, pp. 141–51.
26. *Carteggio*, pp. 328–9, 24 March 1819.
27. *Epistolario*, I. Giordani to G.L., 5 February [1819].
28. Ibid., p. 275, note. 1. Giordani to Brighenti, 25 June 1819.
29. Ibid., 6 July 1819.
30. Carducci, op. cit., p. 201.
31. Ibid., p. 208, quoting from a letter written from Recanati by one of the volunteers.
32. Marc Monnier, *L'Italie est-elle la terre des morts?*
33. Carducci, op. cit., p. 213.
34. L. Settembrini, *Lezioni di letteratura italiana*, p. 354.

CHAPTER SIX

AN ATTEMPT AT FLIGHT

1. *Epistolario*, I, 19 October 1818.
2. Ibid. Carlo Antici to G.L., 26 December 1818.
3. Ibid., 18 January 1819.
4. Ibid., 5 December 1817.

T

5. Ibid., 26 April 1819.

6. Ibid., 21 June 1819.

7. 'What distresses me most of all', he wrote later on, 'is to know that certain literary men . . . have been blamed for this old plan of mine. I swear by all that is most sacred, that none of them have dreamed of giving me such advice—indeed I am certain that if they had known of my plans they would have dissuaded me.' *Epistolario*, I, 13 August 1819.

8. Conte Broglio d'Ajano, whose sons were friends of Giacomo and Carlo, was, like Monaldo, an old-fashioned country gentleman, with a taste for books and for literary Academies, and an agile pen. But unlike him, he was of pronounced Liberal tendencies; he admired the Encyclopædists, he translated Voltaire, and both his sons were *carbonari*.

9. *Epistolario*, I, p. 286. Undated, but written at the end of July 1819.

10. Ibid., p. 288. Written at the same time as the preceding letter.

11. Ibid., 13 August 1819.

12. Ibid., pp. 297–8, note.

13. Ibid., 13 August 1819.

14. *Epistolario*, IV, Conte Monaldo to G.L., 14 July 1828.

15. Avoli, Appendix to Conte Monaldo's *Autobiografia*, p. 304.

16. *Pensieri*, II, *Poesie e Prose*, II, pp. 5–6.

17. *Zibaldone*, I, pp. 162–3, 1 July 1820.

18. Piergili, *Nuovi documenti intorno alla vita e gli scritti di G.L.*, p. 6. Gioberti to De Sinner, 22 August 1838. The passage referred to was in a note to Gioberti's *Teorica del sovrannaturale*: 'A person whose talent, writings, and reputation gave him great authority, determined to render him sceptical; nor did he have much trouble in doing so, owing to his eloquence.' But to De Sinner Gioberti added that though Giordani might have sown the first seeds of doubt, their subsequent growth was due only to Leopardi's own turn of mind, 'since he was not a man to be influenced easily by other men's opinions'.

19. Massari, *Ricordi biografici e carteggio di V. Gioberti*.

20. *Zibaldone*, I, pp. 162–3, 1 July 1820.

21. *Epistolario*, I, 1 November 1819.

22. Ibid., 8 December 1819.

23. *Zibaldone*, I, p. 83.

24. *Epistolario*, I. Giordani to G.L., 8 December [1819].

25. Ibid., 17 December 1819.

26. *Zibaldone*, I, p. 133.

CHAPTER SEVEN

THE POET

The first drafts of practically all Leopardi's poems, or at least the ideas that suggested their main themes, must be sought in the *Zibaldone*, the *Operette Morali*, or in the rough notes or drafts found after the poet's death, and first published in the *Scritti vari inediti dalle carte napolitane* (Firenze, 1906). These have now been grouped together by Prof. Flora in vol. I of *Poesie e Prose*, under the titles '*Argomenti e Abbozzi di Poesie*' and '*Memorie e Disegni Letterari*'.

For the study of Leopardi's methods of composition see Prof. Francesco Moroncini's scholarly edition of *I Canti*, referred to in my Bibliography, p. 264. Valuable, too, for their notes are *I Canti, con l'interpretazione di Giuseppe De Robertis* (Firenze, 1945), and Francesco Flora, *I Canti e le Prose scelte* (Milano, 1950).

1. These *Idylls* are: *L'infinito, Alla luna, La sera del dì di festa, Il sogno, La vita solitaria*, and the fragment which begins, *Odi, Melisso*.

2. *Epistolario*, III, 5 March 1824. To Giuseppe Melchiorri.

3. *Drafts of Idylls* (1819), *Poesie e Prose*, I, p. 377.

4. *Ricordi d'infanzia e di adolescenza* (1819), *Poesie e Prose*, I, p. 674.

5. Ibid., p. 682.

6. *Drafts of Idylls*

7. *Ricordi d'infanzia e di adolescenza*, op. cit., pp. 682–3.

8. Leopardi's *passero* is not a sparrow, but the rock-thrush, *cyadonus-montanus*.

9. 'There are nights when the upper air is windless and the stars in heaven stand out in their full splendour around the bright moon; when every mountain top and headland and ravine starts into sight.' (*Iliad*, Book 8, ll. 551–3, trans. E. V. Rieu.)

10. *Ricordi*, etc.

11. *Zibaldone*, I, p. 1122, 19 September 1821.

12. 'The measure of a nation's genius', he affirmed, 'is the richness of its language, and when a language is insufficient to render in translation the subtleties of another, it is a sure sign that it belongs to a less cultivated people.' *Zibaldone*, I, pp. 730–1, 25 May 1821.

13. Ibid., p. 703, 13 May 1821.

14. For this richness and variety he accounted in various ways, one being 'that we have never given up any of our ancient riches' (unlike

the French language, he maintained, but like the German, which has kept many of its 'deliberate, beautiful and expressive archaisms').

15. Leopardi's notes to the *Canzoni, Poesie e Prose*, I, p. 153.

16. *Zibaldone*, II, p. 389, 1–2 September 1823.

17. A. Momigliano, *La poesia di Leopardi*, in a series of lectures at the Lyceum of Florence.

18. Cf. Flora's Preface to his school edition of *I Canti e le Prose scelte*, pp. 9–14.

19. Flora, Preface to *Poesie e Prose*.

20. *Zibaldone*, I, p. 963.

21. Ibid., p. 156, 24 June 1820.

22. Piccioni, *Lettura Leopardiana*, p. 117.

23. *Zibaldone*, I, p. 963.

24. The equally characteristic adjective '*solingo*' was only reached (in *Bruto Minore*, in the phrase '*solinga sede*') after discarding '*inabitata, invernale, ispida, iberna, nubilosa, nevale, narica, squallida, sassosa, sbigottita, solitaria*'.

25. *Zibaldone*, II, p. 1123.

26. Capponi, *Lettere*, etc., I, p. 322.

27. Flora, Preface to *Poesie e Prose*, p. xliii.

28. *Discorso di un italiano intorno alla poesia romantica*.

29. *Zibaldone*, I, p. 86.

30. Ibid., p. 198.

31. *Saggio sugli errori popolari degli antichi*.

32. *Zibaldone*, II, pp. 1132–3.

33. Notes for *Inni Cristiani, Poesie e Prose*, I, p. 426.

34. *Zibaldone*, I, p. 129.

35. Ibid., I, p. 187. 'Thence', he adds, 'the pleasure I felt as a child and have felt ever since, in seeing the sky through a window or a door.'

36. Ibid., I, p. 198.

37. Ibid., I, p. 953.

38. Ibid., II, p. 1231, 30 November 1828.

CHAPTER EIGHT

TWO WINTERS OF DISCONTENT

1. Carducci, *Le tre canzoni patriotiche di G.L.*, in *Opera*, XVI.

2. Emilio Costa, *Due lettere inedite di Monaldo Leopardi*, 9 April 1820. 'I have little esteem', Monaldo added, 'for naked Literature, and would

always wish to see it allied to some Science. . . . Nevertheless I love my
son very dearly, I am glad that he should satisfy his innocent talents, and
am willing to help him with the means that Providence has given me. . . .
Why then does he remove from me his trust?'

3. *Epistolario*, II, 21 April 1820.

4. Ibid., 24 April 1820.

5. Ibid.

6. Ibid., 28 April 1820.

7. Cf. L. Raffaele, *Una dotta spia dell' Austria* (Roma, 1921), and G.
Bertini, *Un candido amico del Leopardi*, in *Giornale Storico della Letteratura
Italiana*, CVIII, 1936, pp. 80–6.

8. Quoted by Carducci, op. cit., p. 252. This letter was written by
an informer to the Chief of the police in Venice.

9. Byron, *Letters and Journals*, V, pp. 192–3.

10. *Epistolario*, V, 4 July 1828.

11. Ibid., 22 July 1828.

12. *Epistolario*, II. Ferdinanda Melchiorri to G.L., 21 March 1821.

13. Ibid. To Angelo Mai, 30 March 1821.

14. Ibid. To Giulio Perticari, 30 March 1821.

15. Ibid., p. 211, note 2, Monaldo Leopardi to Carlo Antici [1821].

16. Ibid., 6 March 1820.

17. Ibid. Giordani to G.L., 18 June [1820].

18. *Zibaldone*, I, pp. 156–8, 24 June 1820.

19. *Epistolario*, II, 30 June 1820.

20. Its first ponderous title was *Thoughts on Various Forms of Philosophy
and Fine Literature*, but this was soon changed to *Zibaldone*, which the
Vocabolario Fanfani defines as 'A confused mixture of diverse things'.

21. Letter from Vogel to Marchese Filippo Solari, 7 November 1807,
in G. Cugnoni, *Opere Inedite di G.L.* (Halle, 1878).

22. *Zibaldone*, I, p. 108.

23. Ibid., p. 6.

24. Ibid., p. 33.

25. Carducci, Preface to the *Zibaldone*, *Opere*, XI, p. 45.

26. *Zibaldone*, I, p. 218, 14 August 1820.

27. *Zibaldone*, II, p. 1233, 1828. 'Is not this', he added, 'an image of
human life?'

28. Ibid., I, p. 375, 27 December 1820.

29. Ibid., p. 90.

30. Ibid., p. 1453, 5 May 1822.

31. Logan Pearsall-Smith, *Reperusals and Recollections*, p. 34.

32. *Epistolario*, II, 5 January 1821.

33. Ibid., 13 July 1821.

34. They are: *Per le nozze della sorella Paolina, A un vincitore nel pallone, Bruto Minore, Alla Primavera, Ultimo canto di Saffo, Inno ai Patriarchi,* and to those he added the poem *Alla sua donna,* written in September 1823. The same volume also contained the three early patriotic *Canzoni.*

35. Leopardi himself, in a half-ironic tone, wrote some notes for these poems and also for the three earlier *Canzoni. Poesie e Prose,* I, pp. 151-2.

36. Sainte-Beuve, *Leopardi,* in *Portraits Contemporains,* IV.

37. *Disegni letterari* (1821). *Poesie e Prose,* I, p. 700.

38. From Leopardi's notes to the *Canzoni.*

39. Leopardi, Notes to *Alla Primavera,* quoted in Moroncini's critical edition of *I Canti,* p. 277.

40. Leopardi, Notes to the *Canzoni.*

41. Note by Leopardi on the back of the Neapolitan autograph of the *Ultimo canto di Saffo.* Published by Moroncini, *I Canti,* I, p. 347.

42. Various attempts have been made to identify the young women to whom he may, or may not, have paid court, and the story is even told of one lady of Recanati who, according to Giordani, is said to have boasted that she repulsed the advances of the young Conte Leopardi. The incident and the lady's name are of very slight importance; not so the pain aroused.

43. *Zibaldone,* I, p. 101.

44. *Comparison of the speeches of Brutus and Theophrastus at the moment of their death,* published with the *Canzoni* in the edition of 1824. *Poesie e Prose,* I, p. 1037.

45. *Frammento sul suicidio,* found among Leopardi's papers after his death. *Poesie e Prose,* I, p. 1082.

46. *Epistolario,* VI. To De Sinner, 24 May 1832.

47. *Discorsi intorno agli Inni Cristiani e la Poesia cristiana* (1821). *Poesie e Prose,* I, p. 426.

48. Ibid.

49. *Supplemento generale a tutte le mie carte* (1818).

50. *Ricordi d'infanzia e di adolescenza, Poesie e Prose,* I, p. 678.

51. *Epistolario,* III, 25 November 1825.

52. *Saggio sugli errori popolari degli antichi.*

53. 'I do not believe', he wrote, 'that my observation about the falsity of all absolute ideas need destroy the idea of God. . . . I consider God, not as the best of all possible beings (since there is no absolute better or worse) but as holding within himself all possibilities and existing in all possible ways. . . . His relations with human beings and other creatures are perfectly *suitable,* and therefore perfectly good. . . . Thus religion still stands

and the infinite perfection of God, which we deny as absolute, may be affirmed as relative, as perfection in our order of things.' *Zibaldone*, I, pp. 1055–6, 3 September 1821.

54. *Zibaldone*, II, p. 1058, 9 December 1826.

55. N. Serban, *Lettres inédites relatives à G.L.*, p. 6, note 3.

CHAPTER NINE

ROME

Silvagni's *La corte e la società romana nei secoli XVII e XIX* and Stendhal's *Journal d'Italie* and *Promenades dans Rome*, provide a lively picture of the Rome that Leopardi knew. *A Memoir of Baron Bunsen*, by his wife, Frances Bunsen, gives a brief and enthusiastic account of his relationship with Niebuhr.

1. A. Bouché Leclercq, *Giacomo Leopardi*, p. 99.

2. *Epistolario*, II, 25 November [1822]. To Carlo.

3. Ibid.

4. Ibid., 6 December [1822].

5. Ibid., 25 November [1822].

6. Ibid., 9 December 1822.

7. Ibid., 31 December 1822.

8. *Epistolario*, I, 13 August 1819. According to Carlo, Giacomo's sexual development had been unusually precocious, in spite of his fragile health.

9. *Epistolario*, II. To Carlo, 6 December [1822.]

10. Ibid., 25 November [1822].

11. *Zibaldone*, I, pp. 507–8, 5 March 1821.

12. *Zibaldone*, II, p. 1232, 1 December 1828.

13. *Epistolario*, II, 25 November [1822.]

14. Silvagni, op. cit., II, *La restaurazione*.

15. Stendhal, *Promenades dans Rome*, I, pp. 40–2.

16. *Epistolario*, II. To Paolina, 19 March 1823.

17. *Zibaldone*, I, p. 372, 28 December 1820.

18. *Epistolario*, II, 16 April 1823. Neither at this time nor subsequently is it fair, I think, to blame Conte Monaldo for the smallness of Giacomo's allowance. If he did not send him any more money, it was because he had not got it himself. In the very year before Giacomo's visit to Rome,

his family had been obliged to incur some fresh debts, and his mother had sold what was left of her jewellery, to raise 1,000 *scudi*.

19. Ibid., 6 December 1822.

20. Silvagni, op. cit., II, '*Il Carnevale*'.

21. Ibid, II, '*Canova e gli artisti*', and *Epistolario*, II, 15 March 1823.

22. Silvagni, op. cit.

23. Stendhal, op. cit.

24. *Epistolario*, II, 9 December 1822.

25. Ibid., 16 December 1822.

26. Ibid., 22 January 1823.

27. Ibid., 30 December 1822.

28. Frances, Baroness Bunsen, *A Memoir of Baron Bunsen*, I, p. 226. Baroness Bunsen also describes 'the confiding benevolence expressed in Leopardi's countenance'. '*Ese cuerpo*', she quotes from Cervantes, '*que con piadosos ojos estais rimirando, fué depositario de una alma, en quien el Ciel puso infinitas partes de sus riquezas.*'

29. *Epistolario*, II. To Carlo, 12 March 1823. Although gratified by the admiration of this little circle, Leopardi did not over-estimate the value of his philological works. To his brother he wrote, when sending him the article on Eusebius which Niebuhr had admired: 'It will seem rubbish to you, but you must know that it has caused the Minister of Prussia . . . to wish for my acquaintance.'

30. Ibid. Niebuhr himself paid ample tribute to Leopardi's genius in a preface to one of his own works: 'Among the most erudite [of his helpers] I must mention Count Giacomo Leopardi, whom I now present to my compatriots as being already an ornament of Italy, and a man whose reputation is destined, I am sure, to become greater every day. Having had the opportunity of appreciating the charming character and the rare scholarship of this young philologist, I shall rejoice in every honour and success that may come to him.'

31. Ibid. To Carlo, 22 March 1823.

32. Ibid., 12 March 1823.

33. Monaldo Leopardi, *Autobiografia*, p. 287.

34. Epistolario, III, 14 August 1823.

35. Shelley's *Letters* to Peacock, 22 December 1818, at the end of Hogg's *Life of Shelley*, II, pp. 414–5.

36. *Epistolario*, II. To Carlo, 6 December 1822.

37. Ibid., 3 December 1822.

38. *Zibaldone*, II, pp. 1087–8, 14 March 1827.

39. *Epistolario*, II, 20 February 1823.

40. Ibid., 22 March 1823.

41. Ibid., 19 April 1823.

CHAPTER TEN

THE *OPERETTE MORALI*

The most interesting recent Italian remarks on the *Operette Morali* are in Prof. De Robertis's *Saggio su Leopardi*, especially for the relation between the *Operette* and the *Zibaldone*, and in Prof. Flora's Preface to his edition of the *Opere* (pp. xxxii–xlvii). See also Prof. Giovanni Gentile's Preface to his annotated edition of the *Operette Morali* (Bologna, 1918), Benedetto Croce's essay on Leopardi in *Poesia e Non-Poesia* (Bari, 1923), and Karl Vossler, *Leopardi* (translated by T. Gnoli) (Napoli, 1925), A. Zottoli, *Leopardi, Storia di un' anima* (Bari, 1947), and G. Barzellotti, *G.L. e Schopenhauer* (Bologna, 1886).

The English reader is referred to James Thompson, *Essays, Dialogues, and Thoughts of G.L.* (Routledge, 1906) with a preface and brief biography, and to Prof. Bickersteth's Preface to his translation of the *Poems* (Cambridge University Press, 1923).

1. *Epistolario*, IV. To Antonio Stella, 12 March 1826.
2. The *Dialogues between Plotinus and Porphyry* and the *Copernicus* were added in 1827; the *Dialogue between a Seller of Almanacks and a Passer-by* and the *Dialogue between Tristan and a Friend* in 1832.
3. *Dialogue between Tristan and a Friend.*
4. *Epistolario*, III. To Giuseppe Melchiorri, 19 December 1823.
5. Prof. Gentile, in his Preface to the *Operette*, has attempted to prove that the book has also a strict structural unity. He divides the twenty *Operette* into three parts, each with a prologue and epilogue, and declares that each section begins with a negation of life's values, rises to a crisis of despair, and then reconstructs what has been previously destroyed. But the theory is not wholly convincing and more recent critics, such as Flora and De Robertis, have not accepted it.
6. Byron also felt a similar need to escape from tedium by any form of intense activity. 'The great object of life', he wrote to Annabella, 'is sensation—to feel that we exist, even though in pain. It is this "craving void" which drives us to gaming and battle, to travel, and to intemperate, but keenly-felt pursuits of any description, whose principal attraction is the agitation inseparable from their accomplishment.'
7. *Zibaldone*, I, pp. 1071–2, 7 September 1821.
8. *Dialogue between Tasso and his Familiar Spirit.*
9. *Pensieri*, LXVIII (*Poesie e Prose*, II, p. 42).
10. The following passage from Chateaubriand's *Génie du Christianisme*

expresses similar views: 'The more a nation advances in civilization, the more this state of emotions in flux increases. For a very sad thing then occurs: the great number of examples before one's eyes, the great number of books that deal with mankind and its emotions, make a man clever, without giving him experience. He is disenchanted, without having known enjoyment; he still has desires, without any longer having illusions. His imagination is rich, abundant, and wonderful; his life is impoverished, arid, and disenchanted. He lives, with a full heart, in an empty world, and without having made use of anything, he is disillusioned with everything. The bitterness which this state of mind spreads over life is unbelievable; the heart seeks a hundred ways out, a hundred ways of using powers which it feels to have become atrophied.'

11. *Summa*, II, 2; XXXV, 1.

12. 'I have made the acquaintance of a word which describes a condition from which I have been suffering for several months: a very fine word, *anorexie*. That I suffer from it, is saying too much—the worst of it is, that I am hardly aware of it. My lack of physical and intellectual appetite has become such that I sometimes scarcely know what is keeping me alive.' André Gide, *Ainsi soit-il*.

13. Benedetto Croce, *Poesia e Non-Poesia*.

14. *Fragment on Suicide* (1832).

15. See also the *Dialogue between Columbus and Gutierrez*, which exalts the value given to life by the temporary intoxication of danger, and the essay *On Parini*.

16. To quote only two instances: the *Dialogue between Plotinus and Pophyry* developed the apologia for suicide already enounced in *Bruto Minore*, and the main theme of *Tristan and a Friend* was rendered later (and less successfully) in verse in the *Palinodia*.

17. *In Praise of Birds*. They are, the poet wrote, the only living creatures who do not suffer from tedium—'the gayest in the world save only hares'. 'In short—as Anacreon wished to be transformed into a mirror, to be seen constantly by the lady he loved, or into a little gown to cover her, or an ointment to anoint her, or water to cleanse her . . . or even into a shoe, that at least she might press him with her foot—so I wish, at least for a while, to be turned into a bird, to savour their contentment and delight.'

Tommaseo, Leopardi's most savage critic, made short work of all this:

> Esser vorresti uccello?
> Siam lì, sei pipistrello.

(You wish to be a bird? Take comfort: you're a bat.)

18. *Dialogue between Tasso and his Familiar Spirit*.

19. From the note to Thomas's *Éloge de Descartes* which, with Fontenelle's *Éloge de M. Ruysch,* Leopardi cites as the source of his *Dialogue.*

20. *Dialogue between Frederick Ruysch and his Mummies.*

21. *Dialogue between a Seller of Almanacks and a Passer-by.*

22. *Dialogue between Tristan and a Friend.*

CHAPTER ELEVEN

MILAN AND BOLOGNA

An account of Paolina's unhappy romance is to be found in C. Antona-Traversi, *Paolina Leopardi,* and in her own *Lettere a Marianna ed Anna Brighenti.* Antonio Baldini's book of essays, *Il Sor Pietro, Cosimo Papareschi e Tutta di tutti* (Firenze, 1943), contains a lively description of Paolina's tragedies and devotes a chapter to Leopardi's life in Bologna.

1. *Epistolario,* II. Carlo to G.L., 14 April 1823.

2. Paolina was also—at least according to the account of one of her cousins—slightly hunchbacked, like her brother. Antona-Traversi, *Studi,* p. 88.

3. Paolina Leopardi, *Lettere a Marianna ed Anna Brighenti.*

4. *Epistolario,* II, 2 April 1823.

5. Ibid. To Carlo, 19 April 1823.

6. Ibid. To Paolina, 19 April 1823.

7. *Epistolario,* III, Paolina to G.L., 19 August 1825.

8. Ibid., 4 August 1823.

9. Paolina Leopardi, *Lettere.*

10. Antona-Traversi, *Studi,* p. 109.

11. Antona-Traversi, *Paolina Leopardi,* p. 211. Her body was brought back by her nephews to Recanati.

12. *Epistolario,* III, 4 August 1823.

13. Ibid., 23 June 1823.

14. Ibid., 6 May 1825.

15. Ibid., 8 June 1825.

16. Ibid., 19 June 1825.

17. Ibid., 31 July 1825.

18. Ibid., 17 September 1825.

19. Ibid., 21 July 1825. Baroness Bunsen, after describing the efforts made by her husband to obtain this post for Leopardi, writes: 'The

explanation of this tedious course of hope deferred and defeated was simply this, that the court of Rome calculated upon wearing out the opposition made by Leopardi to entering the Church.' Frances, Baroness Bunsen, *Memoir of Baron Bunsen*.

20. She was, in fact, of very modest origins, and had left her husband, a humble clerk of the commune of Modena, in favour of a musical career.

21. *Epistolario*, IV. To Carlo Pepoli, 15 April 1826.

22. *Epistolario*, III. Conte Monaldo to G.L., 6 October 1825.

23. Ibid., III. To Paolina, 9 December 1825.

24. *Zibaldone*, II, p. 1320.

25. Several months after the appearance of these poems, Brighenti was obliged to answer Leopardi's anxious inquiries 'in the language of friendship, that is of sincerity', and to inform him that in Bologna they were thought both obscure and redundant, while in Lombardy they were hardly known at all. 'They [the volumes] are still wandering on the right bank of the Po, like the shades waiting for Charon's bark.' In Tuscany, owing to high praise from Giordani in the *Antologia*, they received greater attention, but, Brighenti added, 'You must be patient, for in Italy many years are needed before the merits of a book are recognized'.

26. *Epistolario*, IV, 16 January 1826.

27. Ibid., 13 January 1825.

28. Ibid., 16 January 1826.

29. Ibid., 6 October 1826.

30. Ibid. To Conte Monaldo, 25 January 1826.

31. Ibid. To Papadopolis, 16 January 1826.

32. Later on he took an active part in the uprisings of 1831, and, after a period of imprisonment, was forced to seek refuge in England and France, where he composed the libretto of Bellini's opera *I Puritani*.

33. *Gli Intronati* (crazy ones) of Siena, *I Trasformati* (transformed) of Milan, *I Gelidi* (frozen ones) of Bologna, *I Pastori Eritrei* (Erithrean shepherds) of Naples, and, as we have seen, *I Disuguali Placidi* of Recanati.

34. Monaldo Leopardi, *Autobiografia*, p. 89.

35. *Pensieri*, XX, *Poesie e Prose*, II, p. 15.

36. *Epistolario*, IV. To Carlo, 4 April, 1826.

37. From the unpublished Diary of Conte Francesco Rangone in the Biblioteca dell' Archiginnasio in Bologna.

38. *Epistolario*, IV, 4 April, 1826.

39. Ibid., 7 April 1826.

40. Ibid., 30 May 1826.

41. Ibid., p. 147. Undated, but probably mid-April 1826.

42. Ibid., 30 May 1826.

43. Ibid., 18 April 1827.

44. Ibid. Undated. Moroncini places it in May 1847.

45. Giordani to Pietro Brighenti, 30 April 1827.

46. *Epistolario*, IV, 5 May 1827.

47. Ibid. VII, p. 83, n. 1062.

48. Teresa Carniani Malvezzi to G.L., 27 May 1830. Quoted by Mestica, *Studi leopardiani*, p. 119.

CHAPTER TWELVE

FLORENCE AND PISA

The picture of the life of Leopardi's friends in Florence is based chiefly on the following books: Paolo Prunas, *L'Antologia di G.P. Vieusseux* (Roma, 1906); Giovanni Gentile, *Gino Capponi e la cultura toscana nel secolo decimonono* (Firenze, 1926); *Lettere di Gino Capponi e di altri a lui*, edited by A. Carraresi (Firenze, 1867); Stendhal, *Rome, Naples, Florence*; Mario Pieri, *Memorie di mia vita*. Cf. also the following articles in periodicals: F. Moroncini, *Uno scritto ignorato di G. Leopardi*, in *Nuova Antologia*, (March–April 1831), and Terenzio Mamiani, *Manzoni e Leopardi*, in *Nuova Antologia* (August 1873). For Leopardi's poem *A Silvia*, see Prof. De Robertis's essay *Sull' autografo del canto 'A Silvia'*, in *Primi Studi Manzoniani* (Firenze, 1949).

1. *Epistolario*, IV, 15 October 1826. Earlier in this same year, too, the Count had written to his son: 'I must weigh in the balance my heart and your mother's good sense. She loves you most tenderly, but believes that your writings are a gold-mine, which make any help unnecessary for you.'

2. *Zibaldone*, II, p. 1055, 16 November 1826.

3. *Epistolario*, IV, 6 December 1826.

4. Ibid., 15 December 1826.

5. Antona-Traversi, *Studi*, pp. 74–5. This story is also confirmed by Alfredo Panzini. He heard it at Recanati from an old man who, in his boyhood, had taken part in the snowballing. Cf. Alfredo Panzini, *Piccole storie del mondo grande*, p. 142.

6. Antona-Traversi, op. cit.

7. *Epistolario*, IV, 9 February 1827.

8. Ibid., 21 April 1827.

9. This story is quoted by Prospero Viani, in the Appendix to his edition of the *Epistolario*, III, p. 494–5.

10. Pieri, *Memorie di mia vita*.

11. Quoted by Baldini, op. cit., p. 15.

12. The 'plan' which Capponi drew up for the review stated that it was to be neither wholly 'classic' nor 'romantic'. Poetry, which had been 'cultivated in recent times to saturation point', was to be set aside while all encouragement was to be given to science, history, economics, and philosophy, 'applied to a knowledge of ourselves and of practical morals, and avoiding the abstruse speculations preferred by German philosophers, which are not to our tastes'.

In the view of the Tuscan Liberals, the time was over when literature could exist on its own merits, dissociated from practical and political life. 'The man who, in the midst of such great conflicts of thought and feeling, of so many tears and so much blood, is able to abstract himself enough from everything around him and to talk of literature or of the exact sciences, as if he had just come out of a hut in the Thebaid—such a man must be either a knave or a fool.' (Introduction to the *Antologia*, II, 1822.) Cf. also *Progetto di un giornale*, Capponi, *Lettere*, V.

13. Vieusseux was constantly hampered by the censorship imposed upon his review from Rome and entrusted to a Scolopian father, Padre Mauro Bernardini, who had been instructed to see that the *Antologia* refrained not only from direct political propaganda, but from all topics that might lead on to dangerous ground. Such topics, at the moment, were not few: anything relating to Napoleon was taboo, and so, of course, were the revolutions in Greece and the discontent in Poland. Religion and education could both only be handled with the greatest care. And when, in May 1821, an anonymous poem was laid on Vieusseux's desk, beginning, '*Ei fu*', Padre Mauro (adding that the composition seemed to him of little merit) promptly required its rejection.

14. *Timander and Eleander, Columbus and Gutierrez*, and *Tasso and his Familiar Spirit*.

15. 'The foolish praise of Giordani has undoubtedly done him much harm,' Vieusseux wrote to Tommaseo. *Il Tommaseo, il Leopardi e il Giordani*, in *Rassegna Storica del Risorgimento*.

16. *Epistolario*, IV, 1 March, 1826. The '*hermite des Apennins*', according to Vieusseux's plan, was to be answered by a 'citizen of the Arno', a role which the candid editor, unaware of Brighenti's activities as a spy, proposed to entrust to the lively advocate. He was to mock the follies of the town; Leopardi, 'more grave, more austere, more misanthropic', to scourge the deeper weakness of human nature, 'egoism and immorality,

fanaticism and atheism, our system of public and private education', etc., etc.

17. He lived first in the Locanda della Fortuna, an old inn dating from the days of Boccaccio, and then moved to lodgings in Via del Fosso (now Via Verdi).

18. *Epistolario*, IV. To Conte Monaldo, 23 June 1827.

19. *Epistolario*, V. 29 July 1828.

20. His publisher had warned him that he must not expect too great a success—'Italy is not yet accustomed to this sort of reading'—and even suggested that the essays (no doubt to make them more digestible) should be published in a *Biblioteca amena*, a collection of light reading suitable for ladies. This Leopardi had refused to allow. 'The lightness of such a collection', he pertinently remarked, 'is a merit in its own kind, but not as applied to my book,' and he added that the essays were intended to be considered as a whole, since they had a complete philosophic structure. But, when the book did appear, he was sadly obliged to admit that some of his publisher's apprehensions had been justified.

21. *L'Antologia*, February 1828. Paolina was so much touched by his praise of her brother that she afterwards declared that merely to see Montani's initials at the foot of an article made her happy. *Epistolario*, V, 12 April 1829.

22. Tommaseo, *Diario intimo*, p. 135.

23. Capponi, op. cit., IV, pp. 416–17. These comments were written in 1875.

24. *Zibaldone*, I, p. 1466–7, 13 May 1822.

25. *Epistolario*, IV, p. 284, note 3.

26. Capponi, op. cit., I, p. 231.

27. Mamiani, op. cit.

28. *Epistolario*, IV. To Puccinotti, 16 August 1827.

29. Ibid., 15 December 1827.

30. Ibid., 24 December 1827.

31. Ibid., 12 November 1827.

32. 'The sentiment of Lord Byron . . . is very little communicated to his readers, and indeed is little suited to be communicated to the feelings of others. And this is because it seems, and perhaps is, dictated by the imagination, rather than by the feelings and the heart . . . and is therefore in itself more suited to affect the reader's imagination than his heart. *Zibaldone*, I, p. 681, 3 November 1823.

33. *Zibaldone*, I, p. 201, 26 July 1820.

34. *Epistolario*, V, 12 November 1827.

35. Ibid.

36. Ettore Botteghi, in *La Gazzetta Letteraria*, 6 October 1898.
37. *Zibaldone*, II, pp. 1143–5, 30 June 1828.
38. *Epistolario*, V, 2 May 1828.

CHAPTER THIRTEEN

REMEMBRANCE

1. *Epistolario*, V, 16 May 1828.
2. Ibid., 26 May 1828.
3. Ibid., 18 May 1828.
4. Ibid., 2 June 1828.
5. Capponi, *Lettere*, op. cit.
6. *Epistolario*, V, 19 June 1828.
7. Ibid., 24 June 1828.
8. Ibid., 5 July 1828.
9. G. Cortese, *La condanna e l'esilio di P. Colletta*.
10. Capponi, *Lettere*.
11. Stendhal, *Rome, Naples, Florence*, p. 215.
12. Gioberti, *Meditazioni*.
13. Gioberti, *Teorica del Sovrannaturale*.
14. *Epistolario*, VI, 30 January 1832.
15. Ibid., V, 28 November 1828.
16. Ibid., 31 December 1828.
17. *Zibaldone*, II, p. 1012, 6 July 1826.
18. Ibid., II, p. 1109, 7 April 1827. The quotation is from *Émile*.
19. *Epistolario*, V, 27 January 1829.
20. Antona-Traversi, *Paolina Leopardi*, p. 101.
21. *Zibaldone*, II, p. 1230, 30 November [1828].
22. Appendix to Prospero Viani's edition of Leopardi's *Epistolario*, III, p. 474.
23. After the death of his first wife Carlo married, at sixty, the housekeeper of a neighbour, Teresa Teja, who was as unpopular in Recanati as himself, and who wrote an amusing, but inaccurate and spiteful book, first published in France with the title *Leopardi et sa famille*. (The Italian edition is referred to here.) When asked in a lady's confession album where he would like to live, Carlo replied: 'Anywhere but in my *patria*, Recanati; which I love as my brother Giacomo loved it.' Appendix to Conte Monaldo's *Autobiografia*, p. 310.

24. Antona-Traversi, *Studi*, pp. 121–2.

25. *Epistolario*, V, 12 April 1829.

26. Ibid., 19 May [1809].

27. *Zibaldone*, II, p. 1092, 24 March 1827.

28. Paolina Leopardi, *Lettere a Marianna ed Anna Brighenti*.

29. *Disegni Letterari, Poesie e Prose*, p. 704.

30. *Ricordi d'infanzia e di adolescenza*.

31. *Zibaldone*, II, p. 1321, 21 May [1829].

32. Carducci, '*Degli spiriti e delle forme nella poesia di G.L.*', *Opere*, XVI.

33. Four years before, in the *Zibaldone*, Leopardi had outlined his theme 'What is our life? The journey of a cripple who, with a great load upon his back, crosses steep mountains and exhausting, perilous passes, beneath snow, ice, rain, wind, and burning sun, yet toils on day and night, without rest—only to arrive at a ditch or precipice into which, unfailingly, he must fall.' *Zibaldone*, II, p. 990, 17 January 1826.

34. Leopardi's Notes to *Canti*, *Poesie e Prose*, I, p. 141, n. xxiii.

35. *Epistolario*, V. To Colletta, 26 April 1829.

36. Ibid., 22 November 1829.

37. Cf. G. Ferretti, '*La fortuna delle Operette Morali e la Crusca*', in *Leopardi, Studi biografici*. 'Your cause', wrote Vieusseux, in imparting the bad news, 'was defended by Capponi and Niccolini—but what could be hoped from the Canons who formed the rest of the assembly?' *Epistolario*, V, 13 February 1830.

38. *Epistolario*, V, 21 March 1830.

39. Ibid., 23 March 1830.

40. Ibid., 2 April 1830.

41. Monaldo Leopardi, *Cenni biografici, Carteggio*, p. 481.

CHAPTER FOURTEEN

RANIERI

Information about this friendship is to be found in Leopardi's and Ranieri's letters to each other (vols. V and VI of the *Epistolario*); in letters to Ranieri from their friends (*Carteggio inedito di vari con G.L., con lettere che lo riguardano* (Torino, 1932)); and in Ranieri's *Sette anni di sodalizio con G.L.* (Napoli, 1880), which must, however, be taken with great caution. The controversy about the relationship between Leopardi and Ranieri has been fully examined by Prof. Francesco Moroncini in his notes

U

to the *Epistolario* and in the following articles: *Nuova Antologia*, 16 March 1932, '*Lettere inedite di G. B. Niccolini ed Antonio Ranieri* (1833–7)'; *Nuova Antologia*, 1 April 1933, '*Il retroscena del sodalizio Ranieri-Leopardi*'; *Nuova Antologia*, 1 March 1934, '*Leggende e verità sulla morte di Giacomo Leopardi*'; *Pegaso*, 8 August 1932, '*Il Leopardi e Ranieri, Fanny e Lenina*'. A clear summing-up of the whole controversy is given by Alberto Consiglio in *La vera storia del sodalizio di Leopardi e Ranieri*, *Italia Letteraria*, 24 December 1933.

De Sinner's friendship with Leopardi and the fate of the manuscripts entrusted to him are fully described by N. Serban in *Leopardi et la France* (Paris, 1913), and in *Lettres inédites relatives à G. L.* (Paris, 1913).

1. On Ranieri's visit to Rome, Leopardi gave him a letter of introduction to the archæologist Visconti, in which he spoke of him as 'a young man of unusual parts, who possesses both a first-rate knowledge of Greek and Latin literature, and a great and noble heart. He wishes to make new acquaintances, especially among young and beautiful women, and to do some research work in libraries.' *Epistolario*, VI, 7 October 1830.

2. Ranieri, *Sodalizio*, pp. 4–5. The implication in this passage that Leopardi was entirely dependent on Ranieri's support has unquestionably been proved untrue. At regular intervals, during the seven years that he lived with Ranieri, Leopardi received from his family sums which Prof. Moroncini (*Nuova Antologia*, 1 April 1933) estimates as amounting, on an average, to 100 *lire* a month; but on the other hand one can hardly argue from this that Leopardi was entirely independent of his friend's help, still less that he positively contributed to the support of Ranieri and his sister.

3. The first two volumes of Leopardi's *Epistolario* were published in 1849, but the letters which most annoyed Ranieri did not appear until 1878, a date which unfortunately coincided with the death of his adored sister Paolina. Ranieri's mental faculties were by then considerably impaired (as is shown by the fact that his will was contested on this ground by his heirs), and this may partly account for the tone of his book.

4. *Epistolario*, VI, 9 September 1830. One at least of these reasons must have become apparent to the citizens of Recanati on reading one passage of *Le ricordanze*:

> Nè mi dicea il cor che l'età verde
> Sarei dannato a consumar in questo
> Natio borgo selvaggio, intra una gente
> Zotica, vil, cui nomi strani, e spesso
> Argomento di riso e di trastullo,
> Son dottrina e saper

(My heart had not warned me that I would be condemned to spend my youth in this wild native village of mine, among people both uncouth and mean, to whom learning and knowledge are unfamiliar names, and often only a subject for laughter and scorn.)

5. Ibid., 15 December 1830.
6. Ibid., 1 April 1831.
7. Ibid., 29 March [1831].
8. Ibid., 24 March 1831.
9. Ibid., 29 March 1831.
10. Ibid., 29 March 1831.
11. Ranieri, *Sodalizio*, pp. 10–11.
12. *Epistolario*, VI, February 1832.
13. Ibid., 22 December 1831.
14. Ibid., 15 October 1831.
15. Ibid., 29 December 1831.
16. Ibid., 9 January 1832.
17. *Carteggio*, pp. 180–1. Fanny Targioni to Ranieri.
18. Gino Doria, '*Antonio Ranieri e i suoi amici di Toscana*', in *Pegaos*, August 1929.
19. 'To other human barbarisms, pederasty must be added—an infamous, unnatural practice which is still very common in the East (to say no more) and appertained not only to barbarians but to a nation as civilized as the Greek. . . . How harmful this infamous vice is to society . . . is manifest.' *Zibaldone*, II, pp. 878–9, 15 March 1824. Cf. also *Zibaldone*, II, pp. 1171–2, 4 October 1821.
20. *Epistolario*, VI, 6 September 1832.
21. Ibid., 15 October 1831.
22. Ranieri, *Sodalizio*, pp. 12–14.
23. Serban, *Lettres inédites relatives à Giacomo Leopardi*, p. 18.
24. The book was signed with the cipher 1150 which in Roman letters, MCL, stood for Monaldo Conte Leopardi. Of the *Little Dialogues* Lammenais wrote: '*Sous des formes tantôt burlesques, tantôt naïvement atroces, ils résument le système entier de l'absolutisme.*'
25. *Epistolario*, VI, 28 May 1832.
26. Ibid. To Giuseppe Melchiorri, 15 May 1832.
27. Ibid., 15 November 1830.
28. Ibid. De Sinner to Giacomo Leopardi, 24 January 1831.
29. Serban, *Leopardi et la France*. The reproaches to De Sinner of Bouché-Leclercq and of others of Leopardi's biographers, are unfair. De Sinner not only persistently attempted to promote his friend's fame during his lifetime, but continued to do so after his death. He tried to

U*

bring about the publication in Paris of a complete edition of Leopardi's works, and when this fell through, largely owing to the opposition of Tommaseo, he showed them to Sainte-Beuve, who first made Leopardi known in France. In De Sinner's later years, however, a tedious controversy took place over Leopardi's philological papers, which were still in his hands. Ranieri asked for them when, in 1848, he began to publish his friend's *Works*; Giordani, too, wanted them for his rival volume. De Sinner refused Giordani and promised the papers to Ranieri; but a painful interlude in his private life prevented him from returning to Italy for many years—and it was not until 1856 that, believing himself to be on the point of death, he presented all Leopardi's manuscripts to Vieusseux. Some months later he returned to Florence to die but, being penniless, accepted (on Vieusseux's advice) the offer of the Tuscan Grand duke's librarian to pay him a small monthly pension, in return for all Leopardi's manuscripts. The papers are now in the *Biblioteca Nazionale* of Florence.

30. *Epistolario*, VI, 24 May 1832.

CHAPTER FIFTEEN

ASPASIA

Inference and surmise must of necessity contribute very largely to any account of this tragic love-affair, but the story, as given here, contains no statements that are not either confirmed by letters or by Leopardi's poems. The main sources are Leopardi's two letters to Fanny Targioni from Rome (quoted in the text), his letters to Ranieri during the winter of 1832–3, and the letters from Fanny Targioni to Ranieri (*Carteggio*, etc.). The relevant poems are: *Il pensiero dominante, Amore e Morte, Consalvo, A se stesso*, and *Aspasia*. Use has also been made of letters from the *Carte Ranieri* quoted by Prof. Moroncini in his article entitled '*Il Leopardi e Ranieri, Fanny e Lenina*' (*Pegaso*, August 1932), and of Prof. Flora's article, '*Aspasia*' (*Nuova Antologia*, Jan. and Feb. 1928), which contains the best summing-up of the story.

1. Charlotte was the daughter of Joseph Bonaparte, and had married her first cousin. Louis Napoleon (the son of the King of Holland), who had recently died in the Romagna, while taking part in the insurrection of 1821.

2. Diego Angeli, *I Bonaparte a Roma*, p. 289.

3. Ranieri, *Notizie intorno alla vita ed agli scritti di G.L.*, printed in an appendix to the *Sodalizio*.

4. Francesco Flora, 'Leopardi e Aspasia', in *Nuova Antologia* (Jan. and Feb. 1928), quoting from a letter of Poerio's to Ranieri (18 May 1830). This letter gives us the approximate date of Leopardi's first sight of Fanny.

5. *Epistolario*, VI. To De Sinner, 1 June 1831.

6. Carducci, *Jaufré Rudel*, *Opere*, X, p. 250. 'But', Carducci added, 'I do not believe it.'

7. Ranieri, Preface to Leopardi's *Works*, repeated as an appendix to the *Sodalizio*, p. 97.

8. The question of Leopardi's 'virginity' has given rise to much controversy among his diligent biographers. Prof. Moroncini maintained ('*Purezza di Leopardi*' in *Italia Letteraria*, 21 May 1933) that here, too, Ranieri was in error. Starting with Carlo's assertion that Giacomo 'very precociously became aware of Nature's sensibility', he quoted passages from Leopardi's letters which, in his opinion, prove that the poet's knowledge of life 'was complete in this respect also'. One, written by Giacomo from Rome to his brother Carlo, ends: 'It is as difficult to accost a woman in Rome as in Recanati, indeed more so, owing to the extreme frivolity and dissipation of these female animals who, except for this, inspire no interest whatever, who are full of hypocrisy, who care for nothing but going about and amusing themselves . . . and who, believe me, do not —— [this word is left in blank] except with as much difficulty as everywhere else. So it all comes back to "*donne pubbliche*", whom I find much more cautious now than they used to be, and who besides are dangerous, as you know.' *Epistolario* II, 6 December 1822. Another letter, says: 'I do not know the —— [word left in blank] of *d'alto affare*, but as to the low ones, I assure you that the ugliest and meanest *coquette* of Recanati is more attractive than the best one in Rome.' *Epistolario*, II, 16 December 1822. From these and other similar passages Moroncini concludes that Ranieri's statement about Leopardi's virginity was not true. The reader must draw his own conclusions. What is certain and more important, is that in none of Leopardi's serious attachments was his love consummated.

9. *Epistolario*, II, 5 April 1823.

10. *Epistolario*, III. To Giuseppe Melchiorri, 19 December 1823.

11. *Zibaldone*, II, p. 253, 16 September 1823.

12. *Epistolario*, VI, 5 December [1831].

13. Ibid., 16 August [1832]. This is the second and last letter from Leopardi to Fanny.

14. Carducci, *Jaufré Rudel*, op. cit., p. 249.

15. *Carteggio*, p. 213. Fanny Targioni to Ranieri, 31 December [1836].

16. Moroncini, op. cit., p. 18, quoting *Carte Ranieri*.

17. Ibid., p. 188. As an explanation of why this letter is in the *Carte Ranieri*, Prof. Moroncini suggests that Niccolini, rather than take the responsibility of giving advice, forwarded the whole letter as it stood to the person whom it most concerned, Ranieri himself.

18. *Epistolario*, VI, 11 December 1832.

19. Ibid., 8 January [1833].

20. Ibid., 5 January [1833].

21. Ibid., 29 January [1833].

22. Prof. Moroncini, op. cit., states that Ranieri, 'probably in agreement with the lady, who had not been ungenerous with her favours to him' proceeded to break with Fanny, in a scene 'which must have been of the same nature as that which ended Giacomo's relations with the Malvezzi in Bologna', but he produces no evidence in confirmation of this statement. The plain truth is that we do not know what happened. The facts to be interpreted are these: after Ranieri's return to Florence (in April 1833) we hear no more of Fanny from Giacomo; in the course of the spring or summer he wrote *A se stesso*, and on the 1st of September Leopardi and Ranieri left Florence for ever.

23. Flora, op. cit., quoting an undated letter of Fanny's in the *Carte Ranieri* (No. 17). In another letter, dated 13 December [1836], she wrote: 'Greet Leopardi for me; I am glad to hear that he is well. I should have liked to write to him on this occasion [the outbreak of cholera in Naples] but I was afraid he would not be glad to receive the letter.' (*Carteggio*, p. 220.)

24. *Carteggio*, pp. 239–40. Fanny Targioni to Ranieri, 21 December 1837.

25. Moroncini, op. cit. The *Carte Ranieri* also contain the rough draft of a letter from Ranieri to Giordani, which plainly show that Leopardi's friends had been persistently asking him, too, to reveal Aspasia's identity. 'How can I tell you who Aspasia is without obtaining her own permission? Many women in the world have been willing to purchase a journey to posterity by a ticket of . . . ['ill-fame'? . . . left in blank in the original] when they cannot get a better one, but it is not a thing one can do without their consent.'

26. Ibid., p. 243. Fanny Targioni to Ranieri, 20 January 1838.

27. Flora, op. cit.

28. *Poesie e Prose*, I, p. 434.

CHAPTER SIXTEEN

HOPE DEFERRED

1. *Sodalizio*, pp. 18–19.
2. *Epistolario*, VI, 23 July 1832.
3. Ibid., 13 September 1832
4. Ibid., 17 November [1832].
5. Flora, '*Leopardi e Aspasia*', in *Nuova Antologia*, February 1928.
6. G. P. Clerici, '*Raspollature da servire alla Biografia di Leopardi*', in *Archivio storico per le provincie parmensi*, XXI, 1921. The friend who described this was Ferdinando Maestri.
7. *Epistolario*, VI, p. 361, note 1.
8. *Epistolario*, V, 5 May 1828. The last words are a quotation from the *canzone* beginning '*In quella parte dove amor mi sprona*' in Petrarca's *Rime*. The line is: '*Ove la stanca mia vita si appoggia.*'
9. *Epistolario*, VI, 6 September [1832].
10. Ibid.
11. All these notes were first published in an appendix to the *Sodalizio* and are now in vol. VI of the *Epistolario*. Those quoted are dated 11, 25, and 27 December 1832; 10 January, 6 and 16 February, 2, 9, and 16 March, 2 and 13 April 1833.
12. *Sodalizio*, p. 23.
13. *Epistolario*, VI, 13 April [1833].
14. 'Believe me, I put my trust only in God and you—that you will tell me precisely what the condition of our dear Giacomo is, and what we may fear or hope. . . . Don't conceal anything, anything at all, and God will give me grace to bear it.' *Epistolario*, VI, p. 252, n. 3.
15. Ibid. Vieusseux to Paolina Leopardi, 4 May 1833.
16. Ibid. G.L. to Paolina, 6 May 1833.
17. Paolina Leopardi, *Lettere*, etc.

CHAPTER SEVENTEEN

TO NAPLES

For Leopardi's last years in Naples the main sources are the letters to him and to Ranieri from their friends (*Carteggio inedito di vari con G.L.*), and his own letters in vol. VI of the *Epistolario*, although these, owing to his failing sight, are fewer and shorter than in previous years, and were often dictated to Ranieri. In addition there is Ranieri's *Sodalizio*, indispensable in spite of the inaccuracies. See also De Sanctis's unfinished autobiography, *La Giovinezza* (edited by Luigi Russo). Lively descriptions of Neapolitan life in the first half of the nineteenth century may be found in Francesco di Bourchard, *Usi e costumi di Napoli descritti e dipinti* (Napoli, 1853–60); Emanuele Bidera, *Passeggiate per Napoli e contorni* (Napoli, 1844); Edmondo Cione, *L'amore per Napoli nei romantici* (Napoli, 1936); Benedetto Croce, *Storie e Leggende Napoletane* (Bari, 1923); August von Platen, *Werke* (Stuttgart, undated); Hans Andersen, *L'Improvvisatore* (Italian translation, Firenze, 1931).

1. *Epistolario*, VI. To Conte Monaldo, 5 October 1833.

2. *Sodalizio*, p. 28.

3. Flora, 'Leopardi e Aspasia', in *Nuova Antologia*, January 1928, quoting *Carte Ranieri*.

4. *Epistolario*, VI, 20 March 1834.

5. Ibid. De Sinner to G.L., 18 May 1834.

6. 'To live tolerably in Naples', Leopardi wrote to De Sinner, 'a single man needs 150 francs a month, to live moderately well 200, and comfortably though not luxuriously, 250.' But the friends certainly did not possess even the smallest of these sums.

7. This included the two later *Operette*: the *Dialogue between Tristan and a Friend*, and *The Seller of Almanacks*.

8. *Sodalizio*, p. 46.

9. *Epistolario*, VI, 22 August 1835.

10. Ibid., 3 February 1835

11. Appendix to *Sodalizio*.

12. Ferretti, *Vita di G.L.*, p. 356.

13. Ibid., p. 357.

14. Giacomo's phrase about the *giunchi marini* (sea reeds) gave particular offence to Ranieri, who took it in the most literal sense and proceeded to apostrophize Leopardi's 'still adored shade', reminding him that he never slept upon reeds, but upon mattresses 'of softest Tunisian wool, especially procured by my Sainted Mother'! This passage is characteristic of the whole controversy, and it is really not necessary to bring such matters into discussion again. Those readers who wish to find out whether the Tunisian mattresses were well- or ill-stuffed are referred to Prof. Moroncini's articles in the *Nuova Antologia*, April 1933.

15. *Epistolario*, IV, 11 December 1836.

16. These errors have been fully noted—not without a certain *Schaden-*

freude—in Prof. Moroncini's edition of *I Canti*. 'Nell' orba fantasia', for instance, turned into 'nell' orbe quanto sia'; many *d's* have become *f's*— whole words are left out. Moroncini was very much annoyed by them. 'Heard wrong and interpreted wrong', he angrily noted in the margin; 'typical example of R's carelessness and irresponsibility', 'no attention to the sense'; 'emphasis and exclamation marks due to R's Neapolitan character', etc., etc.

17. *Sodalizio*, p. 34. Ranieri's and his sister's devotion to each other, which was expressed in terms of the most extreme romanticism, both in Ranieri's book and in his letters, was such that Prof. Moroncini has even gone so far as to hint at an incestuous relation between them. In evidence of this he quotes phrases such as these from Paolina's letters to her brother: 'My soul, my life, light of my eyes, my adored one, do not betray me, as this sorrow would lead me to grave. . . . You cannot believe how great my melancholy is. I adore you. I have nothing on earth but you.' And from Ranieri's letters: 'I love you so much, with so immense, so immeasurable an affection, that you would be a monster of ingratitude if you ever thought the slightest harm of me, or conceived the thought of betraying me.' See Prof. Moroncini, op. cit. There is no other evidence in support of this accusation, which is only quoted here as an example of the lengths to which the attack on Ranieri's character has been carried.

18. *Epistolario*, VI. 27 November 1834.

19. Moroncini, op. cit. It must be said once for all that though Ranieri was undoubtedly a liar, and a hysterical one, all these details have a great verisimilitude, and are hardly likely to have been invented.

20. Sodalizio, p. 54.

21. Ibid., pp. 38–9.

22. Von Platen, *Tagebücher*.

23. *Sodalizio*, p. 37.

24. Sainte-Beuve, *Voyage en Italie*, p. 5.

25. Prof. Moroncini refuses to believe this story, which was told by Ranieri in his old age in a letter to D'Ancona, saying that it is unworthy of so great a man, but it appears to me to be entirely in character.

26. *Zibaldone*, II, pp. 1207–8. And he told the story of how some Neapolitans, after a violent dispute, went one night to wake up the philosopher Genovesi in his bed, to ask him whether, in Tasso's *Gerusalemme liberata*, Rinaldo or Gernando was in the right.

27. Cf. Ferretti, op. cit., p. 350.

28. *Epistolario*, VI, p. 303. De Sinner to G.L., 11 November 1835.

29. Some critics believe that it was the last lines of the *Paralipomeni*, and not of *Il tramonto della luna*, that L. dictated to Ranieri on the last day

of his life. In any case, he was working on them until very shortly before his death.

30. F. de Sanctis, *La Giovinezza*, pp. 95–8.

31. Ibid., p. 228.

32. Ibid., p. 230.

CHAPTER EIGHTEEN

THE SETTING OF THE MOON

1. *Epistolario*, VI. [4 December 1835.]

2. Ibid., 19 February 1836.

3. Ibid., 30 October 1836.

4. Ibid., 9 March 1837.

5. Ranieri, *Sodalizio*, p. 18.

6. *Epistolario*, VI. Charles Lebreton to G.L. [Paris, 8 March 1836.]

7. Ibid., enclosed in a letter to De Sinner, dated 6 April 1836.

8. Flora, in the Preface to his complete edition of Leopardi's *Works*.

9. These theories have been summarized by Dr. G. Pieri, in *G. Leopardi visto da un medico* and *Di quale malattia morì G. Leopardi?* (1937). He does not believe that the poet suffered from rickets in childhood; the evidence, on the contrary, indicates that he was a healthy child, and that all his trouble came from the deformity of his thorax, which did not manifest itself until his adolescence. (Cf. Chap. II.) Dr. Pieri also disagrees with Dr. Arcangeli's hypothesis that the poet suffered from syphilis—either hereditary or acquired from his wet-nurse or through vaccination. Nor is it necessary to pay too much attention to the theories of the psychiatrists (Lombroso, Sergi, and Patrizi) who have attempted to trace, in the poet's heredity, a strain of madness. Renato Bettica, in *Leopardi povero ammalato*, reaches the same conclusions as Dr. Pieri, and so does Prof. Arturo Castiglione, who emphasizes the poet's hyper-sensibility as the chief cause of his pessimism. (*Visita medica a Leopardi* in the *Letture Leopardiane* given in the Lyceum of Florence, 1938.)

10. Monaldo Leopardi, *Cenni Biografici*. Conte Monaldo relates that Giacomo could only manage to urinate by going for long walks (in the company of his father) and 'stealing a moment of inadvertence'.

11. Ibid.

12. See Chap. XV, note 8.

13. De Sanctis, *La Giovinezza*, pp. 100–1.

14. A. Brofferio, *I miei tempi*, p. 81.

15. *Epistolario*, VI, 27 May 1837.

16. Appendix to *Sodalizio*. Letter from Ranieri to Conte Monaldo, 13 January 1837.

17. Wilhelm Schulz, in *Allgemeine Zeitung Beilage*, 1840.

18. Brofferio, op. cit. These remarks were repeated to Brofferio by Ranieri.

19. Ranieri, '*Supplemento alle notizie intorno alla vita e gli scritti di G.L.*', printed as an appendix to the *Sodalizio*, pp. 106–9.

20. *Zibaldone*, II, p. 1333.

21. *Dialogue between Porphyry and Plotinus.*

22. Ibid.

23. *Carteggio*, pp. 215–16, 1 July 1837.

24. Ibid., p. 220, 11 July 1837.

25. Capponi, *Lettere*, IV, p. 418, 9 November 1875.

26. Giordani, *Epistolario*, VI. To Paolo Toschi, 12 July 1837. 'Poor Leopardi,' he wrote in a later letter, 'who died none too soon, having lived in vain.'

27. Gioberti, *Il Gesuita moderno*, preface.

28. Antona-Traversi, *Paolina Leopardi*, pp. 104–5.

29. Paolina Leopardi, *Lettere*, etc., p. 189.

30. Ibid., p. 267. Conte Monaldo survived his son by ten years; Contessa Adelaide, by twenty.

31. Paolina Leopardi, *Lettere*, etc., pp. 316–17.

32. Piergili, *Nuovi documenti*, etc., p. 248.

33. 'I was upset', she wrote, 'by seeing certain details about Giacomo's life, which he was supposed to have told the Father, and in which there is no shadow of truth.' Letter from Paolina to Don Antonio Erculei, quoted by Antona-Traversi, *Paolina Leopardi*, p. 115.

34. Moroncini, *Il retroscena*, etc.

35. Settembrini, *Ricordanze*, quoting Ranieri. 'Thus,' the poet's friend commented, 'thanks to a few fish, Leopardi obtained a tomb.'

36.
AL CONTE GIACOMO LEOPARDI RECANATESE
FILOLOGO AMMIRATO FUORI D'ITALIA
SCRITTORE DI FILOSOFIA E DI POESIE ALTISSIMO
DA PARAGONARE SOLAMENTE COI GRECI
CHE FINÌ DI XXXIX ANNI LA VITA
PER CONTINUE MALATTIE MISERISSIMA
FECE ANTONIO RANIERI
PER SETTE ANNI FINO ALL' ESTREMA ORA CONGIUNTO
ALL'AMICO ADORATO MDCCCXXXVII

37. Letter from Ranieri to De Sinner in 1844, quoted by Dr. Mariotti in his official account of the exhumation of Leopardi's body on 1 July 1900. See Moroncini, 'La Morte, il seppellimento e la tomba di Giacomo Leopardi', Nuova Antologia, 1 March 1934, pp. 58–9.

38. Padre Scarpa's letter, which was published in 1846 in a Neapolitan review, Scienza e Fede, is quoted in full in Bouché-Leclercq, op. cit., Chap. XXII.

39.

> O Death, alone eternal,
> To whom each living thing at last must come,
> In thee, O Death, finds rest
> Our naked being,
> Though joyful not,
> Yet from old anguish free.
>
> *Coro dei Morti.*

INDEX